Major Women Writers
of Seventeenth-Century England

DATE DUE

Major Women Writers of Seventeenth-Century England

EDITED BY

James Fitzmaurice, General Editor
Josephine A. Roberts, Textual Editor
Carol L. Barash
Eugene R. Cunnar
Nancy A. Gutierrez

Ann Arbor

THE UNIVERSITY OF MICHIGAN PRESS

Copyright © by the University of Michigan 1997
All rights reserved
Published in the United States of America by
The University of Michigan Press
Manufactured in the United States of America
⊗ Printed on acid-free paper

2000   1999   1998   1997   4   3   2   1

A CIP catalog record for this book is available from the British Library.

Library of Congress Cataloging-in-Publication Data

Major women writers of seventeenth-century England / edited by James
Fitzmaurice . . . [et al.].
    p.   cm.
  Includes bibliographical references (p.) and index.
  ISBN 0-472-09609-5 (cloth). — ISBN 0-472-06609-9 (pbk.)
  1. English literature—Early modern, 1500–1700.   2. Women—
England—History—17th century—Sources.   3. English literature—
Women authors.   4. Women—Literary collections.   I. Fitzmaurice,
James. 1943–   .
PR1110.W6M35   1997
820.8'0928704—dc21   96-49138
                                                          CIP

IN MEMORIAM
Josephine A. Roberts

In August of 1996, Josephine A. Roberts was killed in an automobile accident. With her passing, the profession loses a fine scholar and good friend. She will be missed by her colleagues who worked on this book.

Acknowledgments

We wish to thank the following scholars for their invaluable assistance: Margaret J. M. Ezell, Margaret W. Ferguson, Douglas Gray, Elizabeth H. Hageman, Paul Hartle, Steven W. May, Mary Ann O'Donnell, Martine Rey, Sara Jayne Steen, Betty S. Travitsky, Susanne Woods, and Susan Wright.

In the preparation of this volume, it has been a genuine pleasure to work with the staff members of the University of Michigan Press, including Joseph Cislo, Richard Isomaki, Kristen Lare, Mary Meade, Kelly Sippell, and Eve Trager. We are particularly grateful for the advice and counsel of the Executive Editor of the Press, LeAnn Fields, who from the beginning has given this project her strong and unwavering support.

James Fitzmaurice wishes to thank the staff of the Cambridge University Library, the Henry E. Huntington Library, and the University of Nottingham Library. He is grateful for summer research assistance from the Organized Research Committee of Northern Arizona University, and for a visiting research fellowship at Gonville and Caius College, Cambridge.

Josephine Roberts acknowledges the generous support of the Newberry Library, Chicago, and the National Endowment for the Humanities. Terry Newgard of the Computing Services, College of Arts and Sciences, Louisiana State University, provided assistance in reconciling many different word processing programs. She is grateful to Jim and John Gaines for their advice and encouragement.

Carol Barash wishes to thank the staffs of the Henry E. Huntington Library, Princeton University Library, Northamptonshire Record Office, Wellesley College Library, and the Folger Shakespeare Library, for kind assistance over many years; and Jason Gieger, for research assistance and wit.

Eugene Cunnar completed part of the research for this project while on a fellowship funded by the Henry E. Huntington Library. He wishes to thank Rebecca L. Tate for her assistance with the textual apparatus for Katherine Philips's poems. He also thanks Merri and Trey, Ralph and Aileen.

Nancy Gutierrez expresses gratitude to Jesse Swan and Jacquelyne Lynch for their hard work in checking references and proofing the final text of *The Tragedy of Mariam*. She is appreciative to the College of Arts and Sciences at Arizona State University for a Minigrant Award that allowed her to complete this project. She would also like to acknowledge the gracious and helpful staff of the Henry E. Huntington Library. She believes that Meg, Hannah, and Beth provided the healthiest of distractions, while James is a reminder of the value of balance. Finally, she will always connect Will with her work on the project.

We jointly dedicate this book to our families.

Contents

Illustrations

Introduction

Amid the excitement and fervor of rewriting literary history, some critics speak of the "discovery" of early women writers, a word that implies an encounter with something previously unknown. But that is not quite the case with the women included here. On the contrary, bits and pieces of their poetry, fiction, and drama have been in print continuously for the last three hundred years. Some of these women have had large segments of what they wrote (even complete works) available for long spans of time. Their lives have been misunderstood and often maligned, but they never have been completely lost.

Why, then, has it taken so long for them to receive serious attention? The answer is simple enough. A genial, patronizing literary establishment saw, and to some extent still sees, them as unimportant. Why, one might go on to ask, were they taken to be unimportant? Here the answers are many, and it is difficult to assign weight among them. In part, over the last three centuries labels gradually became attached to individuals: Aemilia Lanyer was simply Shakespeare's Dark Lady; Mary Wroth was merely "a writer of romances"; Margaret Cavendish, who wore strange clothing, picked up the name "Mad Madge"; and Aphra Behn was a "shady" lady.

Such trivializing labels no longer stick, and the fact is that these, and indeed all, early women writers are now being reassessed. Not all will emerge as significant authors, but each will be more often judged by standards in keeping with what she wrote, and all will be less often belittled by presuppositions about their lives, their gender, and their genres. The methods and the subjects that these women chose are no longer dismissed out of hand. Katherine Philips, for example, wrote about friendship between women, a topic that seemed hardly worth bothering about to many men as they compiled anthologies of the "best" literature a hundred years ago. Now the topic of women's friendship can be studied from a variety of perspectives, like other matters of interest. Similarly, some of Aphra Behn's female characters were dismissed as ungenteel according to the standards of polite conversation accepted in the time of Queen Victoria, but these days the racy remarks of Hellena in *The Rover* seem relatively tame.

Perhaps more damaging to the reputations of early women writers than any prudishness of earlier generations was simply the blindness of critics. Many of those who created standards by which literature was to be judged could see merit in men's writing but were myopic in regard to different sorts of value to be found in what women wrote. These arbiters of taste did not necessarily want to deny the importance of women's literary accomplishments simply for misogynistic reasons, but because they did not always understand what they read.

Sometimes even women misunderstood women writers. Virginia Woolf failed fully to grasp the importance of Aphra Behn, for it was Woolf who attached the tag "shady" lady to her literary ancestor in *A Room of One's Own* (1929). But mostly the problem arose with literary critics who were able to recognize irony in the *Songs and Sonnets* of John Donne but missed out on a different sort of irony in the *Sociable Letters* of Margaret Cavendish. Donne, as a man, they understood. Cavendish, as a woman, they did not.

What, then, are the achievements of the women in this volume? What sort of values should we as readers invoke as we focus on their writings? And, finally, how do these women compare when set beside the canonical figures of the century? In order to find answers or at least seek for aids to understanding, it is probably best to begin with the historical background of women's writing.

In sixteenth-century France, Italy, and Spain, many secular women writers achieved fame, including Marguerite de Navarre, Louise Labé, Veronica Franco, Gaspara Stampa, and Vittoria Colonna. In the international merchant cities, such as Lyon and Venice, the social and economic conditions encouraged the emergence of women writers from the merchant and professional classes, not simply from the elite rank of queens and duchesses. By contrast, their English contemporaries tended to write primarily religious translations and devotional works, under the impact of Protestant teaching. Yet even in early sixteenth-century England there were significant exceptions. One of these was Isabella Whitney (fl. 1567–73), who wrote a number of verse epistles, including a will or testament to London, in which she vividly records all the sights, sounds, and smells of the busy city shops. Another exception is Margaret Tyler, a former servant to the Howard family (perhaps as a lady-in-waiting), who translated the Spanish chivalric romance, *The Mirror of Princely Deeds and Knighthood* (c. 1578). In her prefatory letter, Tyler defends her decision to translate a secular, as opposed to a religious, work. She also boldly argues that "it is all one for a woman to pen a story, as for a man to address his story to a woman." Tyler thus opens the door to other English secular writers of the seventeenth century, including Mary Wroth, Margaret Cavendish, and Aphra Behn.

The public debate over the role of women in society may have also contributed to the emergence of greater numbers of English women writers. The pseudonymous Jane Anger wrote a pamphlet entitled *Jane Anger, her Protection for Women* (1589) in answer to a misogynist tract that has not survived. We do not know whether "Anger" was a man or woman, but the female persona provided a precedent for Rachel Speght, the middle-class daughter of a London cleric. Speght was the first positively identified Englishwoman to write a defense of her sex, in response to Joseph Swetnam's diatribe, *The Arraignment of Lewd, Idle, Froward, and Unconstant Women* (1615).

Speght's accomplishment is all the more impressive because in the period before the English Civil War, the publication of works by women was still a relatively rare occurrence. But the situation changed dramatically after 1640, as the accompanying chart prepared by Patricia Crawford demonstrates (see p. 3). The seventeenth century was indeed a century of revolution for women writers, whose numbers vastly increased, in conjunction with their rising educational opportunities, the increasing literacy rates, and the changing social and economic conditions. It should be noted that this chart records only the

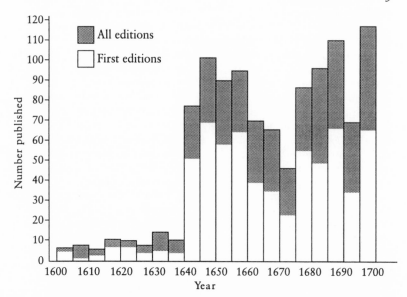

Chart of first editions and all editions of women's works published by half decades in the seventeenth century. (Printed by permission of Patricia Crawford.)

printed editions of women's works and excludes works in manuscript. Throughout the seventeenth century, many women circulated their writings in manuscript copies in coteries, or circles of friends and family members. When Dorothy Leigh published her book of maternal advice, *The Mother's Blessing,* in 1616, she wrote a lengthy self-justification, in which she declared that writing was something "so unusual among us." The strong social pressures against publication may be seen throughout the century, as when Dorothy Osborne reacted negatively to the printing of Margaret Cavendish's verse. Osborne complained to William Temple that Cavendish "could never be so ridiculous else to venture at writing books and in verse too."

As scholars begin to identify women's writing hidden away in manuscript commonplace books, family archives, and county record offices, a more complete account of it can be constructed. The recent identification of manuscripts by such writers as Mary Wroth, Aphra Behn, Katherine Philips, and Anne Finch provides significant new insight into the conflicts these authors faced as they prepared their works for print.

One of the most important predecessors of the authors in this anthology was Mary Sidney, countess of Pembroke (1561–1621), who distinguished herself by completing a verse translation of the Psalms begun by her brother, Sir Philip Sidney. A virtuoso poet, Mary Sidney mastered enormously difficult poetic forms and produced a collection remarkable for its metrical variety. Her elegant and very free rendering of the Psalms drew high praise from John Donne: "They tell us *why* and *how* to sing" ("Upon the Translation of the Psalms by Sir

Philip Sidney, and the Countess of Pembroke his Sister," l. 22). She also wrote a verse dedication to Queen Elizabeth I, containing a subtle political argument on behalf of Protestantism. Although she wrote secular verse, very few of her original poems have been preserved: one example is her pastoral "Dialogue between Two Shepherds," which she may have composed in anticipation of an intended visit by Elizabeth to Wilton House in 1599.

As author and patron, Mary Sidney also championed the genre of Senecan verse drama and boldly published her translation of Robert Garnier's play, *Antonie* (1592). Shakespeare probably drew inspiration from Sidney's translation in his *Antony and Cleopatra*, and a number of other playwrights, including Samuel Daniel, Fulke Greville, and Michael Drayton, followed the example of the countess in composing verse drama. By publishing her *Antonie* (and her translation of Philippe de Mornay's *Discourse of Life and Death*), Mary Sidney provided a significant model to the next generation of women writers, especially Aemilia Lanyer, Elizabeth Cary, and Mary Wroth. She showed the world that a woman might win respect as a writer and helped inspire the literary careers of all three younger women.

In one of the dedications to *Salve Deus Rex Judaeorum* (1611), Aemilia Lanyer self-consciously situates herself as a literary successor to the countess of Pembroke. Lanyer shows her power as a religious poet, as she recounts the story of the Crucifixion from a distinctly female perspective. Focusing on the women surrounding Christ, Lanyer describes the prophetic dream of Pilate's wife, in which she dramatically warns her husband not to let Jesus die. The moral is clear: men should listen to the wisdom of women. Lanyer's "Eve's Apology" can also be considered in the context of earlier defenses of women, such as Jane Anger's argument that men are less pure than women because God made men of mud and women of Adam's rib. Lanyer's contribution to secular literature of the time is represented in this anthology by "The Description of Cookham," perhaps the first country house poem in English and a work that invites comparison with Ben Jonson's "To Penshurst." Unlike Jonson, who joyously celebrates the permanence and continuity of life at the Sidney estate, Lanyer is more somber, recalling better times now fled. Her poem is more in the nostalgic manner of "Prisoned in Windsor" by Henry Howard, earl of Surrey, as she remembers a period of her life, now forever lost, when she belonged to an Edenic paradise of women.

Elizabeth Cary's *The Tragedy of Mariam, The Fair Queen of Jewry* (1613), the first original play in English by a woman to find its way into print, is as compelling to read today as it was in Cary's time. Her play deals with a major figure in religious history, Herod the Great (73–74 B.C.), but the play is only partly the retelling of a story from biblical times. Mostly it treats the subject of marriage in the seventeenth century, as it vividly depicts the conflict that arises among three central and very powerful personalities. Mariam is a beautiful and headstrong woman who begins the drama by describing the love-hate relationship she has had with her husband. Herod's sister Salome (not the woman who asked for the head of John the Baptist) is her powerful antagonist, who makes a convincing case for divorce. Mariam's husband, Herod, is a man for whom love becomes torment. As with Leontes in *The Winter's Tale*, he is driven to madness by jealousy, but the outcome is chilling tragedy rather than the forgiveness and reconciliation of Shakespearean romance. Cary constructs her play so that

Mariam is surrounded by women who may disapprove of her "unbridled speech," but who offer alternatives to her martyrdom. Yet Mariam's resistance to domestic tyranny has profound political implications, and the play invites its audience to identify with a heroine who openly defies society's injunctions to silence and obedience.

Mary Wroth, niece and goddaughter of the countess of Pembroke, wrote in genres more typical of the Elizabethan, rather than the Jacobean, age. *The Countess of Montgomery's Urania* (1621) appeared in print some eighteen years after the death of Elizabeth I, but it is a work of fiction that immediately makes us think of *The Countess of Pembroke's Arcadia*, by Sir Philip Sidney. Although Wroth borrows a number of features from her uncle's work and from other courtly romances—such as the frequent disguises and complicated plots involving aristocratic characters—she highlights the friendship between two women, Pamphilia and Urania. Consisting of a network of over three hundred characters, Wroth's work addresses issues of primary social importance, such as the ills of enforced marriage and the sexual double standard. She thus describes Amphilanthus's mistreatment of Pamphilia with witty irony: "Being a man, it was necessary for him to exceed a woman in all things, so much as inconstancy was fit for him to excel her in."

Wroth's sonnets, which share characters with her fiction, demonstrate the mastery of a supremely difficult poetic form, and thus are like the Psalms of her aunt and uncle. At the same time they show an inversion of some of the usual sonnet conventions. Traditionally, men wrote sonnets to women who, according to the model of Petrarch's *Rime,* were depicted as beautiful, aloof, icy, and unyielding. Men faithfully pined away, while women stood unresponsive on their pedestals. The sonnets that result from this highly artificial view of love are often very beautiful, but even Sir Philip Sidney mocked the conventions in *Astrophil and Stella.* Turning the tradition on its head, Wroth wrote sonnets in which a faithful woman asserts her choice to love, even as the man focuses his attention on other women. If nothing else, these poems provide an incisive commentary on the subject of the "male gaze" as it was manifested in the poems of a great many men who took part in the sonnet craze of the 1590s.

In the thirty years separating the published works of Mary Wroth and Margaret Cavendish, women did a great deal of writing, but mostly not with the printed page in mind. Quaker women constituted an important exception, for they published numerous religious pamphlets, prophetic and mystical discourses, and personal testimonies, which do not fit in the customary literary categories but often reveal a sophisticated command of language. From 1642 until 1660 the theaters were closed, and for much of that time the English civil wars raged. When the wars ended, the literature of the English language was largely divided between those who wrote in exile on the Continent and those who stayed at home living under the Protectorate of Oliver Cromwell. Some writers, like Andrew Marvell, managed to prosper both under Cromwell and after the monarchy came back into power.

During the last half of the 1640s and for the whole of the 1650s, Margaret Cavendish lived in exile in Antwerp with her husband, a civil war commander on the defeated royalist side. She was a woman who had always liked to write, and she came from a family whose widowed mother made the decisions—in spite of the fact that widowed women were expected to find a male relative to provide protection and guidance. Cavendish showed her mother's strength of character by deciding to spend her life writing and publishing what she wrote. She did not write to make a living, but to gain "fame," an end more in keeping with male aspiration in her day than with standards of female modesty. She wrote a great deal and seems to have published nearly all of it, with the result that her work is often uneven in quality. To modern readers her extensive scientific writings are puzzling, but they represent speculations on natural history and atomic theory in the manner of amateur male scientists of the time. On the other hand, today we find her explorations of cross-dressing characters in plays like *The Convent of Pleasure* quite progressive. Arguably her best book, *Sociable Letters* takes a hard look at the institution of marriage, encompassing the basic question of its desirability, and the related issues of divorce, adultery, spousal abuse, and the like. Much of what is said in *Sociable Letters* comes from the mouths of the letter writer's fictional guests, and it is often difficult to assess the degree to which Cavendish agrees with the views she has these characters express. Clearly she is often ironic. Perhaps most surprising is the fact that while ridiculed as Mad Madge, she reached a large reading audience, not all of whom found her so foolish. True, Samuel Pepys was contemptuous of her husband for letting his wife "scribble." The book Pepys so reviled was Cavendish's biography of her husband, which contains a serious and detailed account of the English civil wars. It is an account that, beginning with the noted scholar John Rushworth in the 1680s, has been a respected, if unacknowledged, source of information about England in the 1640s.

Katherine Philips was a near contemporary of Cavendish, but a woman of very different temperament. Philips, who eventually became ambitious for fame herself, was always careful to cultivate an image of modesty. During the 1650s, she was the central figure in a coterie of women and men who wrote poetry on the subjects of love and friendship. By the early 1660s, however, she had turned her pen to political topics, celebrating the coronation of Charles II and generally supporting the newly restored monarchy. Her first large public success was, nonetheless, a translation. The first edition of her version of Corneille's *Pompey* rapidly sold out, and she was in the process of translating Corneille's *Horace* when she suddenly died of smallpox in her early thirties. While a pirated collection of her poems appeared just before her death, Sir Charles Cotterell, a close friend and an influential member of King Charles II's court, thought enough of her work to construct a careful, authorized edition. She gained, albeit posthumously, a wide and admiring audience for her poetry.

Philips's friendship poems—intimate, delicate, and often addressed to other women—are elevated in tone and sometimes remind us of John Donne's Neoplatonic verse. With the restoration of the monarchy in 1660, literary taste had shifted: John Dryden turned away from "metaphysical" or shocking imagery as found in the poem "On the Death of Lord Hastings." Philips's poetry became more public and more like that of her male contemporaries. "To the Countess of Roscommon, with a Copy of Pompey" is smooth and self-assured, written as it is in the heroic couplets that became a staple of poetry in the next 150 years.

Aphra Behn is probably the best known of the women in this volume. She tends to be remembered primarily for her short novel *Oroonoko* and for at least seventeen plays. Mostly she wrote comedies, which were witty, urbane, and racy, in keeping with Restoration taste. Victorian England found Restoration comedy offensive when written by men; such drama was very nearly intolerable as the product of a woman. Taste has changed: Behn's best-known and possibly most memorable play, *The Rover,* is performed before appreciative audiences today. Vivid characters like Willmore, Angellica, and Hellena capture the imagination, but Behn does more than simply create interesting and believable people. She looks at the position of women in marriage, such as Hellena's promise to be "Hellena the Inconstant" or an abused wife's public rejection of her husband in *The Lucky Chance.*

Behn's life, professional and personal, has always been closely tied to her work, and it is clear that she invited this sort of comparison. Exhibiting the daring and intelligence of the heroines of her drama, she traveled by ship to Surinam, a Dutch colony in South America, and worked as a spy for King Charles II in the Netherlands. She was praised by Virginia Woolf, not for what she wrote, but for being paid for writing. Indeed, she was the first clearly professional female writer, the first woman who lived by the pen, and her example was followed to a greater or lesser degree by a number of women whose plays are considered more refined. Her successors—Mary Pix, Catherine Trotter, Delarivier Manley, and Susannah Centlivre—helped make the ten years after the death of Behn in 1689 a time when women playwrights were both abundant and respected.

The literary atmosphere of the 1690s was a good one for women writers. The century had seen women become increasingly esteemed as writers and increasingly able to write and publish on topics that interested them. As the seventeenth century closed, however, gains made by women in the theater were all but wiped away by attacks on the drama for its alleged immorality made by Jeremy Collier in his *Short View of the Immorality and Profaneness of the English Stage* (1698). Nevertheless, women poets and fiction writers continued to find success, notably Anne Finch, countess of Winchilsea.

Writing in the final years of the seventeenth century, Finch was much admired later by the Romantic poet William Wordsworth, who praised her style as "often admirable, chaste, tender, and vigorous." Wordsworth's attention should have brought her the recognition she deserved, but unfortunately he limited himself to praising those passages from her poetry that agreed with his notions of nature. Wordsworth, in fact, rendered Finch's poetry tepid by ignoring her politics; Finch was an ardent supporter of the ill-fated King James II, whose political mistakes resulted in the so-called Glorious Revolution of 1688. Wordsworth also disregarded her many verse references to her female friends. Following Wordsworth's lead, the early twentieth-century editor of her writing, John Middleton Murry, excluded poems on womanly community from his edition of her verse (1928). Unfortunately, because Virginia Woolf used Murry's edition, her assessment of the poet gives an inaccurate and distorted picture of Finch's achievements.

In addition to nature, politics, and female community, Finch considered such issues as death, marriage, language, art, madness, and creativity. Her views on poetic ideals to be found in "To the Nightingale" were reworked by Keats in his ode on the same topic. Her poem "Occasional Reflections" presents an interesting case because it was first written as a multivoiced study of political and linguistic authority in the late seventeenth century. Finch then rewrote it as two poems, "Glass" and "Fragments," in keeping with her artistic development. Her later poems were most appreciated by English Romantics, especially Wordsworth, Shelley, and Keats.

The seventeenth century, then, was a time of enormous change for women's writing. The seven principal authors included in this anthology each produced enough important work to lay claim to being considered major writers of the period. There were, however, hosts of women, especially at the end of the century, who wrote well, and it has not been an easy task for the editors to choose among them in order to produce a book that offers substantial selections from a limited number of figures. We especially regret leaving out the fiction of Jane Barker, as well as the poetry of Anne Killigrew and Anne Wharton, but these are only a few of the very fine writers the century produced.

Editorial Procedure

The texts in this anthology have been edited primarily for an audience of undergraduates and general readers. In each case, we have based our selections on original editions and manuscripts of the works. Although we have modernized spelling, capitalization, punctuation, and word division, we have indicated any departures from the authors' substantive wording by the use of square brackets. In cases where modernizing would change semantic, phonological, or metrical qualities (especially in the case of verse), we have retained the original word(s) and discussed the passage in a note. Brief explanatory notes are also marked by square brackets.

At the end of each selection is a statement identifying the copy-text and discussing any distinctive textual features of the work. Even when modernized, the writings of seventeenth-century women require varying degrees of annotation. In the words of Margaret Cavendish, "Language should be like garments, for though every garment hath a general cut, yet their trimmings may be different, and not go out of the fashion; so wit may place words to its own becoming, delight, and advantage" (*The World's Olio* [1655], 94).

Feminist Criticism and
Seventeenth-Century Women Writers

With few exceptions—perhaps those of Katherine Philips and Aphra Behn—literary scholars have either ignored the women included in this anthology or have determined that they are minor or marginal figures of the age. For this reason, any attention given to these writers is feminist in nature because the attention, whether intended by the critic or not, provides knowledge about women's sensibility in the early modern period—and uncovering knowledge about the lives of women is one explicit tenet of feminist studies. However, since feminist criticism is not a monolithic system, the interrelationship between feminist theory and the practical criticism of seventeenth-century women writers is entangled in the politics and practice of feminist studies in general. Because a kind of dialogue, at times explicit and at other times implicit, characterizes the relationship between the literary scholars working on seventeenth-century women writers and their feminist colleagues specializing in either theory or in other periods, a general discussion of feminist criticism precedes and provides a basis for a more specific survey of scholarship devoted to seventeenth-century women writers.

Feminist criticism must first be described according to its intent, that is, to acknowledge that men and women, because of their different positions and activities in a culture, approach writing and reading from different directions, directions that must be acknowledged in order for a literary analysis to have both theoretical and historical validity. Therefore, in recent years, the term *gender criticism* has frequently replaced feminist criticism, as the more accurate label. However, the very comprehensiveness of the term *gender,* even its neutrality, makes it an oppositional term to feminism in the eyes of some feminist critics, since it deemphasizes the role of women.

Many feminist critics, both theorists and practical critics alike, realize that the foundation for their practice is ideology, that an external political agenda determines their critical practice. As June Howard states, obviously writing for a self-selected feminist audience, "For most of us feminist criticism matters at least in part because it contributes to the feminist political project, to our effort to make a difference in the social world" (168). "Making a difference" quite simply means changing the cultural (i.e., political, economic, social) binarization of gender with its consequent inequities and oppressions, that is, to correct the characterization of the sexes as two separate and unequal entities.

Certain terminology describing this binarization of gender has been incorporated into the very essence of feminist thinking. For example, women are often said to be "marginalized," disallowed a position in the center of things and removed to the sidelines, the margins, where their voices are heard faintly or not at all. Feminists often argue that, because of biology, women are usually associated with the body and with nature: thus, they are considered more emotional, more passionate, more instinctive in behavior than are men. Because they are body, they become "objects" rather than "subjects." In other words, women are not active agents themselves, but are acted upon by "the gaze" of male eyes that effectively creates them. As Laura Mulvey states, "In a world ordered by sexual imbalance, pleasure in looking has been split between active/male and passive/female. The determining male gaze projects its phantasy on to the female figure which is styled accordingly" (11). Feminist literary theory makes central the experience and identity of women in order to assert their subjecthood, an activity that is explicitly political.

In the introduction to their anthology on feminist literary theory, *Making a Difference,* Gayle Greene and Coppélia Kahn succinctly trace the steps from intellectual theorization to political activism. First, they define feminist literary criticism as "one branch of interdisciplinary enquiry which takes gender as a fundamental organizing category of experience." The editors go on to enumerate two related premises about gender: first, that "the inequality of the sexes is neither a biological given nor a divine mandate, but a cultural construct, and therefore a proper subject of study for any humanistic discipline"; and second, that "a male perspective, assumed to be 'universal,' has dominated fields of knowledge, shaping their paradigms and methods." Greene and Kahn conclude their introductory comments by noting feminist scholarship's two concerns: to "[revise] concepts previously thought universal but now seen as originating in particular cultures and serving particular purposes; and [to restore] a female perspective by extending knowledge about women's experience and contributions to culture" (Greene and Kahn 1–2). In her preface to *Sexual/Textual Politics,* Toril Moi more bluntly announces, "The principal objective of feminist criticism has always been political: it seeks to expose, not to perpetuate, patriarchal practices" (xiv).

While there is general agreement, whether implicit or explicit, about these ideological underpinnings of feminist literary criticism, no such unanimity characterizes the critical strategies used to realize such ideological concerns. A primary point of departure is the question of what texts a feminist critic should be examining: texts written by men in which women are depicted; texts written by men in which women are absent; texts written by women; all of these; or only one, and that, obviously, women's writing. Carol Thomas Neely points out the existence of

a division, a professional and critical hiatus between feminist critics who deal with male authors in the traditional canon—Chaucer, Spenser, Shakespeare, Milton—and the larger, better-known group of feminist critics who deal with women authors, mostly from the nineteenth and twentieth centuries. The concerns and even the existence of the first group seem to go largely unacknowledged in many of the best-known discussions of feminist criticism, which often focus on issues not relevant to feminine analysis of traditional male authors on, for example, the nature of the female aesthetic, the female literary tradition, or the reshaping of the canon. (78)

Neely is being kind. Showalter explicitly limits feminist criticism to only women's writings, and asserts that English feminist criticism, French feminist criticism, and American feminist criticism all must become "gynocentric" ("Wilderness" 249). Showalter effectively denies that any critic who examines a male-authored text can be a feminist critic.

A second area of conflict is whether or not a man can possibly be a feminist literary critic. In a dialogue that she initiated in the pages of *Critical Inquiry* in 1975–76 ("Feminist"; "Some Notes"), Annette Kolodny denies the ability of any man, no matter how enlightened, how sensitive, how critically sophisticated, to respond to a text as a true feminist, for no man experiences the internal workings of a woman's body or the external oppressions of a patriarchal structure, and without such knowledge, true feminist reaction is impossible. Further, entry of men into the area of women's studies weakens the very foundations of the enterprise, for the power of women to order and interpret their lives is once again called into question. While Kolodny made her assertions in the early stages of feminist literary activity, and while responsible and intelligent men have indeed practiced what they call "feminist" criticism, this tension is still evident in feminist critical dialogues among men and women critics (Neely, "Feminist Criticism"; Nelson), in conference panels, and even within the critical discourse of the male feminist critics themselves (Waller; Erickson). The publication of *Men in Feminism,* edited by Alice Jardine and Paul Smith, and *Engendering Men,* edited by Joseph A. Boone and Michael Cadden, are important continuations of this dialogue.

A further area of disagreement is whether or not a unified theoretical platform is necessary. In several of her early essays, including her groundbreaking article, "Dancing through the Minefields," first published in 1980, Kolodny states that "feminist literary criticism appear[s] 'more like a set of interchangeable strategies than any coherent school or shared goal orientation'" (159). While Showalter responds to this assessment with a qualified "yes," she argues that a theoretical base that is truly woman-centered is absolutely imperative "if we wish to ask questions about the process and contexts of writing, if we genuinely wish to define ourselves to the uninitiated," as opposed to offering merely an interpretation of literature that competes with other interpretations of literature ("Wilderness" 246). She then offers a theory based on women's culture as the "more complete and satisfying way to talk about the specificity and difference of women's writing than theories based in biology, linguistics, or psychoanalysis," since such a theory could incorporate these disciplines within "the social contexts in which they occur" (258).

Whereas a majority of feminist critics may agree with Showalter's gynocritical emphasis, there is less consensus on the appropriate road to take. The most celebrated conflict within feminist literary criticism is that between Anglo-American feminist criticism and French feminist theory. The Anglo-American school focuses on experience with a sociohistorical emphasis; it includes any mode of criticism that approaches a text with a primary concern for the nature of the female experience in it—the fictional experience of the characters, the deducible or imaginable experience of the author, or the experience implicit in language or structures. The critics associated with this school include Elaine Showalter, Annette Kolodny, Sandra Gilbert and Susan Gubar, among others; compatible methodologies with this point of view include historicist/Marxist criticism and genre criticism. The French school of feminist criticism decries this emphasis upon sociology and history and looks to the unconscious, the deep structures of culture and language by which to describe "the feminine." Julia Kristeva, Hélène Cixous, Luce Irigaray, and Monique Wittig are some of this school's leading critics; their primary methodologies include psychoanalytic criticism and deconstruction.

The conflict between these schools has been addressed by Toril Moi in *Sexual/Textual Politics*. Moi, who explicitly identifies herself with the French feminist position, argues that Anglo-American feminist criticism, while *"politiciz[ing]* existing critical methods and approaches . . . still remains entangled with depoliticizing theoretical paradigms" (87, 88; Moi's emphasis). In other words, Anglo-American feminist critics have challenged the cultural oppression of women by their critical activity, but they have not generated new analytical procedures and thus are still tied to the very systems of thought and behavior they seek to subvert. French feminist theorists, on the other hand, attempt to "deconstruct" the binarization of gender that underlie cultural oppression, thus challenging "the very categories in which feminist politics have usually been understood" (Howard 169).

If the intellectual rigor of the French school seems to have the theoretical edge on the Anglo-American school, it nevertheless has been characterized as being elitist and abstract, that is, that its practice is confined to the well-educated and wealthy intelligentsia of the industrial West and that its philosophical concerns have no effect on political and social institutions and attitudes. In fact, many feminist critics have voiced the need to return to historical context. For example, in *Feminist Literary History,* her self-acknowledged defense of the Anglo-American sociohistorical approach, Janet Todd critiques both French feminist theory and gynocriticism for their basic perception of woman as a kind of single, autonomous entity and advocates instead a "historically specific, archival, ideologically aware but still empirically based enterprise, using a sense of specific genre as well as notions of changing female experience" (7).

Perhaps the confrontation between these two philosophical stances has now passed (as Howard and Felski argue), but in its wake there is greater mutual recognition that the feminist critic must be deeply self-aware about the cultural baggage she brings to her practice, and consequently, she must be unafraid to problematize the system she employs. Further, since gender can never be an isolated variable but exists in contexts informed by multiple other variables, including race, class, and ethnicity, *feminisms* replaces *feminism* as the more accurate term: "the plurality of feminisms is embodied in critical practice" (Capo and Hantzis 249).

These tensions seem inherent between feminism(s) and its oppositional patriarchal structure, as well as within the feminist agenda itself. In fact, it is in the struggle among these points of view that identity may be constructed. Neely articulates the details of such a dialectic.

> I would argue for both separation and assimilation [with patriarchal culture], for the [feminist] movement as a whole and for individuals within it. I see both as necessary personal, critical, pedagogical, and political strategies. I advocate supporting lesbian *and* heterosexual feminists, female *and*

male feminists, white feminists *and* feminists of color, teaching authors of all sexes, races and classes, paying attention to female experience *and* male power, analyzing the patriarchal tradition *and* the history of female resistance to it, allowing the self-confidence and self-knowledge engendered by relationships with women to provide the ground from which to encounter and know men. Neither side of these dichotomies should be abandoned; the tensions between them must be acknowledged, exposed, exploited, and endured. ("Feminist Criticism" 83)

Neely concludes her essay with the realistic and pragmatic conclusion, "no peaceable kingdom this" (83).

As we turn toward a particular focus on how feminist criticism has treated Renaissance women writers, the absence of a peaceable kingdom is pronounced. A gap in understanding seems to characterize, at least partially, the dialogue between scholars working on the writing of women from early periods and those scholars working on the writing of women from later periods. A review of publications over the last twenty years indicates that the writings of women in the nineteenth and twentieth centuries have been privileged over the writings of women prior to these centuries. This privileging seems to be a function of two misconceptions: first, that women of the earlier periods were silenced by the culture's equation of talkativeness with sexual openness, and second, that women who violated this stricture nevertheless are only marginally a part of the "women's tradition in literature" because they were too deeply embedded in the patriarchal culture (Gilbert and Gubar 3–4).

Renaissance scholars are offering a corrective to this statement in two ways. First, they are making accessible the works of Renaissance women by publishing these writings, in many instances, the first printing ever or the first since the seventeenth century. Such a record demonstrates that, regardless of the strictures against writing and publication, many women in fact ignored these cultural constraints (Crawford, "Women's Published Writings 1600–1700"; Smith and Cardinale). Anthologies of these writings include Betty S. Travitsky's *Paradise of Women: Writings by Englishwomen of the Renaissance* (1981; rev. ed. 1989); Angeline Goreau's *The Whole Duty of a Woman: Female Writers in Seventeenth-Century England* (1985); Katharina M. Wilson's *Women Writers of the Renaissance and Reformation* (1987); Wilson and Frank J. Warnke's *Women Writers of the Seventeenth Century* (1989); and *Kissing the Rod: An Anthology of Seventeenth-Century Women's Verse*, edited by Germaine Greer et al. (1988). Certain longer works have been published or are in the process of being published, including Elizabeth Cary's *Mariam* and Mary Wroth's *Urania*. Equally important is the inclusion of works by women writers in comprehensive anthologies of the period, for example the presence of writings by Mary Wroth, Margaret Cavendish, and Aphra Behn in Paul Salzman's *Anthology of Seventeenth-Century Fiction* (1991). Such "mainstreaming" is, unfortunately, still rare. As Barbara Lewalski notes, "early modern women's voices, perspectives, and writings are not adequately brought to bear upon topics which have become central for literary scholars—the power of social and cultural institutions, the ideology of absolutism and patriarchy, the formation of subjectivity, the forms of authorial 'self-fashioning,' the possibility and manifestations of resistance and subversion" ("Lecture" 793).

Along with the discovery of the physical evidence of women's writing is the interpretation of the literary and historical value of these works. For the most part, feminist critics of seventeenth-century women writers are of the Anglo-American school of feminist criticism, focusing on a particular woman writer in a particular age, rather than on the "idea" of woman. These scholars have chosen to rewrite the poststructuralist assertion of Michel Foucault, Roland Barthes, and Jacques Derrida that the author—the notion of a unified subject or center or self from which a piece of literature originates—is dead. An implicit foundation upon which attention to women writers of the early modern period rests is that the sex of the author is the crucial factor in the interpretative process. Thus, personal biography—and especially that part of the biography that is specifically affected by the writer's sex, such as marriage and motherhood—infuses the essays on many of these writers, providing a map by which to read their works.

More recently, following the suggestion of Janet Todd (quoted above), feminist scholars of this period are deliberately taking a view wider than the writer's home and family relationships. As Marilyn L. Williamson, following Linda Alcoff and Teresa de Lauretis, states: "[T]he construction of subjectivity is a continuous process, produced not only by external social patterns and discourses but through the individual's interaction with such discourses and cultural practices. . . . This approach describes a self-analyzing practice that engages the horizons of meanings and practices at a given historical moment in order to position one's self to assume one's feminine identity as a point of departure in political analysis" (10). In practical terms, this kind of criticism attempts to locate a text not only in the more personal and more confined situation of the writer's private relationships and concerns, but also in its specific cultural milieu, thus avoiding reductive generalizations that essentialize either the author or her age.

For example, some scholars argue that Renaissance women were able to demonstrate a separate autonomy by working against patriarchal constructs. Moira Ferguson in her anthology *First Feminists: British Women Writers, 1578–1799* and Hilda Smith in her *Reason's Disciples: Seventeenth-Century English Feminists* argue that explicit feminist attitudes—"those ideas and actions that advocate women's just demands and rights, or that counter or offset, at any level, the socio-cultural, sexual, and psychological oppression and economic exploitation of women" (Ferguson xi)—can be found in the writings of women in early periods. However, this proactive definition of feminism, while apparently appropriate when discussing the lives and works of such "notorious" women writers as Margaret Cavendish and Aphra Behn, who lived their lives in self-conscious opposition to the culture's construction of ideal womanhood, is, for the most part, an inaccurate ideology by which to characterize the lives and works of most seventeenth-century women writers.

More recently, scholars have modified this oppositional aesthetic by contextualizing the writings of Renaissance women within—rather than against—the culture, noting how author and culture intersect in the literary text. Mary Ellen Lamb, for example, sees the Sidney women writers (Mary Sidney and Mary Wroth) as constructing a feminine "heroics of constancy," which works within the cultural construction of woman as chaste, silent, and obedient, at the same time as it opposes the masculine heroics of chivalry. Elaine Hobby shows how seventeenth-century women writers made a "virtue of necessity," using the oppressive cultural definition of woman as the very defense of their writing activity. Marilyn L. Williamson, adopting the historically constructed polar labels for two of the more famous writers of the seventeenth century, argues that women writers of this period legitimized their writing activity by explicitly identifying themselves as followers of either Orinda (Katherine Philips), a proponent of retirement discourse, or Aphra Behn, a follower of the male-identified Cavalier sensibility of political conservatism and libertinism. Tina Krontiris grapples directly with the paradox that the oppressive culture in early modern England simultaneously inhibited women in general from writing and publishing, and yet provided a "congenial" environment essential for the imaginative work of at least a handful of women.

Along with this contextualizing strategy, Renaissance scholars are asking us to rethink the criteria by which such value judgments are made. Janet Todd, writing about "the constructed nature of female consciousness" formed in the fiction of women writers of the eighteenth century (*Sign* 9), queries the historically conditioned and male-defined aesthetic that "eschews the disparate, the sentimental and the moralistic" and privileges "the ironic and the unified work" (6). Margaret Ezell, looking at the production of literature, argues that publication is a false touchstone for assessing the literary value of seventeenth-century writings if it is the only touchstone, since both men and women writers of the age participated in a manuscript culture, which valued both collaborative work and what we might call "marginal" genres, such as letters, diaries, religious writings, and the like ("Myth").

Todd's and Ezell's theses constitute small parts of a more encompassing and more critical issue: the understanding of the seventeenth-century's culture, on both a theoretical and a practical level, of what constituted private and public activities and spaces. Some contemporary historians argue that trying to separate the two spheres of public and private is futile (Willen, "Religion" 156), that the analogy between family and state "means that it is inappropriate to dismiss what happened in the family as 'private'" (Amussen 2). Other historians, however, counter this assessment, asserting that "private and public matters were organized somewhat differently than now but with distinctions that were just as obvious and definitive" (Warnicke, "Private" 23; see also Mendelson, "Diaries," and Schwoerer). This debate not only colors our understanding of women's lives, but also their attitudes toward and practice of writing and/or publication.

Perhaps the most striking aspect of feminist attention to seventeenth-century women writers is its dialogic character. Scholars working in this area are in endless conversation with other scholars—those whose methodology is the same and those whose methodology is different, those who are politically congenial and those who are not. And they are in endless conversation with the subjects of their writing as well as with themselves. The "Recent Studies" lists compiled by Elizabeth H. Hageman and Josephine A. Roberts for *English Literary Renaissance* (Farrell, Hageman, and Kinney), and updated by Georgianna Ziegler and Sara Jayne Steen in *ELR* (1994), attest to the scope and quality of this feminist dialogue. While the course of this literary and political conversation is complex and entangled, its querying nature is nevertheless a constant, constituting its most distinctive and most significant attribute.

INTRODUCTORY BIBLIOGRAPHY

Alcoff, Linda. "Cultural Feminism versus Post-Structuralism: The Identity Crisis in Feminist Theory." *Signs* 13 (spring 1988): 405–23.

Amussen, Susan Dwyer. *An Ordered Society: Gender and Class in Early Modern England*. Oxford: Basil Blackwell, 1988.

Aughterson, Kate, ed. *Renaissance Woman—A Sourcebook*. London: Routledge, 1996.

Ballard, George. *Memoirs of Several Ladies of Great Britain* (1752). Ed. Marilyn L. Williamson. Detroit: Wayne State Univ. Press, 1985.

Beilin, Elaine V. *Redeeming Eve: Women Writers of the English Renaissance*. Princeton: Princeton Univ. Press, 1987.

Bell, Maureen, George Parfitt, and Simon Shepherd. *A Biographical Dictionary of English Women Writers 1580–1720*. Boston: G. K. Hall, 1990.

Belsey, Catherine. *The Subject of Tragedy: Identity and Difference in Renaissance Drama*. London: Methuen, 1985.

Benson, Pamela J. *The Invention of the Renaissance Woman: The Challenge of Female Independence in the Literature and Thought of Italy and England*. University Park, Pa.: Pennsylvania State Univ. Press, 1992.

Benstock, Shari, ed. *Feminist Issues in Literary Scholarship*. Bloomington: Indiana Univ. Press, 1987.

Boone, Joseph A., and Michael Cadden, eds. *Engendering Men: The Question of Male Feminist Criticism*. New York: Routledge, 1990.

Brant, Clare, and Diane Purkiss, eds. *Women, Texts, and Histories, 1575–1760*. London: Routledge, 1992.

Brink, Jean R., ed. *Female Scholars: A Tradition of Learned Women before 1800*. Montreal: Eden Press, 1980.

———, ed. *Playing with Gender: A Renaissance Pursuit*. Urbana: Univ. of Illinois Press, 1991.

———, ed. *Privileging Gender in Early Modern England*. Kirksville, Mo.: Sixteenth-Century Journal Publishers, 1994.

Capo, Kay Ellen, and Darlene M. Hantzis. "(En)Gendered (and Endangered) Subjects: Writing, Reading, Performing, and Theorizing Feminist Criticism." *Text and Performance Quarterly* 11 (1991): 249–66.

Cerasano, S. P., and Marion Wynne-Davies, eds. *Gloriana's Face: Women, Public and Private, in the English Renaissance*. Detroit: Wayne State Univ. Press, 1992.

———, eds. *Renaissance Drama by Women: Texts and Documents*. New York: Routledge, 1996.

Chedgzoy, Kate, Melanie Hansen, and Suzanne Trill, eds. *Voicing Women: Gender and Sexuality in Early Modern Writing*. Staffordshire, England: Keele Univ. Press, 1996.

Clark, Alice. *Working Life of Women in the Seventeenth Century* (1919). Ed. Miranda Chaytor and Jane Lewis. London: Routledge, 1982.

Cotton, Nancy. *Women Playwrights in England, ca. 1363–1750*. Lewisburg, Pa.: Bucknell Univ. Press, 1980.

Crawford, Patricia. *Women and Religion in England, 1500–1720*. London: Routledge, 1993.

———. "Women's Published Writings, 1600–1700." In *Women in English Society, 1500–1800*. Ed. Mary Prior. London: Methuen, 1985. 211–82.

de Lauretis, Teresa, ed. *Feminist Studies/Critical Studies*. Bloomington: Indiana Univ. Press, 1986.

Donovan, Josephine. "Women and the Rise of the Novel: A Feminist-Marxist Theory." *Signs* 16 (1991): 441–62.

Erickson, Peter. *Rewriting Shakespeare, Rewriting Ourselves*. Berkeley and Los Angeles: Univ. of California Press, 1991.

Ezell, Margaret J. M. "The *Gentleman's Journal* and the Commercialization of Restoration Coterie Literary Practices." *Modern Philology* 89 (1992): 323–40.

———. "The Myth of Judith Shakespeare: Creating the Canon of Women's Literature." *New Literary History* 21, no. 3 (spring 1990): 579–92.

———. *The Patriarch's Wife: Literary Evidence and the History of the Family*. Chapel Hill: Univ. of North Carolina Press, 1987.

———. *Writing Women's Literary History*. Baltimore: Johns Hopkins Univ. Press, 1993.

Farrell, Kirby, Elizabeth H. Hageman, and Arthur F. Kinney, eds. *Women in the Renaissance: Selections from "English Literary Renaissance."* Amherst: Univ. of Massachusetts Press, 1990.

Felski, Rita. "The Use and Abuse of History: Recent Developments in Feminist Theory." *Criticism* 31 (1989): 455–63.

Ferguson, Margaret W. "Moderation and Its Discontents: Recent Work on Renaissance Women." *Feminist Studies* 20 (1994): 349–66.

Ferguson, Margaret W., Maureen Quilligan, and Nancy Vickers, eds. *Rewriting the Renaissance: The Discourses of Sexual Difference in Early Modern Europe*. Chicago: Univ. of Chicago Press, 1986.

Ferguson, Moira, ed. *First Feminists: British Women Writers, 1578–1799*. Bloomington: Indiana Univ. Press, 1985.

Fraser, Antonia. *The Weaker Vessel*. New York: Alfred A. Knopf, 1984.

Friedman, Susan Stanford. "Post/Poststructuralist Feminist Criticism: The Politics of Recuperation and Negotiation." *New Literary History* 22, no. 2 (1991): 465–90.

Gallop, Jane. *Thinking through the Body*. New York: Columbia Univ. Press, 1988.

Gardiner, Judith Kegan. "On Female Identity and Writing by Women." *Critical Inquiry* 8, no. 2 (1981): 347–61.

Gartenberg, Patricia, and Nena Whittemore. "A Checklist of English Women in Print, 1475–1640." *Bulletin of Bibliography and Magazine Notes* 34 (1977): 1–13.

Gilbert, Sandra M., and Susan Gubar, eds. *The Norton Anthology of Literature by Women: The Tradition in English*. New York: W. W. Norton and Company, 1985.

Goreau, Angeline. *Reconstructing Aphra: A Social Biography of Aphra Behn*. New York: Dial Press, 1980.

———, ed. *The Whole Duty of a Woman: Female Writers in Seventeenth-Century England*. New York: Dial Press, 1985.

Goulianos, Joan, ed. *By a Woman Writt: Literature from Six Centuries by and about Women.* Baltimore: Penguin, 1973.

Graham, Elspeth, Hilary Hinds, Elaine Hobby, and Helen Wilcox, eds. *Her Own Life: Autobiographical Writings by Seventeenth-Century Englishwomen.* London: Routledge, 1989.

Greene, Gayle, and Coppélia Kahn. "Feminist Scholarship and the Social Construction of Woman." In *Making a Difference: Feminist Literary Criticism.* Ed. Gayle Greene and Coppélia Kahn. London: Methuen, 1985, 1–36.

Greer, Germaine, Susan Hastings, Jeslyn Medoff, and Melinda Sansone, eds. *Kissing the Rod: An Anthology of Seventeenth-Century Women's Verse.* New York: Noonday Press, 1988.

Grundy, Isobel, and Susan Wiseman, eds. *Women, Writing, History, 1640–1740.* Athens: Univ. of Georgia Press, 1992.

Hall, Kim F. *Things of Darkness: Economies of Race and Gender in Early Modern England.* Ithaca: Cornell Univ. Press, 1995.

Hamsten, Elizabeth. "Petticoat Authors: 1660–1720." *Women's Studies* 7 (1980): 21–38.

Hannay, Margaret P., ed. *Silent But for the Word: Tudor Women as Patrons, Translators, and Writers of Religious Works.* Kent, Ohio: Kent State Univ. Press, 1985.

Haselkorn, Anne M., and Betty S. Travitsky, eds. *The Renaissance Englishwoman in Print: Counterbalancing the Canon.* Amherst: Univ. of Massachusetts Press, 1990.

Henderson, Katherine Usher, and Barbara F. McManus, eds. *Half Humankind: Contexts and Texts of the Controversy about Women in England, 1540–1640.* Urbana: Univ. of Illinois Press, 1985.

Hendricks, Margo, and Patricia Parker, eds. *Woman, "Race," and Writing in the Early Modern Period.* London: Routledge, 1994.

Hobby, Elaine. *Virtue of Necessity: English Women's Writing, 1649–1688.* London: Virago Press, 1988.

Howard, June. "Feminist Differings: Recent Surveys of Feminist Literary Theory and Criticism." *Feminist Studies* 14 (1988): 167–90.

Hull, Suzanne W. *Chaste, Silent, and Obedient: English Books for Women, 1475–1640.* San Marino, Calif.: Huntington Library, 1982.

Jardine, Alice, and Paul Smith, eds. *Men in Feminism.* New York: Routledge, 1987.

Jones, Ann Rosalind, ed. "Cluster on Early Modern Women." *PMLA* 109 (1994): 187–237.

———. *The Currency of Eros: Women's Love Lyric in Europe, 1540–1620.* Bloomington: Indiana Univ. Press, 1990.

Jordan, Constance. *Renaissance Feminism: Literary Texts and Political Models.* Ithaca: Cornell Univ. Press, 1990.

Keeble, N. H., ed. *The Cultural Identity of Seventeenth-Century Woman: A Reader.* New York: Routledge, 1994.

Kelly-Gadol, Joan. "Did Women Have a Renaissance?" In *Becoming Visible: Women in European History.* Ed. Renate Bridenthal and Claudia Koonz. Boston: Houghton Miflin, 1977, 137–64.

Kendall. *Love and Thunder: Plays by Women in the Age of Queen Anne.* London: Methuen Drama, 1988.

King, Margaret L. *Women of the Renaissance*. Chicago: Univ. of Chicago Press, 1991.

Kolodny, Annette. "Dancing through the Minefield: Some Observations on the Theory, Practice, and Politics of a Feminist Literary Criticism" (1980). In *The New Feminist Criticism: Essays on Women, Literature, and Theory*. Ed. Elaine Showalter. New York: Pantheon Books, 1985. 144–67.

———. "The Feminist as Literary Critic." *Critical Inquiry* 2 (summer 1976): 821–32.

———. "Some Notes on Defining a 'Feminist Literary Criticism.'" *Critical Inquiry* 2 (fall 1975): 75–92.

Krontiris, Tina. *Oppositional Voices: Women as Writers and Translators of Literature in the English Renaissance*. London: Routledge, 1992.

Labalme, Patricia H. *Beyond Their Sex: Learned Women of the European Past*. New York: New York Univ. Press, 1980.

Lamb, Mary Ellen. *Gender and Authorship in the Sidney Circle*. Madison: Univ. of Wisconsin Press, 1990.

Larsen, Anne R., and Colette H. Winn, eds. *Renaissance Women Writers: French Texts, American Contexts*. Detroit: Wayne State Univ. Press, 1994.

Levin, Carole, and Jeanie Watson, eds. *Ambiguous Realities: Women in the Middle Ages and Renaissance*. Detroit: Wayne State Univ. Press, 1987.

Lewalski, Barbara K. "The 1991 Josephine Waters Bennett Lecture: Writing Women and Reading the Renaissance." *Renaissance Quarterly* 44 (winter 1991): 792–821.

———. *Writing Women in Jacobean England*. Cambridge: Harvard Univ. Press, 1993.

MacCarthy, B. G. *Women Writers: Their Contribution to the English Novel, 1621–1744*. Cork: Cork Univ. Press, 1946.

Mahl, Mary R., and Helen Koon, eds. *The Female Spectator: English Women Writers before 1800*. Bloomington: Indiana Univ. Press, 1977.

Mendelson, Sara Heller. *The Mental World of Stuart Women: Three Studies*. Amherst: Univ. of Massachusetts Press, 1987.

———. "Stuart Women's Diaries and Occasional Memoirs." In *Women in English Society, 1500–1800*. Ed. Mary Prior. London: Methuen, 1985. 181–210.

Miller, Nancy K. *Subject to Change: Reading Feminist Writing*. New York: Columbia Univ. Press, 1988.

———, ed. *The Poetics of Gender*. New York: Columbia Univ. Press, 1986.

Miller, Naomi J., and Gary Waller, eds. *Reading Mary Wroth: Representing Alternatives in Early Modern England*. Knoxville: Univ. of Tennessee Press, 1991.

Moi, Toril. *Sexual/Textual Politics: Feminist Literary Theory* (1985). London: Routledge, 1988.

Morgan, Fidelis. *The Female Wits: Women Playwrights on the London Stage, 1660–1720*. London: Virago, 1981.

Mulvey, Laura. "Visual Pleasure and Narrative Cinema." *Screen* 16, no. 3 (autumn 1975): 6–18.

Neely, Carol Thomas. "Constructing the Subject: Feminist Practice and the New Renaissance Discourses." *English Literary Renaissance* 18 (winter 1988): 5–18.

———. "Feminist Criticism in Motion." In *For Alma Mater: Theory and Practice in Feminist Scholarship*. Ed. Paula A. Treichler, Cheris Kramarae, and Beth Stafford. Urbana: Univ. of Illinois Press, 1985. 69–90.

Nelson, Cary. "Envoys of Otherness: Difference and Continuity in Feminist Criticism." In *For Alma Mater: Theory and Practice in Feminist Scholarship*. Ed. Paula A. Treichler, Cheris Kramarae, and Beth Stafford. Urbana: Univ. of Illinois Press, 1985. 91–118.

Otten, Charlotte F., ed. *English Women's Voices, 1540–1700*. Gainesville: Univ. Press of Florida, 1991.

Pearson, Jacqueline. *The Prostituted Muse: Images of Women and Women Dramatists, 1642–1737*. New York: St. Martin's Press, 1988.

Perry, Ruth. *The Celebrated Mary Astell: An Early English Feminist*. Chicago: Univ. of Chicago Press, 1986.

Poovey, Mary. "Feminism and Deconstruction." *Feminist Studies* 14 (1988): 51–65.

Quilligan, Maureen. *The Allegory of Female Authority: Christine de Pizan's "Cité des Dames."* Ithaca: Cornell Univ. Press, 1991.

Rose, Mary Beth. *The Expense of Spirit: Love and Sexuality in English Renaissance Drama*. Ithaca: Cornell Univ. Press, 1988.

———, ed. *Women in the Middle Ages and the Renaissance: Literary and Historical Perspectives*. Syracuse, N.Y.: Syracuse Univ. Press, 1986.

Roberts, Josephine A., ed. *The Poems of Lady Mary Wroth*. Baton Rouge, La.: Louisiana State Univ. Press, 1983.

Russ, Joanna. *How to Suppress Women's Writing*. London: Women's Press, 1984.

Salzman, Paul, ed. *An Anthology of Seventeenth-Century Fiction*. Oxford: Oxford Univ. Press, 1991.

Schleiner, Louise. *Tudor and Stuart Women Writers*. Bloomington: Indiana Univ. Press, 1994.

Schwoerer, Lois G. *Lady Rachel Russell: "One of the Best of Women."* Baltimore: Johns Hopkins Univ. Press, 1987.

Showalter, Elaine. "Feminist Criticism in the Wilderness" (1981). In *The New Feminist Criticism: Essays on Women, Literature, and Theory*. Ed. Elaine Showalter. New York: Pantheon Books, 1985. 243–70.

———. "Toward a Feminist Poetics" (1979). In *The New Feminist Criticism: Essays on Women, Literature, and Theory*. Ed. Elaine Showalter. New York: Pantheon Books, 1985. 125–43.

———, ed. *The New Feminist Criticism: Essays on Women, Literature, and Theory*. New York: Pantheon Books, 1985.

Smith, Hilda. *Reason's Disciples: Seventeenth-Century English Feminists*. Urbana: Univ. of Illinois Press, 1982.

Smith, Hilda, and Susan Cardinale, comp. *Women and the Literature of the Seventeenth Century: An Annotated Bibliography Based on Wing's "Short-title Catalogue."* New York: Greenwood Press, 1990.

Smith, Sidonie. *A Poetics of Women's Autobiography*. Bloomington: Indiana Univ. Press, 1987.

Spencer, Jane. *The Rise of the Woman Novelist: From Aphra Behn to Jane Austen*. Oxford: Blackwell, 1986.

Spender, Dale. *Mothers of the Novel: One Hundred Good Writers before Jane Austen.* London: Pandora, 1986.

Steen, Sara Jayne. "Recent Studies in Women Writers of the Seventeenth Century, 1604–1674 (1990 to mid-1993)." *ELR* 24 (winter 1994): 243–74.

Sullivan, Patricia A. "Female Writing beside the Rhetorical Tradition: Seventeenth Century British Biography and a Female Tradition in Rhetoric." *International Journal of Women's Studies* 3, no. 2 (March–April 1980): 143–60.

Todd, Janet. *A Dictionary of British and American Women Writers, 1600–1800.* Totowa, N.J.: Rowman and Littlefield, 1985.

———. *Feminist Literary Theory.* New York: Routledge, 1988.

———. *The Sign of Angellica: Women, Writing, and Fiction, 1660–1800.* London: Virago Press, 1989.

Travitsky, Betty S., ed. *The Paradise of Women: Writings by Englishwomen of the Renaissance* (1981). New York: Columbia Univ. Press, 1989.

Travitsky, Betty S., and Adele F. Seeff, eds. *Attending to Women in Early Modern England.* Newark: Univ. of Delaware Press, 1994.

Turner, James Grantham, ed. *Sexuality and Gender in Early Modern Europe: Institutions, Texts, Images.* Cambridge: Cambridge Univ. Press, 1993.

Walker, Cheryl. "Feminist Literary Criticism and the Author." *Critical Inquiry* 16 (spring 1990): 551–71.

Wall, Wendy. *The Imprint of Gender: Authorship and Publication in the English Renaissance.* Ithaca: Cornell Univ. Press, 1993.

———. "Our Bodies/Our Texts?: Renaissance Women and the Trials of Authorship." In *Anxious Power: Reading, Writing, and Ambivalence in Narrative by Women.* Ed. Carol J. Singley and Susan Elizabeth Sweeney. Albany: State Univ. of New York Press, 1993. 51–71.

Waller, Gary F. "Struggling into Discourse: The Emergence of Renaissance Women's Writing." *Silent But for the Word: Tudor Women as Patrons, Translators, and Writers of Religious Works.* Ed. Margaret P. Hannay. Kent, Ohio: Kent State Univ. Press, 1989. 238–56.

Warnicke, Retha. "Private and Public: The Boundaries of Women's Lives in Early Modern England." In *Privileging Gender in Early Modern England.* Ed. Jean R. Brink. Kirksville, Mo.: Sixteenth Century Journal Publishers, 1994.

———. *Women of the English Renaissance and Reformation.* Westport, Conn.: Greenwood Press, 1983.

Warnke, Frank, ed. *Three Women Poets: Louise Labé, Gaspara Stampa, Sor Juanna Ines de la Cruz.* Lewisburg, Pa.: Bucknell Univ. Press, 1987.

Wiesner, Merry E. *Women and Gender in Early Modern Europe.* Cambridge: Cambridge Univ. Press, 1993.

Willen, Diane. "Women and Religion in Early Modern England." In *Women in Reformation and Counter-Reformation Europe: Public and Private Worlds.* Ed. Sherrin Marshall. Bloomington: Indiana Univ. Press, 1989. 140–65.

———. "Women in the Public Sphere in Early Modern England: The Case of the Urban Working Poor." *Sixteenth Century Journal* 19, no. 4 (winter 1988): 559–75.

Williamson, Marilyn L. *Raising Their Voices: British Women Writers, 1650–1750*. Detroit: Wayne State Univ. Press, 1990.

Wilson, Katharina M., ed. *Women Writers of the Renaissance and Reformation*. Athens: Univ. of Georgia Press, 1987.

Wilson, Katharina M., and Frank J. Warnke, eds. *Women Writers of the Seventeenth Century*. Athens: Univ. of Georgia Press, 1989.

Wiltenburg, Joy. *Disorderly Women and Female Power in the Street Literature of Early Modern England and Germany*. Charlottesville: Univ. Press of Virginia, 1992.

Woodbridge, Linda. *Women and the English Renaissance: Literature and the Nature of Womankind, 1540–1620*. Urbana: Univ. of Illinois Press, 1984.

Woolf, Virginia. *A Room of One's Own*. New York: Harcourt, Brace, and Co., 1929.

Zagarell, Sandra A. "Conceptualizing Women's Literary History: Reflections on *The Norton Anthology of Literature by Women*." *Tulsa Studies in Women's Literature* 5 (1986): 273–87.

Ziegler, Georgianna M. "Recent Studies in Women Writers of Tudor England, 1485–1603 (1990 to mid-1993)." *ELR* 24 (winter 1994): 229–42.

AEMILIA LANYER
(1569–1645)

INTRODUCTION

"Eve's Apology in Defense of Women" by Aemilia Lanyer is one of the most eloquent attempts in early seventeenth-century England to counter the misogynistic view of women as weak, seductive, and malicious. Lanyer's defense of Eve forms a central part of a poetic collection, *Salve Deus Rex Judaeorum* (1611), in which she celebrates a community of learned and virtuous women. At the same time as she praises her patrons, Lanyer calls attention, self-consciously and sometimes bitterly, to her own social subordination to the rich ladies she serves.

The author was born into an artistic family, probably of Jewish ancestry: her father was Baptist Bassano, an Italian musician at the Tudor court, and her mother was an Englishwoman named Margaret Johnson. Our major source of information concerning her early life is her poetry, in which she refers to Susan Bertie, dowager countess of Kent, as "the Mistress of my youth, / The noble guide of my ungovern'd days." She may have lived in the countess of Kent's household as a waiting gentlewoman, a position that would provide the opportunity for some education and access to literature.

According to the astrologer Simon Forman, who interviewed Lanyer as one of his clients, she became involved with Henry Carey, first Lord Hunsdon (1526–1596), nearly forty-five years older than Lanyer. Forman records in his diary that when she became pregnant with Hunsdon's child, she was married off to "a minstrel." She was wed in 1592 to Alphonso Lanyer, a military officer and musician who had played at Queen Elizabeth's funeral and who later became one of King James's musicians. Through the intervention of the earl of Southampton, who served with him in Ireland, Lanyer was successful in gaining a straw-weighing monopoly from the Crown in 1604, but the income proved to be insufficient for a family of at least two children: a son Henry, born in 1593, and a daughter Odillya, who died nine months after birth in 1599 (see Woods xxiv–xxv). When Aemilia Lanyer published her slim volume of poems in 1611, she may have been financially motivated to include a large collection of nine dedicatory poems. In her epistle to Anne, countess of Dorset, she bluntly pleads that "God's Stewards must for all the poor provide." Alphonso Lanyer's death in 1613 left his wife and family in severe financial straits.

Lanyer seems to have hoped to support her household by setting up a school for gentlemen's children, but she found herself in court with her landlord, claiming that her repairs to the building should be held against the rent. Between 1635 and 1638, she made repeated applications for her husband's monopoly of weighing straw, but apparently in vain. She was buried at Clerkenwell on April 3, 1645.

Because of her affair with Lord Hunsdon, who was lord chamberlain and

SALVE DEVS
REX IVDÆORVM.

Containing,

1 The Pafsion of Chrift.
2 Eues Apologie in defence of Women.
3 The Teares of the Daughters of Ierufalem.
4 The Salutation and Sorrow of the Virgine Marie.

With diuers other things not vnfit to be read.

Written by Miftris *Æmilia Lanyer*, Wife to Captaine *Alfonfo Lanyer* Seruant to the Kings Majeftie.

At LONDON
Printed by *Valentine Simmes* for *Richard Bonian,* and are to be fold at his Shop in Paules Church-yard. *Anno* 1611.

Title Page of Aemilia Lanyer's *Salve Deus Rex Judaeorum* (1611). (Reproduced by permission of The Huntington Library, San Marino, California.)

patron of Shakespeare's acting company, the historian A. L. Rowse maintained that Aemilia Lanyer was the Dark Lady of Shakespeare's sonnets. He built his case largely on circumstantial evidence, such as her husband's friendship with Southampton, to whom Shakespeare dedicated his long poems, *Venus and Adonis* and *The Rape of Lucrece*. Unfortunately, there is no proof that Aemilia Lanyer even knew Shakespeare, and despite Rowse's valuable research into her life, his identification of her as the Dark Lady has not been generally accepted.

Yet by means of her relationship with Hunsdon, Lanyer gained favor with some of the leading literary women of the court, especially Elizabeth I. In her dedicatory poem to Queen Anne, Lanyer recalls a happier time when "great *Eliza's* favor blest my youth." She was acquainted with the learned Arabella Stuart, niece to James I, and she refers to having read the versified Psalms of Mary Sidney, countess of Pembroke, which circulated only in manuscript. In fact, the countess of Pembroke may have served as a model for Lanyer, since she had boldly published two of her translations in 1592 at a time when few women dared.

Lanyer's only known surviving publication is *Salve Deus Rex Judaeorum* (Hail God, king of the Jews), which is dedicated to Margaret Russell, countess of Cumberland, as a primary patron. Lanyer refers to living with the countess and her daughter, Anne Clifford, at their rented country estate Cookham in Berkshire. She credits the countess with providing her the inspiration to write both her religious poem on Christ's passion (*Salve Deus Rex Judaeorum*), as well as her secular country house poem, "The Description of Cookham." These works, appearing together in the same collection, complement each other in their celebration of feminine heroism. In her meditative poem on Christ's Crucifixion, Lanyer emphasizes the spiritual gifts of women, as seen in the examples of Pilate's wife (who narrates "Eve's Apology"), the daughters of Jerusalem, the Virgin Mary, and the countess of Cumberland. Although the dedicatory epistles may have been included for reasons of patronage, they still create the effect of a larger community of virtuous women, much as the medieval writer Christine de Pisan sought to fashion in her *Book of the City of Ladies* (1405). Two of the epistles are included here, the poetic dream-vision of Mary Sidney, countess of Pembroke, and the prose address "To the Virtuous Reader," in which Lanyer directly insists on the need to recognize female spirituality and to demonstrate the central role of women in the Christian faith.

Located at the heart of Lanyer's religious poem, "Eve's Apology" is not without its contradictions. On the one hand, Lanyer pronounces Eve guiltless of any evil intentions in the Fall, but she cautions her readers, "Let not us Women glory in Men's fall, / Who had power given to over-rule us all" (759–60). This assertion of women's subordination is also implied in the portrait of Adam, who is not deceived by the serpent, whereas Eve innocently fails to detect the evil. Lanyer then argues that because Adam is so strong, wise, and undeceived, he is most to blame. Yet by the end of the apology, Lanyer turns to question the very grounds of subordination: "Your fault being greater, why should you disdain / Our being your equals, free from tyranny?" (829–30). Some of the same spirit of inquiry may be found in the unpublished defense of Eve by Lady Anne Southwell (1573–1636), which appears in her commonplace book (Folger MS V.b.198).

God took a Marble Pillar and did build
  A little world with all perfection fill'd
And brought her unto Adam as a bride;   15
  The text saith she was taken from his side,
A symbol of that side from whence did flow
  Christ's spouse (the Church) as all wise men do know.
But Adam slept, as saith the history,
  Uncapable of such a mystery,   20
And they sleep still that do not understand
  The curious fabric of th'Almighty's hand.

Unlike Lanyer, Southwell refuses to apportion blame for the Fall and maintains that both Adam and Eve "turned fools in Paradise" (32), but she uses her argument, as does Lanyer, to insist on the spiritual equality of men and women.

In "The Description of Cookham," Lanyer evokes a vision of an earthly paradise, inhabited by three women—the countess of Cumberland, her daughter Anne, and the poet. Her work is an example of the country house poem, a genre heavily influenced by the classical models of Horace and Martial, who wrote in praise of rural retirement, as opposed to court or city life. Henry Howard, earl of Surrey, was the first English poet to translate both Horace and Martial, and his own poem "Prisoned in Windsor" contrasts the remembrance of a carefree childhood spent in the "secret groves" and "wild forest" of Windsor with the stark misery of present circumstances, his imprisonment within the same walls. Lanyer similarly sets in opposition her memories of an idyllic existence spent with the countess of Cumberland and her daughter Anne at Cookham and the eventual loss of paradise.

The composition of "The Description of Cookham" may be dated roughly between 1609 (the date of Anne's marriage and departure, alluded to in line 95) and 1610, when *Salve Deus Rex Judaeorum* was entered in the Stationers' Register. Because the date of Ben Jonson's "To Penshurst" is uncertain, we do not know whether the composition of Lanyer's poem preceded it. In any event, Lanyer's poem, published five years before Jonson's, includes many of the features of the country house genre, such as the description of the estate as a *locus amoenus,* the praise of its owners, and the pastoral celebration of the human relation to nature. What sets Lanyer's poem apart from Jonson's is the powerfully elegiac tone in which, after praising the abundance and fertility of the natural world, the poet turns to depict a fallen landscape, in perpetual mourning for the absence of the countess and her daughter.

FROM *SALVE DEUS REX JUDAEORUM* (1611)

The Author's Dream to the Lady Mary, the Countess Dowager of Pembroke

[In keeping with the genre of the dream-vision poem, the speaker falls asleep and, led by Morpheus (god of dreams), travels to Cyprus, where she sees the classical goddesses Minerva, Bellona, Diana, Aurora, and

Flora gather to pay homage to an unnamed mortal, who sits in the seat
of Honor.]

And now me thought I long to hear her name,
Whom wise *Minerva* honored so much,
She whom I saw was crowned by noble Fame,
Whom Envy sought to sting, yet could not touch.   100

Me thought the meager elf did seek by-ways
To come unto her, but it would not be;
Her venom purifi'd by virtue's rays,
She pin'd and starv'd like an anatomy.[1]

While beauteous *Pallas*[2] with this Lady fair,   105
Attended by these nymphs of noble fame,
Beheld those woods, those groves, those bowers
    rare,
By which *Pergusa*, for so hight the name

Of that fair spring, his dwelling place and
    ground;
And through those fields with sundry flowers   110
    clad,
Of sev'ral colors, to adorn the ground,
And please the senses ev'n of the most sad:

He trailed along the woods in wanton wise,
With sweet delight to entertain them all;
Inviting them to sit and to devise   115
On holy hymns; at last to mind they call

Those rare sweet songs which *Israel's* King[3] did
    frame
Unto the Father of Eternity;
Before his holy wisdom took the name
Of great *Messias*, Lord of unity.   120

*The Psalms
written newly
by the
Countess
Dowager of
Penbrooke.*

These holy sonnets they did all agree,
With this most lovely lady here to sing;
That by her noble breasts sweet harmony,
Their music might in ears of angels ring.

While saints like swans about this silver brook   125
Should *Halleluiah* sing continually,
Writing her praises in th'eternal book
Of endless honor, true fame's memory.

Thus I in sleep the heavenli'st music hard,[4]
That ever earthly ears did entertain;   130

1. Skeleton.
2. Minerva, goddess of wisdom.
3. David, the Psalmist.
4. Heard.

And durst not wake, for fear to be debard
Of what my senses sought still to retain.

Yet sleeping, prayed dull Slumber to unfold
Her noble name, who was of all admired;
When presently in drowsy terms he told   135
Not only that, but more than I desired.

This nymph, quoth he, great *Penbrooke*[5] hight by name,
Sister to valiant *Sidney*, whose clear light
Gives light to all that tread true paths of fame,
Who in the globe of heav'n doth shine so bright;   140

That being dead, his fame doth him survive,
Still living in the hearts of worthy men;
Pale Death is dead, but he remains alive,
Whose dying wounds restor'd him life again.

And this fair earthly goddess which you see,   145
Bellona[6] and her virgins do attend;
In virtuous studies of divinity,
Her precious time continually doth spend.

So that a sister well she may be deemd,
To him that liv'd and died so nobly;   150
And far before him is to be esteemd
For virtue, wisdom, learning, dignity.

Whose beauteous soul hath gain'd a double life,
Both here on earth, and in the heav'ns above,
Till dissolution end all worldly strife: 155
Her blessed spirit remains, of holy love,

Directing all by her immortal light,
In this huge sea of sorrows, griefs, and fears;
With contemplation of God's powerful might,
She fills the eyes, the hearts, the tongues, the ears   160

Of after-coming ages, which shall read
Her love, her zeal, her faith, and piety;
The fair impression of whose worthy deed,
Seals her pure soul unto the deity.

That both in heav'n and earth it may remain,   165
Crown'd with her maker's glory and his love;
And this did Father Slumber tell with pain,
Whose dullness scarce could suffer him to move.

When I awaking left him and his bower,
Much grieved that I could no longer stay;   170

5. Alternative spelling of Pembroke.
6. Goddess of war and wisdom.

Senseless was sleep, not to admit me power,
As I had spent the night to spend the day:

Then had God *Morphy* show'd the end of all,
And what my heart desir'd, mine eyes had seen;
For as I wak'd me thought I heard one call   175
For that bright char'ot lent by *Jove's* fair Queen.

But thou, base cunning thief, that robs our sprits[7]
Of half that span of life which years doth give;
And yet no praise unto thyself it merits,
To make a seeming death in those that live.   180

Yea, wickedly thou dost consent to death,
Within thy restful bed to rob our souls;
In Slumber's bower thou steal'st away our breath,
Yet none there is that thy base stealths controls.

If poor and sickly creatures would embrace thee,   185
Or they to whom thou giv'st a taste of pleasure,
Thou fli'st as if *Acteon's* hounds[8] did chase thee,
Or that to stay with them thou hadst no leisure.

But though thou hast depriv'd me of delight,
By stealing from me ere I was aware;   190
I know I shall enjoy the self-same sight,
Thou hast no power my waking sprites to bar.

For to this lady now I will repair,
Presenting her the fruits of idle hours;
Though many books she writes that are more rare,   195
Yet there is honey in the meanest flowers:

Which is both wholesome, and delights the taste:
Though sugar be more finer, higher priz'd,
Yet is the painful bee no whit disgrac'd,
Nor her fair wax, or honey more despis'd.   200

And though that learned damsel and the rest,
Have in a higher style her trophy fram'd;
Yet these unlearned lines being my best,
Of her great wisdom can no whit be blam'd.

And therefore, first I here present my Dream,   205
And next, invite her honor to my feast,
For my clear reason sees her by that stream,
Where her rare virtues daily are increast.

So craving pardon for this bold attempt,
I here present my mirror to her view,   210

7. Spirits.
8. The mythological hunter Actaeon was turned into a stag and devoured by his own dogs.

Whose noble virtues cannot be exempt,
My glass being steel,[9] declares them to be true.

And Madam, if you will vouchsafe that grace,
To grace those flowers that springs from virtue's ground;
Though your fair mind on worthier works is plac'd,   215
On works that are more deep, and more profound;

Yet is it no disparagement to you,
To see your Savior in a shepherd's weed,
Unworthily presented in your view,
Whose worthiness will grace each line you read.   220

Receive him here by my unworthy hand,
And read his paths of fair humility;
Who though our sins in number pass the sand,
They all are purg'd by his divinity.

To the Virtuous Reader

Often have I heard, that it is the property of some women, not only to emulate the virtues and perfections of the rest, but also by all their powers of ill speaking, to eclipse the brightness of their deserved fame: now contrary to this custom, which men I hope unjustly lay to their charge, I have written this small volume, or little book, for the general use of all virtuous Ladies and Gentlewomen of this kingdom; and in commendation of some particular persons of our own sex, such as for the most part, are so well known to myself, and others, that I dare undertake Fame dares not to call any better. And this have I done, to make known to the world, that all women deserve not to be blamed though some forgetting they are women themselves, and in danger to be condemned by the words of their own mouths, fall into so great an error, as to speak unadvisedly against the rest of their sex; which if it be true, I am persuaded they can show their own imperfection in nothing more: and therefore could wish (for their own ease, modesties, and credit) they would refer such points of folly, to be practiced by evil disposed men, who forgetting they were born of women, nourished of women, and that if it were not by the means of women, they would be quite extinguished out of the world, and a final end of them all, do like Vipers deface the wombs wherein they were bred, only to give way and utterance to their want of discretion and goodness. Such as these, were they that dishonored Christ his Apostles and Prophets, putting them to shameful deaths. Therefore we are not to regard any imputations, that

---

9. A steel glass was supposedly a truthful mirror; see George Gascoigne's poem "The Steel Glass" (1576).

they undeservedly lay upon us, no otherwise than to make use of them to our own benefits, as spurs to virtue, making us fly all occasions that may color their unjust speeches to pass current. Especially considering that they have tempted even the patience of God himself, who gave power to wise and virtuous women, to bring down their pride and arrogancy. As was cruell *Cesarus*[1] by the discrete counsel of noble *Deborah*,[2] Judge and Prophetess of Israel: and resolution of *Jael*[3] wife of *Heber* the Kenite: wicked *Haman*,[4] by the divine prayers and prudent proceedings of beautiful *Hester:*[5] blasphemous *Holofernes*,[6] by the invincible courage, rare wisdom, and confident carriage of *Judith:* and the unjust Judges, by the innocency of chaste *Susanna:*[7] with infinite others, which for brevity's sake I will omit. As also in respect it pleased our Lord and Savior Jesus Christ, without the assistance of man, being free from original and all other sins, from the time of his conception, till the hour of his death, to be begotten of a woman, born of a woman, nourished of a woman, obedient to a woman; and that he healed women, pardoned women, comforted women: yea, even when he was in his greatest agony and bloody sweat, going to be crucified, and also in the last hour of his death, took care to dispose of a woman: after his resurrection, appeared first to a woman, sent a woman to declare his most glorious resurrection to the rest of his Disciples. Many other examples I could allege of diverse faithful and virtuous women, who have in all ages, not only been Confessors, but also endured most cruel martyrdom for their faith in Jesus Christ. All which is sufficient to enforce all good Christians and honorable minded men to speak reverently of our sex, and especially of all virtuous and good women. To the modest censures of both which, I refer these my imperfect endeavors, knowing that according to their own excellent dispositions, they will rather, cherish, nourish, and increase the least spark of virtue where they find it, by their favorable and best interpretations, than quench it by wrong constructions. To whom I wish all increase of virtue, and desire their best opinions.

---

1. Cesarus (Sisera) was a Canaanite military leader (12th century B.C.), who was defeated by the Israelites, led by Deborah and Barak.
2. Deborah, a judge and prophetess of Israel, united the various tribes in opposition to the Canaanites. A prose narrative of the exploit appears in Judges 4, and a descriptive poem in Judges 5.
3. Jael, wife of Heber the Kenite, killed Sisera by luring him into her tent and driving a nail through his temple into the ground (Judges 4).
4. Haman, the highest ranking prince of the court of the Persian king Ahasuerus (Xerxes I), devised a plot to destroy the Jews, but Esther revealed it to the king and had Haman executed on his own gallows.
5. Hester (Esther) was the Jewish wife of King Ahasuerus (5th century B.C.).
6. Holofernes, an Assyrian leader (5th century B.C.), was decapitated by Judith (*Apocrypha*, Book of Judith).
7. Susanna was a Jewish wife (6th century B.C.) falsely accused of adultery and condemned to death by the elders. The judge Daniel saved her by revealing the elders' lies (*Apocrypha*, Book of Susanna).

Salve Deus Rex Judaeorum

Sith *Cynthia*[1] is ascended to that rest
Of endless joy and true Eternity,
That glorious place that cannot be exprest
By any wight clad in mortality,
In her almighty love so highly blest,   5
And crown'd with everlasting Sov'reignty;
 Where Saints and Angels do attend her Throne,
 And she gives glory unto God alone.

To thee great Countess now I will apply   *The Lady*
My Pen, to write thy never dying fame;   10   *Margaret*
That when to Heav'n thy blessed Soul shall fly,   *Countess*
These lines on earth record thy reverend name: *Dowager of*
And to this task I mean my Muse to tie,   *Cumberland*[2]
Though wanting skill I shall but purchase blame:
 Pardon (dear Lady) want of woman's wit   15
 To pen thy praise, when few can equal it.

And pardon (Madam) though I do not write
Those praiseful lines of that delightful place,[3]
As you commanded me in that fair night,
When shining *Phoebe* gave so great a grace,   20
Presenting *Paradise* to your sweet sight,
Unfolding all the beauty of her face
 With pleasant groves, hills, walks, and stately trees,
 Which pleasures with retired minds agrees.

Whose Eagle's eyes behold the glorious Sun   25
Of th'all-creating Providence, reflecting
His blessed beams on all by him, begun;
Increasing, strength'ning, guiding and directing
All worldly creatures their due course to run,
Unto His pow'rful pleasure all subjecting: 30
 And thou (dear Lady) by his special grace,
 In these his creatures dost behold his face.

[Then follows extended praise of the countess, who has retired from
the court to the country, where she spends her time in religious meditation. Lanyer inveighs against "outward beauty unaccompanied with
virtue." She then invokes divine inspiration to describe Christ's Passion
and to condemn Pontius Pilate, who fails to follow his wife's advice.]

1. Cynthia, the goddess of the moon, was frequently identified with Queen Elizabeth, who died in
1603.
2. Margaret, countess dowager of Cumberland (1560–1616), was married in 1577 to George
Clifford, third earl of Cumberland, sea dog and adventurer. Margaret lived apart from her husband
and was reconciled to him only on his deathbed in 1605.
3. Lanyer is probably referring to Cookham; see "The Description of Cookham," which she apparently wrote at the countess's request.

Now *Pontius Pilate* is to judge the Cause 745
Of faultless *Jesus,* who before him stands;
Who neither hath offended Prince, nor Laws,
Although he now be brought in woeful bands:
O noble Governor, make thou yet a pause,
Do not in innocent blood imbrue thy hands; 750
    But hear the words of thy most worthy wife,
    Who sends to thee, to beg her Savior's life.

Let barb'rous cruelty far depart from thee,
And in true Justice take affliction's part;
Open thine eyes, that thou the truth may'st see, 755
Do not the thing that goes against thy heart,
Condemn not him that must thy Savior be;
But view his holy Life, his good desert.
    Let not us Women glory in Men's fall,
    Who had power given to over-rule us all. 760

Till now your indiscretion sets us free,   *Eve's*
And makes our former fault much less appear;   *Apology*
Our Mother *Eve,* who tasted of the Tree,
Giving to *Adam* what she held most dear,
Was simply good, and had no power to see, 765
The after-coming harm did not appear:
    The subtle Serpent that our Sex betrayed,
    Before our fall so sure a plot had laid.

That undiscerning Ignorance perceav'd
No guile, or craft that was by him intended; 770
For had she known, of what we were bereav'd,
To his request she had not condescended.
But she (poor soul) by cunning was deceav'd,[4]
No hurt therein her harmless Heart intended:
    For she alleg'd God's word, which he denies, 775
    That they should die, but even as Gods, be wise.

But surely *Adam* cannot be excus'd,
Her fault though great, yet he was most to blame;
What Weakness offer'd, Strength might have refus'd,
Being Lord of all, the greater was his shame: 780
Although the Serpent's craft had her abus'd,
God's holy word ought all his actions frame,
    For he was Lord and King of all the earth,
    Before poor *Eve* had either life or breath.

Who being fram'd by God's eternal hand, 785
The perfect'st man that ever breath'd on earth;

---

4. Lanyer's account of Eve as deceived may derive from 1 Timothy 2:14.

And from God's mouth receiv'd that straight command,
The breach whereof he knew was present death:
Yea having power to rule both Sea and Land,
Yet with one Apple won to lose that breath   790
    Which God had breathed in his beauteous face,
    Bringing us all in danger and disgrace.

And then to lay the fault on Patience back,
That we (poor women) must endure it all;
We know right well he did discretion lack,   795
Being not persuaded thereunto at all;
If *Eve* did err, it was for knowledge sake,
The fruit being fair persuaded him to fall:
    No subtle Serpent's falsehood did betray him,
    If he would eat it, who had power to stay him?   800

Not *Eve*, whose fault was only too much love,[5]
Which made her give this present to her Dear,
That what she tasted, he likewise might prove,
Whereby his knowledge might become more clear;
He never sought her weakness to reprove,   805
With those sharp words, which he of God did hear:
    Yet Men will boast of Knowledge, which he took
    From *Eve's* fair hand, as from a learned Book.

If any Evil did in her remain,
Being made of him, he was the ground of all;   810
If one of many Worlds could lay a stain
Upon our Sex, and work so great a fall
To wretched Man, by Satan's subtle train;
What will so foul a fault amongst you all?
    Her weakness did the Serpent's words obey,   815
    But you in malice God's dear Son betray.

Whom, if unjustly you condemn to die,
Her sin was small, to what you do commit;
All mortal sins that do for vengeance cry,
Are not to be compared unto it: 820
If many worlds would altogether try,
By all their sins the wrath of God to get;
    This sin of yours, surmounts them all as far
    As doth the Sun, another little star.

Then let us have our Liberty again,   825
And challenge to yourselves no Sov'reignty;
You came not in the world without our pain,

5. Whereas Lanyer regards Eve's fault as "too much love" in offering the apple to Adam, Milton
presents a far darker interpretation of Eve's motivation in *Paradise Lost*, for he sees her driven by
fear and jealousy that Adam may replace her with another Eve (IX.826–33). Lanyer's portrayal of
Adam as "most to blame" (l. 778) also differs from Milton's account of him as "fondly overcome
with female charm" (IX.999).

Make that a bar against your cruelty;
Your fault being greater, why should you disdain
Our being your equals, free from tyranny?   830
  If one weak woman simply did offend,
  This sin of yours hath no excuse, nor end.

To which (poor souls) we never gave consent,
Witness thy wife (O *Pilate*) speaks for all;
Who did but dream, and yet a message sent,[6]   835
That thou should'st have nothing to do at all
With that just man; which, if thy heart relent,
Why wilt thou be a reprobate with *Saul?*
  To seek the death of him that is so good,
  For thy soul's health to shed his dearest blood.   840

Yea, so thou may'st these sinful people please,
Thou art content against all truth and right,
To seal this act, that may procure thine ease
With blood, and wrong, with tyranny, and might;
The multitude thou seekest to appease,   845
By base dejection of this heavenly Light:
  Demanding which of these that thou should'st loose,
  Whether the Thief, or Christ King of the Jews.

Base *Barabas* the Thief, they all desire,
And thou more base than he, perform'st their will;   850
Yet when thy thoughts back to themselves retire,
Thou art unwilling to commit this ill:
Oh that thou couldst unto such grace aspire,
That thy polluted lips might never kill
  That Honor, which right Judgment ever graceth,   855
  To purchase shame, which all true worth defaceth.

Art thou a Judge, and asketh what to do
With one, in whom no fault there can be found?
The death of Christ wilt thou consent unto,
Finding no cause, no reason, nor no ground?   860
Shall he be scourg'd, and crucified too?
And must his miseries by thy means abound?
  Yet not asham'd to ask what he hath done,
  When thine own conscience seeks this sin to shun.

Three times thou ask'st, What evil hath he done?   865
And sayst, thou find'st in him no cause of death,
Yet wilt thou chasten God's beloved Son,
Although to thee no word of ill he saith:
For Wrath must end, what Malice hath begun,
And thou must yield to stop his guiltless breath.   870

6. Matthew 27:19 describes how Pilate's wife sent a message to her husband concerning her dream
and warned him to have nothing to do with Christ, "that just man."

This rude tumultuous rout doth press so sore,
That thou condemnest him thou shouldst adore.

Yet *Pilate*, this can yield thee no content,
To exercise thine own authority,
But unto *Herod* he must needs be sent, 875
To reconcile thyself by tyranny:
Was this the greatest good in Justice meant,
When thou perceiv'st no fault in him to be?
    If thou must make thy peace by Virtue's fall,
    Much better 'twere not to be friends at all. 880

Yet neither thy stern brow, nor his great place,
Can draw an answer from the Holy One:
His false accusers, nor his great disgrace,
Nor *Herod's* scoffs; to him they are all one:
He neither cares, nor fears his own ill case, 885
Though being despis'd and mockt of every one:
    King *Herod's* gladness gives him little ease,
    Neither his anger seeks he to appease.

Yet this is strange, that base Impiety
Should yield those robes of honor, which were due; 890
Pure white, to show his great Integrity,
His innocency, that all the world might view;
Perfection's height in lowest penury,
Such glorious poverty as they never knew:
    Purple and Scarlet well might him beseem, 895
    Whose precious blood must all the world redeem.

And that Imperial Crown of Thorns he wore,
Was much more precious than the Diadem
Of any King that ever liv'd before,
Or since his time, their honor's but a dream 900
To his eternal glory, being so poor,
To make a purchase of that heavenly Realm;
    Where God with all his Angels lives in peace,
    No griefs, nor sorrows, but all joys increase.

Those royal robes, which they in scorn did give, 905
To make him odious to the common sort,
Yield light of Grace to those whose souls shall live
Within the harbor of this heavenly port;
Much do they joy, and much more do they grieve,
His death, their life, should make his foes such sport: 910
    With sharpest thorns to prick his blessed face,
    Our joyful sorrow, and his greater grace.

Three fears at once possessed *Pilate's* heart;
The first, Christ's innocency, which so plain appears;

The next, That he which now must feel this　　915
　　smart,
Is God's dear Son, for anything he hears:
But that which prov'd the deepest wounding dart,
Is People's threat'nings, which he so much fears,
　　That he to *Caesar* could not be a friend,
　　Unless he sent sweet JESUS to his end.　　920

Now *Pilate* thou art prov'd a painted wall,
A golden Sepulcher with rotten bones;
From right to wrong, from equity to fall:
If none upbraid thee, yet the very stones
Will rise against thee, and in question call　　925
His blood, his tears, his sighs, his bitter groans:
　　All these will witness at the latter day,
　　When water cannot wash thy sin away.

Canst thou be innocent, that gainst all right,
Wilt yield to what thy conscience doth with-　　930
　　stand?
Being a man of knowledge, power, and might,
To let the wicked carry such a hand,
Before thy face to blindfold Heav'n's bright light,
And thou to yield to what they did demand?
　　Washing thy hands, thy conscience cannot　　935
　　　clear,
　　But to all worlds this stain must needs appear.

For lo, the Guilty doth accuse the Just,
And faulty Judge condemns the Innocent;
And willful Jews to exercise their lust,
With whips and taunts against their Lord are　　940
　　bent;
He basely us'd, blasphemed, scorn'd, and curst,
Our heavenly King to death for us they sent:
　　Reproaches, slanders, spittings in his face,
　　Spite doing all her worst in his disgrace.

And now this long expected hour draws near,　　945　*Christ going*
When blessed Saints with Angels do condole;　　　　　*to death*
His holy march, soft pace, and heavy cheer,
In humble sort to yield his glorious soul,
By his deserts the foulest sins to clear;
And in th'eternal book of heaven to enroll　　950
　　A satisfaction till the general doom,
　　Of all sins past, and all that are to come.

[Lanyer then praises the daughters of Jerusalem, who show compassion
for Christ, in contrast with the men who torment and mock him. She

describes the grief of the Virgin Mary, "all comfortless in depth of
sorrow drowned." Following the account of Christ's crucifixion and
resurrection, she draws upon the Song of Solomon to portray Christ
as a Bridegroom, whose spiritual beauty is engraved in the heart
of the countess of Cumberland. The poem concludes by praising the
countess as a pattern of virtue, superior to Deborah, Judith, Esther, and
Susanna, the biblical women mentioned in Lanyer's prose preface.]

The Description of Cookham[1]

Farewell (sweet *Cookham*) where I first obtain'd
Grace from that Grace[2] where perfect Grace remain'd;
And where the Muses gave their full consent,
I should have power the virtuous to content:
Where princely Palace will'd me to indite,   5
The sacred Story[3] of the Soul's delight.
Farewell (sweet Place) where Virtue then did rest,
And all delights did harbor in her breast:
Never shall my sad eyes again behold
Those pleasures which my thoughts did then unfold: 10
Yet you (great Lady) Mistress of that Place,
From whose desires did spring this work of Grace;
Vouchsafe to think upon those pleasures past,
As fleeting worldly Joys that could not last:
Or, as dim shadows of celestial pleasures,   15
Which are desir'd above all earthly treasures.
Oh how (me thought) against you thither came,
Each part did seem some new delight to frame!
The House receiv'd all ornaments to grace it,
And would endure no foulness to deface it.   20
The Walks put on their summer Liveries,
And all things else did hold like similes:
The Trees with leaves, with fruits, with flowers clad,
Embrac'd each other, seeming to be glad,
Turning themselves to beauteous Canopies,   25
To shade the bright Sun from your brighter eyes:
The crystal Streams with silver spangles graced,
While by the glorious Sun they were embraced:
The little Birds in chirping notes did sing,

1. Unfortunately the manor house at Cookham no longer exists. The manor belonged to the Crown
and was annexed to Windsor Castle in 1540. Members of Margaret Clifford's family lived there
from time to time (although it was not their family seat), and her daughter Anne Clifford records a
visit to Cookham in 1603 in her diary. The area, located on the Thames a few miles from Maid-
enhead, is still a place of great natural beauty, with dense woodlands, rolling meadows, and high
hills to the west.
2. Margaret Clifford, countess of Cumberland.
3. Lanyer's religious poem, *Salve Deus Rex Judaeorum.*

To entertain both You and that sweet Spring.   30
And *Philomela*[4] with her sundry lays,
Both You and that delightful Place did praise.
Oh how me thought each plant, each flower, each tree
Set forth their beauties then to welcome thee:
The very Hills right humbly did descend,   35
When you to tread upon them did intend.
And as you set your feet, they still did rise,
Glad that they could receive so rich a prize.
The gentle Winds did take delight to be
Among those woods that were so grac'd by thee.   40
And in sad murmur utter'd pleasing sound,
That Pleasure in that place might more abound:
The swelling Banks deliver'd all their pride,
When such a *Phoenix* once they had espied.
Each Arbor, Bank, each Seat, each stately Tree,   45
Thought themselves honor'd in supporting thee.
The pretty Birds would oft come to attend thee,
Yet fly away for fear they should offend thee:
The little creatures in the Burrough[5] by
Would come abroad to sport them in your eye;   50
Yet fearful of the Bow in your fair Hand,
Would run away when you did make a stand.[6]
Now let me come unto that stately Tree,
Wherein such goodly Prospects you did see;
That Oak that did in height his fellows pass,   55
As much as lofty trees, low growing grass:
Much like a comely Cedar straight and tall,
Whose beauteous stature far exceeded all:
How often did you visit this fair tree,
Which seeming joyful in receiving thee,   60
Would like a Palm tree spread his arms abroad,[7]
Desirous that you there should make abode:
Whose fair green leaves much like a comely vail,
Defended *Phoebus* when he would assail:
Whose pleasing boughes did yield a cool fresh air,   65
Joying his happiness when you were there.
Where being seated, you might plainly see,
Hills, vails, and woods, as if on bended knee
They had appear'd, your honor to salute,
Or to prefer some strange unlook'd for suit: 70

4. Philomela, the daughter of an Athenian king, was raped by her brother-in-law Tereus, who cut out her tongue, but she was transformed into a nightingale; see l. 189.
5. Burrow.
6. A place from which a hunter may shoot game.
7. Symbol of marriage. In a poem from the *Old Arcadia*, Sir Philip Sidney observes, "Palms do rejoyce to be joined by the match of a male to a female" (13). Lanyer may be referring ironically to the countess's estrangement from her husband, with whom she quarreled in an effort to maintain her daughter's rights of inheritance.

All interlac'd with brooks and crystal springs,
A Prospect fit to please the eyes of Kings:
And thirteen shires[8] appear'd all in your sight,
Europe could not afford much more delight.
What was there then but gave you all content,   75
While you the time in meditation spent,
Of their Creator's power, which there you saw,
In all his Creatures held a perfect Law;
And in their beauties did you plain descry,
His beauty, wisdom, grace, love, majesty.   80
In these sweet woods how often did you walk,
With Christ and his Apostles there to talk;
Placing his holy Writ in some fair tree,
To meditate what you therein did see:
With *Moses* you did mount his holy Hill,   85
To know his pleasure, and perform his Will.
With lovely *David* you did often sing,
His holy Hymns to Heaven's Eternal King.[9]
And in sweet music did your soul delight,
To sound his praises, morning, noon, and night.   90
With blessed *Joseph*[10] you did often feed
Your pined brethren, when they stood in need.
And that sweet Lady sprung from *Clifford's* race,[11]
Of noble *Bedford's* blood,[12] fair stem[13] of Grace;
To honorable *Dorset* now espous'd,[14]   95
In whose fair breast true virtue then was hous'd:
Oh what delight did my weak spirits find
In those pure parts of her well framed mind:
And yet it grieves me that I cannot be
Near unto her, whose virtues did agree   100
With those fair ornaments of outward beauty,
Which did enforce from all both love and duty.
Unconstant Fortune, thou art most to blame,
Who casts us down into so low a frame:
Where our great friends we cannot daily see,   105
So great a diff'rence is there in degree.
Many are placed in those Orbs of state,
Parters[15] in honor, so ordain'd by Fate;
Nearer in show, yet farther off in love,

8. Probably an exaggeration, but "shire" could refer to a town.
9. The countess of Cumberland's daughter, Anne Clifford, wrote in her diary that her mother was very devout: "the death of her two sons did so much affect her as that ever after the book of Job was her daily companion."
10. Joseph's generosity to the poor is recorded in Genesis 47:12.
11. Anne Clifford (1590–1676) was the daughter of George Clifford, third earl of Cumberland, and Margaret Russell.
12. Margaret Russell was the youngest daughter of Francis Russell, second earl of Bedford.
13. Lineage.
14. Anne Clifford married Richard Sackville, earl of Dorset, on February 25, 1609.
15. Dividers.

In which, the lowest always are above.   110
But whither am I carried in conceit?
My Wit too weak to conster[16] of the great.
Why not? although we are but born of earth,
We may behold the Heavens, despising death;
And loving heaven that is so far above,   115
May in the end vouchsafe us entire love.
Therefore sweet Memory do thou retain
Those pleasures past, which will not turn again:
Remember beauteous *Dorset's* former sports,[17]
So far from being toucht by ill reports;   120
Wherein myself did always bear a part,
While reverend Love presented my true heart:
Those recreations let me bear in mind,
Which her sweet youth and noble thoughts did find:
Whereof depriv'd, I evermore must grieve,   125
Hating blind Fortune, careless to relieve.
And you sweet Cookham, whom these Ladies leave,
I now must tell the grief you did conceive
At their departure; when they went away,
How everything retain'd a sad dismay: 130
Nay long before, when once an inkling came,
Me thought each thing did unto sorrow frame:
The trees that were so glorious in our view,
Forsook both flow'rs and fruit, when once they knew
Of your depart, their very leaves did wither,   135
Changing their colors as they grew together.
But when they saw this had no power to stay you,
They often wept, though speechless, could not pray you;
Letting their tears in your fair bosoms fall,
As if they said, Why will ye leave us all?   140
This being vain, they cast their leaves away,
Hoping that pity would have made you stay:
Their frozen tops, like Age's hoary hairs,
Shows their disasters, languishing in fears:
A swarthy riveld rine[18] all overspread,   145
Their dying bodies half alive, half dead.
But your occasions call'd you so away,
That nothing there had power to make you stay:
Yet did I see a noble grateful mind,
Requiting each according to their kind,   150
Forgetting not to turn and take your leave
Of these sad creatures, powerless to receive
Your favor, when with grief you did depart,

16. Construe.
17. The sports could be outdoor activities such as hunting and field games, or dancing and masquing.
18. A wrinkled bark that covers the trees, like a frost.

Placing their former pleasures in your heart;
Giving great charge to noble Memory,   155
There to preserve their love continually:
But specially the love of that fair tree,
That first and last you did vouchsafe to see:
In which it pleas'd you oft to take the air,
With noble *Dorset,* then a virgin fair: 160
Where many a learned Book was read and scann'd
To this fair tree, taking me by the hand,
You did repeat the pleasures which had past,
Seeming to grieve they could no longer last.[19]
And with a chaste, yet loving kiss took leave,   165
Of which sweet kiss I did it soon bereave:
Scorning a senseless creature should possess
So rare a favor, so great happiness.
No other kiss it could receive from me,
For fear to give back what it took of thee: 170
So I ingrateful Creature did deceive it,
Of that which you vouchsaft in love to leave it.
And though it oft had giv'n me much content,
Yet this great wrong I never could repent:
But of the happiest made it most forlorn,   175
To show that nothing's free from Fortune's scorn,
While all the rest with this most beauteous tree,
Made their sad consort[20] Sorrow's harmony.
The Flow'rs that on the banks and walks did grow,
Crept in the ground, the Grass did weep for woe.   180
The Winds and Waters seem'd to chide together,
Because you went away they knew not whither:
And those sweet Brooks that ran so fair and clear,
With grief and trouble wrinkled did appear.
Those pretty Birds that wonted were to sing,   185
Now neither sing, nor chirp, nor use their wing;
But with their tender feet on some bare spray,
Warble forth sorrow, and their own dismay.
Fair *Philomela* leaves her mournful Ditty,
Drown'd in dead sleep, yet can procure no pity: 190
Each arbor, bank, each seat, each stately tree,
Looks bare and desolate now for want of thee;
Turning green tresses into frosty gray,
While in cold grief they wither all away.

19. Anne Clifford continued the practice of meditating in a garden, long after her departure from Cookham. In her diary for April 1616 she records, "About this time I used to rise early in the morning and go to the standing in the garden, and taking my prayer book with me, beseech God to be merciful to me in this and to help me as he always hath done."
20. Concert.

The Sun grew weak, his beams no comfort gave,   195
While all green things did make the earth their grave:
Each briar, each bramble, when you went away,
Caught fast your clothes, thinking to make you stay:
Delightful Echo wonted to reply
To our last words, did now for sorrow die: 200
The house cast off each garment that might grace it,
Putting on Dust and Cobwebs to deface it.
All desolation then there did appear,
When you were going whom they held so dear.
This last farewell to *Cookham* here I give,   205
When I am dead thy name in this may live,
Wherein I have perform'd her noble hest,[21]
Whose virtues lodge in my unworthy breast,
And ever shall, so long as life remains,
Tying my heart to her by those rich chains.   210

Finis

To the doubtful Reader[1]

Gentle Reader, if thou desire to be resolved, why I give this Title, *Salve Deus Rex Judaeorum,* know for certain, that it was delivered unto me in sleep many years before I had any intent to write in this manner, and was quite out of my memory, until I had written the Passion of Christ, when immediately it came into my remembrance, what I had dreamed long before; and thinking it a significant token, that I was appointed to perform this Work, I gave the very same words I received in sleep as the fittest Title I could devise for this Book.

TEXTUAL NOTES

Copy-text: Lanyer's *Salve Deus Rex Judaeorum* (1611) survives in two different issues: the first with a 4-line imprint on the title-page (see p. 24), and the second (more common) with a 5-line imprint. This edition is based on the Huntington Library's copy of the second issue of *Salve* (STC 15227; RB62139), which has been collated with the copies at the British Library, the Victoria and Albert Museum (Dyce Collection), and the Bodleian Library. Ellipsis in noun and verb forms has been retained for the purpose of rhyme and meter.
Textual Notes:
30.19   this custom] their custom BL, V&A, O
31.17   healed women] *ed.;* healed woman *all copies*

21. Behest, command.
  1. Lanyer's account of her dream, in which she received the title for her religious poem, parallels her earlier account of the dream of Pontius Pilate's wife (ll.834–37) and her dedicatory dream-vision of Mary Sidney, countess of Pembroke. Lanyer's defense, "To the doubtful reader," may be compared with Milton's account of the "nightly visitation" that inspired *Paradise Lost* (IX.20–24).

BIBLIOGRAPHY

Editions

Purkiss, Diane, ed. *Renaissance Women: The Plays of Elizabeth Cary and The Poems of Aemilia Lanyer.* London: Pickering and Chatto, 1994.

Rowse, A. L., ed. *The Poems of Shakespeare's Dark Lady: "Salve Deus Rex Judaeorum."* New York: Clarkson N. Potter, 1979.

Woods, Susanne, ed. *The Poems of Aemilia Lanyer: "Salve Deus Rex Judaeorum."* New York: Oxford Univ. Press, 1993.

Secondary Works

Beilin, Elaine V. "The Feminization of Praise: Aemilia Lanyer." In *Redeeming Eve: Women Writers of the English Renaissance.* Princeton: Princeton Univ. Press, 1987.

Coiro, Ann Baines. "Writing in Service: Sexual Politics and Class Position in the Poetry of Aemilia Lanyer and Ben Jonson." *Criticism* 35 (1993): 357–76.

Dubrow, Heather. "The Country-House Poem: A Study in Generic Development." *Genre* 12 (1977): 153–79.

Greer, Germaine, Susan Hastings, Jeslyn Medoff, and Melinda Sansone, eds. *Kissing the Rod: An Anthology of Seventeenth-Century Women's Verse.* New York: Farrar Straus Giroux, 1988. 44–53.

Hibbard, G. R. "The Country House Poem of the Seventeenth Century," *Journal of the Warburg and Courtauld Institutes* 19 (1956): 159–77.

Hutson, Lorna. "Why the Lady's Eyes Are Nothing Like the Sun." In *New Feminist Discourses.* Ed. Isobel Armstrong. London: Routledge, 1992. 154–75.

Krontiris, Tina. *Oppositional Voices: Women as Writers and Translators of Literature in the English Renaissance.* London: Routledge, 1992. 102–20.

Lewalski, Barbara K. "The Lady of the Country-House Poem." In *The Fashioning and Functioning of the British Country House.* Ed. Gervase Jackson-Stops, Gordon J. Schochet, Lena Cowen Corlin, and Elisabeth Blair MacDoughall. Washington, D.C.: National Gallery of Art, 1989. 261–75.

——. "Of God and Good Women: The Poems of Aemilia Lanyer." In *Silent but for the Word: Tudor Women as Patrons, Translators, and Writers of Religious Works.* Ed. Margaret P. Hannay. Kent, Ohio: Kent State Univ. Press, 1985. 203–24.

——. "Re-writing Patriarchy and Patronage: Margaret Clifford, Anne Clifford, and Aemilia Lanyer." *Yearbook of English Studies* 21 (1991): 87–106.

——. *Writing Women in Jacobean England.* Cambridge: Harvard Univ. Press, 1993. 213–41; 321–22.

Mahl, Margaret, and Helene Koon, eds. *The Female Spectator: English Women Writers before 1800.* Bloomington: Indiana Univ. Press, 1977. 73–87.

McClung, William Alexander. *The Country House in English Renaissance Poetry.* Berkeley and Los Angeles: Univ. of California Press, 1977.

McGrath, Lynette. "'Let Us Have Our Libertie Againe': Amelia Lanier's Seventeenth-Century Feminist Voice." *Women's Studies* 20 (1992): 331–48.

———. "Metaphoric Subversions: Feasts and Mirrors in Amelia Lanier's *Salve Deus Rex Judaeorum.*" *Literature, Interpretation, Theory* 3 (1991): 101–13.

McGuire, Mary Ann C. "The Cavalier Country-House Poem: Mutations on a Jonsonian Tradition." *Studies in English Literature* 19 (1979): 93–108.

Molesworth, Charles. "Property and Virtue: The Genre of the Country-House Poem in the Seventeenth Century." *Genre* 1 (1968): 141–57.

Mueller, Janel. "The Feminist Poetics of Aemilia Lanyer's *Salve Deus Rex Judaeorum.*" In *Feminist Measures: Soundings in Poetry and Theory.* Ed. Lynn Keller and Cristianne Miller. Ann Arbor: Univ. of Michigan Press, 1994. 208–36.

Prior, Roger. "More (Moor? Moro?) Light on the Dark Lady." *Financial Times* (London), Oct. 10, 1987, 17.

Rowse, A. L. *Simon Forman: Sex and Society in Shakespeare's Age.* London: Weidenfeld and Nicholson, 1974. 96–117.

Schleiner, Louise. "Women's Household Circles as a Gendered Reading Formation: Whitney, Tyler, and Lanyer." In *Tudor and Stuart Writers.* Bloomington: Indiana Univ. Press, 1994.

Travitsky, Betty, ed. *The Paradise of Women: Writings by Englishwomen of the Renaissance.* 2d ed. New York: Columbia Univ. Press, 1989. 97–103.

Wall, Wendy. *The Imprint of Gender: Authorship and Publication in the English Renaissance.* Ithaca: Cornell Univ. Press, 1993. 319–30.

———. "Our Bodies/Our Texts?: Renaissance Women and the Problem of Publication." In *Anxious Power: Reading, Writing, and Ambivalence in Narrative by Women.* Ed. Carol J. Singley and Susan Elizabeth Sweeney. Albany: State Univ. of New York Press, 1993. 51–71.

Woods, Susanne. "Aemilia Lanyer." *Dictionary of Literary Biography.* Vol. 121: *Seventeenth-Century British Nondramatic Poets.* Ed. M. Thomas Hester. Detroit: Gale Research, 1992. 213–20.

———. "Aemilia Lanyer and Ben Jonson: Patronage, Authority, and Gender." *Ben Jonson Journal* 1 (1994): 15–30.

Elizabeth Cary, Viscountess Falkland by T. Athow from a
painting by Paul Van Somer. Sutherland Collection, Ashmolean
Museum, Oxford. (Reproduced by permission of the
Ashmolean.)

ELIZABETH CARY
VISCOUNTESS FALKLAND
(1585?–1639)

INTRODUCTION

The Tragedy of Mariam, The Fair Queen of Jewry is the first known original play written in English by a woman. It was probably written about 1603, when Elizabeth Cary was living with her mother-in-law, while her new husband was traveling on the Continent. Based on a story in Josephus's *Jewish Antiquities,* translated by Thomas Lodge and published in 1602, *Mariam* may be viewed as Cary's creative effort to describe her situation and explore the various options open to her as a woman and as a wife: a sheltered bride who had not yet lived alone with her husband; a young girl (about the age of seventeen) who enjoyed learning in an age that did not value educated women; a possible recusant Catholic, that is, a secret follower of the Roman Church in a country politically and ideologically opposed to that institution.

Mariam is outspoken and rebellious to her husband, yet a chaste woman; Salome is an adulteress and a murderess, who manipulates men in order to serve her own political and sexual desires; Graphina is a silent, obedient, and chaste woman, who follows the will of Pheroras, her lover; Doris, the scorned first wife of Herod, is willing to put her own life in jeopardy for her son; Alexandra, Mariam's mother, behaves according to what is politically expedient. The male characters also serve as foils for Mariam, particularly in their attitudes and behavior toward Herod. Consequently, the play presents a complex picture of both the private and public tensions in marriage.

While the biography of Cary certainly is a useful starting point in thinking about the play, the cultural context is also important in evaluating the literary and historical importance of *Mariam.* A so-called closet drama, that is, a Senecan-influenced dramatic piece, written mostly for the purposes of reading aloud rather than for performance, *Mariam* is one of twelve such plays written (or translated from the French playwright, Robert Garnier) between 1591 and 1607. These plays are primarily intellectual and even lyric, rather than dramatic, as they initiate a problem at the beginning, which is then debated at length by the various characters in long verse declamations; the reader/audience is very much a part of the action, as the play often suffers limited closure, in that the resolution of the problem is unsatisfying or discomfiting.

Mary Sidney, countess of Pembroke, initiated the writing of such compositions, when she translated *The Tragedy of Antonie* (published 1592, 1595). She commissioned Samuel Daniel to write a companion piece, *Cleopatra* (1595). The ten other plays, probably not directly commissioned by the countess but most probably influenced by her effort and interest, in general focus too on the collapse of the Roman Empire, and in particular, on the dilemmas of women who find themselves torn between family and state obligations. Cary's *Mariam* seems written in response to these plays, and in particular, in response to the

47

depiction of the female protagonists, who, for the most part, determine that family takes priority over state responsibility.

A second cultural context is that of the political use of the sonnet form. A lyric convention that describes the situation and feelings of a male lover pursuing a cold and chaste mistress, the sonnet also can depict the anxieties of a male courtier suing for patronage in the political realm. Consequently, the sonnet is an ideal vehicle for exposing the clash of private and public priorities. Further, because she is a woman, Cary subverts the inherent power structure of the form, since she is its subject and creator, rather than the passive love object. The verse form of *Mariam* consists of iambic pentameter lines rhyming *abab;* however, the sonnet form intrudes frequently throughout the play, either in full or in truncated versions. In fact, the first fourteen lines of the play are a sonnet.

Mariam was published in 1613 without the permission of Cary or her family, according to the biography of Cary written by one of her daughters. Apparently it was withdrawn from circulation almost immediately, and it was not printed again until the Malone Society issued an edition in 1914. Cary lived with her husband until 1626, supporting him in all of his state duties and bearing him eight children. In 1626, however, she publicly acknowledged her Catholicism and was immediately cast off by her husband. Although they reconciled shortly before Henry Cary's death in 1631, she suffered severe financial hardship until her own death in 1639. Her extant writings include a childhood translation of Abraham Ortelius's *Mirroir du Monde;* an epitaph on George Villiers, duke of Buckingham (c. 1628); a prose history of Edward II, written in 1627 and published twice in 1680 (but not attributed to Cary until 1935); and a translation of the *Reply of the Cardinall of Perron to the Answeare of the King of Great Britaine,* published at Douay in 1630.

THE TRAGEDY OF MARIAM,
THE FAIR QUEEN OF JEWRY (1613)

To Diana's earthly deputess, and my worthy sister, Mistress Elizabeth Cary[1]

When cheerful Phoebus[2] his full course hath run,
His sister's[3] fainter beams our hearts doth cheer:
So your fair brother[4] is to me the sun,
And you his sister as my moon appear.

You are my next belov'd, my second friend,   5
For when my Phoebus' absence makes it night,
Whilst to th'Antipodes[5] his beams do bend,
From you my Phoebe,[6] shines my second light.

---

1. Probably the sister-in-law of Elizabeth Cary, also Elizabeth Cary, who married her husband's brother, Philip, in 1609.
2. The sun.
3. I.e., the moon's.
4. Henry Cary, the author's husband.
5. The opposite ends of the earth.
6. The moon.

He like to Sol, clear-sighted, constant, free,
You Luna-like, unspotted, chaste, divine: 10
He shone on Sicily,[7] you destin'd be,
T'illumine the now obscur'd Palestine.[8]
My first was consecrated to Apollo,[9]
My second to Diana[10] now shall follow.

                                        E. C.

The Names of the Speakers.
Herod, King of Judea.
Doris, his first wife.
Mariam, his second wife.
Salome, Herod's sister.
Antipater, his son by [Doris].
Alexandra, Mariam's mother.
Silleus, Prince of Arabia.
Constabarus, husband to Salome.
[Pheroras], Herod's brother.
Graphina, his love.
Babus' first son.
Babus' second son.
[Ananell], the high priest.
Sohemus, a counselor to Herod.
Nuntio.
Bu[tler], another messenger.
Chorus, a company of Jews.

The Argument

Herod, the son of Antipater (an Idumean),[11] having crept by the favor of the Romans into the Jewish monarchy, married Mariam, the [grand]daughter[12] of Hircanus, the rightful king and priest, and for her (besides her high blood, being of singular beauty) he repudiated Doris, his former wife, by whom he had children.

This Mariam had a brother called Aristobolus, and next him and Hircanus, his grandfather, Herod in his wife's right had the best title. Therefore, to remove them, he charged the [second] with treason and put him to death, and drowned the [first] under color of sport. Alex-

7. Cary apparently had dedicated to her husband an earlier play, now lost, whose action took place in Sicily.
8. The setting of *Mariam*.
9. The god of the sun, whom Cary is likening to her husband.
10. The goddess of the moon, whom Cary is likening to her sister-in-law.
11. Idumea, the homeland of Herod, was the district south of Jerusalem and Bethlehem. The Idumeans were descendants of the Old Testament Edomites, who, it was said, urged the Babylonian destroyers of Jerusalem. For whatever reason, the Jews hated them. The Idumeans were forcibly converted to Judaism by John Hyrcanus I (134–104 B.C.), but the prejudice against them died hard, as is seen in Mariam's attitude toward Salome.
12. Emended in accordance with Cary's source, Josephus.

andra, daughter to the one and mother to the other, accused him for their deaths before Anthony.

So when he was forc'te[13] to go answer this accusation at Rome, he left the custody of his wife to Josephus, his uncle, that had married his sister, Salome, and out of a violent affection (unwilling any should enjoy her after him), he gave strict and private commandment that if he were slain she should be put to death. But he returned with much honor, yet found his wife extremely discontented to whom Josephus had (meaning it for the best, to prove Herod loved her) revealed his charge.

So by Salome's accusation he put Josephus to death, but was reconciled to Mariam, who still bare the death of her friends exceeding hardly.

In this meantime, Herod was again necessarily to revisit Rome, for Caesar having overthrown Anthony, his great friend, was likely to make an alteration of his fortune.

In his absence, news came to Jerusalem that Caesar had put him to death; their willingness it should be so together with the likelihood gave this rumor so good credit, as Sohemus that had succeeded Josephus' charge succeeded him likewise in revealing it. So at Herod's return which was speedy and unexpected, he found Mariam so far from joy that she showed apparent signs of sorrow. He still desiring to win her to a better humor, she being very unable to conceal her passion, fell to upbraiding him with her brother's death. As they were thus debating came in a fellow with a cup of wine who, hired by Salome, said first it was a love potion which Mariam desired to deliver to the King: but afterwards he affirmed that it was a poison and that Sohemus had told her somewhat which procured the vehement hate in her.

The King hearing this, more moved with jealousy of Sohemus than with this intent of poison, sent her away, and presently after by the instigation of Salome she was beheaded. Which rashness was afterward punished in him with an intolerable and almost frantic passion for her death.

Actus Primus. Scena Prima.   [Act I, scene i]

Mariam sola.[14]

Mar. How oft have I with public voice run on,
To censure Rome's last hero[15] for deceit,
Because he wept when Pompey's[16] life was gone,
Yet when he liv'd, he thought his name too great.
But now I do recant, and Roman Lord,   5
Excuse too rash a judgment in a woman:

---

13. See the textual notes for an explanation of spelling.
14. Alone.
15. Marc Anthony.
16. Caesar's great antagonist, who was murdered in 48 B.C. after the battle of Pharsalus.

My sex pleads pardon, pardon then afford,
Mistaking is with us, but too too common.
Now do I find by self-experience taught,
One object yields both grief and joy: ` 10
You wept indeed, when on his worth you thought,
But joy'd that slaughter did your foe destroy.
So at his death your eyes true drops did rain,
Whom dead, you did not wish alive again.
When Herod liv'd, that now is done to death, 15
Oft have I wisht that I from him were free,
Oft have I wisht that he might lose his breath,
Oft have I wisht his carcass dead to see.
Then rage and scorn had put my love to flight,
That love which once on him was firmly set: 20
Hate hid his true affection from my sight,
And kept my heart from paying him his debt.
And blame me not, for Herod's jealousy
Had power even constancy itself to change:
For he by barring me from liberty, 25
To shun my ranging, taught me first to range.
But yet too chaste a scholar was my heart,
To learn to love another than my Lord:
To leave his love, my lesson's former part,
I quickly learn'd, the other I abhorr'd. 30
But now his death to memory doth call,
The tender love, that he to Mariam bare:
And mine to him, this makes those rivers fall,
Which by another thought unmoist'ned are.
For Aristobolus,[17] the lowliest youth 35
That ever did in angel's shape appear,
The cruel Herod was not mov'd to ruth;
Then why grieves Mariam Herod's death to hear?
Why joy I not the tongue no more shall speak,
That yielded forth my brother's latest doom: 40
Both youth and beauty might thy fury break,
And both in him did ill befit a tomb.
And worthy Grandsire[18] ill did he requite,
His high ascent alone by thee procur'd,
Except he murd'red thee to free the sprite 45
Which still he thought on earth too long immur'd.
How happy was it that Sohemus' [mind]
Was mov'd to pity my distrest estate?
Might Herod's life a trusty servant find,
My death to his had been unseparate. 50

---

17. Mariam's brother, killed by Herod. Previous editors Dunstan and Greg emended "lowliest" (found in 1613 text) to "loveliest."
18. Hyrcanus, Mariam's grandfather, killed by Herod.

These thoughts have power, his death to make me bear,
Nay more, to wish the news may firmly hold:
Yet cannot this repulse some falling tear,
That will against my will some grief unfold.
And more I owe him for his love to me,   55
The deepest love that ever yet was seen:
Yet had I rather much a milkmaid be,
Than be the monarch of Judea's queen.
It was for nought but love, he wisht his end
Might to my death, but the vaunt-currier[19] prove: 60
But I had rather still be foe than friend,
To him that saves for hate, and kills for love.
Hard-hearted Mariam, at thy discontent,
What floods of tears have drencht his manly face?
How canst thou then so faintly now lament,   65
Thy truest lover's death, a death's disgrace:
[Aye], now mine eyes you do begin to right
The wrongs of your admirer and my Lord;
Long since you should have put your smiles to flight,
Ill doth a widowed eye with joy accord.   70
Why now methinks the love I bare him then,
When virgin freedom left me unrestrain'd,
Doth to my heart begin to creep again,
My passion now is far from being feign'd.
But tears fly back, and hide you in your banks,   75
You must not be to Alexandra seen:
For if my moan be spi'd, but little thanks
Shall Mariam have, from that incensed Queen.

Actus Primus. Scena Secunda.   [Act I, scene ii]

Mariam. Alex[andra.]

Alex. What means these tears? My Mariam doth mistake,
The news we heard did tell the tyrant's end:
What, weepst thou for thy brother's murther's sake,
Will ever wight[20] a tear for Herod spend?
My curse pursue his breathless trunk and spirit,   5
Base Edomite[21] the damned Esau's heir:[22]
Must he ere Jacob's child[23] the crown inherit?
Must he, vile wretch, be set in David's chair?[24]
No, David's soul within the bosom plac'te,

---

19. A soldier sent out in advance of an army; a forerunner.
20. Person.
21. Herod.
22. The Edomites were the descendants of Esau, the eldest son of Isaac.
23. The brother of Esau, who founded the twelve tribes of Israel.
24. David was the second king of Israel and Judah.

Of our forefather Abram[25] was asham'd   10
To see his seat with such a toad disgrac'te,
That seat that hath by Judas' race[26] been fain'd.[27]
Thou fatal enemy to royal blood,
Did not the murther of my boy suffice,
To stop thy cruel mouth that gaping stood?   15
But must thou dim the mild Hircanus' eyes,
My gracious father, whose too ready hand
Did lift this Idumean[28] from the dust:
And he ungrateful caitiff[29] did withstand,
The man that did in him most friendly trust.   20
What kingdom's right could cruel Herod claim,
Was he not Esau's issue, heir of hell?
Then what succession can he have but shame?
Did not his ancestor his birthright sell?
Oh yes, he doth from Edom's name derive,   25
His cruel nature which with blood is fed:
That made him me of sire and son deprive,
He ever thirsts for blood, and blood is red.
Weepst thou because his love to thee was bent?
And read'st thou love in crimson characters?   30
Slew he thy friends to work thy heart's content?
No: hate may justly call that action hers.
He gave the sacred priesthood for thy sake,
To Aristobolus. Yet doom'd him dead:
Before his back the ephod[30] warm could make,   35
And ere the miter settled on his head.
Oh, had he given my boy no less than right,
The double oil should to his forehead bring
A double honor, shining doubly bright,
His birth anointed him both priest and king.   40
And say my father, and my son he slew,
To royalize by right your prince-born breath:
Was love the cause, can Mariam deem it true,
That [Herod] gave commandment for her death?
I know by fits, he show'd some signs of love,   45
And yet not love, but raging lunacy:
And this his hate to thee may justly prove,
That sure he hates Hircanus' family.
Who knows if he, unconstant wavering Lord,
His love to Doris had renew'd again?   50

25. Later known as Abraham, first patriarch and father of the Jewish people.
26. The tribe of Judas, or Judah, the fourth son of Jacob and Leah, became preeminent among the
    twelve tribes of Israel; his name is consequently frequently used to signify the entire Hebrew
    people.
27. Enjoyed.
28. Herod.
29. Mean, evil, and cowardly person.
30. Richly embroidered outer vestment, worn by Jewish priests in ancient times.

And that he might his bed to her afford,
Perchance he wisht that Mariam might be slain.
[Mar.] Doris, alas her time of love was past,
Those coals were rakte in embers long ago
[Of] Mariam's love and she was now disgrast,   55
Nor did I glory in her overthrow.
He not a whit his firstborn son esteem'd,
Because as well as his he was not mine:
My children only for his own he deem'd,
These boys that did descend from royal line.   60
These did he style his heirs to David's throne,
My Alexander if he live, shall sit
In the majestic seat of Solomon;[31]
To will it so, did Herod think it fit.
Alex. Why? Who can claim from Alexander's[32] brood   65
That gold adorned lion-guarded chair?
Was Alexander not of David's blood?
And was not Mariam Alexander's heir?
What more than right could Herod then bestow,
And who will think except for more than right,   70
He did not raise them, for they were not low,
But born to wear the crown in his despite:
Then send those tears away that are not sent
To thee by reason but by passion's power:
Thine eyes to cheer, thy cheeks to smiles be bent,   75
And entertain with joy this happy hour.
Felicity, if when she comes, she finds
A mourning habit and a cheerless look,
Will think she is not welcome to thy mind,
And so perchance her lodging will not brook.   80
Oh, keep her whilest thou hast her. If she go
She will not easily return again:
Full many a year have I endur'd in woe,
Yet still have su'd her presence to obtain:
And did not I to her as presents send   85
A table,[33] that best art did beautify
Of two,[34] to whom Heaven did best feature lend,
To [woo] her love by winning Anthony:
For when a prince's favor we do crave,
We first their minions' loves do seek to win: 90
So I, that sought felicity to have,

31. King of Israel, the son of David, noted for his wealth and wisdom.
32. Alexander was the father of Mariam.
33. A board or other flat surface upon which a picture is painted; hence, the picture itself.
34. Aristobolus and Mariam. Alexandra sent these portraits to Anthony at the suggestion of Quintus Dellius, a friend of Anthony, who happened to be visiting Jerusalem. Anthony apparently requested that Aristobolus be sent to him, but Herod denied the request, Josephus asserts, so that the young man would not be defiled.

Did with her minion Anthony begin.
With double [sleight]³⁵ I sought to captivate
The warlike lover, but I did not right:
For if my gift had borne but half the rate,   95
The Roman had been overtaken quite.
But now he fared like a hungry guest,
That to some plenteous festival is gone,
Now this, now that, he deems to eat were best,
Such choice doth make him let them all alone.   100
The boy's large forehead first did fairest seem,
Then glaunst his eye upon my Mariam's cheek:
And that without comparison did deem,
What was in either but he most did [seek].
And thus distracted, either's beauties' might   105
Within the other's excellence was drown'd:
Too much delight did [bar] him from delight,
For either's love, the other's did confound.
Where, if thy portraiture had only gone,
His life from Herod, Anthony had taken: 110
He would have loved thee, and thee alone,
And left the brown Egyptian³⁶ clean forsaken.
And Cleopatra then to seek had been,
So firm a lover of her waned³⁷ face:
Then great Anthonius' fall we had not seen,   115
By her that fled to have him hold the chase.³⁸
Then Mariam in a Roman's chariot set,
In place of Cleopatra might have shown:
A mart of beauties in her visage met,
And part in this, that they were all her own.   120
Mar. Not to be empress of aspiring Rome,
Would Mariam like to Cleopatra live:
With purest body will I press my tomb,
And wish no favors Anthony could give.
Alex. Let us retire us, that we may resolve   125
How now to deal in this reversed state:
Great are th'affairs that we must now revolve,
And great affairs must not be taken late.

Actus Primus. Scena Tertia.   [Act I, scene iii]

Mariam. Alexandra. Salome.

Sal. More plotting yet? Why? Now you have the thing

35. Cunning or deceit; 1613 text reads "slight."
36. Cleopatra.
37. Becoming less bright and strong; aging.
38. In the sea battle of Actium, Anthony followed Cleopatra's fleeing ship, thus losing the battle and the war to Octavius. He subsequently committed suicide.

For which so oft you spent your suppliant breath:
And Mariam hopes to have another king,
Her eyes do sparkle joy for Herod's death.
Alex. If she desir'd another king to have,   5
She might before she came in Herod's bed
Have had her wish. More kings than one did crave,
For leave to set a crown upon her head.
I think with more than reason she laments,
That she is freed from such a sad annoy: 10
Who is't will weep to part from discontent,
And if she joy, she did not causeless joy.
Sal. You durst not thus have given your tongue the rein,
If noble Herod still remain'd in life:
Your daughter's betters far I dare maintain,   15
Might have rejoic'd to be my brother's wife.
Mar. My betters far, base woman 'tis untrue,
You scarce have ever my superiors seen:
For Mariam's servants were as good as you,
Before she came to be Judea's queen.   20
Sal. Now stirs the tongue that is so quickly mov'd,
But more than once your choler have I borne:
Your fumish[39] words are sooner said than prov'd,
And Salome's reply is only scorn.
Mar. Scorn those that are for thy companions held,   25
Though I thy brother's face had never seen,
My birth, thy baser birth so far excell'd,
I had to both of you the princess been.
Thou parti-Jew, and parti-Edomite,
Thou mongrel:[40] issu'd from rejected race,   30
Thy ancestors against the Heavens did fight,
And thou like them wilt heavenly birth disgrace.
Sal. Still twit you me with nothing but my birth,
What odds betwixt your ancestors and mine?
Both born of Adam, both were made of earth,   35
And both did come from holy Abraham's line.
Mar. I favor thee when nothing else I say,
With thy black acts I'll not pollute my breath:
Else to thy charge I might full justly lay
A shameful life, besides a husband's death.   40
Sal. 'Tis true indeed, I did the plots reveal,
That pass'd betwixt your favorites and you:
I meant not I, a traitor to conceal.

---

39. Offensive.
40. Like Herod, her brother, Salome is Idumean. Technically, she is completely Jewish, but her Edomite heritage makes her a "mongrel" in Mariam's eyes.

Thus Salome your minion Joseph[41] slew.
Mar. Heaven, dost thou mean this infamy to smother?   45
Let sland'red Mariam ope thy closed ear:
Self-guilt hath ever been [suspicion's] mother,
And therefore I this speech with patience bear.
No, had not Salome's unsteadfast heart,
In Josephus' stead her Constabarus plast,   50
To free herself, she had not us'd the art,
To slander hapless Mariam for unchaste.
Alex. Come Mariam, let us go: it is no boot
To let the head contend against the foot.

Actus Primus. Scena Quarta.   [Act I, scene iv]

Salome, Sola.

Sal. Lives Salome, to get so base a style
As foot, to the proud Mariam? Herod's spirit
In happy time for her endured exile,
For did he live she should not miss her merit:
But he is dead, and though he were my brother,   5
His death such store of cinders cannot cast
My coals of love to quench: for though they smother
The flames a while, yet will they out at last.
Oh blest Arabia, in best climate plast,
I by the fruit will censure of the tree: 10
'Tis not in vain, thy happy name thou hast,
If all Arabians like Silleus[42] be:
Had not my fate been too too contrary,
When I on Constabarus first did gaze,
Silleus had been object to mine eye: 15
Whose looks and personage must [all eyes] amaze.
But now ill-fated Salome, thy tongue
To Constabarus by itself is ti'd:
And now except I do the Ebrew[43] wrong
I cannot be the fair Arabian bride: 20
What childish lets[44] are these? Why stand I now
On honorable points? 'Tis long ago
Since shame was written on my tainted brow:
And certain 'tis, that shame is honor's foe.
Had I upon my reputation stood,   25

41. Salome's first husband, slain by Herod. Upon leaving for an earlier trip to Rome, Herod had secretly charged Joseph to kill Mariam if he himself were killed. Joseph revealed this to Mariam to prove Herod's love for her, but it only increased her anger toward her husband. When Herod returned, he killed Joseph for revealing this secret charge.
42. Chief minister to King Obodas of Arabia, who asked for Salome in marriage several years after the event in question (about 25 B.C.). However, the marriage was not approved by Herod, since Salome would have had to give up her Jewish faith.
43. A variant of *Hebrew.*
44. Obstacles; impediments.

Had I affected an unspotted life,
Josephus' veins had still been stuft with blood,
And I to him had liv'd a sober wife.
Then had I never cast an eye of love,
On Constabarus' now detested face,   30
Then had I kept my thoughts without remove,
And blusht at motion of the least disgrace.
But shame is gone, and honor wipt away,
And Impudency[45] on my forehead sits:
She bids me work my will without delay,   35
And for my will I will employ my wits.
He loves, I love; what then can be the cause,
Keeps me [from] being the Arabian's wife?
It is the principles of Moses' laws,
For Constabarus still remains in life.   40
If he to me did bear as earnest hate,
As I to him, for him there were an ease:
A separating bill might free his fate,[46]
From such a yoke that did so much displease.
Why should such privilege to man be given?   45
Or given to them, why barr'd from women then?
Are men than we in greater grace with Heaven?
Or cannot women hate as well as men?
I'll be the custom-breaker: and begin
To show my sex the way to freedom's door,   50
And with an off'ring will I purge my sin,
The law was made for none but who are poor.
If Herod had liv'd, I might to him accuse
My present lord. But for the future's sake
Then would I tell the King he did refuse   55
The sons of Baba[47] in his power to take.
But now I must divorce him from my bed,
That my Silleus may possess his room:
Had I not begg'd his life he had been dead,
I curse my tongue, the hind'rer of his doom,   60
But then my wand'ring heart to him was fast,
Nor did I dream of change: Silleus said,
He would be here, and see he comes at last,
Had I not nam'd him, longer had he stay'd.

---

45. An obsolete form of impudence.
46. Jewish law allowed a man to divorce his wife, but did not allow a woman to divorce her husband.
47. A variant of *Babus,* the name of a Hasmonaean family, antagonistic to Herod, who held Jerusalem before Herod captured the city in a siege in 37 B.C. and assumed the position of tetrarch of Judea given to him by Anthony. Constabarus had been responsible for hunting down and destroying the Hasmoneans and their supporters, but had secreted these boys instead.

Actus Primus. Scena Quinta.   [Act I, scene v]

Salome. Silleus.

Sill. Well found, fair Salome, Judea's pride,
Hath thy innated wisdom found the way
To make Silleus deem him deified,
By gaining thee a more than precious prey?
Sal. I have devis'd the best I can devise,   5
A more imperfect means was never found:
But what cares Salome? It doth suffice
If our endeavors with their end be crown'd.
In this our land we have an ancient use,
Permitted first by our law giver's head: 10
Who hates his wife, though for no just abuse,
May with a bill divorce her from his bed.
But in this custom women are not free,
Yet I for once will wrest it. Blame not thou
The ill I do, since what I [do is] for thee;   15
Though others blame, Silleus should allow.
Sill. Thinks Salome, Silleus hath a tongue
To censure her fair actions? Let my blood
Bedash my proper brow; for such a wrong,
The being yours, can make even vices good: 20
Arabia joy, prepare thy earth with green,
Thou never happy wert indeed till now:
Now shall thy ground be trod by beauty's queen,
Her foot is destin'd to depress thy brow.
Thou shalt, fair Salome, command as much   25
As if the royal ornament were thine:
The weakness of Arabia's king is such,
The kingdom is not his so much as mine.
My mouth is our Obodas'[48] oracle,
Who thinks not ought but what Silleus will.   30
And thou rare creature, Asia's miracle,
Shalt be to me as it: Obodas' still.
Sal. 'Tis not for glory I thy love accept,
Judea yields me honor's worthy store:
Had not affection in my bosom crept,   35
My native country should my life deplore.
Were not Silleus he with [whom] I go,
I would not change my Palestine for Rome:
Much less would I a glorious state to show,
Go far to purchase an Arabian tomb.   40
Sill. Far be it from Silleus so to think,
I know it is thy gratitude requites

48. Obodas was king of Arabia, who was entirely ruled by Silleus.

The love that is in me, and shall not shrink
Till death do sever me from earth's delights.
Sal. But whist;[49] methinks the wolf is in our talk.   45
Be gone, Silleus. Who doth here arrive?
'Tis Constabarus that doth hither walk,
I'll find a quarrel, him from me to drive.
Sill. Farewell, but were it not for thy command,
In his despite Silleus here would stand.   50

Actus Primus. Scena Sexta.   [Act I, scene vi]

Salome. Constabarus.

Const. Oh Salome, how much you wrong your name,
Your race, your country, and your husband most?
A stranger's private conference is shame,
I blush for you, that have your blushing lost.
Oft have I found, and found you to my grief,   5
Consorted with this base Arabian here:
Heaven knows that you have been my comfort chief,
Then do not now my greater plague appear.
Now by the stately carved edifice
That on Mount Sion makes so fair a show,   10
And by the Altar fit for sacrifice,
I love thee more than thou thyself doest know.
Oft with a silent sorrow have I heard
How ill Judea's[50] mouth doth censure thee:
And did I not thine honor much regard,   15
Thou shouldst not be exhorted thus for me.
Didst thou but know the worth of honest fame,
How much a virtuous woman is esteem'd,
Thou wouldest like hell eschew deserved shame,
And seek to be both chaste and chastely deem'd.   20
Our wisest Prince did say, and true he said,
A virtuous woman crowns her husband's head.[51]
Sal. Did I for this, uprear thy low estate?
Did I for this requital[52] beg thy life,
That thou hadst forfeited hapless fate,   25
To be to such a thankless wretch the wife?
This hand of mine hath lifted up thy head,
Which many a day ago had fall'n full low,
Because the sons of Baba are not dead,
To me thou doest both life and fortune owe.   30

49. Be quiet; silence.
50. Judea is the southern section of ancient Palestine, used here to refer to the entire Jewish people.
51. Proverbs 12:4 (Geneva Bible): "A virtuous woman is the crown of her husband: but she that maketh him ashamed, is as corruption in his bones."
52. Reproval; retaliation.

Const. You have my patience often exercis'd,
Use make my choler keep within the banks:
Yet boast no more, but be by me advis'd.
A benefit upbraided, forfeits thanks:
I prithee, Salome, dismiss this mood,   35
Thou doest not know how ill it fits thy place:
My words were all intended for thy good,
To raise thine honor and to stop disgrace.
Sal. To stop disgrace? Take thou no care for me,
Nay do thy worst, thy worst I set not by: 40
No shame of mine is like to light on thee,
Thy love and admonitions I defy.
Thou shalt no hour longer call me wife,
Thy jealousy procures my hate so deep,
That I from thee do mean to free my life,   45
By a divorcing bill before I sleep.
Const. Are Hebrew women now transform'd to men?
Why do you not as well our battles fight,
And wear our armor? Suffer this, and then
Let all the world be topsy-turved quite.   50
Let fishes graze, beasts, swine, and birds descend,
Let fire burn downwards whilst the earth aspires:
Let winter's heat and summer's cold offend,
Let thistles grow on vines, and grapes on briars,
Set us to spin or sow, or at the best   55
Make us wood-hewers, waters-bearing wights:
For sacred service let us take no rest,
Use us as Joshua⁵³ did the Gibonites.
Sal. Hold on your talk, till it be time to end,
For me I am resolv'd it shall be so: 60
Though I be first that to this course do bend,
I shall not be the last full well I know.
Const. Why then be witness, Heav'n, the judge of sins,
Be witness spirits that eschew the dark:
Be witness angels, witness cherubins,   65
Whose semblance sits upon the holy ark:
Be witness earth, be witness Palestine,
Be witness David's city, if my heart
Did ever merit such an act of thine:
Or if the fault be mine that makes us part.   70
Since mildest Moses,⁵⁴ friend unto the Lord,

53. Moses' successor and leader of the Israelites into the Promised Land. The Gibonites (or people of Gibeon) came to Joshua, after the Hebrews had destroyed the cities of Jericho and Hai, pretending to be inhabitants of a faraway land who had heard of the Israelites' god and who wanted to join the Israelite forces. When Joshua realized that they were natives of the land, he condemned them to perpetual slavery for their deceit, making them "hewers of wood and drawers of water," proverbial terms for the lowest social class in the Israelite community. See Joshua 9.
54. Lawgiver who led the Israelites out of Egypt.

Did work his wonders in the land of Ham,[55]
And slew the firstborn babes without a sword,
In sign whereof we eat the holy lamb;
Till now that fourteen hundred years are past,   75
Since first the Law with us hath been in force:
You are the first, and will I hope be last,
That ever sought her husband to divorce.
Sal. I mean not to be led by precedent,
My will shall be to me instead of Law.   80
Const. I fear me much you will too late repent,
That you have ever liv'd so void of awe:
This is Silleus' love that makes you thus
Reverse all order: you must next be his.
But if my thoughts aright the cause discuss,   85
In winning you, he gains no lasting bliss;
I was Silleus, and not long ago
Josephus then was Constabarus now:
When you became my friend you prov'd his foe,
As now for him you break to me your [vow].   90
Sal. If once I lov'd you, greater is your debt:
For certain 'tis that you deserved it not.
And undeserved love we soon forget,
And therefore that to me can be no blot.
But now fare ill, my once beloved lord,   95
Yet never more belov'd than now abhorr'd.
                                              (*Exit Salome.*)
Const. Yet Constabarus biddeth thee farewell.
Farewell, light creature. Heaven forgive thy sin:
My prophesying spirit doth foretell
Thy wavering thoughts do yet but new begin.   100
Yet I have better 'scap'd than Joseph did,
But if our Herod's death had been delay'd,
The valiant youths that I so long have hid,
Had been by her and I for them betray'd.
Therefore in happy hour did Caesar give   105
The fatal blow to wanton Anthony:
For had he lived, our Herod then should live,
But great Anthonius' death made Herod die.
Had he enjoyed his breath, not I alone
Had been in danger of a deadly fall: 110
But Mariam had the way of peril gone,
Though by the tyrant most belov'd of all.
The sweet-fac'd Mariam as free from guilt
As Heaven from spots, yet had her lord come back
Her purest blood had been unjustly spilt.   115

55. Egypt, so called because the Egyptians were said to be descendants of Ham, the second son of Noah.

And Salome it was would work her wrack.
Though all Judea yield her innocent,
She often hath been near to punishment.

Chorus. Those minds that wholly dote upon delight,
Except they only joy in inward good,
Still hope at last to hop upon the right,
And so from sand they leap in loathsome mud:
    Fond wretches, seeking what they cannot find,   5
    For no content attends a wavering mind.

If wealth they do desire, and wealth attain,
Then wondrous fain[56] would they to honor [leap]:
Of mean degree they do in honor gain,
They would but wish a little higher step.   10
    Thus step to step, and wealth to wealth they add,
    Yet cannot all their plenty make them glad.

Yet oft we see that some in humble state,
Are cheerful, pleasant, happy, and content:
When those indeed that are of higher state,   15
With vain additions do their thoughts torment.
    Th'one would to his mind his fortune bind,
    Th'other to his fortune frames his mind.

To wish variety is sign of grief,
For if you like your state as now it is,   20
Why should an alteration bring relief?
Nay, change would then be fear'd as loss of bliss.
    That man is only happy in his fate,
    That is delighted in a settled state.

Still Mariam wisht she from her Lord were free,   25
For expectation of variety:
Yet now she sees her wishes prosperous be,
She grieves, because her Lord so soon did die.
    Who can those vast imaginations feed,
    Where in a property, contempt doth breed?   30

Were Herod now perchance to live again,
She would again as much be grieved at that:
All that she may, she ever doth disdain,
Her wishes guide her to she knows not what.
    And sad must be their looks, their honor sour,   35
    That care for nothing being in their power.

56. With eagerness; gladly.

Actus Secundus. Scena Prima.   [Act II, scene i]

Pheroras and Graphina.

Pher. 'Tis true, Graphina, now the time draws nigh
Wherein the holy priest with hallowed rite,
The happy long-desired knot shall tie,
Pheroras and Graphina to unite:
How oft have I with lifted hands implor'd   5
This blessed hour, till now implor'd in vain,
Which hath my wished liberty restor'd,
And made my subject self my own again.
Thy love, fair maid, upon mine eye doth sit,
Whose nature hot doth dry the moisture all,   10
Which were in nature and in reason fit
For my [monarchal] brother's death to fall:
Had Herod liv'd, he would have pluckt my hand
From fair Graphina's palm perforce and ti'd
The same in hateful and despised band,   15
For I had had a baby to my bride:[57]
Scarce can her infant tongue with easy voice
Her name distinguish to another's ear.
Yet had he liv'd, his power and not my choice
Had made me [solemnly] the contract swear.   20
Have I not cause in such a change to joy?
What? Though she be my niece, a princess born:
Near blood's without respect, high birth a toy,
Since love can teach blood and kindred's scorn.
What booted it that he did raise my head,   25
To be his realm's copartner,[58] kingdom's mate,
Withal,[59] he kept Graphina from my bed,
More wisht by me than thrice Judea's state.
Oh, could not he be skillful judge in love,
That doted so upon his Mariam's face?   30
He for his passion Doris did remove.
I needed not a lawful wife displace.
It could not be but he had power to judge,
But he that never grudg'd a kingdom's share,
This well-known happiness to me did grudge: 35
And meant to be therein without compare.
Else had I been his equal in love's host,
For though the diadem on Mariam's head
Corrupt the vulgar judgments, I will boast

---

57. Pheroras had been betrothed to one of Herod's daughters.
58. Cary must be referring to Herod's installation of Pheroras as tetrarch of Perea; however, this did not occur until 20 B.C.
59. Despite that.

[Graphina's] brow's as white, her cheeks as red.   40
Why speaks thou not, fair creature? Move thy tongue,
For silence is a sign of discontent:
It were to both our loves too great a wrong
If now this hour do find thee sadly bent.
Graph. Mistake me not my Lord, too oft have I   45
Desir'd this time to come with winged feet,
To be enrapt with grief when 'tis too nigh,
You know my wishes ever yours did meet:
If I be silent, 'tis no more but fear
That I should say too little when I speak: 50
But since you will my imperfections bear,
In spite of doubt I will my silence break:
Yet might amazement tie my moving tongue,
But that I know before Pheroras' mind,
I have admired your affection long,   55
And cannot yet therein a reason find.
Your hand hath lifted me from lowest state,
To highest eminency wondrous grace,
And me your handmaid have you made your mate,
Though all but you alone do count me base.   60
You have preserved me pure at my request,
Though you so weak a vassal might constrain
To yield to your high will; then last not best
In my respect a princess you disdain.
Then need not all these favors study crave,   65
To be requited by a simple maid:
And study still you know must silence have,
Then be my cause for silence justly weigh'd;
But study cannot boot nor I requite,
Except your lowly handmaid's steadfast love   70
And fast obedience may your mind delight,
I will not promise more than I can prove.
Pher. That study needs not let Graphina smile,
And I desire no greater recompense:
I cannot vaunt me in a glorious style,   75
Nor show my love in farfetcht eloquence:
But this, believe me, never Herod's heart
Hath held his prince-born beauty-famed wife
In nearer place than thou fair virgin art,
To him that holds the glory of his life.   80
Should Herod's body leave the sepulcher,
And entertain the sever'd ghost again:
He should not be my nuptial hinderer,
Except he hind'red it with dying pain.
Come, fair Graphina, let us go in state,   85
This wish-endeared time to celebrate.

Actus 2. Scena 2.   [Act II, scene ii]

Constabarus and Babus' Sons.

Son 1. Now, valiant friend, you have our lives redeem'd,
Which lives as sav'd by you, to you are due:
Command and you shall see yourself esteem'd,
Our lives and liberties belong to you.
This twice six years with hazard of your life,   5
You have conceal'd us from the tyrant's sword:
Though cruel Herod's sister were your wife,
You durst in scorn of fear this grace afford.
In recompense we know not what to say,
A poor reward were thanks for such a merit,   10
Our truest friendship at your feet we lay,
The best requital to a noble spirit.
Const. Oh, how you wrong our friendship, valiant youth,
With friends there is not such a word as debt:
Where amity is ti'd with bond of truth,   15
All benefits are there in common set.
Then is the golden age[60] with them renew'd,
All names of properties are banisht quite:
Division and distinction are eschew'd:
Each hath to what belongs to others right.   20
And 'tis not sure so full a benefit,
Freely to give, as freely to require:
A bounteous act hath glory following it,
They cause the glory that the act desire.
All friendship should the pattern imitate,   25
Of Jesse's son[61] and valiant Jonathan:
For neither sovereign's nor father's hate,
A friendship fixt on virtue sever can.
Too much of this, 'tis written in the heart,
And need no amplifying with the tongue: 30
Now may you from your living tomb depart,
Where Herod's life hath kept you overlong.
Too great an injury to a noble mind,
To be quick buried. You had purchast fame
Some years ago, but that you were confin'd,   35
While thousand meaner did advance their name.
Your best of life, the prime of all your years,
Your time of action is from you bereft.
Twelve winters have you [overpast] in fears:
Yet if you use it well, enough is left.   40

---

60. In classical mythology, the first age of the world, an untroubled and prosperous era during which the human race lived in ideal happiness.
61. David. The friendship between David and Jonathan, the son of Saul, David's enemy, was considered exemplary.

And who can doubt but you will use it well?
The sons of Babus have it by descent:
In all their thoughts each action to excel,
Boldly to act, and wisely to invent.
Son 2. Had it not like the hateful cuckoo been,   45
Whose riper age his infant nurse doth kill:[62]
So long we had not kept ourselves unseen,
But Constabarus safely crost our will:
For had the tyrant fixt his cruel eye
On our concealed faces, wrath had sway'd   50
His justice so, that he had forst us die.
And dearer price than life we should have paid,
For you our truest friend had fall'n with us:
And we much like a house on pillars set,
Had clean deprest our prop, and therefore thus   55
Our ready will with our concealment met.
But now that you, fair Lord, are dangerless,
The sons of Baba shall their rigor show:
And prove it was not baseness did oppress
Our hearts so long, but honor kept them low.   60
Son 1. Yet do I fear this tale of Herod's death,
At last will prove a very tale indeed:
It gives me strongly in my mind his breath
Will be preserv'd to make a number bleed:
I wish not therefore to be set at large,   65
Yet peril to myself I do not [fear]:
Let us for some days longer be your charge,
Till we of Herod's state the truth do hear.
Const. What, art thou turn'd a coward, noble youth,
That thou beginst to doubt undoubted truth?   70
Son 1. Were it my brother's tongue that cast this doubt,
I from his heart would have the question out
With this keen fauchion;[63] but 'tis you, my Lord,
Against whose head I must not lift a sword,
I am so ti'd in gratitude.   75
Const.   Believe
You have no cause to take it ill,
If any word of mine your heart did grieve
The word dissented from the speaker's will,
I know it was not fear the doubt begun,
But rather valor and your care of me,   80
A coward could not be your father's son.
Yet know I doubts unnecessary be:

---

62. The cuckoo lays its eggs in the nests of smaller birds, and the young birds consequently devour
their first caregivers. Cf. *King Lear* I.iv.215–16: "The hedge-sparrow fed the cuckoo so long, /
That it had it head bit off by it young."
63. A short broadsword with a convex cutting edge and a sharp point, used in medieval times.

For who can think that in Anthonius' fall,
Herod, his bosom friend, should 'scape unbruis'd:
Then, Caesar, we might thee an idiot call,   85
If thou by him should'st be so far abus'd.
Son 2. Lord Constabarus, let me tell you this,
Upon submission Caesar will forgive:
And therefore, though the tyrant did amiss,
It may fall out that he will let him live.   90
Not many years agone it is since I,
Directed thither by my father's care,
In famous Rome for twice twelve months did live,
My life from Hebrews' cruelty to spare;
There, though I were but yet of boyish age,   95
I bent mine eye to mark, mine ears to hear.
Where I did see Octavius,[64] then a page,
When first he did to Julion's[65] sight appear:
Methought I saw such mildness in his face,
And such a sweetness in his looks did grow,   100
Withal, commixt with so majestic grace,
His [phisnomy][66] his fortune did foreshow:
For this I am indebted to mine eye,
But then mine ear receiv'd more evidence,
By that I knew his love to clemency,   105
How he with hottest choler could dispense.
Const. But we have more than barely heard the news.
It hath been twice confirm'd. And though some tongue
Might be so false, with false report t'abuse,
A false report hath never lasted long.   110
But be it so that Herod have his life,
Concealment would not then a whit avail:
For certain 'tis, that she that was my wife,
Would not to [let] her accusation fail.
And, therefore, now as good the venture give,   115
And free ourselves from blot of cowardice:
As show a pitiful desire to live,
For who can pity but they must despise?
Son 1. I yield, but to necessity I yield,
I dare upon this doubt engage mine arm: 120
That Herod shall again this kingdom wield,
And prove his death to be a false alarm.
Son 2. I doubt it too: God grant it be an error,
'Tis best without a cause to be in terror:
And rather had I, though my soul be mine,   125

64. Augustus Caesar, 63 B.C.–A.D. 14, the adopted son of Julius Caesar, who founded the imperial Roman government.
65. "Julion": Julius Caesar.
66. A shortened variant of *physiognomy*, meaning facial features, especially when regarded as revealing character.

My soul should lie, than prove a true divine.
Const. Come, come, let fear go seek a dastard's nest,
Undaunted courage lies in a noble breast.

Actus 2. Scena 3.   [Act II, scene iii]

Doris and Antipater.

Dor. [You] royal buildings, bow your lofty side,
And [stoop] to her that is by right your queen:
Let your humility upbraid the pride
Of those in whom no due respect is seen:
Nine times⁶⁷ have we with trumpets' haughty sound,   5
And banishing sour leaven from our taste,
Observ'd the feast that takes the fruit from ground.⁶⁸
Since I, fair city, did behold thee last,
So long it is since Mariam's purer cheek
Did rob from mine the glory. And so long   10
Since I return'd my native town to seek:
And with me nothing but the sense of wrong.
And thee, my boy, whose birth though great it were,
Yet have thy after fortunes prov'd but poor:
When thou wert born how little did I fear   15
Thou shouldst be thrust from forth thy father's door.
Art thou not Herod's right begotten son?
Was not the hapless Doris Herod's wife?
Yes: ere he had the Hebrew kingdom won,
I was companion to his private life.   20
Was I not fair enough to be a queen?
Why ere thou wert to me false monarch ti'd,
My [lack] of beauty might as well be seen,
As after I had liv'd five years thy bride.
Yet then thine oath[s] came pouring like the rain,   25
Which all affirm'd my face without compare:
And that if thou might'st Doris' love obtain,
For all the world besides thou didst not care.
Then was I young, and rich, and nobly born,⁶⁹
And therefore worthy to be Herod's mate: 30
Yet thou, ungrateful, cast me off with scorn,
When Heaven's purpose rais'd your meaner fate.
Oft have I begg'd for vengeance for this fact,
And with dejected knees, aspiring hands

---

67. Nine years, although thirteen years had actually passed. The events of the play take place in 29 B.C. In 42 B.C. Doris had been divorced from Herod and forbidden to appear in Jerusalem except on days of public festival.
68. Passover.
69. In *The Jewish Wars*, Josephus describes Doris as a "native of Jerusalem" and "a Jewess of some standing" (I, 241, 432), although modern historians assert that she more likely than not came from a royal Idumean family.

Have pray'd the highest power to enact   35
The fall of her that on my trophy stands.
Revenge I have according to my will,
Yet where I wisht this vengeance did not light:
I wisht it should high-hearted Mariam kill.
But it against my whilom[70] Lord did fight.   40
With thee, sweet boy, I came and came to try
If thou before his bastards might be plac'd
In Herod's royal seat and dignity.
But Mariam's infants here are only grac'd,
And now for us there doth no hope remain: 45
Yet we will not return till Herod's end
Be more confirm'd. Perchance he is not slain.
So glorious fortunes may my boy attend,
For if he live, he'll think it doth suffice
That he to Doris shows such cruelty: 50
For as he did my wretched life despise,
So do I know I shall despised die.
Let him but prove as natural to thee,
As cruel to thy miserable mother:
His cruelty shall not upbraided be   55
But in thy fortunes. I his faults will smother.
Ant. Each mouth within the city loudly cries
That Herod's death is certain: therefore we
Had best some subtle hidden plot devise,
That Mariam's children might subverted be   60
By poison's drink or else by murtherous knife;
So we may be advanc'd, it skills not how:
They are but bastards, you were Herod's wife,
And foul adultery blotteth Mariam's brow.
Dor. They are too strong to be by us remov'd,   65
Or else revenge's foulest spotted face,
By our detested wrongs might be approv'd,
But weakness must to greater power give place.
But let us now retire to grieve alone,
For solitariness best fitteth moan.   70

Actus Secundus. Scena 4.   [Act II, scene iv]

Silleus and Constabarus.

Sill. Well met, Judean Lord, the only wight
Silleus wisht to see. I am to call
Thy tongue to strict account.
Const.   For what despite
I ready am to hear, and answer all.

70. Former.

But if directly at the cause I guess 5
That breeds this challenge, you must pardon me:
And now some other ground of fight profess,
For I have vow'd, vows must unbroken be.
Sill. What may be your expectation? Let me know.
Const. Why? Aught concerning Salom, my sword 10
Shall not be wielded for a cause so low,
A blow for her my arm will scorn t'afford.
Sill. It is for slandering her unspotted name,
And I will make thee in thy vow's despite,
Suck up the breath that did my mistress blame, 15
And swallow it again to do her right.
Const. I prithee give some other quarrel ground
To find beginning: rail against my name,
Or strike me first, or let some scarlet wound
Enflame my courage, give me words of shame, 20
Do thou our Moses' sacred laws disgrace,
Deprave our nation, do me some despite:
I'm apt enough to fight in any case,
But yet for Salome I will not fight.
Sill. Nor I for aught but Salome: my sword 25
That owes his service to her sacred name
Will not an edge for other cause afford,
In other fight I am not sure of fame.
Const. For her, I pity thee enough already,
For her, I therefore will not mangle thee: 30
A woman with a heart so most unsteady,
Will of herself sufficient torture be.
I cannot envy for so light a gain,
Her mind with such unconstancy doth run:
As with a word thou didst her love obtain, 35
So with a word she will from thee be won.
So light as her possessions for most day
Is her affections lost, to me 'tis known:
As good go hold the wind as make her stay,
She never loves, but till she call her own. 40
She merely is a painted sepulcher,
That is both fair and vilely foul at once:
Though on her outside graces garnish her,
Her mind is fill'd with worse than rotten bones.
And ever ready lifted is her hand, 45
To aim destruction at a husband's throat:
For proofs, Josephus and myself do stand,
Though once on both of us she seem'd to dote.
Her mouth, though serpent-like it never hisses,
Yet like a serpent poisons where it kisses. 50
Sill. Well, Hebrew, well. Thou bark'st, but wilt not bite.

Const. I tell thee still for her I will not fight.
Sill. Why then I call thee coward.
Const.   From my heart
I give thee thanks. A coward's hateful name,
Cannot to valiant minds a blot impart,   55
And therefore I with joy receive the same.
Thou know'st I am no coward: thou wert by
At the Arabian battle th'other day,
And saw'st my sword with daring valiancy,
Amongst the faint Arabians cut my way.   60
The blood of foes no more could let it shine,
And 'twas enameled with some of thine.
But now have at thee; not for Salome
I fight but to discharge a coward's style.
Here 'gins the fight that shall not parted be,   65
Before a soul or two endure exile. *[They fight.]*
Sill. Thy sword hath made some windows for my blood,
To show a horrid crimson phisnomy.
To breathe for both of us methinks 'twere good.
The day will give us time enough to die.   70
Const. With all my heart, take breath. Thou shalt have time,
And if thou list, a twelve month; let us end.
Into thy cheeks there doth a paleness climb.
Thou canst not from my sword thyself defend.
What needest thou for Salome to fight?   75
Thou hast her, and may'st keep her, none strives for her.
I willingly to thee resign my right,
For in my very soul I do abhor her.
Thou seest that I am fresh, unwounded yet.
Then not for fear I do this offer make.   80
Thou art with loss of blood to fight unfit,
For here is one, and there another take.
Sill. I will not leave, as long as breath remains
Within my wounded body: spare your words,
My heart in blood's stead courage entertains,   85
Salome's love no place for fear affords.
Const. Oh, could thy soul but prophesy like mine,
I would not wonder thou should'st long to die.
For Salome if I aright divine
Will be than death a greater misery.   90
Sill. Then list, I'll breathe no longer.
Const.   Do thy will,
I hateless fight, and charitably kill.
[They fight.]
Pity thyself, Silleus. Let not death
Intrude before his time into thy heart.
Alas it is too late to fear. His breath   95

Is from his body now about to part.
How far'st thou, brave Arabian?
Sill.   Very well,
My leg is hurt, I can no longer fight.
It only grieves me, that so soon I fell,
Before fair Salom's wrongs I came to right.   100
Const. Thy wounds are less than mortal. Never fear,
Thou shalt a safe and quick recovery find:
Come, I will thee unto my lodging bear,
I hate thy body, but I love thy mind.
Sill. Thanks, noble Jew, I see a courteous foe,   105
Stern enmity to friendship can no art.
Had not my heart and tongue engag'd me so,
I would from thee no foe, but friend depart.
My heart to Salome is ti'd so fast,[71]
To leave her love for friendship, yet my skill   110
Shall be employ'd to make your favor last,
And I will honor Constabarus still.
Const. I ope my bosom to thee, and will take
Thee in, as friend, and grieve for thy complaint,
But if we do not expedition make,   115
Thy loss of blood I fear will make thee faint.

Chorus. To hear a tale with ears prejudicate,
It spoils the judgment and corrupts the sense:
That human error given to every state,
Is greater enemy to innocence.
 It makes us foolish, heady, rash, unjust.   5
 It makes us never try before we trust.

It will confound the meaning, change the words,
For it our sense of hearing much deceives:
Besides no time to judgment it affords,
To weigh the circumstance our ear receives.   10
 The ground of accidents it never tries,
 But makes us take for truth ten thousand lies.

Our ears and hearts are apt to hold for good,
That we ourselves do most desire to be,
And then we drown objections in the flood   15
Of partiality. 'Tis that we see
 That makes false rumors long with credit past,
 Though they like rumors must conclude at last.

The greatest part of us prejudicate,
With wishing Herod's death do hold it true: 20
The being once deluded doth not bate,
The credit to a better likelihood due.

71. I.e., too fast.

Those few that wish it, not the multitude,
Do carry headlong, so they doubts conclude.

They not object the weak uncertain ground,   25
Whereon they built this tale of Herod's end.
Whereof the author scarcely can be found,
And all because their wishes that way bend.
　　They think not of the peril that ensu'th,
　　If this should prove the contrary to truth.   30

On this same doubt, on this so light a breath,
They pawn their lives and fortunes. For they all
Behave them as the news of Herod's death,
They did of most undoubted credit call:
　　But if their actions now do rightly hit,   35
　　Let them commend their fortune, not their wit.

Actus Tertius. Scena Prima.　　　　　　　　**[Act III, scene i]**

Pheroras. Salome.

Pher. Urge me no more Graphina to forsake,
Not twelve hours since I married her for love,
And do you think a sister's power [can make]
A resolute decree so soon remove?
Sal. Poor minds they are that honor not affects.   5
Pher. Who hunts for honor, happiness neglects.
Sal. You might have been both of felicity,
And honor too in equal measure seiz'd.
Pher. It is not you can tell so well as I,
What 'tis can make me happy or displeas'd.   10
Sal. To match for neither beauty nor respects
One mean of birth, but yet of meaner mind,
A woman full of natural defects,
I wonder what your eye in her could find.
Pher. Mine eye found loveliness, mine ear found wit,   15
To please the one, and to enchant the other:
Grace on her eye, mirth on her tongue doth sit,
In looks a child, in wisdom's house a mother.
Sal. But say you thought her fair, as none thinks else,
Knows not, Pheroras, beauty is a blast: 20
Much like this flower which today excels,
But longer than a day it will not last.
Pher. Her wit exceeds her beauty.
Sal.　　　　　　　　　　　　Wit may show
The way to ill, as well as good you know.
Pher. But wisdom is the porter of her head,   25
And bars all wicked words from issuing thence.

Sal. But of a porter, better were you sped,
If she against their entrance made defense.
Pher. But wherefore comes the sacred Ananell,[72]
That hitherward his hasty steps doth bend?   30
Great sacrificer, y'are arrived well.
Ill news from holy mouth I not attend.

Actus Tertius. Scena 2.   [Act III, scene ii]

Pheroras. Salome. Ananell.

Anan. My lips, my son, with peaceful tidings blest,
Shall utter honey to your list'ning ear.
A word of death comes not from priestly breast,
I speak of life: in life there is no fear.
And for the news I did the heavens salute,   5
And fill'd the Temple with my thankful voice:
For though that mourning may not me pollute,
At pleasing accidents I may rejoice.
Pher. Is Herod then reviv'd from certain death?
Sal. What? Can your news restore my brother's breath?   10
Anan. Both so, and so the King is safe and sound,
And did such grace in royal Caesar meet,
That he, with larger style than ever crown'd,
Within this hour Jerusalem will greet.
I did but come to tell you and must back   15
To make preparatives for sacrifice:
I knew his death your hearts like mine did rack,[73]
Though to conceal it prov'd you wise.
                                        (Exit Ananell.)
Sal. How can my joy sufficiently appear?
Pher. A heavier tale did never pierce mine ear.   20
Sal. Now Salome of happiness may boast.
Pher. But now Pheroras is in danger most.
Sal. I shall enjoy the comfort of my life.
Pher. And I shall lose it, losing of my wife.
Sal. Joy heart, for Constabarus shall be slain.   25
Pher. Grieve soul, Graphina shall from me be ta'en.
Sal. Smile cheeks, the fair Silleus shall be mine.
Pher. Weep eyes, for I must with a child combine.
Sal. Well, brother, cease your moans; on one condition
I'll undertake to win the King's consent: 30
Graphina still shall be in your tuition,[74]
And her with you be ne'er the less content.
Pher. What's the condition? Let me quickly know,

---

72. High priest, who replaced Aristobolus.
73. Torture; torment.
74. Guardianship; protection.

That I as quickly your command may act:
Were it to see what herbs in Ophir[75] grow,   35
Or that the lofty Tyrus[76] might be sackt.
Sal. 'Tis no so hard a task: it is no more,
But tell the King that Constabarus hid
The sons of Baba, done to death before,
And 'tis no more than Constabarus did.   40
And tell him more that [we], for Herod's sake,
Not able to endure [our] brother's foe,
Did with a bill our separation make,
Though loath from Constabarus else to go.
Pher. Believe this tale for told. I'll go from hence,   45
In Herod's ear the Hebrew to deface,
And I that never studied eloquence,
Do mean with eloquence this tale to grace.
(Exit.)
Sal. This will be Constabarus' quick dispatch,
Which from my mouth would lesser credit find.   50
Yet shall he not decease without a match,[77]
For Mariam shall not linger long behind.
First jealousy, if that avail not, fear
Shall be my minister to work her end.
A common error moves not Herod's ear,   55
Which doth so firmly to his Mariam bend.
She shall be charged with so horrid crime,
As Herod's fear shall turn his love to hate.
I'll make some swear that she desires to climb,
And seeks to poison him for his estate.   60
I scorn that she should live my birth t'upbraid,
To call me base and hungry Edomite.
With patient show her choler I betray'd,
And watcht the time to be reveng'd by [sleight].
Now tongue of mine with scandal load her name,   65
Turn hers to fountains, Herod's eyes to flame.
Yet first I will begin Pheroras' suit,
That he my earnest business may effect.
And I of Mariam will keep me mute,
Till first some other doth her name detect.   70
Who's there, Silleus' man? How fares your Lord,
That your aspects do bear the badge of sorrow?
Man. He hath the marks of Constabarus' sword,
And for a while desires your sight to borrow.
Sal. My heavy curse the hateful sword pursue,   75
My heavier curse on the more hateful arm

75. A land rich in gold. See 1 Kings 9:28, 10:11.
76. Famous maritime and commercial city of the Phoenicians.
77. Companion.

That wounded my Silleus. But renew
Your tale again. Hath he no mortal harm?
Man. No sign of danger doth in him appear,
Nor are his wounds in place of peril seen.   80
He bids you be assured you need not fear.
He hopes to make you yet Arabia's queen.
Sal. Commend my heart to be Silleus' charge.
Tell him my brother's sudden coming now
Will give my foot no room to walk at large,   85
But I will see him yet ere night I vow.

Actus 3. Scena 3.   [Act III, scene iii]

Mariam and Sohemus.

Mar. Sohemus, tell me what the news may be
That makes your eyes so full, your cheeks so blue?
Soh. I know not how to call them. Ill for me
'Tis sure they are. Not so I hope for you.
Herod.   5
Mar.   Oh, what of Herod?
Soh.   Herod lives.
[Mar.] How! Lives? What, in some cave or forest hid?
Soh. Nay, back return'd with honor. Caesar gives
Him greater grace than ere Anthonius did.
Mar. Foretell the ruin of my family,
Tell me that I shall see our city burn'd,   10
Tell me I shall a death disgraceful die,
But tell me not that Herod is return'd.
Soh. Be not impatient, Madam, be but mild,
His love to you again will soon be bred.
Mar. I will not to his love be reconcil'd,   15
With solemn vows I have forsworn his bed.
Soh. But you must break those vows.
Mar.   I'll rather break
The heart of Mariam. Cursed is my fate,
But speak no more to me. In vain ye speak[78]
To live with him I so profoundly hate.   20
Soh. Great Queen, you must to me your pardon give,
Sohemus cannot now your will obey.
If your command should me to silence drive,
It were not to obey, but to betray.
Reject and slight my speeches, mock my faith,   25
Scorn my observance, call my counsel naught.
Though you regard not what Sohemus saith,
Yet will I ever freely speak my thought.

78. Try to convince me.

I fear ere long I shall fair Mariam see
In woeful state, and by herself undone.   30
Yet for your issues' sake more temp'rate be,
The heart by affability is won.
Mar. And must I to my prison turn again?
Oh, now I see I was an hypocrite.
I did this morning for his death complain,   35
And yet do mourn because he lives ere night.
When I his death believ'd, compassion wrought,
And was the stickler 'twixt my heart and him.
But now that curtain's drawn from off my thought,
Hate doth appear again with visage grim,   40
And paints the face of Herod in my heart,
In horrid colors with detested look.
Then fear would come, but scorn doth play her part,
And saith that scorn with fear can never brook.
I know I could enchain him with a smile,   45
And lead him captive with a gentle word.
I scorn my look should ever man beguile,
Or other speech than meaning to afford.
Else Salome in vain might spend her wind,
In vain might Herod's mother⁷⁹ whet her tongue,   50
In vain had they complotted and combin'd,
For I could overthrow them all ere long.
Oh, what a shelter is mine innocence,
To shield me from the pangs of inward grief.
'Gainst all mishaps it is my fair defense,   55
And to my sorrows yields a large relief.
To be commandress of the triple earth⁸⁰
And sit in safety from a fall secure,
To have all nations celebrate my birth,
I would not that my spirit were impure.   60
Let my distressed state unpitied be,
Mine innocence is hope enough for me.
(Exit.)
Soh. Poor guiltless Queen. Oh, that my wish might place
A little temper now about thy heart:
Unbridled speech is Mariam's worst disgrace,   65
And will endanger her without desert.
I am in greater hazard. O'er my head,
The fatal axe doth hang unsteadily.
My disobedience once discovered,
Will shake it down: Sohemus so shall die.   70
For when the King shall find we thought his death
Had been as certain as we see his life,

---

79. Cyprus, most probably an Arabian woman.
80. The known world: Europe, Asia, and Africa.

And marks withal[81] I slighted so his breath,
As to preserve alive his matchless wife,
Nay more, to give to [Alexandra's] hand   75
The regal dignity,[82] the sovereign power,
How I had yielded up at her command,
The strength of all the city, David's Tower,
What more than common death may I expect,
Since I too well do know his cruelty?   80
'Twere death, a word of Herod's to neglect,
What then to do directly contrary?
Yet, life, I [quit] thee with a willing spirit,
And think thou could'st not better be employ'd.
I forfeit thee for her that more doth merit.   85
Ten such were better dead than she destroy'd.
But fare thee well, chaste Queen, well may I see
The darkness palpable and rivers part,
The sun stand still. Nay more, retorted[83] be,
But never woman with so pure a heart.   90
Thine eyes' grave majesty keeps all in awe,
And cuts the wings of every loose desire.
Thy brow is table to the modest law,
Yet though we dare not love, we may admire.
And if I die, it shall my soul content,   95
My breath in Mariam's service shall be spent.

Chorus. 'Tis not enough for one that is a wife
To keep her spotless from an act of ill,
But from suspicion she should free her life,
And bare herself of power as well as will.
    'Tis not so glorious for her to be free,   5
    As by her proper self restrain'd to be.

When she hath spacious ground to walk upon,
Why on the ridge should she desire to go?
It is no glory to forbear alone,
Those things that may her honor overthrow.   10
    But 'tis thank-worthy, if she will not take
    All lawful liberties for honor's sake.

That wife her hand against her fame doth rear,
That more than to her Lord alone will give
A private word to any second ear.   15
And though she may with reputation live,
    Yet though most chaste, she doth her glory blot,
    And wounds her honor, though she kills it not.

---

81. Besides.
82. Apparently Sohemus had given over the rule of Jerusalem to Alexandra. This is not in Josephus.
83. Turned backward.

When to their husbands they themselves do bind,
Do they not wholly give themselves away? 20
Or give they but their body not their mind,
Reserving that though[t] best for others' prey?
    No sure, their thoughts no more can be their own,
    And therefore should to none but one be known.

Then she usurps upon another's right, 25
That seeks to be by public language grac't.
And though her thoughts reflect with purest light,
Her mind if not peculiar is not chaste.
    For in a wife it is no worse to find,
    A common body, than a common mind. 30

And every mind though free from thought of ill,
That out of glory seeks a worth to show,
When any's ears but one therewith they fill,
Doth in a sort her pureness overthrow.
    Now Mariam had (but that to this she bent) 35
    Been free from fear, as well as innocent.

Actus Quartus. Scena Prima.   **[Act IV, scene i]**

Enter Herod and his attendants.

Her. Hail, happy city, happy in thy store,
And happy that thy buildings such we see.
More happy in the Temple where w'adore,
But most of all that Mariam lives in thee.
Art thou return'd? How fares my Mariam? 5

Enter Nuntio.

Nun. She's well my Lord, and will anon be here
As you commanded.
Her.   Muffle up thy brow,
Thou day's dark taper.[84] Mariam will appear,
And where she shines, we need not thy dim light.
Oh, haste thy steps, rare creature, speed thy pace, 10
And let thy presence make the day more bright,
And cheer the heart of Herod with thy face.
It is an age since I from Mariam went.
Methinks our parting was in David's days,[85]
The hours are so increast by discontent. 15
Deep sorrow, Joshua-like[86] the season stays,

---

84. Herod calls the sun a taper or candle, a dim light in contrast to Mariam's brightness.
85. As long ago as when David lived.
86. For a long time, as long as Joshua's lifetime. See Joshua 24:29 (Geneva Bible): "And after these things Joshua the son of Nun, the servant of the Lord died, being an hundreth and ten years old."

But when I am with Mariam, time runs on.
Her sight can make months, minutes, days of weeks.
An hour is then no sooner come than gone,
When in her face mine eye for wonders seeks.   20
You world-commanding city,[87] Europe's grace,
Twice hath my curious eye your streets survey'd,
And I have seen the statue-filled place,[88]
That once if not for grief had been betray'd.
I all your Roman beauties have beheld,   25
And seen the shows your aediles[89] did prepare.
I saw the sum of what in you excell'd,
Yet saw no miracle like Mariam rare.
The fair and famous Livia,[90] Caesar's love,
The world's commanding mistress did I see,   30
Whose beauties both the world and Rome approve.
Yet, Mariam, Livia is not like to thee.
Be patient but a little, while mine eyes
Within your compass limits be contain'd.
That object straight shall your desires suffice,   35
From which you were so long a while restrain'd.
How wisely Mariam doth the time delay,
Lest sudden joy my sense should suffocate.
I am prepar'd. Thou needst no longer stay.
Who's there? My Mariam, more than happy fate?   40
Oh no, it is Pheroras. Welcome, Brother.
Now for a while, I must my passion smother.

Actus Quartus. Scena Secunda.   [Act IV, scene ii]

Herod. Pheroras.

Pher. All health and safety wait upon my Lord,
And may you long in prosperous fortunes live
With Rome-commanding Caesar at accord,
And have all honors that the world can give.
Her. Oh Brother, now thou speakst not from thy heart.   5
No, thou hast strook a blow at Herod's love,
That cannot quickly from my memory part,
Though Salome did me to pardon move.
Valiant Phasaelus,[91] now to thee farewell.
Thou wert my kind and honorable brother.   10
Oh hapless hour, when you self-stricken fell,
Thou father's image, glory of thy mother.

87. Rome.
88. The Roman Forum.
89. Roman officials in charge of buildings, roads, sanitation, public games, etc.
90. The wife of Augustus Caesar.
91. Herod's elder brother and former governor of Jerusalem, killed in 40 B.C. by anti-Roman forces. Herod is comparing his dead heroic brother to the weak-willed and lovesick Pheroras.

Had I desir'd a greater suit of thee,
Than to withhold thee from a harlot's bed,
Thou wouldst have granted it. But now I see   15
All are not like that in a womb are bred.
Thou wouldst not, hadst thou heard of Herod's death,
Have made his burial time, thy bridal hour.
Thou wouldst with clamors, not with joyful breath,
Have show'd the news to be not sweet but sour.   20
Pher. Phasaelus' great worth I know did stain
Pheroras' petty valor. But they lie
(Excepting you yourself) that dare maintain,
That he did honor Herod more than I.
For what I show'd, love's power constrain'd me show,   25
And pardon loving faults for Mariam's sake.
Her. Mariam, where is she?
Pher.   Nay, I do not know,
But absent use of her fair name I make.
You have forgiven greater faults than this,
For Constabarus that against you[r] will   30
Preserv'd the sons of Baba, lives in bliss,
Though you commanded him the youths to kill.
Her. Go, take a present order for his death,
And let those traitors feel the worst of fears.
Now Salome will whine to beg his breath,   35
But I'll be deaf to prayers, and blind to tears.
Pher. He is, my Lord, from Salom divorst,
Though her affection did to leave him grieve.
Yet was she by her love to you enforst,
To leave the man that would your foes relieve.   40
Her. Then haste them to their death. I will requite
Thee, gentle Mariam. Salom, I mean.
The thought of Mariam doth so steal my spirit,
My mouth from speech of her I cannot wean.
                                                 (Exit.)

Actus 4. Scena 3.   [Act IV, scene iii]

Herod. Mariam.

Her. And here she comes indeed. Happily met,
My best and dearest half. What ails my dear?
Thou doest the difference certainly forget
'Twixt dusky habits[92] and a time so clear.
Mar. My Lord, I suit my garment to my mind,   5
And there no cheerful colors can I find.
Her. Is this my welcome? Have I long'd so much

92. Apparently Mariam is dressed in black.

To see my dearest Mariam discontent?
What is't that is the cause thy heart to touch?
Oh speak, that I thy sorrow may prevent.   10
Art thou not Jewry's queen, and Herod's too?
Be my commandress, be my sovereign guide.
To be by thee directed I will woo,
For in thy pleasure lies my highest pride.
Or if thou think Judea's narrow bound,   15
Too strict a limit for thy great command,
Thou shalt be empress of Arabia crown'd,
For thou shalt rule, and I will win the land.
I'll rob the holy David's sepulcher
To give thee wealth, if thou for wealth do care.   20
Thou shalt have all they did with him inter,
And I for thee will make the Temple bare.
Mar. I neither have of power nor riches want.
I have enough, nor do I wish for more.
Your offers to my heart no ease can grant,   25
Except they could my brother's life restore.
No, had you wisht the wretched Mariam glad,
Or had your love to her been truly ti'd,
Nay, had you not desir'd to make her sad,
My brother nor my grandsire had not di'd.   30
Her. Wilt thou believe no oaths to clear thy Lord?
How oft have I with execration sworn,
Thou art by me belov'd, by me ador'd,
Yet are my protestations heard with scorn.
Hircanus plotted to deprive my head   35
Of this long settled honor that I wear,
And therefore I did justly doom him dead,
To rid the realm from peril, me from fear.
Yet I for Mariam's sake do so repent
The death of one whose blood she did inherit,   40
I wish I had a kingdom's treasure spent,
So I had ne'er expell'd Hircanus' spirit.[93]
As I affected that same noble youth,
In lasting infamy my name enroll,
If I not mourn'd his death with hearty truth.   45
Did I not show to him my earnest love
When I to him the priesthood did restore,
And did for him a living priest remove,
Which never had been done but once before?
Mar. I know that mov'd by importunity,   50
You made him priest, and shortly after die.
Her. I will not speak, unless to be believ'd.

---

93. The disrupted rhyme scheme suggests that a line may be missing after this one.

This froward[94] humor will not do you good.
It hath too much already Herod griev'd,
To think that you on terms of hate have stood.   55
Yet smile, my dearest Mariam, do but smile,
And I will all unkind conceits[95] exile.
Mar. I cannot frame disguise, nor never taught
My face a look dissenting from my thought.
Her. By Heav'n, you vex me. Build not on my love.   60
Mar. I will not build on so unstable ground.
Her. Naught is so fixt, but peevishness may move.
Mar. 'Tis better [slightest] cause than none were found.
Her. Be judge yourself if ever Herod sought
Or would be mov'd a cause of change to find.   65
Yet let your look declare a milder thought,
My heart again you shall to Mariam bind.
How oft did I for you my mother chide,
Revile my sister, and my brother rate,
And tell them all my Mariam they beli'd.   70
Distrust me still, if these be signs of hate.

Actus 4. Scena 4.   [Act IV, scene iv]

Herod. [Mariam.] Bu[tler. Soldier].

Her. What hast thou here?
Bu.   A drink procuring love.
The Queen desir'd me to deliver it.
Mar. Did I? Some hateful practice this will prove,
Yet can it be no worse than heavens permit.
Her. Confess the truth, thou wicked instrument   5
To her outrageous will. 'Tis passion sure.
Tell true, and thou shalt 'scape the punishment,
Which if thou do conceal, thou shalt endure.
Bu. I know not, but I doubt it be no less.
Long since the hate of you her heart did cease.   10
Her. Know'st thou the cause thereof?
Bu.   My Lord, I guess
Sohemus told the tale that did displease.
Her. Oh Heaven! Sohemus false! Go let him die.
Stay not to suffer him to speak a word.
Oh damned villain, did he falsify   15
The oath he swore ev'n of his own accord?
Now do I know thy falsehood, painted devil,
Thou white enchantress. Oh, thou art so foul

94. Stubborn; willful; contrary.
95. Opinions; thoughts; ideas.

That hyssop[96] cannot cleanse thee worst of evil.
A beauteous body hides a loathsome soul.   20
Your love, Sohemus, mov'd by his affection,
Though he have ever heretofore been true,
Did blab forsooth, that I did give direction,
If we were put to death to slaughter you.
And you in black revenge attended now   25
To add a murther to your breach of vow.
Mar. Is this a dream?
Her.   Oh Heaven, that 'twere no more,
I'll give my realm to who can prove it so.
[I] would I were like any beggar poor,
So I for false my Mariam did not know.   30
Foul pith contain'd in the fairest rind,
That ever grac'd a cedar. Oh, thine eye
Is pure as Heaven, but impure thy mind,
And for impurity shall Mariam die.
Why didst thou love Sohemus?   35
Mar.   They can tell
That say I lov'd him. Mariam says not so.
Her. Oh, cannot impudence the coals expel,
That for thy love in Herod's bosom glow.
It is as plain as water, and denial
Makes of thy falsehood but a greater trial.   40
Hast thou beheld thyself and couldst thou stain
So rare perfection? Even for love of thee
I do profoundly hate thee. Wert thou plain,
Thou should'st the wonder of Judea be.
But oh, thou art not. Hell itself lies hid   45
Beneath thy heavenly show. Yet never wert thou chaste.
Thou might'st exalt, pull down, command, forbid,
And be above the wheel of fortune plast.
Hadst thou complotted Herod's massacre,
That so thy son a monarch might be styl'd,   50
Not half so grievous such an action were,
As once to think that Mariam is defil'd.
Bright workmanship of nature sulli'd o'er
With pitched darkness, now thine end shall be.
Thou shalt not live, fair fiend, to cozen more,   55
With heavy semblance, as thou coz'nedst me.[97]
Yet must I love thee in despite of death,
And thou shalt die in the despite of love,
For neither shall my love prolong thy breath,
Nor shall thy loss of breath my love remove.   60

---

96. An unidentified plant mentioned in the Bible as a source of twigs used for sprinkling in certain Hebraic purificatory rites. See Exodus 12:22.
97. Cf. *Othello* V.ii.106: "Yet she must die, else she'll betray more men."

I might have seen thy falsehood in thy face.
Where could'st thou get thy stars that serv'd for eyes,
Except by theft, and theft is foul disgrace?
This had appear'd before, were Herod wise.
But I'm a sot, a very sot, no better.   65
My wisdom long ago a wand'ring fell.
Thy face encount'ring it, my wit did fetter,
And made me for delight my freedom sell.
Give me my heart, false creature, 'tis a wrong
My guiltless heart should now with thine be slain.   70
Thou hadst no right to [lock] it up so long,
And with usurper's name I Mariam stain.

Enter Bu[tler.]

Her. Have you design'd Sohemus to his end?
Bu. I have, my Lord.
Her.   Then call our royal guard
To do as much for Mariam. They offend⁹⁸   75
Leave ill unblam'd, or good without reward.
Here take her to her death. Come back, come back.
What meant I to deprive the world of light,
To muffle iv'ry in the foulest black,
That ever was an opposite to white.   80
Why whither would you carry her?
Sold.   You bade
We should conduct her to her death, my Lord.
Her. Why sure I did not. Herod was not mad.
Why should she feel the fury of the sword?
Oh, now the grief returns into my heart,   85
And pulls me piecemeal. Love and hate do fight
And now hath [love] acquir'd the greater part.
Yet now hath hate affection conquer'd quite.
And therefore bear her hence. And Hebrew, why
Seize you with lion's paws the fairest lamb   90
Of all the flock? She must not, shall not, die.
Without her I most miserable am.
And with her more than most. Away, away,
But bear her but to prison not to death.
And is she gone indeed? Stay, villains, stay.   95
Her looks alone preserv'd your sovereign's breath.
Well, let her go, but yet she shall not die.
I cannot think she meant to poison me.
But certain 'tis she liv'd too wantonly,
And therefore shall she never more be free.   100

98. Ellipsis of the word "who" after "offend."

Actus 4. Scena 5.   [Act IV, scene v]

[Butler].

Bu. Foul villain, can thy pitchy-colored soul
Permit thine ear to hear her [causeless]⁹⁹ doom,
And not enforce thy tongue that tale control,
That must unjustly bring her to her tomb?
Oh, Salome, thou hast thyself repaid,   5
For all the benefits that thou hast done.
Thou art the cause I have the Queen betray'd.
Thou hast my heart to darkest falsehood won.
I am condemn'd. Heav'n gave me not my tongue
To slander innocents, to lie, deceive,   10
To be the hateful instrument to wrong,
The earth of greatest glory to bereave.
My sin ascends and doth to Heav'n cry,
It is the blackest deed that ever was.
And there doth sit an angel notary,   15
That doth record it down in leaves of brass.
Oh, how my heart doth quake. Achitophel,¹⁰⁰
Thou [found'st] a means thyself from shame to free,
And sure my soul approves thou didst not well.
All follow some, and I will follow thee.   20

Actus 4. Scena 6.   [Act IV, scene vi]

Constabarus, Babus' sons, and their guard.

Const. Now here we step our last, the way to death.
We must not tread this way a second time.
Yet let us resolutely yield our breath.
Death is the only ladder, Heav'n to climb.
Son 1. With willing mind I could myself resign.   5
But yet it grieves me with a grief untold,
Our death should be accompani'd with thine.
Our friendship we to thee have dearly sold.
Const. Still wilt thou wrong the sacred name of friend?
Then should'st thou never style it friendship more,   10
But base mechanic traffic that doth lend,
Yet will be sure they shall the debt restore.
I could with needless compliment return.
'Tis for thy ceremony I could say.
'Tis I that made the fire your house to burn,   15

---

99. Or "callous." The Huntington text reads "caules."
100. Traitorous counselor to David, who deserted to David's son, Absalom, during the latter's attempted usurpation of his father. Achitophel hanged himself when his advice was disregarded. See 2 Samuel 17.

For but for me she would not you betray.
Had not the damned woman sought mine end,
You had not been the subject of her hate.
You never did her hateful mind offend,
Nor could your deaths have freed [her] nuptial fate.   20
Therefore, fair friends, though you were still unborn,
Some other subtlety devis'd should be,
[Whereby] my life, though guiltless should be torn.
Thus have I prov'd, 'tis you that die for me,
And therefore should I weakly now lament.   25
You have but done your duties, friends should die.
Alone their friends' disaster to prevent,
Though not compell'd by strong necessity.
But now farewell, fair city, never more
Shall I behold your beauty shining bright.   30
Farewell of Jewish men, the worthy store,
But no farewell to any female wight.
You wavering crew, my curse to you I leave.
You had but one to give you any grace,
And you yourselves will Mariam's life bereave.   35
Your commonwealth doth innocency chase,
You creatures made to be the human curse,
You tigers, lionesses, hungry bears,
Tear-massacring hyenas[101]—nay far worse,
For they for prey do shed their feigned tears.   40
But you will weep (you creatures cross to good)
For your unquenched thirst of human blood.
You were the angels cast from Heaven for pride,
And still do keep your angels' outward show,
But none of you are inly beautifi'd,   45
For still your heav'n-depriving pride doth grow.
Did not the sins of many require a scourge,
Your place on earth had been by this withstood.
But since a flood no more the world must purge,[102]
You stay'd in office of a second flood.   50
You giddy creatures, sowers of debate,
You'll love today, and for no other cause,
But for you yesterday did deeply hate.
You are the wreak[103] of order, breach of laws.
[Your] best are foolish, froward, wanton, vain.   55
Your worst adulterous, murderous, cunning, proud.

101. The hyena "gobbles up [its prey] with hypocritical sobs," according to the twelfth-century
    work, *The Book of Beasts* (trans. T. H. White, 1984, p. 31). This animal is also marked with
    duplicity and inconstancy, two characteristics often ascribed to women.
102. A reference to the flood God sent to destroy the world in Noah's time. God then made a
    covenant with Noah, promising that He would never destroy the world with water again. See
    Genesis 6–9.
103. Destruction.

And Salome attends the latter train,
Or rather [s]he their leader is allow'd.
I do the sottishness of men bewail,
That do with following you enhance your pride.   60
'Twere better that the human race should fail,
Than be by such a mischief multipli'd.
Cham's servile curse[104] to all your sex was given,
Because in Paradise you did offend.
Then do we not resist the will of Heaven,   65
When on your wills like servants we attend?
You are to nothing constant but to ill.
You are with naught but wickedness endu'd.[105]
Your loves are set on nothing but your will,
And thus my censure I of you conclude.   70
You are the least of goods, the worst of evils,
Your best are worse than men, your worst than devils.
Son 2. Come, let us to our death. Are we not blest?
Our death will freedom from these creatures give,
Those trouble-quiet sowers of unrest.   75
And this I vow that had I leave to live,
I would forever lead a single life
And never venture on a devilish wife.

Actus 4. Scena 7.   **[Act IV, scene vii]**

Herod and Salome.

Her. Nay, she shall die. Die, quoth you, that she shall.
But for the means. The means! Methinks 'tis hard
To find a means to murther her withal.
Therefore, I am resolv'd [she] shall be spar'd.
Sal. Why? Let her be beheaded.   5
Her.   That were well.
Think you that swords are miracles like you?
Her skin will ev'ry curtal ax[106] edge [repel],
And then your enterprise you well may rue.
What if the fierce Arabian notice take
Of this your wretched weaponless estate?   10
They answer when we bid resistance make,
That Mariam's skin their fanchions[107] did rebate.
Beware of this. You make a goodly hand,
If you of weapons do deprive our land.
Sal. Why drown her then.   15

104. Cham (a variant of *Ham*) was the second son of Noah. When Cham discovered his father naked in his tent, he laughed, and Noah subsequently cursed him, saying that he would be the servant of his brothers. See Genesis 9:25.
105. Clothed; endowed.
106. Short, heavy sword with a curved single-edged blade, once used as weapon by sailors; cutlass.
107. Same as *fauchion;* see note 63.

Her.   Indeed, a sweet device.
Why? Would not ev'ry river turn her course
Rather than do her beauty prejudice,
And be reverted to the proper source?
So not a drop of water should be found
In all Judea's quondam fertile ground.   20
Sal. Then let the fire devour her.
Her.   'Twill not be.
Flame is from her deriv'd into my heart.
Thou nursest flame. Flame will not murther thee,
My fairest Mariam, fullest of desert.
Sal. Then let her live for me.   25
Her.   Nay, she shall die.
But can you live without her?
Sal.   Doubt you that?
Her. I'm sure I cannot, I beseech you try.
I have experience but I know not what.
Sal. How should I try?
Her.   Why, let my love be slain.
But if we cannot live without her sight   30
You'll find the means to make her breathe again,
Or else you will bereave my comfort quite.
Sal. Oh [aye,] I warrant you.
Her.   What, is she gone?
And gone to bid the world be overthrown?
What? Is her heart's composure hardest stone?   35
To what a pass are cruel women grown?
She is return'd already. Have you done?
Is't possible you can command so soon
A creature's heart to quench the flaming sun,
Or from the sky to wipe away the moon?   40
Sal. If Mariam be the sun and moon, it is,
For I already have commanded this.
Her. But have you seen her cheek?
Sal.   A thousand times.
Her. But did you mark it, too?
Sal.   [Aye,] very well.
Her. What is't?   45
Sal.   A crimson bush, that ever limes[108]
The soul whose foresight doth not much excel.
Her. Send word she shall not die. Her cheek a bush—
Nay, then I see indeed you markt it not.
Sal. 'Tis very fair, but yet will never blush,
Though foul dishonors do her forehead blot.   50
Her. Then let her die. 'Tis very true indeed,

---

108. Catches; ensnares, as with bird lime on twigs in a bush.

And for this fault alone shall Mariam bleed.
Sal. What fault my Lord?
Her.   What fault is't? You that ask,
If you be ignorant, I know of none.
To call her back from death shall be your task.   55
I'm glad that she for innocent is known.
For on the brow of Mariam hangs a fleece,[109]
Whose slenderest twine is strong enough to bind
The hearts of kings. The pride and shame of Greece,
Troy-flaming Helen's,[110] not so fairly shin'd.   60
Sal. 'Tis true indeed. She lays them out for nets
To catch the hearts that do not shun a bait.
'Tis time to speak, for Herod sure forgets
That Mariam's very tresses hide deceit.
Her. Oh, do they so? Nay, then you do but well.   65
In sooth I thought it had been hair.
Nets call you them? Lord, how they do excel.
I never saw a net that show'd so fair.
But have you heard her speak?
Sal.   You know I have.
Her. And were you not amaz'd?   70
Sal.   No, not a whit.
Her. Then 'twas not her you heard. Her life I'll save,
For Mariam hath a world-amazing wit.
Sal. She speaks a beauteous language, but within
Her heart is false as powder, and her tongue
Doth but allure the auditors to sin,   75
And is the instrument to do you wrong.
Her. It may be so. Nay, 'tis so. She's unchaste.
Her mouth will ope to ev'ry stranger's ear.
Then let the executioner make haste,
Lest she enchant him if her words he hear.   80
Let him be deaf, lest she do him surprise
That shall to free her spirit be assign'd.
Yet what boots deafness if he have his eyes?
Her murtherer must be both deaf and blind.
For if he see, he needs must see the stars   85
That shine on either side of Mariam's face,
Whose sweet aspect will terminate the wars,
Wherewith he should a soul so precious chase.
Her eyes can speak, and in their speaking move.
Oft did my heart with reverence receive   90
The world's mandates. Pretty tales of love

---

109. Hair; also suggestive of the Golden Fleece, the fleece of pure gold taken from a miraculous winged ram, which Jason and the Argonauts stole from Colchis and returned to Iolcus.
110. Helen of Troy, the wife of Menelaus, was kidnapped by Paris, one of the sons of King Priam of Troy.

They utter which can human bondage weave.
But shall I let this Heaven's model die
Which for a small self-portraiture she drew:
Her eyes like stars, her forehead like the sky.   95
She is like Heaven and must be heavenly true.
Sal. Your thoughts do rave with doting on the Queen.
Her eyes are ebon-hew'd, and you'll confess
A sable star hath been but seldom seen.
Then speak of reason more, of Mariam less.   100
Her. Yourself are held a goodly creature here,
Yet so unlike my Mariam in your shape,
That when to her you have approached near,
Myself hath often ta'en you for an ape.
And yet you prate of beauty. Go your ways.   105
You are to her a sunburnt blackamoor.
Your paintings[111] cannot equal Mariam's praise.
Her nature is so rich, you are so poor.
Let her be stay'd from death, for if she die,
We do we know not what to stop her breath.   110
A world cannot another Mariam buy.
Why stay you ling'ring? Countermand her death.
Sal. Then you'll no more remember what hath past.
Sohemus' love and hers shall be forgot.
'Tis well in truth. That fault may be her last   115
And she may mend though yet she love you not.
Her. Oh God! 'Tis true. Sohemus. Earth and Heav'n,
Why did you both conspire to make me curst?
In coz'ning me with shows and proofs unev'n,
She show'd the best and yet did prove the worst.   120
Her show was such as had our singing king,
The holy David, Mariam's beauty seen,
The Hittites had then felt no deadly sting,
Nor Bethsabe had never been a queen.[112]
Or had his son,[113] the wisest man of men,   125
Whose fond delight did most consist in change,
Beheld her face, he had been stay'd again.
No creature having her can wish to range.
Had Asuerus seen my Mariam's brow,
The humble Jew,[114] she might have walkt alone.   130
Her beauteous virtue should have stay'd below,
Whiles Mariam mounted to the Persian throne.
But what avails it all? For in the weight

111. Salome's use of cosmetics.
112. David had an adulterous affair with Bethsabe, the wife of Uriah the Hittite, whom David
    deliberately had killed in battle.
113. Solomon.
114. Esther, a Jewish woman who became queen of Persia when Asuerus, the king of Persia, married
    her for her beauty. She subsequently saved her people from annihilation. See the Book of Esther.

She is deceitful, light as vanity.
Oh, she was made for nothing but a bait   135
To train some hapless man to misery.
I am the hapless man that have been train'd
To endless bondage. I will see her yet.
Methinks I should discern her if she feign'd.
Can human eyes be daz'd by woman's wit?   140
Once more these eyes of mine with hers shall meet,
Before the headsman do her life bereave.
Shall I forever part from thee, my sweet,
Without the taking of my latest leave?
Sal. You had as good resolve to save her now.   145
I'll stay her death. 'Tis well determined,
For sure she never more will break her vow.
Sohemus and Josephus both are dead.
Her. She shall not live, nor will I see her face.
A long-heal'd wound, a second time doth bleed.   150
With Joseph I remember her disgrace.
A shameful end ensues a shameful deed.
Oh, that I had not call'd to mind anew
The discontent of Mariam's wavering heart.
'Twas you, you foul-mouth'd Ate,[115] none but you,   155
That did the thought hereof to me impart.
Hence from my sight, my black tormentor, hence,
For hadst not thou made Herod unsecure,
I had not doubted Mariam's innocence,
But still had held her in my heart for pure.   160
Sal. I'll leave you to your passion. 'Tis no time
To purge me now though of a guiltless crime.
(Exit.)
Her. Destruction take thee. Thou hast made my heart
As heavy as revenge. I am so dull,
Methinks I am not sensible of smart,   165
Though hideous horrors at my bosom pull.
My head weighs downwards. Therefore will I go
To try if I can sleep away my woe.

Actus 4. Scena. 8.   [Act IV, scene viii]

Mariam. [Doris.]

Mar. Am I the Mariam that presum'd so much,
And deem'd my face must needs preserve my breath?
[Aye, I] it was that thought my beauty such,
[As] it alone could countermand my death.
Now death will teach me. He can pale as well   5

115. Goddess of discord.

A cheek of roses, as a cheek less bright,
And dim an eye whose shine doth most excel,
As soon as one that casts a meaner light.
Had not myself against myself conspir'd,
No plot, no adversary from without   10
Could Herod's love from Mariam have retir'd,
Or from his heart have thrust my semblance out.
The wanton queen that never lov'd for love,
False Cleopatra, wholly set on gain,
With all her [sleights] did prove, yet vainly prove,   15
For her the love of Herod to obtain.
Yet her allurements, all her courtly guile,
Her smiles, her favors, and her smooth deceit,
Could not my face from Herod's mind exile,
But were with him of less than little weight.   20
That face and person that in Asia late
For beauty's goddess, Paphos' Queen,[116] was ta'en,
That face that did captive great Julius' fate,
That very face that was Anthonius' bane,
That face that to be Egypt's pride was born,   25
That face that all the world esteem'd so rare,
Did Herod hate, despise, neglect, and scorn,
When with the same he Mariam's did compare.
This made that I improvidently wrought,
And on the wager even my life did pawn,   30
Because I thought, and yet but truly thought,
That Herod's love could not from me be drawn.
But now though out of time[117] I plainly see
It could be drawn, though never drawn from me.
Had I but with humility been grac'te,   35
As well as fair I might have prov'd me wise,
But I did think because I knew me chaste,
One virtue for a woman might suffice.
That mind for glory of our sex might stand,
Wherein humility and chastity   40
Doth march with equal paces hand in hand.
But one if single seen, who setteth by?
And I had singly one, but 'tis my joy,
That I was ever innocent, though sour,
And therefore can they but my life destroy,   45
My soul is free from adversaries' power.

Enter Doris.

---

116. Venus, so called because it was believed that the goddess rose from the sea off the coast of
Cyprus near Paphos.
117. I.e., too late.

You princes great in power and high in birth,
Be great and high. I envy not your hap.
Your birth must be from dust, your power on earth.
In Heav'n shall Mariam sit in Sara's[118] lap.   50
Dor. [In] Heav'n! Your beauty cannot bring you thither.
Your soul is black and spotted, full of sin.
You in adult'ry liv'd nine year together
And Heav'n will never let adult'ry in.
Mar. What art thou that dost poor Mariam pursue?   55
Some spirit sent to drive me to despair,
Who sees for truth that Mariam is untrue?
If fair she be, she is as chaste as fair.
Dor. I am that Doris that was once belov'd,
Belov'd by Herod, Herod's lawful wife.   60
'Twas you that Doris from his side remov'd,
And robb'd from me the glory of my life.
Mar. Was that adult'ry? Did not Moses say,
That he that being matcht did deadly hate,
Might by permission put his wife away,   65
And take a more belov'd to be his mate?
Dor. What did he hate me for, for simple truth?
For bringing beauteous babes for love to him?
For riches? Noble birth, or tender youth?
Or for no stain did Doris' honor dim?   70
Oh, tell me Mariam, tell me if you know,
Which fault of these made Herod Doris' foe.
These thrice three years have I with hands held up,
And bowed knees fast nailed to the ground,
Besought for thee the dregs of that same cup,   75
That cup of wrath that is for sinners found.
And now thou art to drink it. Doris' curse
Upon thyself did all this while attend,
But now it shall pursue thy children worse.
Mar. Oh Doris, now to thee my knees I bend.   80
That heart that never bow'd to thee doth bow.
Curse not mine infants. Let it thee suffice,
That Heav'n doth punishment to me allow.
Thy curse is cause that guiltless Mariam dies.
Dor. Had I ten thousand tongues, and ev'ry tongue   85
Inflam'd with poison's power and steept in gall,
My curses would not answer for my wrong,
Though I in cursing thee employ'd them all.
Hear thou that didst Mount Gerarim[119] command,
To be a place whereon with cause to curse.   90

118. Sara was Mariam's grandmother.
119. Mount Gerizim, on which a shrine holy to the Samaritans had been located until destroyed by
    John Hyrcanus I in 128 B.C.

Stretch thy revenging arm. Thrust forth thy hand,
And plague the mother much, the children worse.
Throw flaming fire upon the baseborn heads
That were begotten in unlawful beds.
But let them live till they have sense to know   95
What 'tis to be in miserable state.
Then be their nearest friends their overthrow.
Attended be they by suspicious hate.[120]
And Mariam, I do hope this boy of mine
Shall one day come to be the death of thine.
(Exit.)   100
Mar. Oh! Heaven forbid. I hope the world shall see
This curse of thine shall be return'd on thee.
Now earth farewell. Though I be yet but young,
Yet I methinks have known thee too too long. *(Exit.)*

Chorus. The fairest action of our human life,
Is [scorning] to revenge an injury.
For who forgives without a further strife,
His adversary's heart to him doth tie.
    And 'tis a firmer conquest truly said,   5
    To win the heart than overthrow the head.

If we a worthy enemy do find,
To yield to worth, it must be nobly done.
But if of baser metal be his mind,
In base revenge there is no honor won.   10
    Who would a worthy courage overthrow,
    And who would wrastle with a worthless foe?

We say our hearts are great and cannot yield.
Because they cannot yield it proves them poor.
Great hearts are task't beyond their power, but seld[121]   15
The weakest lion will the loudest roar.
    Truth's school for certain doth this same allow.
    High-heartedness doth sometimes teach to bow.

A noble heart doth teach a virtuous scorn:
To scorn to owe a duty overlong,   20
To scorn to be for benefits forborne,[122]
To scorn to lie, to scorn to do a wrong,
    To scorn to bear an injury in mind,
    To scorn a freeborn heart slave-like to bind.

But if for wrongs we needs revenge must have,   25
Then be our vengeance of the noblest kind.
Do we his body from our fury save,

---

120. Mariam's two sons, Alexander and Aristobolus, were executed by Herod in 7 B.C. for treason.
121. Obsolete form of "seldom."
122. Tolerated; endured.

And let our hate prevail against our mind?
   What can 'gainst him a greater vengence be,
   Than make his foe more worthy far than he?   30

Had Mariam scorn'd to leave a due unpaid,
She would to Herod then have paid her love,
And not have been by sullen passion sway'd
To fix her thoughts all injury above
   [In] virtuous pride. Had Mariam thus been prov'd,   35
   Long famous life to her had been allow'd.

Actus Quintus. Scena Prima.   [Act V, scene i]

Nuntio. [Herod.]

Nun. When, sweetest friend, did I so far offend
Your heavenly self, that you my fault to quit
Have made me now relator of her end,
The end of beauty, chastity and wit?
Was none so hapless in the fatal place,   5
But I, most wretched, for the Queen t'choose?
'Tis certain I have some ill-boding face
That made me cull'd to tell this luckless news.
And yet no news to Herod. Were it new,
To him unhappy ['t had] not been at all.   10
Yet do I long to come within his view,
That he may know his wife did guiltless fall.
And here he comes. Your Mariam greets you well.

Enter Herod.

Her. What? Lives my Mariam? Joy, exceeding joy.
She shall not die.   15
Nun.   Heav'n doth your will repel.
Her. Oh, do not with thy words my life destroy.
I prithee tell no dying-tale. Thine eye
Without thy tongue doth tell but too too much,
Yet let thy tongue's addition make me die.
Death welcome comes to him whose grief is such.   20
Nun. I went amongst the curious gazing troop,
To see the last of her that was the best,
To see if death had heart to make her stoop,
To see the sun-admiring Phoenix'[123] nest.
When there I came, upon the way I saw   25
The stately Mariam not debas'd by fear.

---

123. The bird in Egyptian mythology that consumed itself by fire after five hundred years and rose renewed from its ashes, a symbol of Christ. Hence, a person or thing of unsurpassed beauty or excellence; a paragon.

Her look did seem to keep the world in awe,
Yet mildly did her face this fortune bear.
Her. Thou dost usurp my right. My tongue was fram'd
To be the instrument of Mariam's praise.   30
Yet speak. She cannot be too often-fam'd.
All tongues suffice not her sweet name to raise.
Nun. But as she came she Alexandra met,
Who did her death (sweet Queen) no whit bewail,
But as if nature she did quite forget,   35
She did upon her daughter loudly rail.
Her. Why stopt you not her mouth? Where had she words
To dark that, that Heaven made so bright?
Our sacred tongue no epithet affords
To call her other than the world's delight.   40
Nun. She told her that her death was too too good,
And that already she had liv'd too long.
She said, she sham'd to have a part in blood
Of her that did the princely Herod wrong.
Her. Base pickthank[124] devil. Shame, 'twas all her glory,   45
That she to noble Mariam was the mother.
But never shall it live in any story.
Her name, except to infamy I'll smother.
What answer did her princely daughter make?
Nun. She made no answer but she lookt the while,   50
As if thereof she scarce did notice take,
Yet smil'd a dutiful, though scornful smile.
Her. Sweet creature. I that look to mind do call.
Full oft hath Herod been amaz'd withal.
Go on.   55
Nun.   She came unmov'd with pleasant grace,
As if to triumph her arrival were,
In stately habit, and with [cheerful] face.
Yet ev'ry eye was moist, but Mariam's there.
When justly opposite to me she came,
She pickt me out from all the crew.   60
She beck'ned to me, call'd me by my name,
For she my name, my birth, and fortune knew.
Her. What, did she name thee? Happy, happy man.
Wilt thou not ever love that name the better?
But what sweet tune did this fair dying swan   65
Afford thine ear. Tell all. Omit no letter.
Nun. "Tell thou my Lord," said she.
Her.   Me, meant she me?
Is't true? The more my shame. I was her Lord.
Were I not made her Lord, I still should be.

---

124. Flatterer; sycophant.

But now her name must be by me ador'd. 70
Oh say, what said she more? Each word she said
Shall be the food whereon my heart is fed.
Nun. "Tell thou my Lord thou saw'st me [lose] my breath."
Her. Oh, that I could that sentence now control.
Nun. "If guiltily, eternal be my death. . ." 75
Her. I hold her chaste ev'n in my inmost soul.
Nun. "By three days hence if wishes could revive,
I know himself would make me oft alive."
Her. Three days! Three hours, three minutes, not so much,
A minute in a thousand parts divided! 80
My penitency for her death is such,
As in the first I wisht she had not died.
But forward in thy tale.
Nun.   Why, on she went,
And after she some silent prayer had said,
She did as if to die she were content, 85
And thus to heav'n her heav'nly soul is fled.
Her. But art thou sure there doth no life remain?
Is't possible my Mariam should be dead?
Is there no trick to make her breathe again?
Nun. Her body is divided from her head. 90
Her. Why yet methinks there might be found by art,
Strange ways of cure. 'Tis sure rare things are done
By an inventive head and willing heart.
Nun. Let not, my Lord, your fancies idly run.
It is as possible it should be seen 95
That we should make the holy Abraham live,
Though he entomb'd two thousand years had been,
As breath again to slaught'red Mariam give.
But now for more assaults prepare your ear . . .
Her. There cannot be a further cause of moan. 100
This accident shall shelter me from fears.
What can I fear? Already Mariam's gone.
Yet tell ev'n what you will.
Nun.   As I came by,
From Mariam's death, I saw upon a tree
A man that to his neck a cord did tie, 105
Which cord he had design'd his end to be.
When me he once discern'd, he downwards bow'd,
And thus with fearful voice [he] cri'd aloud:
"Go tell the King, he trusted ere he tri'd.
I am the cause that Mariam causeless di'd." 110
Her. Damnation take him, for it was the slave
That said she meant with poison's deadly force
To end my life that she the crown might have,
Which tale did Mariam from herself divorce.

Oh pardon me, thou pure unspotted ghost.   115
My punishment must needs sufficient be,
In missing that content I valued most,
Which was thy admirable face to see.
I had but one inestimable jewel,[125]
Yet one I had no monarch had the like,   120
And therefore may I curse myself as cruel.
'Twas broken by a blow myself did strike.
I gaz'd thereon and never thought me blest,
But when on it my dazzled eye might rest.
A precious mirror made by wonderous art,   125
I priz'd it ten times dearer than my crown,
And laid it up fast-folded in my heart.
Yet I in sudden choler cast it down,
And pasht it all to pieces. 'Twas no foe,
That robb'd me of it. No Arabian host,   130
Nor no Armenian guide hath us'd me so,
But Herod's wretched self hath Herod crost.
She was my graceful moiety,[126] me accurst,
To slay my better half and save my worst.
But sure she is not dead; you did but jest,   135
To put me in perplexity a while.
'Twere well indeed if I could so be drest.
I see she is alive. Methinks you smile.
Nun. If sainted Abel yet deceased be,
'Tis certain Mariam is as dead as he.   140
Her. Why, then go call her to me. Bid her now
Put on fair habit, stately ornament,
And let no frown o'ershade her smoothest brow.
In her doth Herod place his whole content.
Nun. She'll come in stately weeds to please your sense,   145
If now she come attir'd in robe of Heaven.
Remember you yourself did send her hence,
And now to you she can no more be given.
Her. She's dead. Hell take her murderers, she was fair.
Oh, what a hand she had! It was so white,   150
It did the whiteness of the snow impair.
I never more shall see so sweet a sight.
Nun. 'Tis true, her hand was rare.
Her.   Her hand? Her hands.
She had not singly one of beauty rare,
But such a pair as here where Herod stands,   155
He dares the world to make to both compare.
Accursed Salome, hadst thou been still,
My Mariam had been breathing by my side.

125. Cf. *Othello*, V.ii.347–48: "Like the base Judean, threw a pearl away / Richer than all his tribe."
126. A half; one of two equal parts.

Oh, never had I, had I had my will,
Sent forth command that Mariam should have di'd.   160
But Salome thou didst with envy vex,
To see thyself out-matched in thy sex.
Upon your sex's forehead Mariam sat,
To grace you all like an imperial crown.
But you, fond fool, have rudely pusht thereat,   165
And proudly pull'd your proper glory down.
One smile of hers—nay, not so much, a look—
Was worth a hundred thousand such as you.
Judea, how canst thou the wretches brook,
That robb'd from thee the fairest of the crew?   170
You dwellers in the now-deprived land,
Wherein the matchless Mariam was bred,
Why grasp not each of you a sword in hand,
To aim at me, your cruel sovereign's head?
Oh, when you think of Herod as your King   175
And owner of the pride of Palestine,
This act to your remembrance likewise bring.
'Tis I have overthrown your royal line.
Within her purer veins the blood did run,
That from her Grandam Sara she deriv'd,   180
Whose beldame age the love of kings hath won.
Oh, that her issue had as long been liv'd.
But can her eye be made by death obscure?
I cannot think but it must sparkle still.
Foul sacrilege to rob those lights so pure,   185
From out a temple made by heav'nly skill.
I am the villain that have done the deed,
The cruel deed, though by another's hand.
My word though not my sword made Mariam bleed.
Hircanus' grandchild [died] at my command,   190
That Mariam that I once did love so dear,
The partner of my now-detested bed.
Why shine you, Sun, with an aspect so clear?
I tell you once again my Mariam's dead.
You could but shine, if some Egyptian blowse,[127]   195
Or Ethiopian dowdy lose her life.
This was—then wherefore bend you not your brows—
The King of Jewry's fair and spotless wife.
Deny thy beams, and moon refuse thy light.
Let all the stars be dark. Let Jewry's eye   200
No more distinguish which is day and night,
Since her best birth did in her bosom die.
Those fond idolators, the men of Greece,

---

127. Beggar wench; wench; slattern.

Maintain these orbs are safely governed,
That each within themselves have gods apiece,   205
By whom their steadfast course is justly led.
But were it so, as so it cannot be,
They all would put their mourning garments on.
Not one of them would yield a light to me,
To me that is the cause that Mariam's gone.   210
For though they [feign][128] their Saturn melancholy,
Of sour behaviors, and of angry mood,
They [feign] him likewise to be just and holy,
And justice needs must seek revenge for blood.
Their Jove, if Jove he were, would sure desire,   215
To punish him that slew so fair a lass,
For Leda's[129] beauty set his heart on fire,
Yet she not half so fair as Mariam was.
And Mars would deem his Venus had been slain,
Sol to recover her would never stick,   220
For if he want the power her life to gain,
Then physic's god is but an empiric.[130]
The Queen of love would storm for beauty's sake,
And Hermes[131] too since he bestow'd her wit.
The night's pale light for angry grief would shake,   225
To see chaste Mariam die in age unfit.
But oh, I am deceiv'd. She past them all
In every gift, in every property.
Her excellencies wrought her timeless fall,
And they rejoic'd, not griev'd to see her die.   230
The Paphian goddess[132] did repent her waste,
When she to one such beauty did allow.
Mercurius thought her wit his wit surpast,
And Cynthia[133] envi'd Mariam's brighter brow.
But these are fictions. They are void of sense.   235
The Greeks but dream and dreaming falsehoods tell.
They neither can offend nor give defense,
And not by them it was my Mariam fell.
If she had been like an Egyptian black,
And not so fair, she had been longer liv'd.   240
Her overflow of beauty turned back,
And drown'd the spring from whence it was deriv'd.

128. Imagine; relate or represent in fiction; fable. Two spellings of this word occur in the extant editions: "faine" and "fame," in lines 212 and 214. While validity can be ascribed to both "feign" and "fame," "feign" appears to be the more appropriate reading here, for the following lines allude to various classical myths that Cary then terms "fictions" in line 235.
129. Leda was the wife of King Tyndareus of Sparta; to her Zeus appeared in the form of a swan, and she bore Zeus two sons, Castor and Pollux.
130. Charlatan; quack.
131. The messenger god; also the god of cunning. Herod asserts that Mariam's intellect and wit are the gifts of Hermes. Hermes' Roman name is Mercury. See line 233.
132. Venus. See note 116.
133. Goddess of chastity and the moon.

Her heav'nly beauty 'twas that made me think
That it with chastity could never dwell.
But now I see that Heav'n in her did link,   245
A spirit and a person to excel.
I'll muffle up myself in endless night,
And never let mine eyes behold the light.
Retire thyself, vile monster, worse than he
That stain'd the virgin earth with brother's blood.   250
Still in some vault or den enclosed be
Where with thy tears thou may'st beget a flood,
Which flood in time may drown thee. Happy day
When thou at once shalt die and find a grave.
A stone upon the vault, someone shall lay,   255
Which monument shall an inscription have.
And these shall be the words it shall contain,
"Here Herod lies, that hath his Mariam slain."

Chorus. Who ever hath beheld with steadfast eye,
The strange events of this one only day?
How many were deceiv'd? How many die,
That once today did grounds of safety lay?
   It will from them all certainty bereave,   5
   Since twice six hours so many can deceive.

This morning Herod held for surely dead,
And all the Jews on Mariam did attend,
And Constabarus rise from Salom's bed,
And neither dream'd of a divorce or end.   10
   Pheroras joy'd that he might have his wife,
   And Babus' sons for safety of their life.

Tonight our Herod doth alive remain,
The guiltless Mariam is depriv'd of breath,
Stout Constabarus both divorst and slain,
The valiant sons of Baba have their death.   15
   Pheroras sure his love to be bereft,
   If Salome her suit unmade had left.

Herod this morning did expect with joy,
To see his Mariam's much beloved face.   20
And yet ere night he did her life destroy,
And surely thought she did her name disgrace.
   Yet now again so short do humors last,
   He both repents her death and knows her chaste.

Had he with wisdom now her death delay'd,   25
He at his pleasure might command her death.
But now he hath his power so much betray'd,
As all his woes cannot restore her breath.
   Now doth he strangely, lunatic'ly rave,

Because his Mariam's life he cannot save.   30

This day's events were certainly ordain'd,
To be the warning to posterity.
So many changes are therein contain'd,
So admirably strange variety,
      This day alone, our sagest Hebrews shall   35
      In after times the school of wisdom call.

Finis.

TEXTUAL NOTES

Copy-text: The Huntington Library copy of *The Tragedie of Mariam, The Faire Queene of Jewry* (1613).

In this modernized text, verb endings have been normalized except in the following instances. Apostrophes have been retained when they indicate the loss of a syllable (for example, "-'n" for "-en," "-'d" for "-ed," and "list'ning" for "listening"). For verbs in the past tense ending in "-d" rather than "-ed," an apostrophe is inserted (for example, "liv'd" for "livd"). For verbs ending in "-de," the ending has been changed to "-'d" since the loss of the final "-ed" appears to be pointed. For verbs ending with the sound "-st," "-pt," or "-kt," the original spelling has been retained (for example, "plast," "wipt," and "rakte").

Misplaced or absent apostrophes that do not affect sense or scansion have been silently corrected (for example, "'tis" for "t'is," "ne'er" for "nere," "o'er" for "oe'r" or "ore," and "liv'd" for "li'vd"). Apostrophes have also been inserted where the absence of a vowel indicates the loss of a syllable (for example, "wand'ring" for "wandring"). Capitalization has been normalized.

Emendations

Speakers.6	Doris] Salome
Speakers.10	Pheroras] Pharoras
Speakers.14	Ananell] Annanell
Speakers.17	Butler] Bu.
Argument	granddaughter] daughter
Argument	second] first
Argument	first] second
1.1.47	mind] maide
1.1.67	Aye] I
1.2.44	Herod] Mariam
1.2.53 s.p.	Mar.] Nun.
1.2.55	Of] If
1.2.88	woo] woe
1.2.93	sleight] slight
1.2.104	seek] leeke
1.2.107	bar] bare

1.3.47	suspicion's] suspitious
1.4.16	all eyes] allyes
1.4.38	from] for
1.5.15	do is] do'es
1.5.37	whom] home
1.6.90	vow] vowd
1.chorus.8	leap] lep
2.1.12	monarchal] monachall
2.1.20	solemnly] solembly
2.1.40	Graphina's] Graphina:
2.	overpast] operpast
2.2.66	fear] leare
2.2.75	The text contains no punctuation after gratitude, eliding these two speeches.
2.2.102	phisnomy] phismony
2.2.114	let] set
2.3.1	You] Your
2.3.2	stoop] scope
2.3.23	lack] lake
2.3.25	oaths] oath
2.4.66	They fight.] Not printed in text.
2.4.92 s.d.	They fight.] I, I, They fight.
3.1.3	can make] cane mak
3.2.41	we] he
3.2.42	our] his
3.2.64	sleight] slite
3.3.6 s.p.	Mar] no speech prefix in text.
3.3.75	Alexandra's] Alexander's
3.3.83	quit] quite
3.Chorus.22	thought] though
4.2.30	your] you
4.3.63	slightest] sleightest
4.4.s.d.	*Herod. Mariam. Butler. Soldier.*] Herod.
4.4.29	I] not printed in the text
4.4.71	lock] looke
4.4.87	love] bove
4.5.2	causeless] caules
4.5.18	found'st] founds
4.6.20	her] your
4.6.23	Whereby] Were by
4.6.55	Your] You
4.6.58	she] he
4.7.4	she] the
4.7.7	repel] refell
4.7.33	aye] I:
4.7.44	Aye,] I
4.8.3	Aye, I] I, I
4.8.4	As] At
4.8.15	sleights] slights

4.8.51	In] I
4.Chorus.2	scorning] scorniug
4.Chorus.35	In] Is
5.1.s.d.	*Herod.*] not printed in text.
5.1.10	't had] t'had
5.1.55	This entire line is given to Nuntio.
5.1.57	cheerful] cheefull
5.1.73	lose] loose
5.1.108	he] she
5.1.190	died] did
5.1.211, 213	feign] fame

BIBLIOGRAPHY

Editions

Cerasano. S. P., and Marion Wynne-Davies, eds. *Renaissance Drama by Women: Texts and Documents.* London: Routledge, 1996.

Dunstan, Arthur C., and W. W. Greg, eds. *The Tragedy of Mariam.* Oxford: Oxford Univ. Press for the Malone Society, 1914. Rpt. 1992, with an introd. by Marta Straznicky and Richard Rowland.

Purkiss, Diane, intro. and ed. *Renaissance Women: The Plays of Elizabeth Cary and the Poems of Aemilia Lanyer.* London: Pickering and Chatto, 1994.

Weller, Barry, and Margaret W. Ferguson, eds. *The Tragedy of Mariam, The Fair Queen of Jewry.* Berkeley and Los Angeles: Univ. of California Press, 1993.

Wright, Stephanie, ed. *Elizabeth Cary: The Tragedy of Mariam.* Keele: Keele Univ. Press, 1996.

Secondary Works

Beilin, Elaine V. "Elizabeth Cary and *The Tragedie of Mariam.*" *Papers on Language and Literature* 16 (1980): 45–64.

———. *Redeeming Eve: Women Writers of the English Renaissance.* Princeton: Princeton Univ. Press, 1987. 157–76.

Belsey, Catherine. *The Subject of Tragedy: Identity and Difference in Renaissance Drama.* London: Methuen, 1985.

Berry, Boyd M. "Feminine Construction of Patriarchy; Or What's Comic in *The Tragedy of Mariam.*" *Medieval and Renaissance Drama in England* 7 (1995): 257–74.

Brackett, Virginia. "Elizabeth Cary, Drayton, and Edward II." *Notes and Queries* 41 (Dec. 1994): 517–19.

Brashear, Lucy. "A Case for the Influence of Lady Cary's *Tragedy of Mariam* on Shakespeare's *Othello.*" *Shakespeare Newsletter* 26 (1976): 31.

Callaghan, Dympna. "Re-reading Elizabeth Cary's *The Tragedie of Mariam, Faire Queene of Jewry.*" In *Woman, "Race," and Writing in the Early Modern Period.* Ed. Margo Hendricks and Patricia Parker. London: Routledge, 1994. 163–77.

Cotton, Nancy. *Women Playwrights in England, c. 1363–1750.* Lewisburg, Pa.: Bucknell Univ. Press, 1980, 31–37.

Dunstan, Arthur Cyril. *Examination of Two English Dramas: "The True Tragedy of Mariam" by Elizabeth Carew; and "The True Tragedy of Herod and Antipater: With the Death of Faire Mariam," by Gervase Markham, and William Sampson.* Konigsberg: Hartungsche Buchdruckerei, 1908.

Ferguson, Margaret W. "A Room Not Their Own: Renaissance Women as Readers and Writers." In *The Comparative Perspective on Literature: Approaches to Theory and Practice.* Eds. Clayton Koelb and Susan Noakes. Ithaca: Cornell Univ. Press, 1988. 93–116.

———. "Running On with Almost Public Voice: The Case of 'E.C.'" In *Tradition and the Talents of Women.* Ed. Florence Howe. Urbana: Univ. of Illinois Press, 1991. 37–67.

———. "The Spectre of Resistance: *The Tragedy of Mariam* (1613)." In *Staging the Renaissance: Reinterpretations of Elizabethan and Jacobean Drama.* Ed. David Scott Kastan and Peter Stallybrass. New York: Routledge, 1991. 235–50.

Fischer, Sandra K. "Elizabeth Cary and Tyranny, Domestic and Religious." In *Silent but for the Word: Tudor Women as Patrons, Translators, and Writers of Religious Works.* Ed. Margaret P. Hannay. Kent, Ohio: Kent State Univ. Press, 1985. 225–37.

Fullerton, Lady Georgiana. *The Life of Elisabeth Lady Falkland, 1585–1639.* London: Burns and Oates, 1883.

Goreau, Angeline. "Two English Women in the Seventeenth Century: Notes for an Anatomy of Feminine Desire." In *Western Sexuality: Practice and Precept in Past and Present Times.* Ed. Philippe Ariès and Andre Béjin. Trans. Anthony Forster. Oxford: Basil Blackwell, 1985. 103–13.

Gutierrez, Nancy A. "Valuing *Mariam*: Genre Study and Feminist Analysis." *Tulsa Studies in Women's Literature* 10 (1991): 233–51.

Holdsworth, R. V. "Middleton and *The Tragedy of Mariam*." *Notes and Queries* 33.3 (1986): 379–80.

Kennedy, Gwynne. "Feminine Subjectivity in the Renaissance: The Writings of Elizabeth Cary, Lady Falkland, and Lady Mary Wroth." Ph.D. diss., Univ. of Pennsylvania, 1989. DAI 50:9 (1990).

———. "Lessons of the 'Schools of Wisedome.'" In *Sexuality and Politics in Renaissance Drama.* Ed. Carole Levin and Karen Robertson. Lewiston, N.Y.: Mellen, 1991. 113–36.

Krontiris, Tina. *Oppositional Voices: Women as Writers and Translators of Literature in the English Renaissance.* New York: Routledge, 1992. 78–101.

———. "Reading with the Author's Sex: A Comparison of Two Seventeenth-Century Texts." *Gamma* 1 (1993): 123–36.

Lewalski, Barbara K. *Writing Women in Jacobean England.* Cambridge: Harvard Univ. Press, 1993. 179–211.

Lunn, David. *Elizabeth Cary, Lady Falkland (1586/7–1639).* Royal Stuart Papers 11. Ilford, Essex: Royal Stuart Society, 1977.

Murdock, Kenneth B. "Passion and Infirmities." In *The Sun at Noon: Three Biographical Sketches: Elizabeth Cary, Viscountess Falkland, 1585–1639;*

*Lucius Cary, Viscount Falkland, 1610–1643; John Wilmot, Earl of Roches-
ter, 1647–1680.* New York: Macmillan, 1939.

Pearse, Nancy Cotton. "Elizabeth Cary, Renaissance Playwright." *Texas Studies in Literature and Language* 18, no. 4 (winter 1977): 601–8.

Quilligan, Maureen. "Staging Gender: William Shakespeare and Elizabeth
Cary." In *Sexuality and Gender in Early Modern Europe: Institutions,
Texts, Images.* Ed. James Grantham Turner. Cambridge: Cambridge Univ.
Press, 1993. 208–32.

Raber, Karen L. "Gender and the Political Subject in *The Tragedy of Mariam.*"
Studies in English Literature 35 (1995): 321–43.

Schleiner, Louise. "Lady Falkland's Reentry into Writing: Anglo-Catholic Con-
sensual Discourse and Her *Edward II* as Historical Fiction." In *The Witness
of Times: Manifestations of Ideology in Seventeenth-Century England.* Ed.
Katherine Z. Keller and Gerald J. Schiffhorst. Pittsburgh: Duquesne Univ.
Press, 1993. 201–17.

———. "Popery and Politics: Lady Falkland's Return to Writing." In *Tudor
and Stuart Women Writers.* Bloomington: Indiana Univ. Press, 1994.

Shannon, Laurie J. "*The Tragedie of Mariam*: Cary's Critique of the Terms of
Founding Social Discourses." *English Literary Renaissance* 24 (1994):
135–53.

Simpson, Richard, ed. *The Lady Falkland: Her Life. From a MS. in the Imperial Archives at Lille.* London: Catholic Publishing and Bookselling Company, 1861.

Straznicky, Marta. " 'Profane Stoical Paradoxes': *The Tragedie of Mariam* and
Sidnean Closet Drama." *English Literary Renaissance* 24 (1994): 104–34.

Swan, Jesse. "*The Life, Reign, and Death of Edward II*: A Critical Edition."
Ph.D. diss., Arizona State Univ., 1993. DAI 54:7 (1994).

Travitsky, Betty S. "The *Feme Covert* in Elizabeth Cary's *Mariam.*" In *Ambiguous Realities: Women in the Middle Ages and Renaissance.* Ed. Carole
Levin and Jeanie Watson. Detroit: Wayne State Univ. Press, 1987. 184–96.

———. "Husband-Murder and Petty Treason in English Renaissance Tragedy." *Renaissance Drama* n.s. 21 (1990): 171–98.

Valency, Maurice Jacques. *The Tragedies of Herod and Mariamne.* Columbia
Univ. Studies in English and Comparative Literature 145. New York: Columbia Univ. Press, 1940.

Warnicke, Retha. *Women of the English Renaissance and Reformation.* Westport, Conn.: Greenwood Press, 1983.

Witherspoon, Alexander Maclaren. *The Influence of Robert Garnier on Elizabethan Drama* (1924). New York: Phaeton Press, 1968.

LADY MARY WROTH
(1587?–1653?)

INTRODUCTION

Although earlier women writers of the sixteenth century had mainly explored the genres of translation, dedication, and epitaph, Lady Mary Wroth openly and boldly transgressed the traditional boundaries by writing secular love poetry and romances. Her verse was celebrated by the leading poets of the age, including Ben Jonson, George Chapman, Joshua Sylvester, and others. Yet the publication in 1621 of her major work of fiction, *The Countess of Montgomery's Urania*, the first known original work of fiction by an Englishwoman, created a controversy in the Jacobean court that was to have enormous impact on Wroth's literary career.

The eldest daughter of Sir Robert Sidney and Lady Barbara Gamage, she was probably born on October 18, 1587, a date derived from the Sidney correspondence. She belonged to a prominent literary family, known for its patronage of the arts. One of the most powerful forces in shaping Wroth's career was her aunt and godmother, Mary Sidney, who was married to Henry Herbert, second earl of Pembroke. Their country estate at Wilton served as a gathering place for a diverse number of poets, theologians, and scientists. The countess of Pembroke wrote poetry and translations from French and Italian, but even more importantly, she bravely chose to publish her works under her own name. Her decision inspired a number of early seventeenth-century women writers, including Aemilia Lanyer (who praised the Countess for the "many books she writes" in a dedicatory epistle in *Salve Deus Rex Judaeorum*) and Elizabeth Cary. Wroth drew even greater attention to her aunt as a model by including her name on the title-page to the *Urania* (see p. 110).

Her uncle, Sir Philip Sidney, was a leading Elizabethan poet, statesman, and soldier, whose tragic death in the Netherlands elevated him to the status of national hero. A number of her uncle's literary works influenced Wroth, including his sonnet sequence, *Astrophil and Stella*; a prose romance, intermingled with poetry, *The Countess of Pembroke's Arcadia* (existing in two distinct versions); and a pastoral entertainment, *The Lady of May*.

Wroth's father, Sir Robert Sidney, was also a poet, although his verse survived in a single manuscript and did not appear in print until 1984. Following the death of Philip, Robert was appointed to fill his brother's post of governor of Flushing in the Netherlands, where he served throughout much of Wroth's childhood. He kept in close touch with his family through visits and letters; his friend and advisor Rowland Whyte wrote Sidney frequent reports concerning his eldest child, whom he affectionately nicknamed "little Mall."

Wroth's education was largely informal, obtained from household tutors under the guidance of her mother. Her family negotiated her marriage in 1604 to Sir Robert Wroth, son of a wealthy landowner, but the union was a mismatch from the start, for Robert Wroth was primarily concerned with hunting

The
Countesse
of Mountgomeries
URANIA.
Written by the right honorable the Lady
MARY WROATH.
Daughter to the right Noble Robert
Earle of Leicester.
And Neece to the ever famous, and re-
nowned Sr Phillips Sidney knight. And to
ye most exellt Lady Mary Countesse of
Pembroke late decea sed.

LONDON
Printed for IOH MARRIOTT
and IOHN GRISMAND. And
are to bee sould at theire shop-
pes in St Dunstons Church-
yard in Fleetstreet and in
Poules Ally at ye signe of
the Gunn.

1621

Simo Passaus sculp

Title Page of Lady Mary Wroth's *The Countess of Montgomery's Urania* (1621). Engraved by Simon van de Passe. (Reproduced by permission of the Huntington Library, San Marino, California.)

and had few literary interests; throughout his entire career, only one book was dedicated to him—a treatise on mad dogs. For her part, Mary Wroth maintained a close attachment to her first cousin, William Herbert, third earl of Pembroke, whom she had known from childhood. The two shared an avid interest in poetry and music, and both actively participated in court entertainments; Wroth danced with Queen Anne and her ladies in the first masque written by Ben Jonson in collaboration with Inigo Jones, *The Masque of Blackness* (1605), while Pembroke also performed in many jousts, tournaments, and masques.

Following the death of her husband in 1612, Wroth was left with a son James, only a month old, and enormous debts of twenty-three thousand pounds. The death of James two years later increased her financial troubles because the estate fell into the hands of Robert Wroth's uncle. Despite the severity of her situation, Mary Wroth insisted on handling the problems herself, but she spent much of the rest of her life struggling to settle her debts. She was now financially unable to participate in the lavish court spectacles, but her affair with Pembroke may also have contributed to her decline in royal favor. In the years after her husband's death, Wroth bore two illegitimate children by Pembroke: a son, William, and a daughter, Catherine. Although Pembroke eventually abandoned Wroth for other lovers, his family continued to take an interest in the welfare of her son William, even after Pembroke's death in 1630.

Wroth's sonnet sequence *Pamphilia to Amphilanthus* describes the troubled relationship between Pamphilia, whose name means "all loving," and the unfaithful Amphilanthus ("lover of two"). Wroth radically revises the Petrarchan model of the male lover in pursuit of a cold, unpitying lady by completely omitting the rhetoric of wooing and courtship. She addresses her sonnets to Cupid, night, grief, fortune, or time, rather than directly to Amphilanthus, whose name appears only in the title of the sequence. The poems reveal Pamphilia's conflicting emotions as she attempts to resolve the struggle between passionate surrender and self-affirmation. Her "Crown of Sonnets" represents a technical tour de force, as well as a central turning point in her internal debate, wherein she attempts to redirect her thoughts to spiritual love. The effort is not entirely successful, for Pamphilia ends trapped in fearful perplexity: "In this strange labyrinth how shall I turn?" (the line that opens and closes the "Crown"). Although Wroth does not explicitly identify Amphilanthus as Pembroke within the sequence, she perhaps hints at the possibility in a pun found in the final sonnet: "The endless gain which never *will* remove" (italics added).

The intense, ambivalent passion of Pamphilia for Amphilanthus formed the nucleus of Wroth's prose romance, *The Countess of Montgomery's Urania*. Within the fiction Pamphilia is the eldest daughter of the king of Morea, and her unmarried uncle designates her as the heir to his kingdom of Pamphilia (an actual country located on the south coast of Asia Minor). Despite her vow to serve her country as a virgin queen (in imitation of Elizabeth I), Pamphilia falls in love with Amphilanthus, who among his many virtues has one major flaw, inconstancy.

A brief summary does not do justice to the intricate plot of the *Urania* (over six hundred thousand words in length), with many first-person narratives and inset tales. Wroth emphasizes the social conditions that oppressed early seventeenth-century women, especially their lack of freedom to choose a marital partner. A number of the tales appear to be autobiographical, but Wroth mingles fact and fantasy in the portraits of herself by carefully modifying and refashioning the major events of her life. Pamphilia herself tells the tale of Lindamira (an anagram for Lady Mary), in which she traces her own career as a courtier and poet, along with a strong protest against her loss of royal favor. Lindamira concludes her tale with a group of seven sonnets, as a mirror of the larger *Urania*, which was first printed in 1621, with the sequence *Pamphilia to Amphilanthus* appended to part I of the romance.

The publication of the *Urania* unleashed a storm of criticism from powerful noblemen at court, who believed that Wroth had thinly veiled their private affairs under the guise of fiction. Sir Edward Denny, baron of Waltham, launched a vicious attack against the author and circulated a verse diatribe, from which this brief excerpt is taken.

To Pamphilia from the father-in-law of Seralius

Hermaphrodite in show, in deed a monster
   (As by thy words and works all men may conster),
Thy wrathful spite conceived an Idle book,
   Brought forth a fool which like the dam doth look.

Yet Wroth was not intimidated by Denny's power, influence, or insults. She responded by turning the verses back against him, word for word.

Railing Rhymes Returned upon the Author by Mistress Mary Wroth

Hermaphrodite in sense in Art a monster
   (As by your railing rhymes the world may conster),
Your spiteful words against a harmless book
   Shows that an ass much like the sire doth look.

Regardless of her show of courage, Wroth was obliged to send letters to her friends and to the duke of Buckingham, to intercede with King James I on her behalf. She assured Buckingham that she never meant for her *Urania* to offend anyone and that the books "were sold against my mind I never purposing to have had them published." Yet, significantly, the hostile reception did not stop her from composing a second part of the *Urania* (240,000 words in length), which survives today in a unique autograph manuscript at the Newberry Library, Chicago.

While at work on the second part of *Urania* in the 1620s, Wroth also completed a five-act play, *Love's Victory,* a pastoral tragicomedy probably designed for private presentation at a country house. The drama depicts four contrasting couples who illustrate a variety of human responses to love.

Little evidence survives of Wroth's later life, except that she lived in Woodford, where her name appears in connection with tax rolls and the sale of lands.

The only record of her death is a chancery deposition, which states that the event occurred in 1651, or more probably in 1653. Clearly Wroth's creative accomplishments—her sonnet sequence, her prose fiction, and pastoral drama—opened the possibilities for women writers of succeeding generations.

SONNETS FROM *PAMPHILIA TO AMPHILANTHUS* (1621)

P1

When night's black mantle could most darkness prove,
    And sleep, death's Image, did my senses hire
    From knowledge of myself, then thoughts did move
    Swifter than those most swiftness need require.

In sleep, a Chariot drawn by wing'd desire   5
    I saw:[1] where sate bright Venus Queen of love,
    And at her feet her son, still adding fire
    To burning hearts which she did hold above,[2]

But one heart flaming more than all the rest
    The goddess held, and put it to my breast,   10
    "Dear son, now shut," said she, "thus must we win."

He her obey'd, and martyr'd my poor heart,
    I, waking, hop'd as dreams it would depart
    Yet since, O me, a lover I have been.

P8

Love leave to urge, thou know'st thou hast the hand;
    Tis cowardice, to strive where none resist:
    Pray thee leave off, I yield unto thy band;
    Do not thus, still, in thine own power persist.

Behold I yield: let forces be dismist;   5
    I am thy subject, conquer'd, bound to stand,
    Never thy foe, but did thy claim assist,
    Seeking thy due of those who did withstand.

But now, it seems, thou would'st I should thee love;
    I do confess, twas thy will made me choose;   10

1. In Pamphilia's dream-vision, Venus appears drawn in a chariot by doves (a traditional representation found in Ovid). The opening of Wroth's sequence may recall the dream-vision found in the first sonnet of Dante's *Vita Nuova*, in which Cupid holds a burning heart that he forces the lady to eat.
2. On the title page of the *Urania* (see fig. 4), Venus holds aloft a flaming heart.

And thy fair shows made me a lover prove
When I my freedom did, for pain refuse.

Yet this, Sir God,[3] your boyship I despise;
Your charms I obey, but love not want of eyes.

P22

Come darkest night, becoming sorrow best;
   Light, leave thy light, fit for a lightsome soul;
   Darkness doth truly suit with me opprest,
   Whom absence power doth from mirth control:

The very trees with hanging heads condole   5
   Sweet summer's parting, and of leaves distrest
   In dying colors make a grief-full role;
   So much (alas) to sorrow are they prest.

Thus of dead leaves her farewell carpet's made:
   Their fall, their branches, all their mournings prove;   10
   With leafless, naked bodies, whose hues vade[4]
   From hopeful green, to wither in their love.

If trees, and leaves for absence, mourners be
No marvel that I grieve, who like want see.

P25

Like to the Indians, scorched with the sun,[5]
   The sun which they do as their God adore,
   So am I us'd by love, for evermore
   I worship him, less favors have I won.

Better are they who thus to blackness run,   5
   And so can only whiteness want[6] deplore
   Than I who pale, and white am with griefs' store
   Nor can have hope, but to see hopes undone;

Besides their sacrifice receivd's[7] in sight
   Of their chose saint: mine hid as worthless rite;   10
   Grant me to see where I my off'rings give,

Then let me wear the mark of Cupid's might

---

3. Pamphilia's mocking address ("Sir God") recalls Astrophil's jibe at Cupid ("sir foole") in Sir Philip Sidney's *Astrophil and Stella*, 53.7.
4. Fade, decay.
5. Wroth herself assumed the disguise of a Moor in the first performance of Ben Jonson's *Masque of Blackness* at court in 1605. She may also be alluding to the dark-skinned Indians of the New World.
6. Lack of whiteness.
7. Received is.

In heart as they in skin of Phoebus' light,
Not ceasing off'rings to love while I live.

P26

When everyone to pleasing pastime hies
    Some hunt, some hawk, some play, while some delight
    In sweet discourse, and music shows joy's might,
    Yet I my thoughts do far above these prize.

The joy which I take, is that free from eyes   5
    I sit, and wonder at this daylike night,
    So to dispose themselves, as void of right;
    And leave true pleasure for poor vanities.

When others hunt, my thoughts I have in chase;
    If hawk, my mind at wished end doth fly;   10
    Discourse, I with my spirit talk, and cry
    While others, music choose as greatest grace.

O God, say I, can these fond pleasures move?
Or music be but in sweet thoughts of love?

P32

Grief, killing grief: have not my torments been
    Already great, and strong enough: but still
    Thou dost increase, nay glory in mine ill,
    And woes new past afresh new woes begin!

Am I the only purchase thou canst win?   5
    Was I ordain'd to give despair her fill
    Or fittest I should mount misfortune's hill
    Who in the plain of joy cannot live in?

If it be so: Grief come as welcome guest
    Since I must suffer, for another's rest: 10
    Yet this, good Grief, let me entreat of thee,

Use still thy force, but not from those I love.
    Let me all pains and lasting torments prove
    So I miss these, lay all thy weights on me.

P40

False hope which feeds but to destroy, and spill
    What it first breeds;[8] unnatural to the birth

8. An image of miscarriage or infanticide.

Of thine own womb; conceiving but to kill,
And plenty gives to make the greater dearth,[9]

So Tyrants do who falsely ruling earth   5
   Outwardly grace them, and with profits fill
   Advance those who appointed are to death
   To make their greater fall to please their will.

Thus shadow they their wicked vile intent
   Coloring evil with a show of good   10
   While in fair shows their malice so is spent;
   Hope kills the heart, and tyrants shed the blood.

For hope deluding brings us to the pride
Of our desires the farther down to slide.

A Crown of Sonnets Dedicated to Love[10]

P77

In this strange labyrinth how shall I turn?
   Ways are on all sides while the way I miss:
   If to the right hand, there, in love I burn;
   Let me go forward, therein danger is;

If to the left, suspicion hinders bliss,   5
   Let me turn back, shame cries I ought return
   Nor faint though crosses with my fortunes kiss;
   Stand still is harder, although sure to mourn;

Thus let me take the right, or left hand way;
   Go forward, or stand still, or back retire;   10
   I must these doubts endure without allay
   Or help, but travail[11] find for my best hire;

Yet that which most my troubled sense doth move
Is to leave all, and take the thread of love.[12]

P78

Is to leave all, and take the thread of love
   Which line straight leads unto the soul's content

9. Famine.
10. Wroth's "Crown of Sonnets" is based on the Italian poetic form, the *corona*, in which the last line of each sonnet serves as the first line of the succeeding one. Both her father and her uncle attempted the intricate poetic form, although Robert Sidney's *corona* is incomplete. Among John Donne's divine poems is a collection of seven linked sonnets, "La Corona."
11. The Elizabethan word *travail* meant both labor and travel.
12. Wroth alludes to Ariadne's thread, given to Theseus to lead him out of the labyrinth, or maze, enclosing the Minotaur.

Where choice delights with pleasure's wings do move,
And idle phant'sie[13] never room had lent.

When chaste thoughts guide us then our minds are bent   5
   To take that good which ills from us remove,
   Light of true love, brings fruit which none repent
   But constant lovers seek, and wish to prove;

Love is the shining star of blessing's light;
   The fervent fire of zeal, the root of peace,   10
   The lasting lamp fed with the oil of right;
   Image of faith, and womb for joy's increase.

Love is true virtue, and his ends delight;
His flames are joys, his bands true lovers' might.[14]

P79

His flames are joys, his bands true lovers' might,
   No stain is there but pure, as purest white,
   Where no cloud can appear to dim his light,
   Nor spot defile, but shame will soon requite.

Here are affections, tried by love's just might   5
   As gold by fire, and black discern'd by white,
   Error by truth, and darkness known by light,
   Where faith is valued for love to requite.

Please him, and serve him, glory in his might,
   And firm he'll be, as innocency white,   10
   Clear as th'air, warm as sun beams, as day light,
   Just as truth, constant as fate, joy'd to requite.

Then love obey, strive to observe his might,
And be in his brave court a glorious light.[15]

P80

And be in his brave court a glorious light,
   Shine in the eyes of faith, and constancy,
   Maintain the fires of love still burning bright
   Not slightly sparkling but light flaming be

Never to slack till earth no stars can see,   5

13. "Phant'sie" (or fancy) is sensuous love.
14. Pamphilia shifts from mocking Cupid as the mischievous blind boy to praising him as a mature, noble monarch, the embodiment of spiritual love.
15. Wroth creates a monorhymed sonnet, with only four ending words: *might, white, light, requite*. This poem may be patterned on Sir Philip Sidney's monorhymed sonnet from the *Old Arcadia*, 42, which uses only the *light-might* rhymes.

Till Sun, and Moon do leave to us dark night,
And second Chaos[16] once again do free
Us, and the world from all division's spite.

Till then, affections which his followers are
Govern our hearts, and prove his powers' gain,   10
To taste this pleasing sting seek with all care
For happy smarting is it with small pain,

Such as although, it pierce your tender heart
And burn, yet burning you will love the smart.

P81

And burn, yet burning you will love the smart,
When you shall feel the weight of true desire,
So pleasing, as you would not wish your part
Of burden should be missing from that fire;

But faithful and unfeigned heat aspire   5
Which sin abolisheth, and doth impart
Salves to all fear, with virtues which inspire
Souls with divine love, which shows his chaste art,

And guide he is to joyings; open eyes
He hath to happiness, and best can learn[17]   10
Us means how to deserve, this he descries
Who blind yet doth our hiddenest thoughts discern.

Thus we may gain since living in blest love
He may our Prophet,[18] and our Tutor prove.

P82

He may our Prophet, and our Tutor prove
In whom alone we do this power find,
To join two hearts as in one frame to move;[19]
Two bodies, but one soul to rule the mind;

Eyes which must care to one dear object bind   5
Ears to each other's speech as if above
All else they sweet, and learned were; this kind
Content of lovers witnesseth true love.

16. The state out of which the world was created; hence "second chaos" is the ultimate destruction of
    the world.
17. Teach.
18. The manuscript spelling is "profitt," a pun on gain and prophet.
19. An Elizabethan ideal of love was one soul in two bodies. A lyric entitled "On one heart made of
    two" has been attributed to Wroth's lover, William Herbert, third earl of Pembroke, in the 1660
    edition of his poems.

It doth enrich the wits, and make you see
    That in yourself, which you knew not before,   10
    Forcing you to admire such gifts should be
    Hid from your knowledge, yet in you the store;

Millions of these adorn the throne of Love,
How blest be they then, who his favors prove.

P83

How blest be they then, who his favors prove
    A life whereof the birth is just desire,
    Breeding sweet flame which hearts invite to move
    In these lov'd eyes which kindle Cupid's fire,

And nurse his longings with his thoughts entire,   5
    Fix'd on the heat of wishes form'd by love,
    Yet whereas fire destroys this doth aspire,
    Increase, and foster all delights above;

Love will a painter make you, such, as you
    Shall able be to draw your only dear   10
    More lively, perfect, lasting, and more true
    Than rarest workman, and to you more near.

These be the least, then all must needs confess
He that shuns love doth love himself the less.

P84

He that shuns love doth love himself the less
    And cursed he whose spirit not admires
    The worth of love, where endless blessedness
    Reigns, and commands, maintain'd by heav'nly fires

Made of virtue, join'd by truth, blown by desires,   5
    Strengthened by worth, renewed by carefulness,
    Flaming in never changing thoughts, briars
    Of jealousy shall here miss welcomeness;

Nor coldly pass in the pursuits of love
    Like one long frozen in a sea of ice,   10
    And yet but chastely let your passions move
    No thought from virtuous love your minds entice.

Never to other ends your phant'sies place
But where they may return with honor's grace.

P85

But where they may return with honor's grace
Where Venus' follies can no harbor win
But chased are as worthless of the face
Or style of love who hath lascivious been.

Our hearts are subject to her son; where sin   5
Never did dwell, or rest one minute's space;
What faults he hath, in her, did still begin,
And from her breast he suck'd his fleeting pace.

If lust be counted love 'tis falsely nam'd
By wickedness a fairer gloss to set   10
Upon that vice, which else makes men asham'd
In the own phrase to warrant but beget

This child for love,[20] who ought like monster born
Be from the court of Love, and reason torn.

P86

Be from the court of Love, and reason torn
For Love in reason now doth put his trust,
Desert[21] and liking are together born
Children of love and reason, parents just.

Reason advisor is, love ruler must   5
Be of the state, which crown he long hath worn,
Yet so as neither will in least mistrust
The government where no fear is of scorn,

Then reverence both their mights thus made of one,
But wantonness, and all those errors shun,   10
Which wrongers be, impostures, and alone
Maintainers of all follies ill begun;

Fruit of a sour,[22] and unwholesome ground
Unprofitably pleasing, and unsound.

P87

Unprofitably pleasing, and unsound

20. These lines can be read: "If lust be counted love, it's falsely named by wickedness in order to set a
fairer gloss upon that vice, which otherwise makes men ashamed in the same word to identify lust
as love's child." The poem contrasts two figures of Cupid, the mischievous boy discussed in these
lines and the medieval figure of Cupid as a mature monarch in the court of love.
21. Merit.
22. Cold and wet.

When heaven gave liberty to frail dull earth
To bring forth plenty that in ills abound
Which ripest yet do bring a certain dearth.

A timeless, and unseasonable birth   5
  Planted in ill, in worse time springing found,
  Which hemlock-like might feed a sick-wit's mirth
  Where unrul'd vapors swim in endless round,

Then joy we not in what we ought to shun
  Where shady pleasures show, but true born fires   10
  Are quite quench'd out, or by poor ashes won
  Awhile to keep those cool, and wan desires.

O no, let love his glory have and might
Be given to him who triumphs in his right.

P88

Be given to him who triumphs in his right
  Nor vading be, but like those blossoms fair
  Which fall for good, and lose their colors bright
  Yet die not but with fruit their loss repair

So may love make you pale with loving care   5
  When sweet enjoying shall restore that light
  More clear in beauty than we can compare
  If not to Venus in her chosen night,

And who so give themselves in this dear kind
  These happinesses shall attend them still   10
  To be supply'd with joys, enrich'd in mind
  With treasures of content, and pleasures fill,

Thus love to be divine doth here appear
Free from all fogs but shining fair, and clear.

P89

Free from all fogs but shining fair, and clear
  Wise in all good, and innocent in ill
  Where holy friendship is esteemed dear
  With truth in love, and justice in our will,

In love these titles only have their fill   5
  Of happy life maintainer, and the mere
  Defense of right, the punisher of skill,
  And fraud; from whence directions doth appear.

To thee then lord commander of all hearts,
   Ruler of our affections kind, and just   10
   Great King of Love, my soul from feigned smarts
   Or thought of change I offer to your trust

This crown, myself, and all that I have more
Except my heart which you bestow'd before.

P90

Except my heart which you bestow'd before,
   And for a sign of conquest gave away
   As worthless to be kept in your choice store[23]
   Yet one more spotless with you doth not stay.

The tribute which my heart doth truly pay   5
   Is faith untouch'd, pure thoughts discharge the score
   Of debts for me, where constancy bears sway,
   And rules as Lord, unharm'd by envies sore,

Yet other mischiefs fail not to attend,
   As enemies to you, my foes must be;   10
   Curst jealousy doth all her forces bend
   To my undoing; thus my harms I see.

So though in Love I fervently do burn,
In this strange labyrinth how shall I turn?

P93

Come merry spring delight us
For winter long did spite us
In pleasure still persever,
Thy beauties ending never,
   Spring, and grow   5
   Lasting so
With joys increasing ever.

Let cold from hence be banisht
Till hopes from me be vanisht,
But bless thy dainties growing   10
In fullness freely flowing
   Sweet birds sing
   For the spring

23. Treasure.

All mirth is now bestowing.

Philomel in this arbor[24]   15
Makes now her loving harbor
Yet of her state complaining
Her notes in mildness straining
   Which though sweet
   Yet do meet   20
Her former luckless paining.

P96

Late in the Forest I did Cupid see
   Cold, wet, and crying he had lost his way,
   And being blind was farther like to stray:
   Which sight a kind compassion bred in me.

I kindly took, and dried him, while that he   5
   Poor child complain'd he starved was with stay,[25]
   And pin'd for want of his accustom'd prey,
   For none in that wild place his host would be.

I glad was of his finding, thinking sure
   This service should my freedom still procure,   10
   And in my arms I took him then unharm'd,

Carrying him safe unto a Myrtle bower,[26]
   But in the way he made me feel his power,
   Burning my heart who had him kindly warm'd.

P102

How glowworm-like the sun doth now appear,
   Cold beams do from his glorious face descend
   Which shows his days, and force draw to an end,
   Or that to leave taking his time grows near;

This day his face did seem but pale though clear,   5
   The reason is he to the north must lend
   His light, and warmth must to that climate bend
   Whose frozen parts could not love's heat hold dear.

24. According to Ovid, following the rape of Philomela by Tereus, she was transformed into a
nightingale. Unlike male poets who often celebrated Philomela as a harbinger of spring, Wroth
emphasizes Philomela's continued suffering.
25. Wroth's depiction of Cupid as a beggar boy who ungratefully wounds his benefactor derives
ultimately from the Greek *Anacreontea*, 33.
26. The myrtle tree was held sacred to Venus and used as an emblem of love.

Alas, if thou (bright sun) to part from hence
   Grieve so, what must I hapless who from thence   10
   Where thou dost go my blessing shall attend.

Thou shalt enjoy that sight for which I die,
   And in my heart thy fortunes do envy,
   Yet grieve, I'll love thee, for this state may mend.

P103

My muse now happy, lay thyself to rest,
   Sleep in the quiet of a faithful love,
   Write you no more, but let these phant'sies move
Some other hearts, wake not to new unrest,

But if you study, be those thoughts addrest   5
   To truth, which shall eternal goodness prove;
Enjoying of true joy, the most, and best,
   The endless gain which never will remove.[27]

Leave the discourse of Venus, and her son
   To young beginners, and their brains inspire   10
   With stories of great love, and from that fire
Get heat to write the fortunes they have won,

And thus leave off; what's past shows you can love,
   Now let your constancy your honor prove,
Pamphilia.[28]

TEXTUAL NOTES

Copy-text: Wroth's sonnet sequence, *Pamphilia to Amphilanthus,* survives in two different versions: an autograph manuscript at the Folger Library (V.a.104), and a printed text that appears at the end of *The Countess of Montgomery's Urania* (1621). The Folger manuscript appears to be the earlier text since most of the author's handwritten corrections were incorporated into the published version. This modernized text of Wroth's sonnets is based on the critical edition found in *The Poems of Lady Mary Wroth,* rev. ed. (Baton Rouge: Louisiana State Univ. Press, 1992). Ellipsis in noun and verb forms has been retained for the purpose of rhyme and meter. Only substantive variants are listed below; deletions in the manuscript appear in angle brackets.

P 1.14	I have] 1621; have I F
P 8.6	thy] 1621; your F
	to] 1621; doe F
P 8.7	thy foe] 1621; your foe F

27. Possibly a pun on the name of William Herbert.
28. At the end of the first book of the 1621 *Urania,* Pamphilia accepts the keys to the Throne of Love, "at which instant *Constancy* vanished, as metamorphosing herself into her breast" (141). In the Folger manuscript, the signature "Pamphilia" appears at the end of the sequence.

	thy claim] 1621; your claim F
P 8.8	thy] 1621; your F
P 8.9	thou would'st] 1621; you would F
	thee] 1621; you F
P 8.10	thy will made me] 1621; you, made mee first F
P 8.11	thy] 1621; your F
P 25.4	favors] 1621; favor F
P 25.9	receavd's] F; receiv'd 1621
P 25.13	of] 1621; doe F
P 26.4	do] 1621; ⟨did⟩ doe F
P 26.12	choose as] 1621; is theyr F
P 26.14	sweet] 1621; deere F
P 32.3	mine] 1621; my F
P 32.5	thou canst] 1621; you can F
P 40.8	their greater] 1621; the greater F
P 40.10	a show] 1621; the mask F
P 77.7	with] F; which 1621
P 78.2	line] F; ⟨path⟩ line F
P 78.3	with] 1621; ⟨on⟩ with F
P 78.11	The] 1621; ⟨the⟩ that F
P 79.5	tried] 1621; tried ⟨are⟩ F
P 79.11	sun] F; sun's 1621
P 81.7	fear] 1621; feares F
P 81.12	thoughts] 1621; thought F
P 81.13	we may] 1621; may wee F
P 81.14	Prophet] 1621; profitt F
P 82.1	Prophet] 1621; profitt F
P 82.5	which must] 1621; with much F
P 82.9	make] 1621; makes F
P 82.14	be] F; are 1621
P 83.3	flame] 1621; flames F
P 83.4	these] 1621; those F
	kindle] 1621; kindles F
P 83.7	whereas] 1621; as wher F
	aspire] 1621; respire F
P 83.12	workman] 1621; woorkmen F
P 83.13	all must needs] 1621; needs must all F
P 85.5	subject] 1621; subjects F
	son] 1621; sunn F
P 85.6	or] 1621; nor F
P 86.9	of] 1621; butt F
P 88.2	vading] F; fading 1621
P 88.8	night,] F; might. 1621
P 88.12	content] 1621; contents F
P 89.8	directions] 1621; directnes F
P 90.6	Is faith untouch'd] 1621; faith untouch'd is F
P 96.12	safe] 1621; *om.* F
P 102.5	This] F; The 1621
P 103.9	son] 1621; sunn F

FROM *THE COUNTESS OF MONTGOMERY'S URANIA* (1621)

[The Tale of the Cephalonian Lovers]

[The *Urania* opens with the lament of the shepherdess Urania, who is in search of her true identity. When she finds a knight in mourning, she attempts to give him counsel, but he rebuffs her once he realizes that she is not a spirit: "But now I see you are a woman, and therefore not much to be marked and less resisted" (p. 4). Despite his denigrating remark, Urania proves that she is indeed capable of heroic action. She eventually discovers that she is the daughter of the king of Naples and that she had been kidnapped as a child, sent to sea in a basket, and saved by an old shepherdess and his wife, who reared her. Urania develops a strong and mutually supportive friendship with Pamphilia, who is secretly in love with the unfaithful Amphilanthus, Urania's brother. Meanwhile Leandrus, prince of Achaya, originally betrothed to Antissia, falls in love with Pamphilia and vainly begs her to marry him. In this excerpt (from part I, book I, pp. 34–36), Leandrus delivers a first-person narrative of the star-crossed lovers he meets on the Greek island of Cephalonia; this tale of unhappy love mirrors his own condition.]

"But being in the island of Cephalonia,[1] there was a solemn and magnificent feast held, which was by reason of a marriage between the lord's daughter of that island and the lord of Zante's son, a fine and sprightful youth, jousts, tilts, and all other such warlike exercises being proclaimed. Hearing this, I would needs show myself one, as forward as any stranger to honor the feast. The first day (which was the wedding day) arms were laid aside, and only dancing and feasting exercised, after supper everyone preparing for the dancing again. With the sound of trumpets, there entered one in habit and fashion like a commander of horse, who delivered some few lines to the new married pair, dedicated as to their honor and joy, which they received most thankfully, promising freedom and welcome to the whole company.

"Then entered in twenty gentlemen presenting soldiers, and so danced in their kind, making a brave and commendable demonstration of courtship in the bravest profession, honor abounding most, where nobleness in valor and bounty in civility agree together. After they went to a rich banquet: the brave masquers, discovering themselves, were found to be gentlemen of both islands, equally divided in number, as their affections ought to be to either, and therefore had put themselves into the evenest and perfectest number of ten and ten.[2]

"But to leave sport, and come to earnest, the manner of that place

1. Cephalonia is the largest of the Ionian islands off the western coast of Greece; it is located eight miles to the north of Zante, a smaller Ionian island.
2. Masques were frequently performed during wedding celebrations (as in *The Tempest*). Although the number of masquers was typically twelve, they entered in procession arranged in pairs.

was that from the banquet the bride must be stolen away (to bed the meaning is), but she took to the fields. Most did miss her, for there wanted no respective care of her, but all were satisfied with the fashion, correcting such as spake suspiciously, and expecting to be called to see her in bed, waited the calling. But the time being long, some hastier than the rest went to the chamber, where they found she had not been. This was instantly blown abroad; all betook themselves to arms who could bear any, the ladies to their tears, everyone amazed, and chiefly the bridegroom perplexed, the old fathers vexed, the mothers tore their gray locks, such disorder in general, as cannot be expressed, but by the picture of the same accident. Some mistrusted the masquers, but soon they cleared themselves, putting on arms and being as earnest as any in the search.

"I, a stranger, and loving business, would needs accompany them (which the favor of a nobleman, with whom I had got some little acquaintance, did well aid me in), whose fortunes were in finding them, more happy than any others, overtaking them, when they thought themselves most secure, being together laid within a delicate vineyard, a place able to hide them, and please them with as much content, as Paris felt, when he had deceived the Greek king of his beautiful Helen,[3] laughing at the fine deceit and pitying in a scornful fashion those who with direct pain and meaning followed them, commending their subtleties and fine craftiness in having so deceived them. Kissing and embracing, they joyfully remained in their stolen comforts till we, rudely breaking in upon them, made them as fearfully rush up, as a tapist[4] buck will do, when he finds his enemies so near. Yet did not our coming any whit amaze them, but that they were well able to make use of the best sense at that time required for their good, which was speech, uttering it in this manner.

"'My Lords,' said they, 'if ever you have known love, that will (we hope) now withhold you from crossing lovers. We confess, to the law we are offenders, yet not to the law of love. Wherefore as you have loved, or do, or may, pity us, and be not the means that we too soon sacrifice our bloods on the cruel altar of revenge, while we remain the faithful vassals of Venus. Let not your hands be soiled in the blood of lovers. What can wash away so foul a stain? You may bring us (it is true) unto our just deserved ends, but then take heed of a repentant, gnawing spirit, which will molest you, when you shall be urged to remember that you caused so much faithful and constant love to be offered to the triumph of your conquest over a lover unarmed, wanting all means of resistance, but pure affections to defend himself withal, and a woman only strong in truth of love.'

"For my part, she won me; my companion was by him gained, so as

---

3. The Trojan Paris deceived Menelaus, king of Sparta, in kidnapping his wife Helen, an incident that precipitated the Trojan War.
4. Hidden, lying close to the ground.

promising assistance in place of arms and help instead of force, we sat down together, he beginning his discourse in this manner:

" 'To make long speeches, striving to be held an orator, or with much delicacy to paint this story, the time affords not the one, our truth and love requires not the other. Wherefore as plainly as truth itself demands, I will tell you the beginning, success, and continuance of our fortunate (though crossed) affections. I loved this lady before she had seen this young lord. She likewise had only seen my love, and only tied her self to that, before he saw her. Love made me her slave, while she suffered as by the like authority. I sued, she granted; I loved, she requited, happiness above all blessings to be embraced. Our eyes kept just measure of looks, being sometimes so enchained in delightful links of each other's joy-tying chain (for so we made up the number of our beholdings), as hard it was to be so unkindly found, as to separate so dear a pleasure. Our hearts held even proportion with our thoughts and eyes, which were created, nursed, and guided by those, or rather one heart's power.

" 'But parents having (were it not for Christianity, I should say) a cruel and tyrannical power over their children, brought this (to us) disastrous fortune, for discovering our loves, set such spies over us (scorning that I, being the younger brother to an earl, should have such happiness, as to enjoy my princess) as we could never come to enjoy more than bare looks, which yet spake our true meanings after it was discovered. This course enraged us, vowing to have our desires upon any terms whatsoever, always considered with true nobleness and virtue. Thus resolved, we continued till her father, concluding this match, shut her up in a tower, wherein he then kept (in her) his choicest treasure, till this day of her marriage, which opportunity we took, purposing—'

"More he would have said, as it seemed, truly to manifest the virtuous determination they had, in their accomplishment of their desires, when he was hindered by the rushing in of others with their horses. Rising, we discerned the deceived youth with some others in his company, fate, like his love, having guided him to that place. In charity we could not leave our first professed friends, nor could I part myself from such and so true love; wherefore resolutely taking my companion's part, defended the lovers, pity then taking the place of justice in our swords. The husband being unfortunately slain by my companion, truly I was sorry for him, and glad it was not I had done it.

"But soon followed a greater and more lamentable misfortune. For one of the young lord's servants, seeing his master slain, pressed in, unregarded or doubted, upon the unarmed lover, who was this while comforting his mistress and not expecting danger, was on the sudden thrust into the back, as he was holding his only comfort in his arms. He soon (alas, and so forever) left his dear embracement, turning on him who hurt him, repaying the wrong with giving him his death, but then soon followed his own, the wound being mortal which he had received, yet not so suddenly, but that he saw the destruction of his enemies. We being as fierce, as rage and revenge could make us, then he remaining alone (besides myself) alive, and yet dying, giving me infinite thanks for my love and willing rescue lent him, with many doleful and (in affection) lamentable groans and complaints, he took his leave of his only and best beloved, then of me, to whom he committed the care of her and his body, then kissing her, departed.

"But what shall I say of her? Imagine, great Prince and all this brave company, what she did. You will say, she wept, tore her hair, rent her clothes, cried, sobbed, groaned. No, she did not thus; she only embraced him, kissed him, and with as deadly a paleness, as death could with most cunning counterfeit, and not execute, she entreated me to conduct her to the next religious house, where she would remain till she might follow him. I admired her patience, but since more wondered at her worth. O women, how excellent are you, when you take the right way? Else, I must confess, you are the children of men, and like them fault-full.

"The body we took with the help of a litter which passed by (having before conveyed a hurt knight to the same monastery next to that place), and in that we conveyed it thither, where we buried him and almost drowned him in our tears. Thinking then to have removed, she fell ill, not sick in body, but dead in heart, which appeared, for within two days she died, leaving this world, to meet and once more joy in him, who more than a world, or ten thousand worlds, she loved and still desired, which made her choose death, being her then greater joy, burying them together a little without the house (the order of that place not permitting them to be laid within it.)"

[The Throne of Love]

[Urania and her friends venture within sight of Cyprus, where they observe a burning ship in the harbor; no sooner do they arrive than their own boat is inflamed, and they flee to land. "Thus, on they went (but as in a Labyrinth without a thread) till they came within sight of a rare and admirable Palace." See the title page of the *Urania* (fig. 4) for an illustration of this episode from part I, book I.]

It was situated on a hill, but that hill formed, as if the world would needs raise one place of purpose to build Love's throne upon, all the country besides humbly plain, to show the subjection to that powerful dwelling. The hill whereon this palace stood was just as big as to hold the house, three sides of the hill made into delicate gardens and orchards; the further side was a fine and stately wood. This sumptuous house was square, set all upon pillars of black marble, the ground paved with the same, everyone of those pillars presenting the lively image (as perfectly as carving could demonstrate) of brave and mighty men, and sweet and delicate ladies, such as had been conquered by love's power, but placed there, as still to maintain and uphold the honor and house of Love.

Coming towards it, they imagined it some magical work, for so daintily it appeared in curiosity, as it seemed as if it hung in the air, the trees, fountains, and all sweet delicacies being discerned through it. The upper story had the gods most fairly and richly appearing in their thrones; their proportions such as their powers and qualities are described, as Mars in arms, weapons of war about him, trophies of his victories, and many demonstrations of his war-like godhead; Apollo with music; Mercury, Saturn, and the rest in their kind. At the foot of this hill ran a pleasant and sweetly passing river, over which was a bridge, on which were three towers.

Upon the first was the image of Cupid, curiously carved with his bow bent, and quiver at his back, but with his right hand pointing to the next tower, on which was a statue of white marble, representing Venus, but so richly adorned, as it might for rareness and exquisiteness have been taken for the goddess herself, and have caused as strange an affection as the image did to her maker, when he fell in love with his own work.[1] She was crowned with myrtle and pansies, in her left hand holding a flaming heart, her right directing to the third tower, before which, in all dainty riches and rich delicacy, was the figure of Constancy, holding in her hand the keys of the palace, which showed that place was not to be open to all, but to few possessed with that virtue.[2]

They all beheld this place with great wonder, Parselius[3] resolving it was some enchantment, wherefore was the nicer how they proceeded in the entering of it. While they were thus in question, there came an aged man with so good a countenance and grave aspect, as it struck reverence into them, to be showed to him, by them. He saluted them thus:

"Fair company, your beholding this place with so much curiosity, and besides your habits, makes me know you are strangers, therefore fit to let you understand the truth of this brave building, which is dedicated to Love. Venus (whose priest I am) thinking herself in these latter times, not so much, or much less honored than in ages past, hath built this, calling it the Throne of Love. Here is she daily served, by myself and others of my profession, and here is the trial of false or faithful lovers.

"Those that are false may enter this tower, which is Cupid's Tower, or the Tower of Desire, but therein once enclosed, they endure torments fit for such a fault. Into the second any lover may enter, which is the Tower of Love, but there they suffer inexpressible tortures, in sev-

---

1. Spenser tells how the Greek sculptor Phidias fell in love with the statue he created of Venus (*Faerie Queene* IV.x.40). Pliny recounts a similar story of a statue of Venus by Praxiteles (*Natural History* XXXVI.21).

2. See sonnet 103 of *Pamphilia to Amphilanthus*.

3. Parselius, eldest son of the king of Morea, is Pamphilia's brother; he initially loves Urania but later abandons her when he meets Dalinea, whom he eventually marries (see excerpt, "The Tomb of Love").

eral kinds as their affections are most incident to, as jealousy, despair, fear, hope, longings, and such like. The third, which is guarded by Constancy, can be entered by none, till the valiantest knight with the loyalest lady come together and open that gate, when all these charms shall have conclusion. Till then, all that venture into these towers remain prisoners; this is the truth. Now if your hearts will serve you, adventure it."

They thanked the old man for his relation, but told him they had some vows to perform first, which ended, they would adventure for imprisonment in so rare a prison. The old priest left them, and they, weary, laid them down near the Tower of Desire, refreshing themselves with some little meat which Urania's maid had in her scrip,[4] but wanting drink, they all went to the river, whereof they had but drunk, when in them several passions did instantly abound.

Parselius forgot all but his promise to the dead King of Albania for the settling his sons in that kingdom. Leandrus, afflicted with the loss of Antissia, must straight into Morea to find her and take her from Amphilanthus. Steriamus and Selarinus would not be refused the honor of knighthood, Mars having so possessed them with his warlike disposition, as worlds to their imaginations were too little to conquer; therefore Albania was already won. Urania, whose heart before was only fed by the sweet looks and pleasing conversation of Parselius, loves him now so much, as she imagines she must try the adventure to let him see her loyalty is such, as for his love and by it she would end the enchantment. Selarina thought she saw within the gardens a young prince with a crown upon his head who beckoned to her, wherefore she would go at such a call. Urania's maid beheld, as she believed, Allimarlus in the second tower, kissing and embracing a black-moor,[5] which so far enraged her, being passionately in love with him, as she must go to revenge herself of that injury.

These distractions carried them all, as their passions guided them. Parselius, having knighted the two princes, took their way to the next port, Urania now not seen or thought on. Leandrus hasting another way, to find means for his journey. Selarina to the tower and knocked with that fervent desire to accomplish her end as the gate opened. All the three[6] rushed in, striving who should be first. But Selarina was then soon made to know she should not contend with Urania, wherefore she was locked into the first tower, burning with desire to come to that sweet prince, which still she sees before her, he calling, she with incessant desire striving to go to him.

Urania went on, when entering the second tower, guarded by Venus, she was therein enclosed, when as thus much sense came to her, as to know she had left Parselius, which strake her into a mourning passion, confessing that an unpardonable fault, and what he in justice could not

4. A small bag or satchel.
5. Dark-skinned person.
6. The three women: Selarina, Urania, and Urania's maid.

excuse. Then despair possessed her so, as there she remained, loving in despair, and despairing mourned. The shepherdess her servant continuing her first passion got into that tower too, where she still saw her affliction, striving with as much spiteful jealousy as that fury could vex her withal, to come at the moor to pull her from her knight. Thus were the women for their punishment left prisoners in the Throne of Love, which throne and punishments are daily built in all humane[7] hearts.

[The Tale of Veralinda and Leonia]

[The young knight Leonius, Amphilanthus's brother, arrives in Arcadia, where he rescues the shepherdess Veralinda from a bear, only to fall in love with her. When he becomes so tongue-tied that he cannot woo her, he decides to assume the disguise of a shepherdess named Leonia. This excerpt (from part I, book III, pp. 369–72) opens with Veralinda as she passes by a fountain and overhears the supposed nymph Leonia, who laments his/her unrequited love.]

As she went on sadly bemoaning her solitary thoughts, she heard as pitiful a voice utter these imperfect joined words.

"Leonia, poor nymph," said it, "where is thy vow? Must Venus make thee change? O love, coward love to steal thus to my heart, couldst thou not have come bravely, and contended with me in the chase, or taken me in the time when I did revile thee and scorn thy power? But to set upon me when I was quiet, and safe as I thought, treacherously to lie in wait and betray me when I was unarmed, naked, and without power to resist, and more for my shame when I had sworn to Diana, what punishment will that chaste goddess lay upon me for this offence? But fool, why talk I of these poor things which in comparison of my woe are but blossoms? I love, and must love, what then? I will love, and die in love, then shall that cruel[1] see written in my heart that murder thus committed. Unkind, alas, my soul melts as these tears, and yet to thee my pains are no more weighed than bubbles. My heart weeps blood, pity me then; say you do pity and save me."

"Pity," said the shepherdess, "is that I want. What new companion in my woe have I found here?"

With that she went towards the place from whence as she imagined that sad voice did proceed, when as a little from the bank under the shade of myrtle trees, which made as it were a cabin of themselves, lay a forest nymph, her apparel of color and fashion like Diana, buskins[2] upon her legs of white, her hair tied up, only some of the shortest, and about the temples curled, crowned with roses and hyacinths. She lay with her head toward her, who with a soft pace went on till she came just behind her, then viewing her earnestly, her eyes being so full of love,

---

7. In the early seventeenth century the word meant both "human" and "compassionate."
1. Cruel one (i.e., beloved).
2. Boots that reach to the calf or knee.

as all loving creatures found a power in them to draw them to her call, especially those eyes which were so much hers as they could not stir but to her will, commanding them so, as she could with her looking on them with loving force, bring them to her own. And so it now proved, for those eyes which full of tears were seeing themselves in the stream, showing their watery pictures to each other, her earnest viewing the nymph with a natural humbleness to hers, drew her looks to her. Joy then appeared in the nymph's face, yet straight was that clouded with sorrow. She rose, and with a timorous (though she imagined bashful) countenance and fashion, saluted her.

"I did think, fair nymph," said the loving shepherdess, "that it had been impossible for me to find any so like myself unhappily wounded."

"Why are you hurt, fair shepherdess?" said she. "Alas, I am sorry for you, and wish your remedy, for none knows the torment of despair like to myself, and therefore in charity would have none else afflicted with it, but it is very strange that such beauty should complain."

"Alas," said she, "oft times perfection is turned to the contrary, and so is it in me, if in me be that you spake of. But I pray, sweet nymph, let me take boldness to demand of you, of whence you are and what hath brought you hither."

"Love," said she, "for this must be the first and last of my discourse, all other matters how great soever, being but dependances of this. My name," said she, "is Leonia, my profession was what my habits tell me to be, but love hath altered me. No more must I abuse my mistress who I served,[3] since I have left her and a new one now have gained, a poor change (yet the fruit of change), when for liberty and pleasure I get beggary and slavery. Shun then this passion, rare shepherdess, for nothing but misery follows it."

"Alas, it is too late," said she, "you give this counsel out of time, for I am in the prison too fast locked, by any means but by love to be freed."

"Are you in love then?" said Leonia.

"Oh hapless me, why," said the shepherdess, "doth that grieve you?"

"It grieves me that such sweetness should be vexed. It grieves me more," cried she, "that I love in despair. Thus both afflict me," said Leonia, "and on these do I plain, and in them die."

"Let us sit down and tell our woes?" said she.

"Mine are all endless," said the nymph, "yet I will not refuse to do what you command, for you may help me if you will but pity me."

"I pity you," said she, "and love you, for in you I see (O dear remembrance) many things which represent thy love unto mine eyes."

With that the nymph did blush, the shepherdess went on: "Be not offended sweetest nymph," said she, "for he was excellent whom I did

---

3. As one of Diana's servants, she had taken a vow of chastity.

love, and do love, rare for true beauty and valor, and O, too brave for me."

"None can be so," sighed she, "fair shepherdess, for the fairest and bravest must sue to you for grace. But I did blush to hear that I should seem so favorably blessed in your all-conquering eyes, as to be thought but to resemble him that happy man whom your great goodness loves. But to go on, I was by my own suit to my parents chosen a nymph, and accepted into the number and service of Diana's servants, being given to all those sports that goddess did affect, but especially to throwing my dart at marks, and shooting in my bow at beasts, or anything, so cunning I was in that exercise, as I could hit a bird at great distance. Oft times I would take my greyhounds and course[4] the deer or hare, being so nimble, as I could follow them where ere they went. These and many other harmless delights I lived in, till one day sacrificing to Diana, unhappily for me, there came a youth, who having killed a terrible beast, offered it to the goddess as the princess of the woods and deserts.[5] This offering proved strange, making my heart the victim bleeding and lying on the Altar, dedicated to his love; thus doubly had he conquered. I fainted, fearing the chaste goddess, yet I was rescued by Venus, who promised her assistance, but not so well armed by her as not afraid of Diana, I fled from those parts, and since have I roamed about, directed by mine own despair, for never since have I seen my love. The forgetful goddess (having enough in winning, but scorning too much care) hath, I fear, forgotten me, contented with my yielding, but careless of my proceeding. I seek still, but I know not with what hope. I have wept and grieved, and so I fear still must, and thus lives and perpetually laments the poor unblessed Leonia."

The shepherdess catching her in her arms, "Ah my companion in my woes," said she, "let us still live together fittest for our fortunes, let our tears be shed together, our sighs breathed together, and let us never part, but always keep together."

This was what the nymph desired, being so glad of that embracement, as she could have found in her heart to have forgot her habits, but danger of losing all, if not governed with modesty, till apter time gain fitter opportunity of discovery, she only with an affectionate kiss, and that she would not suffer herself to miss, being such a one, as liked Veralinda (for so the shepherdess was called) better than any of her fellows' kisses, for this seemed more passionately kind, gave liberty to that, and then began her own discourse thus.

"My name is Veralinda; daughter I am to the King's shepherd, who dwells upon yonder hill. His place, estate in goods, and some kind of thing in me which these people here call beauty, hath made me to be sought by many, but I have still refused all, truly I must say with some

4. Hunt with hounds.
5. Leonia describes the earlier episode when he had saved Veralinda from the bear. The episode recalls the transformation of Musidorus from prince to shepherd in Sir Philip Sidney's *Arcadia*, but Wroth provides for a change in both class and gender.

neglectiveness, for which I am punished. And if I flatter not myself above my merit, the pain being more than the offence, for I am made to love in despair, to hope in loss, and affect one I know not, or can aspire to thought of ever seeing him again, destiny prevailing in this, and I am left a poor example of the fates' tyranny. For how can I hope, that if I meet him, he could fancy me? He a knight, I a poor Maid; he a prince it may be, and surely is, for princely virtues dwell in him, beauty inexpressible, and such as but in you I never saw any like him, and so like are you, as I love you for his sake so much, as love can command love to the image of their dear.

"Valiant he is above expression, and mild, and courteous, but what doth grieve my soul most, is, he surely loves."

"And surely would love you," said the nymph, "if he could be but happy with the knowledge. In the mean space grace me with your favor, which I will strive like him to merit. Let me enjoy those sweet embracements you would yield to him, and think I am your love, which I will do by you, and in that thought till we be blessed with perfecter enjoyings, we shall have some ease."

She condescended, and so they kissed again, wishing and loving, they remained, passing many such pleasant times, till at last the wonder of such affection twixt women was discovered, and it may be, had then been brought to light, had not the shepherdesses arrived to his grief, and no way to her content, who truly loved the sweet conversation and discourse of this nymph. To the fountain they then altogether took their way, the nymph setting herself so, as she might both see and touch the loved shepherds, all the rest beholding this stranger with as much admiration, as she did their mistress, thinking no difference between them in beauty, save that the new guest's fairness seemed more masculine, as fitted with her estate, yet full of grave, modest, and seemly bashfulness. Thus they beheld each other, the shepherdess passionately beholding Leonia in memory of her love, and the nymph amorously gazing on her in her own passions, till the music a little awaked them, making their ears prove traitors to their hearts, for letting in anything to them but love.

[The Tale of Lindamira]

[Betrayed by her lover Amphilanthus, who has forsaken her for other women, Queen Pamphilia conceals the causes of her grief from even her closest friends. In this episode (from part I, book III, pp. 423–25), she agrees to tell her companion Dorolina the tale of Lindamira, which is a mirror of her own experience.]

As they walked, discoursing of their loves and torments for it, Dorolina besought the Queen to honor her with the repeating of some of her verses. She answered, she was grown weary of rhyme, and all things but that which wearied her life, and yet for cruelty's sake would not take it. She would not be answered so, but urged her again, hoping to take her this way something from her continual passions, which not uttered did wear her spirits and waste them, as rich embroideries will spoil one another, if laid without papers between them, fretting each other, as her thoughts and imaginations did her rich and incomparable mind. But as yet Dorolina could not prevail for the part of poetry, yet she gained so much, as Pamphilia sat down and told her this tale, feigning it to be written in a French story.

"There was," said she, "in France for many years, many kings, that country being divided into several kingdoms. Several nations there were likewise which spake different languages, some of these had kings, the others only princes, but in success of time, all came happily under the rule and government of one king; care only had then by marriages to make a perpetual union, which only length of time could do. Among these marriages there was one from which grew both good and ill. A brave young lord of the isle of France, second son to a famous nobleman, and one who had great employment under the King, being counted the bravest man of the kingdom,[1] was by the means of a brother-in-law of his married to a great heir in little Brittany, of rich possessions.[2]

"This lady was wooed and sought by many; one she affected and so much loved, as she was contented to think him worthy to be her husband, and so for worth, he was. Miserably hard her father kept her and close, yet so much liberty she gained, as she had almost tied herself never but by death to be released. Yet her fortunes were not meant thus to be disposed of, for her father dying, and she thinking she was a little, or much, neglected by her first servant,[3] who came not according to appointment to attend her, she changed her mind and gave herself to valiant and lovely Bersindor the Frenchman,[4] leaving the other, as he had her, at home to learn better breeding.

"Into France she came, where she was by Bersindor's father and mother cherished with all affection and love, her husband kind and as respective as she merited. Many fair and sweet children they had to their comforts and their friends, and so bred they were, as all companies coveted their presence, being like sweet delights to sad eyes. The eldest daughter was called Lindamira; she was so much favored by the Queen of France,[5] as by no means she must be absent from the court, which indeed was the fittest place for her, being a lady of great spirit,

---

1. Wroth's father, Sir Robert Sidney, was the second son of Sir Henry Sidney, who served Elizabeth I as lord deputy of Ireland.

2. Sir Robert Sidney's brother-in-law, Henry Herbert, second earl of Pembroke, acted as an intermediary in arranging his marriage to Barbara Gamage, a wealthy Welsh heiress.

3. The first servant was probably Herbert Croft, grandson of the comptroller of the royal household. Barbara was originally betrothed to him, but she apparently changed her mind; when Croft learned the news, he attempted to stop the marriage by appealing to Queen Elizabeth, whose messenger arrived too late, two hours after the ceremony had already taken place.

4. "Bersindor" is most likely an anagram for Robert Sidney.

5. Lady Mary ("Lindamira") performed with Queen Anne in several of her court masques. One of Wroth's letters to Queen Anne survives in which she requested (apparently successfully) the queen's assistance in obtaining funds for the restoration of her home, Loughton Hall.

excellent qualities, and beautiful enough to make many in love with her. But she loved only one, and that one she had loved many years before any mistrusted it, or himself knew it.[6] He was likewise favored by the Queen Mother, whose husband dead, had leisure to bestow her eyes upon the loveliest object, and this Lord was well enough contented, spending his time after his own desire.[7]

"Lindamira served the Queen faithfully and so affectionately, as she had no love but them two of either sex. Yet was she careful to give no dislike to her mistress, whom she would not injure, or indeed at that time herself, for she was married, he not thinking that it was himself she loved, though he knew she was somewhere bound in those fetters. A careful eye he carried over her, not that it appeared he loved her much more than as her deserts, which her noble and free carriage deserved, yet he was desirous to find her love.[8] Once he thought it was the husband of a lady she had made her chosen friend, but after he found the contrary, to his own comfort. For the Queen, how well assured soever she was, or rather might have been in her fidelity, yet love she knew had commanded her, who born a princess and matched to a king, yet could not resist his power, might with greater ease soveraignize over a subject. But in Love's Court all are fellow-subjects, and thus her majesty was deceived in her greatness, which could not, as she thought, be subject, and therefore though others must be vassals, when they are all companions and serve alike.

"This suspicion was first put into her mind by a malicious lady, who envied sweet Lindamira. But so was it believed and followed by the Queen, as all her favor was withdrawn as suddenly and directly as if never had, Lindamira remaining like one in a gay masque, the night passed, they are in their old clothes again, and no appearance of what was. She yet was grieved to the heart because she truly loved her mistress, as her disgrace went further than only discontent for the loss, or the note the world might take of it, which must like their reports be wiped away, or washed like linen, which would be as white again as ever. But these pierced her heart, and she was inly[9] afflicted, at all times she nevertheless attended, never failing her duty, yet desirous to know the cause of this her misfortune. She employed many to move the Queen, only to know why she was offended, that if she were guilty she might ask forgiveness and make humble submission, but this would not serve. She, poor lady, ignorant of the cause, desired the lord for whom she suffered to do the like for her. He did, but returned as the others did to her, telling her the Queen's answer was, that she should not know the

---

6. Probably William Herbert, third earl of Pembroke.
7. The seventeenth-century historian Arthur Wilson claimed that whereas Queen Anne "had her *Favourites* in one place, the King had his in another. She lov'd the elder Brother, the Earl of *Pembroke*; he the younger, whom he made Earl of *Montgomery*, and Knight of the *Garter*." Wroth's inconsistency in referring first to the Queen Mother and then to the queen may reflect her efforts to obscure the charge of adultery.
8. According to Ben Jonson's *Conversations with Drummond*, Wroth was "unworthily married" to a jealous husband.
9. "was inly": inwardly felt.

cause, therefore willed her to be satisfied with that, and with knowledge that she was, and had just cause to be offended.

"Lindamira then asked leave to retire; she had permission, and withal her majesty, when she gave her her hand to kiss (which favor she was contented to allow her), she told her she should do well to stay till she was sent for. She humbly, and with tears in her eyes, answered she would obey, and so she departed going home, and soon after with a husband like her last fortune, went to live with him, whither soon came all her friends to visit her, and by him were nobly entertained. The lord, whom she so much loved and was accused for, likewise came with that lady her dear friend. Among many discourses they fell upon this of her disgrace, Lindamira saying that the thing itself did not now so much afflict her, as the ignorance of it.

" 'None,' said he, 'that dares tell you the cause knows it, and some that do, dare not.'

" 'What should fear them?' said she. 'If mistrust of my secrecy, I will give them cause to take away that suspicion of weakness in me; other reason I cannot guess.'

" 'If I should go further,' said he, 'you might imagine me one could tell.'

" 'I am verily persuaded of that,' said she.

" 'But I fear your displeasure,' said he.

" 'Why,' said Lindamira, 'concerning none but poor me, how can anything trouble you?'

" 'It may be,' said he, 'it toucheth others, and so much as you will hate them for suffering for them.'

" 'I have no reason for that,' said she, 'though it may be I shall be angry with myself for giving cause.'

" 'Then,' said he, 'with your pardon, I will tell you that I am enjoined not to let you of any know; to secrecy I will not bind you, for the business itself hath power to do that.'

"Wherewith the friend lady rose, and he proceeding told her all that had passed. 'But now,' said he, 'I fear you will hate me for this.'

" 'Pardon me, my lord,' answered she, 'I am only sorry that you should suffer for me, so unworthy of your favor, but for being offended, I protest I love her displeasure, since she hath honored me with this worthy opinion, rather than I loved her greatest grace. And more noble is my fall, than my time of favor was.'

"He did not, it seemed, lose that opportunity, nor was she nice[10] to let him know her long love; expressions of it and embracing affections wanted of neither side. What happiness this was to sweet Lindamira that constant woman, if such an other there be who loved five years undiscovered, and then on such an unlooked for occasion revealed so great a secret, may judge. This showed a strange happiness to befall them, that a jealous woman whose doubt of loss brought her losing and

10. Shy, reserved.

Lindamira's gain. Thus you may see the effects of that base humor, but alas, what succeeded all this? Your fortune, dear Dorolina, and mine, for after she had lost the Queen's favor, endured an unquiet life and miserable crosses from her husband possessed with like or more furious madness in jealousy, her honor not touched, but cast down and laid open to all men's tongues and ears, to be used as they pleased. Lastly, after fourteen years' unchanged affection, he cast her off contemptuously and scornfully, she complained, which complaint, because I liked it, or rather found her estate so near agree with mine, I put into sonnets. This course I might call ungratefulness in him and give all ill names to it, but I will with the story conclude my rage[11] against him, for thus the book leaves her; the complaint is thus divided into seven sonnets."

[The Tomb of Love]

[Parselius, king of Achaya, and his Queen Dalinea, now happily married, reflect on the perils of their earlier courtship. They travel together into a wilderness, where an old woman lures Dalinea into "a little round place, green as fresh grass could make it, and as circular as those places feigned to be made by the fairy company to dance in." In the center of the woods, Dalinea arrives at a white stone, with a set of stairs carved and decorated with gold (from part I, book IV, pp. 441–45).]

Those stairs she was to descend, which she did, entering then into a delicate fine gallery, as curious and costly all on pillars of gold; out of this into a garden, such as the perfectest was described to be; thence into a tarras,[1] the rails, pillars, and all of the same continued richness; out of that into a large and spacious hall, the inside for engraving and curiosity, like or surpassing the others, the very benches and thresholds being pure gold, the walls enriched and adorned with precious stones. In the midst of this, or rather at the upper end, was an altar or the proportion of one, six candlesticks with wax lights in them upon it but not burning. A book in the midst lay open which she took up, and reading in it, instantly a delicate sound of music was heard, and then appeared an ancient graveful[2] old man speaking these words.

"Great and rightful Queen of Achaya, blessed be your days, and happy may your issue be. Know from me that you were here foretold us many years since, to witness which this book shall give you understanding," taking that on the altar in his hand, "but till your own, and by your self chosen lord come, I must not discover the secrets unto you."

As thus they were in discourse, a strange noise of several sorts of trumpets and other wind instruments were heard, whereat entered the King Parselius, who hunting was brought by a like train into that place.

---

11. Pamphilia's sudden slippage of pronouns, from third to first person ("my rage"), reveals her strong identification with Lindamira.
1. Terrace.
2. Full of gravity.

He beheld her, and she him, but as two statues, set with their eyes one upon the other without power to speak, so stood they, admiration filling them as they were but wonder.

The old man thus said, "Since my lord the King is now likewise present, I may lawfully go forward, and fulfill the charge left unto me, which hath lain in my hands these many years. Your grandfather, brave Queen, had a brother named Distantes; he was a brave and valiant gentleman, as this kingdom ever knew, but his misfortune was to fall in love with a lady, wife to another man, whose deserts especially for love and truth to him (worthiness above all to be prized) merited what? So much love as was in him (and that was as much as ever man carried or suffered for woman) could demand, and she had such requital from him. He had loved her before her marriage, she had likewise dearly loved him, and gave so lively proofs of it, as he was made possessor of what was most desired by him. And the other only made a color for their loves, losing what was by marriage his due, but the others by the right of love, so as he was the right husband, the other the servant that had but by stealth, Distantes possessing freely.

This proceeded, and she was with child. The good man rejoiced at it, she was heartily glad, and the prince thought himself blessed, who at the same time also had his wife with child, who died in child-bed, leaving a fair and delicate daughter as years after manifested. His mistress had a son who were brought up together, the prince desiring her as a friend to bring up his daughter, having by that a fair occasion to visit her whom he loved more than any other, or himself which is easily to be beloved, since himself, he, nor any lover will spare in comparison of love to the beloved. These children continually nourished, fed, and conversing together, did breed, feed, and discourse affections by this means, growing like trees insensible yet to perfection, and flourishing. Such roots they had planted, as could not without perishing both branches be decayed, yet time made them fearful, by reason that she was so much greater and above him. In her it made her love the stronger, thinking it an honor to her, to advance by her favor a man fit in worth, though below her in dignity, the other being above all degrees.

One day she was in the garden by a delicate fountain, combing her hair and braiding it into several braids, tying at each end a delicate rich pearl. He came near her enough to behold her, but not so near (for his own happiness) to hinder her, or make delays from so delicate a work, with which she knotted and tied up his heart in as many bonds as her fingers made plaits, and wound them at last all round to crown her victory and his bondage.

When she had done, he went to her; she with smiles and pleasant discourse welcomed him, with such sweet and familiar affection, as bade him boldly sit by her, take her hand, kiss it, and so discourse of love. So far he proceeded, and so willingly she embraced his desires, as she yielded as far as chaste love did warrant, promise of marriage passing between them. This continued till the prince having provided a fit marriage for her, came and propounded it unto her, little imagining what had passed between his children. Glad he was to see their loves, which nature told him was necessary, but not (alas) the least misdoubting the mischief committed, till she seemed so nice and unwilling to be persuaded, as he grew offended, yet feared not such a misadventure. Then did he set his mistress, her husband, and the youth their son to work with her. They all promised their helps, except the young man, who modestly excused it as well as he could, confessing his want of power with her and unwillingness to offend her. This did not dislike the prince, who went away hoping for all that to win her in time, which he was resolved not by force to purchase, but if by persuasions not else to compass.

The love increased between the two young ones, as warmth in the spring, but the misery at last grew to their loss. Yet gain in this kind by sad discourse making them know the ill they had run into, and the sin they had committed, which by this chance happened unto them. The lady, mother to the youth and governess to the princess, began to discern they loved, then doubted where, then guessed, and so grieved, and more was perplexed, not being able to find a way out of this maze of trouble, nor an end to wind the skein upon any bottom,[3] but destruction and ruin. She could not find a friend to trust with it, to reveal her suspicion to her beloved. Not being sure of the ill, she thought it not fit, since a just tax might be laid upon her judgment, and an incurable wound given to him to think of the offence, and deep, though deserved punishment on him and her, whose sins had bred flowers to poison themselves withal and brought forth joys to be their overthrows.

In these perplexities she remained till a night or two before the prince was to come again, in the evening, or rather so late as might be called night, she went into the garden to breathe her complaints in the sweet and silent air. But what hour can be so late or early, that (if profitable) lovers will not find convenient?

She had not walked one alley, but in a close delicate covered walk, she heard a whispering which made her stand still, and not unmannerly, but only for knowledge sake listen who they were, when against her will (as often that happens), she heard these words.

"My dear," said one of them, "what strange mistrust is this, that lately is fallen into my mother's breast, to make her so curiously watch, and as it were strive to deprive us of our loved meetings? Can she be unkind to her own son? Or thinks she that I am not worthy of thee? Can she which cherished me with such hearty love, envy or seek undeservedly to bar my chiefest blessing? The earth holds not that treasure I prize like thee, the heavens but in themselves can give me such content as thy presence fills me withal. Joy is not but in thy sight, nor

3. Base on which to wind thread.

am I ought if not with thee; bar me thy conversation and imprison me. Let me be banished thee and murther me; let me not enjoy thee, and let me perish in perpetual accursedness. What shall I say? I cannot say I am worthy of thee; then should I flatter myself, and wrong thee. I cannot think I merit speech for me, yet since thou gracest me, why should any else envy or grudge my fortune? As thou art matchless, so are thy favors, and I am blessed, enriched, and ennobled with them. Why then should purblind chance or fond policy hinder me? Tricks of state, as being tricks, are to be condemned. I am true, thou excellent; I loyal, thou affectionate. What crocodile treason[4] should howl to bewray and destroy our contents? Weep not, dear eyes—"

With that he kissed the tears, and like nectar drank them, corsives[5] to see her shed them, but cordials as shed for him, and he permitted to take them.

"O my dear life," cried he, "tear not my soul with thy sorrow; let me not see thee mourn unless I may with that die."

He still kissed her, I know not whether more molested with her pain or joyed with that liberty of kissing, she at last kissing his eyes which likewise accompanied hers in showers.

"My joy," said she, "why make you these questions? May there be any accident that can hinder our loves? Our wills and desires, 'tis true there may, but be confident no further than absenting can gain, for never shall I be in heart and soul but yours. The least thing that belongs to you is dear to me, how infinitely dear then is your self. Mine eyes are not so dear, my heart so well beloved (but that you cherish it) as is your sight and dearest self to me. I think not of a fortune which is not with you and for you, I dream not but of you, I joy not but in you, nor am I ought else but your self metamorphosed wholly into you, and your love."

Then sat they down by a delicate fountain at the side of that walk, there they wailed again, there testified their woes in sighs and tears.

"At last," cried she, "but if my father take me hence, will not you forget me? Shall not absence work in you?"

"Yes," said he, "in admiration of thee, to think how chaste, how excellent thou art, how happy I was in thy loved sight, and so by that, see more and more cause always to lament. Other effects when absence brings to me, let ruin follow, or come jointly with it. If room be found for foul forgetfulness, let me of heaven be unremembered; thy beauty printed in my heart shall still before my soul call thoughts of love. Mistrust not me sweet life unless thou mean to martyr me. I can love none, I nere loved any, or ere will live to think so shameful and detestable a thought, as change in love procures. No, I was born just, I am just, and will die just."

She wrung his hand, "And these am I," cried she.

---

4. According to medieval bestiaries, the crocodile had the ability to shed tears in order to attract foolishly sympathetic humans, who would be swallowed up unawares.
5. Corrosives.

Then they embraced, with which the mother came unto them, who seemed like a great shower in harvest, grievous to their covetous desires of being by themselves. The moon shined so as all things appeared as clear as in the day. They were in innocence ashamed to be heard and found alone, yet love made them only desire that. Affection in a mother made tears to fall for fear and love for him; respect unto the other, as child of him she most loved, made her weep also for her. Both brought passions, as for both she suffered, she could not speak; her breath was stopped, and she was choked with kindness. She fell upon their necks as they together kneeled unto her, their eyes did say they fain would speak, and they begged for them, hers promised will to grant, and sorrow to deny. All three were in an ecstasy,[6] not knowing what to do, speech failed, senses lost their use, and they were like the images that in resemblance of the substances implored good, but dumb as they were, gained little, and thus did they remain till he spake.

"Madam," said he, "the bringer of me forth, the kind nourisher of me in youth and till this time, undo not your first work, nor make me wish I never had been born, which I must do if I be hindered from enjoying this sweet lady, mistress of my life. You have tenderly bred me with affection, and can be as tender over me still; then let my sufferings in love be as the dangers you sought to prevent, and so protect me still. I did amiss in beginning without your knowledge, but she loves me (Madam) that speaks for me, and therein am I richer than in kingdoms, if else where. She wishes what I seek, and desires what I wish; you have charity to strangers, let not your son be a greater stranger to you. His life lies on it, and so yours; if you do hold me but as dear as you did lately protest I was, you have power and means to effect this. What can you desire of my lord that he will not consent to? What entreat of her father that he will refuse? We both petition, both beseech your aid; you may assist and save us, else let us faint and perish in dismay."

The lady then grew more passionate at his speeches, than before the plain suit and confession being delivered by his own tongue, desirous she was to help and succor him, but assured she was it lay not in her power. Nor had she use of speech, only tears freely served her, so as if one would dream of the ancient changes, one might think she had been instantly ready to be transformed into a fountain. Her silence gave the young lady opportunity, who thus discoursed her passions.

"Mother," said she, "to my perfecter self, disdain not nor refuse the petition of my heart thus made, while that is prostrate to you; hear and grant my suit, use the power of love that no question you have employed by your own sufferings, judge mine, and for them both command redress. Love dares not deny you, who can and have in my hearing given proofs of his respects due unto you. Let him now show what is your due, and allow it you, but employ it to our profits, seeing thus before you, the two purest lovers his power ever touched or

---

6. A state of mystical rapture, in which the body is supposed to become incapable of sensation, while the soul is focused on divine contemplation.

brought under his obedience. Behold our pains as yours, for so they are since jointly his, and pity mine as hers, bred by your hand, like a lamb, till seized by the wolf of love, which (though fierce) yet kind and sweet are those claws that hold me fast to him. He hath told you your power; I can but beseech your favor, and beg it for love, and your own love's sake. Think how miserable the death of lovers will be, and how unfortunate when caused by a mother and a friend to love?"

"A friend to love," cried the old woman, "and a mother? 'Tis true I am both, and they have brought my misery. O my children, how miserable am I in this? I might (did not my own guiltiness condemn me) think myself and call myself your mother, but my shame makes my sorrow, and your loss must proceed from my infamy. Grieved I am in soul to tell the truth, for you must and cannot choose but hate me, when I shall say, what yet my heart, loath to let me speak? My eyes will waste themselves in streams before I can utter it and my soul rend when I must say, you cannot be blessed in love, your woeful and sinful mother being the cause and root of all this mischief. I blush in foul guiltiness, I mourn in the knowledge of my sin, I am more faulty than ever woman was, and a mere stain to my sex. You cannot, my dearest heart, enjoy this lady, nor you (sweet lady) have your love. I am the monster that keeps the gates against you, and the serpent that deserves death from you for double injury."

Then kneeled she down. "Pardon me," cried she, "you perfectest and best, though most unfortunate lovers, I am the wretch that hath undone you and myself; your love's unlawful, I am the shameful cause thereof; your loves cannot embrace, I am the divorcer; your wishes, if granted, would be wickedness, and I am the ground brought forth this poison. Wonder not, but shun me as the pestilence. I am not to be nearer suffered than the plague, for such I am to you, to you (dear two) the life of my poor life. The reason of all this was love, and your love by this sinful love is crossed. You are, poor souls, deceived and cozened.[7] Turn your affections now to chaste and just desires, for you are (ah that I must say so) brother and sister, children to one man."

They, miserable souls, could not look upon each other, the ground was their highest object, swell and almost burst they did with grief, their senses shut up as in an apoplexy.[8] At last, all rose from the earth, into which they rather would have gone, the old woman to her chamber, where falling into passions her weakness could not sustain, but she with heart afflicted, oppressed with shame and insufferable woe, died, being found in the morning in her bed a pitiful corpse of an afflicted mind. The youth and his sister wept, and sat that night together wringing their hands, as their hearts and souls smarted for this harm. In the morning, for fear of spies, they parted their misery, being to show themselves as careful as before, their honors and the parents lying on it, though their woeful fortunes might have given liberty, which was their

7. Cheated.
8. A type of stroke in which the powers of sense and motion are lost.

greatest prison; liberty they before did covet, now had, is only hated. Sobs and groans were the words they said farewell withal, their eyes so filled with clouds of tears, as if yet pity were had, not to let them see their extremest misery, but through a scarf of love-shed water.

The noise of the lady's death was soon spread abroad the house, coming to the young lord's ears, who with much sorrow, which he dissembled not (his supposed father being absent) took order for her burial, himself soon after went thence privately, like Caunus from Byblis.[9] Yet the comparison holds not clearly, because these lovers were chaste and pure after the secret was disclosed. Wandering about, he happened on this desert, and into a little round place in proportion, like this you came from, where you descended the stairs. She followed him, or fortune whither she would guide her, who was too kind as to bring her to this place where they continued some short space, life not allowing too much sorrow to such unfortunate though worthy creatures, but would, to assist them, lose itself, parting with them, leaving their bodies clear reliques[10] of spotless truth, and crossed affections' malice. They saw each other and bewailed their chance, but to favor each other, came no nearer than through those bushes to behold their woeful selves, as in moonshine glimmering, and as cold. At last, as they had justly at once begun their loves, they justly at one instant died a little before meeting, pity not letting the one outlive the other, or love covetous, would receive both parts at once again into possession, loath to spare any part of such perfection.

The bodies by divine providence kept safe, the woeful prince, father to them, by destiny brought to them, having searched, and all his servants for them. Under a great cypress tree which grew where the stone is now, they lay entwined in each other's arms, dying with as chaste, and in as chaste embracements as they had lived. Her groans of death called him, who had as little life, yet something more strength, finding her end coming, he kissed her hand and dying lips, then tore some of those branches down, honoring again poor Cyparissus,[11] wearing his funeral memory, making two coronets, one for her, another for himself, and so crowned, but most with loyal spotless love, they ended, leaving no stain but misfortune to touch them withal and much honor to be rendered to their loves.

TEXTUAL NOTES

Copy-text: This modernized text is based on a collation of the twenty-nine surviving copies of the 1621 *Urania*. The volume was heavily corrected, with over 1,500 stop-press variants; readings from the uncorrected sheets are listed as *uncor* below. One copy contains Wroth's own handwritten corrections, and

---

9. According to Ovid (*Metamorphoses* IX.446–665), Byblis is in love with her brother Caunus, and when he attempts to flee from her, she pursues him until she collapses and is changed into a spring of water.
10. Relics.
11. Ovid describes how Cyparissus accidentally killed his favorite stag, was overcome by grief, and transformed into a cypress tree (*Metamorphoses* X.120).

these have been incorporated and identified as *author's cor*. In modernizing the author's punctuation, direct speech has been indicated with quotation marks, and paragraphing has been added to distinguish direct from indirect discourse. Wroth's sentences are notoriously difficult to punctuate because of the accumulation of subsidiary clauses and asides. The italicization of all proper names has been removed, and capitalization has been normalized. The spelling has been modernized to distinguish between such forms as then/than, to/too, and of/off; dialect and obsolete words have been retained, but are glossed in the commentary.

"The Tale of the Cephalonian Lovers"
126.24   tilts] *ed.;* tilt *all copies*

"The Throne of Love"
130.33   in these] these *uncor*
131.4   charms] charm *uncor*
131.34   knocked] knocke *uncor*

"The Tale of Veralinda and Leonia"
132.30   no more] no *uncor*
132.39   and] *author's cor; om.* 1621
133.27   Shun] *author's cor; om.* 1621
133.42   represent thy] *author's cor;* report sent my 1621
135.30   shepherdess] *author's cor;* shepheards 1621

"The Tale of Lindamira"
139.7   he cast] *ed.;* she cast
139.12   thus] *ed.;* this

"The Tomb of Love"
140.37   braids] *ed.;* breads
143.25   to | you.] *ed.;* to | yon.
143.26   you did] *ed.;* yon did
143.38   not] *ed.;* no
143.44   your due] *ed.;* your dure

BIBLIOGRAPHY

Editions

Brennan, Michael G., ed. *Lady Mary Wroth's "Love's Victory": The Penshurst Manuscript*. London: Roxburghe Club, 1988.

Cerasano, S. P., and Marion Wynne-Davies, eds. *Renaissance Drama by Women*. New York: Routledge, 1996. [Modernized text of *Love's Victory*].

Hannay, Margaret P. "Lady Mary Wroth." In *Women Writers of the Renaissance and Reformation*. Ed. Katharina M. Wilson. Athens: Univ. of Georgia Press, 1987. 548–65.

Pritchard, R. E., ed. *Lady Mary Wroth: Poems: A Modernized Edition*. Keele: Keele Univ. Press, 1996.

Roberts, Josephine A., ed. *The Poems of Lady Mary Wroth*. Rev. ed. Baton Rouge: Louisiana State Univ. Press, 1992.

——, ed. *The First Part of the Countess of Montgomery's Urania*. Binghamton: Medieval and Renaissance Texts and Studies for the Renaissance English Text Society, 1995.

——, ed. *The Countesse of Mountgomeries Urania*. London: Scolar Press, 1996. [A facsimile of the 1621 edition].

Salzman, Paul, ed. Book 1 of *The Countess of Montgomery's Urania*. In *An Anthology of Seventeenth-Century Fiction*. Oxford: Oxford Univ. Press, 1991. 3–208.

Waller, Gary, ed. *Pamphilia to Amphilanthus by Lady Mary Wroth*. Salzburg: Institut für Englishche Sprache und Literatur, Universität Salzburg, 1977.

Secondary Works

Beilin, Elaine V. "Heroic Virtue: Mary Wroth's *Urania* and *Pamphilia to Amphilanthus*." In *Redeeming Eve: Women Writers of the English Renaissance*. Princeton: Princeton Univ. Press, 1987.

Cavrell, Jennifer. "A Pack of Lies in a Looking Glass: Lady Mary Wroth's *Urania* and the Magic Mirror of Romance." *Studies in English Literature* 34 (1994): 79–107.

Dubrow, Heather. *Echoes of Desire: English Petrarchism and Its Counterdiscourses*. Ithaca: Cornell Univ. Press, 1995.

Hackett, Helen. "'Yet Tell Me Some Such Fiction': Lady Mary Wroth's *Urania* and the 'Femininity' of Romance." In *Women, Texts, and Histories, 1575–1760*. Ed. Clare Brant and Diane Purkiss. London: Routledge, 1992. 39–68.

Hall, Kim F. "'I Rather Would Wish to Be a Black-moor': Beauty, Race, and Rank in Lady Mary Wroth's *Urania*." In *Women, "Race," and Writing in the Early Modern Period*. Ed. Margo Hendricks and Patricia Parker. London: Routledge, 1994. 178–94.

——. *Things of Darkness: Economies of Race and Gender in Early Modern England*. Ithaca: Cornell Univ. Press, 1995.

Hannay, Margaret P. "'O Daughter Heare': Reconstructing the Lives of Aristocratic Englishwomen." In *Attending to Women in Early Modern England*. Ed. Betty S. Travitsky and Adele Seeff. Newark: Univ. of Delaware Press, 1994. 35–63.

Hanson, Ellis. "Sodomy and Kingcraft in *Urania* and *Antony and Cleopatra*." In *Homosexuality in Renaissance and Enlightenment England: Literary Representations in Historical Context*. Ed. Claude J. Summers. New York: Haworth Press, 1992. 235–51. Published simultaneously in *Journal of Homosexuality* 23 (1992).

Jones, Ann Rosalind. "Feminine Pastoral as Heroic Martyrdom: Gaspara Stampa and Mary Wroth." In *The Currency of Eros: Women's Love Lyric in Europe, 1540–1620*. Bloomington: Indiana Univ. Press, 1990.

Krontiris, Tina. *Oppositional Voices: Women as Writers and Translators of Literature in the English Renaissance*. London: Routledge, 1992. 102–40.

Lamb, Mary Ellen. *Gender and Authorship in the Sidney Circle*. Madison: Univ. of Wisconsin Press, 1990.

Lewalski, Barbara K. "Revising Genres and Claiming the Woman's Part: Mary Wroth's Oeuvre." In *Writing Women in Jacobean England*. Cambridge: Harvard Univ. Press, 1993.

MacArthur, Janet. "A *Sydney*, Though Un-Named: Lady Mary Wroth and Her Poetical Progenitors." *English Studies in Canada* 15 (1989): 12–20.

McLaren, Margaret Anne. "An Unknown Continent: Lady Mary Wroth's Forgotten Pastoral Drama, *Love's Victorie*." In *The Renaissance Englishwoman in Print: Counterbalancing the Canon*. Ed. Anne M. Haselkorn and Betty S. Travitsky. Amherst: Univ. of Massachusetts Press, 1990. 295–310.

Miller, Naomi J. *Changing the Subject: Mary Wroth and Figurations of Gender in Early Modern England*. Lexington: Univ. of Kentucky Press, 1996.

———. " 'Not Much to Be Marked': Narrative of the Woman's Part in Lady Mary Wroth's *Urania*." *Studies in English Literature* 29 (1989): 121–37.

———. "Rewriting Lyric Fictions: The Role of the Lady in Mary Wroth's *Pamphilia to Amphilanthus*." In *The Renaissance Englishwoman in Print: Counterbalancing the Canon*. Ed. Anne M. Haselkorn and Betty S. Travitsky. Amherst: Univ. of Massachusetts Press, 1990. 295–310.

———, and Gary F. Waller, eds. *Representing Alternatives: Lady Mary Wroth*. Knoxville: Univ. of Tennessee Press, 1991.

O'Connor, John J. "James Hay and the Countess of Montgomery's *Urania*." *Notes and Queries* 200 (1955): 150–52.

Parry, Graham. "Lady Mary Wroth's *Urania*." *Proceedings of the Leeds Philosophical and Literary Society* 16 (1975): 51–60.

Paulissen, May Nelson. *The Love Sonnets of Lady Mary Wroth: A Critical Introduction*. Salzburg: Institut für Englische Sprache und Literatur, Universität Salzburg, 1982.

Pigeon, Renée. "Manuscript Notations in an Unrecorded Copy of Lady Mary Wroth's *The Countess of Mountgomeries Urania* (1621)." *Notes and Queries* 236 (1991): 81–82.

Quilligan, Maureen. "The Constant Subject: Instability and Female Authority in Wroth's *Urania* Poems." In *Soliciting Interpretation: Literary Theory and Seventeenth-Century English Poetry*. Ed. Elizabeth D. Harvey and Katharine Eisaman Maus. Chicago: Univ. of Chicago Press, 1990. 307–35.

———. "Lady Mary Wroth: Female Authority and the Family Romance." In *Unfolded Tales: Essays on Renaissance Romance*. Ed. George M. Logan and Gordon Teskey. Ithaca: Cornell Univ. Press, 1989. 257–80.

Roberts, Josephine A. "The Biographical Problem of *Pamphilia to Amphilanthus*." *Tulsa Studies in Women's Literature* 1 (1982): 43–53.

———, and James F. Gaines. "The Geography of Love in Seventeenth-Century Women's Fiction." In *Sexuality and Gender in Early Modern Europe: Institutions, Texts, Images*. Ed. James Grantham Turner. Cambridge: Cambridge Univ. Press, 1993. 289–309.

———. "The Huntington Manuscript of Lady Mary Wroth's Play, *Loves Victorie*." *Huntington Library Quarterly* 46 (1983): 56–84.

———. "Labyrinths of Desire: Lady Mary Wroth's Reconstruction of Romance." *Women's Studies* 19 (1991): 183–92.

———. "Lady Mary Wroth." *Dictionary of Literary Biography*. Vol. 121: *Seventeenth-Century Nondramatic Poets*. Ed. M. Thomas Hester. Detroit: Gale Research, 1992. 296–309.

———. "Lady Mary Wroth's *Urania*: A Response to Jacobean Censorship." In *New Ways of Looking at Old Texts: Papers of the Renaissance English Text Society, 1985–1991.* Ed. W. Speed Hill. Binghamton: Medieval and Renaissance Texts and Studies, 1993. 125–29.

———. "Radigund Revisited: Perspectives on Women Rulers in Lady Mary Wroth's *Urania*." In *The Renaissance Englishwoman in Print: Counterbalancing the Canon.* Ed. Anne M. Haselkorn and Betty S. Travitksy. Amherst: Univ. of Massachusetts Press, 1990. 187–207.

Salzman, Paul. "Contemporary References in Mary Wroth's *Urania*." *Review of English Studies* 29 (1978): 178–81.

———. "Talking/Listening: Anecdotal Style in Recent Australian Women's Fiction." *Southerly* 4 (1989): 539–53.

———. "*Urania* and the Tyranny of Love." In *English Prose Fiction, 1558–1700: A Critical History.* Oxford: Clarendon Press, 1985.

Schleiner, Louise. "Parlor Games and Male Self-Imaging as Government: Jonson, Bulstrode, and Ladies Southwell and Wroth" and "Factional Identities and Writers' Energies: Wroth, the Countess of Bedford, and Donne." In *Tudor and Stuart Women Writers.* Bloomington: Indiana Univ. Press, 1994.

Shapiro, Michael. "Lady Mary Wroth Describes a 'Boy Actress.'" *Medieval and Renaissance Drama in England* 4 (1987): 187–94.

Shaver, Anne. "A New Woman of Romance." *Modern Language Studies* 21 (1991): 63–71.

Swift, Carolyn Ruth. "Feminine Identity in Lady Mary Wroth's Romance *Urania*." *English Literary Renaissance* 14 (1984): 328–46.

———. "Feminine Self-Definition in Lady Mary Wroth's *Love's Victorie* (c. 1621)." *English Literary Renaissance* 19 (1989): 171–88.

Wall, Wendy. *The Imprint of Gender: Authorship and Publication in the English Renaissance.* Ithaca: Cornell Univ. Press, 1993.

Waller, Gary. "Mother/Son, Father/Daughter, Brother/Sister, Cousins: The Sidney Family Romance." *Modern Philology* 88 (1991): 401–14.

———. *The Sidney Family Romance: Mary Wroth, William Herbert, and the Early Modern Construction of Gender.* Detroit: Wayne State Univ. Press, 1993.

Wynne-Davies, Marion. "The Queen's Masque: Renaissance Women and the Seventeenth-Century Court Masque." In *Gloriana's Face: Women, Public and Private, in the English Renaissance.* Ed. S. P. Cerasano and Marion Wynne-Davies. Detroit: Wayne State Univ. Press, 1992. 79–104.

Studious She is and all Alone,
Most visitants, when She has none,
Her Library on which She looks
It is her Head her Thoughts her Books.
Scorninge dead Ashes without fire
For her owne Flames doe her Inspire.

Margaret Cavendish, Duchess of Newcastle. Frontispiece portrait
from *Philosophical and Physical Opinions* (1655) by Abraham
van Diepenbeke. Engraved by Peter van Schuppen. (Reproduced
by permission of The Huntington Library, San Marino, California.)

MARGARET CAVENDISH
DUCHESS OF NEWCASTLE
(1623–1673)

INTRODUCTION

Margaret Cavendish was born Margaret Lucas, the eighth and last child of Thomas Lucas of Colchester. Although various accounts suggest that Thomas was a titled aristocrat, he was not. An affluent man, he died two years after Margaret's birth, and her mother, Elizabeth Leighton Lucas, took over control of the family estates. Her mother's ability to move effectively in the male world of farm management left a lasting impression on Margaret. When she was a woman of twenty and a Maid of Honor, Margaret Lucas followed Queen Henrietta Maria into exile in France, even as the royalist forces collapsed during the English civil wars. There Margaret met and married William Cavendish, then marquis of Newcastle and something of a war hero. Newcastle's was a literary family, and several of its women wrote well. What makes Margaret Cavendish unique in the family and gives her a permanent place in the history of English literature is that so many of her books were published not just with her consent, but with her active involvement in the process of publication. From the date of her first volume of poetry in 1653 until her death in 1673, fourteen separate titles in twenty-two editions came into print.

Margaret Cavendish was an eccentric, partly in craft and partly in actuality. Undoubtedly she enjoyed the attention her peculiarities of dress and of behavior drew. Dorothy Osborne, a contemporary, felt Cavendish belonged in Bedlam but actively tried to obtain a copy of the poems of this "mad woman." Cavendish, in short, was not just an author but a phenomenon, who caused a great stir as her coach drove though Hyde Park for the May Day celebration of 1667. Samuel Pepys, the famous diarist, spent most of that day trying to catch a glimpse of her. In the same year, she paid a call on the Royal Society in grand style, the first woman to visit this venerable bastion of scientific thought.

She published fiction, drama, poetry, essays on science, an autobiography, and a biography. Her scientific writing, interwoven with the curious "virtuoso" ideas of her day, poses difficulties for modern readers. Her plays are often enjoyable, although they were thought by many later historians of the drama to be too racy. Most interesting today are her letters, largely written not as actual letters to real people, but as imaginary correspondence between two fictional women. In these letters, she probes deeply into contemporary social institutions and explores the difficulties of marriage in particular. What, for instance, happens when a man marries a kitchen wench? Why might he choose a partner of another social station? Can it be a good marriage? What about adultery and the keeping of mistresses? The answers Cavendish provides to questions like these are almost always surprising and frequently have about them the ring of truth. Other letters discuss literature, as with her defense of Shakespeare's lower-class and low-life characters. Restoration critics disliked what they saw as Shakespeare's lack of refinement, and characters who displayed such behavior were often eliminated from actual stage productions. Cavendish is witty, arch, ironic, and fun. Above all, she is not easy to pin down. One should should never underestimate the "mad" duchess and never assume that a naive narrator is the author herself.

In recent years, Cavendish's reputation has gained in stature, with special interest directed to her science fiction novel *The Blazing World* and to *The Convent of Pleasure,* a play with scenes important for those who study cross-dressing and the theory of gender. She remains one of the most vividly memorable women writers of the century.

FROM *CCXI SOCIABLE LETTERS* (1664)

Prefatory Letter from Cavendish to Her Husband

My Lord,

It may be said to me, as one said to a lady, "Work lady, work.[1] Let writing books alone, for surely wiser women ne'r writ one." But your Lordship never bid me to work, nor leave writing, except when you would persuade me to spare so much time from my study as to take the air for my health. The truth is, my Lord, I cannot work. I mean such works as ladies use to pass their time withal, and, if I could, the materials of such works would cost more than the work would be worth, besides all the time and pains bestow'd upon it. You may ask me, what works I mean. I answer, "Needle-works, spinning-works, preserving-works, as also baking and cooking-works, as making cakes, pies, puddings, and the like, all which I am ignorant of." And as I am ignorant in these employments, so I am ignorant in gaming, dancing, and revelling. But yet, I must ask you leave to say that I am not a dunce in all employments, for I understand the keeping of sheep and ordering of a grange indifferently well, although I do not busy myself much with it by reason my scribbling takes away the most part of my time.[2] Perchance some may say that if my understanding be most of sheep and a grange it is a beastly understanding. My answer is, "I wish men were as harmless as most beasts are." Then surely the world would be more quiet and happy than it is, for then there would not be such pride, vanity, ambition, covetousness, faction, treachery, and treason, as is now. Indeed one might very well say in his prayers to God, "O Lord God, I beseech thee of thy infinite mercy, make man so and order his mind, thoughts, passions, and appetites like beasts that they may be temperate, socia-

---

1. "Work lady, work," alludes to lines in a poem by Lord Denny that attack Lady Mary Wroth. Because Wroth was a woman and a writer, he said that she was a "hermaphrodite."
2. Cavendish actually did concern herself with farm management, and she was especially good at spotting dishonest stewards. She may have learned early from her mother, who "was very skillful in leases, and in setting of lands [planting], and court [farmyard] keeping, ordering of stewards, and the like affairs."

ble, laborious, patient, prudent, provident, brotherly-loving, and neighborly-kind, all which beasts are, but most men not." But leaving most men to beasts, I return to your Lordship, who is one of the best of men, whom God hath fill'd with heroic fortitude, noble generosity, poetical wit, moral honesty, natural love, neighborly-kindness, great patience, loyal duty, and celestial piety. And I pray God as zealously and earnestly to bless you with perfect health and long life, as becomes,

Your Lordship's

honest wife and

humble servant,

M. Newcastle.

Letter 4

Madam,

The other day was here the Lady J.O. to see me and her three daughters, which are called the three graces. The one is black, the other brown, the third white, all three different colored beauties.[3] Also they are of different features, statures, and shapes, yet all three so equally handsome that neither judgment nor reason can prefer one before another. Also their behaviors are different. The one is majestical, the other gay and airy, the third meek and bashful; yet all three graceful, sweet, and becoming. Also their wits are different. The one propounds well, the other argues well, the third resolves well, all which make a harmony in discourse. These three ladies are resolved never to marry, which makes many sad lovers. But whilst they were here, in comes the Lord S.C. and discoursing with them at last he asks them whether they were seriously resolved never to marry. They answered, they were resolved never to marry. "But, ladies," said he, "consider, time wears out youth and fades beauty, and then you will not be the three young fair graces." "You say true, my lord," answered one of them, "but when we leave to be the young fair graces, we shall then be the old wise sibyls." By this answer you may perceive that, when our sex cannot pretend to be fair, they will pretend to be wise. But it matters not what we pretend to, if we be really virtuous, which I wish all our sex may be, and rest,

Madam,

Your very faithful friend

and servant.

Letter 5

Madam,

In my opinion the marriage between Sir A.G. and Mrs. F.S. is no ways agreeable, wherefore not probable to be blessed with a happy union

---

3. "Black": "brunette." In this letter Cavendish anticipates Mary Astell by suggesting that women need not marry.

though she is likelier to be the happier of the two. For 'tis better to have an old doting fool than a wanton young filly. But he will be very unhappy through jealousy, what with his dotage and her freedom, which will be like fire and oil to set his mind on a flame and burn out the lamp of his life. Truly I did wonder when I heard they were married, knowing her nature and his humor, for she loves young masculine company, and he loves only a young female companion. So that he cannot enjoy her to himself unless she bar herself from all other men for his sake, which I believe she will not do. For she will not bury her beauty, nor put her wit to silence for the sake of her husband. For if I be not mistaken, she will love a young servant better than an old husband. Nay, if her husband were young, she would prefer variety of servants before a single husband insomuch that if she had been made when there was but one man, as Adam, she would have done like her grandmother Eve, as to have been courted by the devil and would betray her husband for the devil's sake rather than want a lover. But leaving the discourse of jealousy, age, courtship, and devils, I rest,

Madam,

Your very faithful Fr. and S.

Letter 30

Madam,

Yesterday being not in the humor of writing, I took *Plutarch's Lives* or as some call them Plutarch's lies. But lives or lies or a mixture of both, I read part of the day in that book, and it was my chance to read the life of Pericles the Athenian in which story he is commended for his gravity, government, and wisdom. This Pericles I did much admire all the time I read of him until I did read where it was mentioned of his marrying Aspasia, a famous courtesan, and then I did not think him so wise a man as I did before, in that he could not rule his passion better but to marry a whore.[4] Neither doth gravity and wantonness suit well together, for to my imagination a grave cuckold doth appear most ridiculous. And although she was constant to him, yet the lewdness of her former life could not but be a great blemish to him as to marry the dregs and leavings of other men. But it seemed that she had an attractive power especially on such as they call wise men, as statesmen, philosophers, and governors, and all this power lay in her tongue, which was a bawd for the other end. Nay, so well (it is said) she could speak, that not only such men as forementioned did come to hear her and to learn to speak eloquently by her, but many also brought their wives to hear her, which in my opinion was dangerous, lest they might learn her vice with her rhetoric. But it seems the Grecians were not like the Italians

---

4. The story of Aspasia told here draws from North's translation of Plutarch. Cavendish often found parallels between mistresses and courtesans, and many mistresses, as was the case with Nell Gwyn, had significant social standing as well as power.

concerning their wives, although they were like them concerning their courtesans.[5] But honest women take not so much care to speak well as to do that which is virtuous. And so leaving Aspasia and Pericles in Plutarch's history, I rest,

Madam,

Your faithful friend
and servant.

Letter 32

Madam,

Sir D.D. and his lady had invited a great many of their friends to a feasting dinner, and being set they fell to eating and soon after to talking, for talking accompanies eating and drinking, especially at a feast. But amongst other discourses, they were speaking of marriage, husbands and wives, where Sir D.D. said somewhat that his wife had great reason to take unkindly, knowing her virtue had deserved more loving expressions from him, especially in an open assembly. Which unkindness forced tears through her eyes, but they were becoming tears for they did not cause the feature[s] in her face to be distorted. For she appeared in her countenance sweet and amiable, as if there had been no discontent in her mind. Neither did she show any discontent in her words or behavior, for she neither complained, nor railed at her husband, nor quarreled with him, nor rose from the table in a passion to the disturbance of the company, as most women would have done and often do when they are displeased or angered. But she wiped the tears from her eyes and addrest herself as she did before to entertain her friends civilly and courteously, and when they had all dined and the cloth taken away, she asked pardon of her friends for her tears, saying her tears had made their meeting appear rather as a funeral condoling than a merry feasting. "But truly," said she, "I could not help it, for they would not be restrained, do what I could, for some words my husband spoke caused a storm of grief in my mind which raised up billows of tears that overflowed my eyes. Yet," said she, "the dearest and lovingest friends will both take and give cause of exception sometimes, for not any man or woman is so perfect as not to err." And thus her discretion did not suffer her passion to disturb her guests, and her good nature did excuse her husband's folly, and her love did forgive his disrespect to her. But the Lady C.C. did not behave herself so, for her husband, Sir G.C., and she had invited many of their friends to a feasting dinner, and she, as the mistress to order all affairs belonging to a wife, took upon her to order the feast. And being a mode-lady, would have a mode-feast.[6] But the cook, knowing his master loved roast beef, sent in a chine of roast beef to the table, and when her guests were all

---

5. A number of Italian courtesans were highly respected women of letters, most notably Veronica Franco.
6. "mode": "modish" or "trendy."

set and beginning to eat, she spied the chine of beef, whereat she was very angry to have as she thought her feast disgraced with an old English fashion and not only an old but a country fashion to have beef served to their table. Wherefore she, to show herself a courtier rather than a country lady, commanded one of the waiters to take the beef from the table. Sir G.C., her husband, desired not to have it taken away for, said he, "I love beef better than any other meat," but she to express she had a lady's nice stomach or rather a nice lady's stomach[7] said the beef was fulsome to her eyes and made her stomach sick to see it. Her husband bad her to look upon some of the other meat, and to give him leave to eat of what he liked. But she would not agree to that, for, said she, the very smell was offensive to her, and therefore she would have it taken away. He said it should not be taken away until he had eaten as much as he would. But in fine, their words multiplied and gathered together in an outrageous tumult, raised their voices into an uproar, and then from words they went to blows, flinging whatsoever came next to hand at one another's head. Their guests, being in danger to be hurt, rose from the table, and Sir G.C. and his lady rose also and went to cuffs. But their friends did soon part them, and the lady went crying into her chamber and was sick because she had not her will. At least, feigned herself sick. As for their guests, they were rather invited to fast than to feast as it fell out, for all the fine quelquechose was spoiled and overthrown in the hurly-burly,[8] but the beef was so substantial and solid as it strongly kept its place on which the guests might have fed. But fright, noise and disorder had taken away their appetite to eating. Thus, madam, I have related these feasts and entertainings to let you know the different humors and behaviors of these two ladies, the one having cause to be angry did patiently and discreetly pass over her injury, appearing celestial. The other out of a vain humor fell into a raging passion. The truth is she showed herself a fool and behaved herself as mad. But leaving the angelic lady to be a pattern to her sex, I rest,

    Madam,

Your faithful Fr. & S.

Letter 34

Madam,
You were pleased to express to me in your last letter that you have been in the country to see the Lady M.L., who seems melancholy since she was married—which is a sign she is not pleased with the condition of

---

7. Cavendish puns on two meanings of "nice": "dainty" and "foolish."
8. "quelquechose": French for "something." Cavendish suggests that the wife is overly fond of French cooking. "Hurly-burly": tumult or uproar.

her life.[9] I believe one of the causes of her melancholy is that she is in the country, wherein is little resort, especially of courting gallants. For most women love variety of company and much company, even married wives as well as maids. Neither do all widows shun company. As for maids, they have an excuse to get them husbands, and widows are at liberty to make a second, third, or fourth choice, when their husbands are dead, but wives have no excuse for the company of courting servants[10] and merry meetings, but only the spleen,[11] which nothing can cure but company and jollity to divert melancholy and to remove the splenetic obstructions and crude vapors. For which, dancing, feasting, gaming, and the like is the best cure, *probatum est*.[12] Whereas the lone company of a husband is so far from working any cure as it is many times the cause of the disease. But if her melancholy proceed from want of variety of company, I pity both her husband and attendants, for most commonly a peevish frowardness[13] doth attend that melancholy. They will quarrel with everything and not be pleased with any, take exceptions at every word, complain of being sick, but know not where their pains are even as weary of themselves, which makes their husbands many times weary of them. And to divert the grief of their wives' troubles, they solace with their wives' maids, who are more pleasant company being not troubled with the spleen as not having a husband. Nay, when they do marry, their minds are so employed about getting a livelihood as they have not time to think of their spleens. Besides, they are forced to labor and work for their living, which keeps them from such obstructions or disease. And the spleen is a disease which is only amongst the noble and rich, whose wealth makes them idle, and their idleness begets an appetite to variety of diets, clothes, and company, whereas poor, laborious people know not such disease. But leaving this theme, give me leave to welcome you out of the country and to acquaint you that I will shortly personally wait upon you as is the duty of,
Madam,

Your faithful friend.

Letter 35

Madam,
Sir W.C.'s wife you know hath a conversable and ingenious wit, yet not being very handsome her husband hath got him a mistress, who is very

9. The story of M.L. involves self-parody, for Cavendish was M.L., or Margaret Lucas, prior to her marriage. She lived in the country after the Restoration, and she writes elsewhere of suffering from melancholy. For more on M.L., see letter 113.
10. A "servant" was a man who paid amorous attention to his "mistress." Sometimes such attentions were platonic and sometimes not.
11. Victims of spleen were unpleasant to be around: the condition was related to melancholia. See Aphra Behn's "The Spleen," in this anthology.
12. "It is proven." Cavendish is having fun by ironically invoking the Latin of formal debate.
13. *Froward* meant "perverse" and was often used to describe women who would not subordinate themselves to men.

beautiful and handsome, but yet she is a fool. A friend of his asked him why he chose a fool for his mistress. He said he did not court her for her wit but for her beauty. "For," said he, "now I have a mistress for delight and a wife for conversation. I have a mistress to look on and admire and a wife to listen to and discourse with and both to embrace at my pleasure." "But," said his friend, "if your wife should come to know you have a mistress, you will not take much pleasure in her conversation, unless you account mourning complaints of or to you, exclamations and curses against you, cross speeches, opposite actions, and hideous noise to be conversable and delightful. For the truth is," said he, "your wife's words will be so salt, sharp, and bitter as they will corrode your mind, leaven your thoughts, and make your life unpleasant." "My wife," said Sir W.C., "shall not know I have a mistress." His friend replied, "Your often absence will betray you, or else some other will tell her, for adultery is like murder. It seldom escapes finding out." And since that time Sir W.C.'s lady hath heard of her husband's mistress. But she seems not to be angry at it, but talks of it with great patience, saying that if her husband takes pleasure in variety he will be more delighted with her wit than with his mistress's beauty and will sooner be tired with gazing on one object than in hearing divers discourses and diversions of wit, sense, reason, judgment, fancy, and speech. "Besides," said she, "wit attracts the mind more to love than beauty to admiration. And if my husband loves me best," said she, "I am well content he should admire her beauty most, as also to embrace her as much as he pleases, for I am so delighted and wedded to my own wit that I regard not my husband's amours nor embracings. For wit is spiritual and not corporeal. It lives with the mind and not with the body, being not subject to the gross senses. For though wit," said she, "may be known by words and actions, yet those are but the pictures of wit's works, not wit itself. For that cannot be drawn. It is beyond all drafts. And so much difference," said she, "is between my husband's mistress and his wife as a picture and an invisible spirit, which spirit can both help and hurt, delight and terrify, damn and glorify. But howsoever," said she, "my wit shall not be my husband's evil spirit neither to reproach him nor to disgrace, reprove, delude, or anger him. But it shall be always ready to defend, commend, inform, delight, and, if it could, to reform him. But I believe," said she, "that is past the power of my wit, for it is a hard matter to restrain nature from liberty especially of the appetites. For the passions of the mind are more easily governed than the appetites of the body. For they are sensual and brutal, wherefore time is a better reformer of the appetites than reason." But, madam, this is to let you know the Lady W.C.'s wit, discretion, and temper, which is more than most of our sex hath. And so leaving her to her wit, and her husband to reformation, and his mistress's beauty to time, I rest,

Madam,

Your most faithful
friend and servant.

Letter 36

Madam,

You were pleased in your last Letter to express how Mr. P.C. is persecuted by another man's whore, which is not usual. For though many men are persecuted by their own whores both in body, mind, course of life, and estate, diseasing the one, vexing the other, opposing the third, and spending the fourth, yet not usually by any other man's but their own, at least believing them to be only theirs. But I believe Mr. P.C. will not easily clear himself from her, for courtesans are often assisted by the powerful.[14] Insomuch as in any law suit or petitioning request, they shall be heard and their suit granted although against all law or right. Such power and favor hath concupiscence, as to corrupt magistrates, bribe judges, fee lawyers, flatter courtiers, and the truth is entice, allure, and persuade most of mankind. But although there be in all ages and nations, courtesans, and men liable to be tempted, yet men have not been frequently tempted, persuaded, or allured to marry courtesans unless in this age, wherein courtesans are so prevalent and fortunate as they do not only get themselves husbands when beauty and lovers begin to leave them, but marry more richly and honorably for dignities than honest, chaste widows or pure and innocent virgins. Which is apt to make honest and chaste women to doubt, their honesty and chastity is not blest with such good fortune as dishonesty is. Insomuch as those that are not honest merely and for no other end than for honesty's sake may be corrupted through hopes of good fortune. But where virtue takes a thorough possession, it never leaves the habitation. Yet many that have been base, wicked, and of beastly lives may be reformed, so as to become very honest, worthy, and pure. And such reclaimed persons ought to be esteemed and respected, for I am not of Mrs. F.R.'s humor, who hates a reformado. But some men are of that humor as they hate honest, chaste women not only out of a despair of their enjoyments, but that they love the company and conversation of wanton and free women. Insomuch that a courtesan shall have a greater and stronger power to cause and persuade men to do actions not only to the ruin of their estates and families, but to the ruin of their honors and reputation, nay, to make them unnatural, extravagant or base, than an honest, chaste wife hath to persuade her husband to keep his estate, honor, or honesty. For many a worthy and honorable person hath degenerated from his birth and breeding, from his natural courage and generosity, from his loyalty and duty, from his natural affection and sacred vows, from his honor and reputation through the persuasion of whores. Nay, many men love a whore so much more than an honest and chaste woman as many make better husbands and are more fond and kinder to their wives if they be libertines than if they were honest and true to their marriage bed. But leaving such men to their own heads, and their wives to their neighbors' beds, I rest,

14. See note 4 above on the power of courtesans and mistresses.

Madam,

Your faithful friend
and servant.

Letter 39

Madam,

I may give the Lady F.L. joy of her second marriage, for I hear she is married again. But I fear it will be applied to her what is said of another lady who married first very well for title and wealth, her husband being in years but she very poor. And amongst much company it was told she seemed to be a crafty, witty woman that she could get such an husband. "No," said one man, "it was not the wit or craft of the lady that got her such a husband, but the folly of the man that married such a wife." And after he died and left her very rich, she married a young man that had no estate, and then they said that it seemed her second husband was a wise man that he could get so rich a wife. "No," said the former man, "it was not the wisdom of the man but the folly of the woman that caused that match." So she was even with her first husband in folly, for he played the fool to marry her, and she played the fool to marry her second husband. Thus most of the world of mankind is mistaken, for what they attribute to some men's wit is other men's folly. But for marriages, the truth is that folly makes more marriages than prudence. As for example, Mr. A.B. hath married a common courtesan. If she had been particular, it had been more excusable. But all men are not so foolish, for I hear that Sir W.S. will rather endure the persecution of his own courtesan than marry her. But leaving the Lady F.L. to her new husband, and Mr. A.B. to his new wife, and Sir W.S. to his pursuing whore, I rest,

Madam,

Your most faithful
friend and servant.

Letter 42

Madam,

I am sorry Sir F.O. hath undervalued himself so much below his birth and wealth as to marry his kitchen maid, but it was a sign he had an hungry appetite, or that he lived a solitary life seeing no better company or conversed not with women of quality.[15] Or else he hath been too privately kind and was loath to have it publicly known, or he hath tried her virtue and so married her for chastity, though many women will

---

15. Perhaps the best-known event of this nature to take place during the Restoration involved George Monck, duke of Albemarle, who married a "vociferous" laundress named Nan Clarges (George deF. Lord, *Poems on Affairs of State*, xvii).

deny some and grant to others. Or else he married her for beauty or wit or both, although the inferior or meaner sort of people, especially women, are oftener owners of beauty than wit. And if they have some wit, it is only sharp replies, which are a kind of a scolding. And I have heard that the way or manner of courtship amongst the inferior sort of people in E. is scolding. They scold themselves into matrimony, or at least make love[16] in a rough, rude style. But perchance Sir F.O. married his kitchen maid in hopes she would make a nimble and obedient wife, which he might fear one of equal birth would not be. Indeed he hath chosen one out of the humblest offices or household employments, for the kitchen for the most part is the lowest room in a house. Yet I write not this as believing he may not be happy in his choice, for 'tis likely the match may be more happy than honorable, and if he thinks it no disgrace or cares not for disgrace all is well, for it only concerns himself, as having no parents living to grieve or anger, nor no former children to suffer by. But though her office and birth were both dripping or basting, yet his dignity and wealth hath made her a gay lady. And so leaving him to his dish of brewess,[17] I rest,

Madam,

Your faithful friend
and servant.

Letter 46

Madam,

I have observed that in all combustions and wars those get more favor and profit that enter into them latest, for those that are at the beginning for the most part are losers, either in lives or estates or both, and are least favored by those they fight or adventure for.[18] Nay, most commonly they are disfavored. Wherefore, if honor and honesty would give leave, were I a man, I would not enter until the last course, for that is sweetest like a banquet. But because honor and honesty would exclaim against me for preferring profit and promotion before them, therefore a man ought to do his endeavor in a just cause for honor and honesty's sake, although he were sure to lose his liberty, estate, or life. But leaving war, loss, disfavor and preferment to worthy persons and unjust states and princes, I rest,

Madam,

Your faithful friend
and servant.

16. "make love": court or woo.
17. His "dish of brewess" recalls *Antony and Cleopatra*, where Cleopatra is Antony's "Egyptian dish" (II.vi.126). Brewess (brewis) is bread soaked in boiling fat that drips from meat.
18. William Cavendish was an important commander in the early parts of the English civil wars. His army was decimated at the battle of Marston Moor, and he fled to the Continent. After the Restoration, he expected to be rewarded for his heroism and to be compensated for his losses, but he met instead with promises and delays. Margaret Cavendish was understandably bitter about the shabby treatment he received from Charles II.

Letter 47

Madam,

The other day the Lady S.M. was to visit me, and I gave her joy. She said she should have joy indeed if it were a son. I said I bid her joy of her marriage, for I had not seen her since she was a wife and had been married, which was some four weeks ago, wherefore I did not know she was with child.[19] But she rasping wind out of her stomach, as childing women usually do, making sickly faces to express a sickly stomach, and fetching her breath short, and bearing out her body, drawing her neck downward, and standing in a weak and faint posture, as great bellied wives do bearing a heavy burden in them, told me she had been with child a fortnight, though by her behavior one would not have thought she had above a week to go or to reckon. But she is so pleased with the belief she is with child (for I think she cannot perfectly know herself, at most it is but breeding child)[20] as she makes or believes herself bigger than she appears and says she longs for every meat that is difficult to be gotten and eats and drinks from morning till night with very little intermission and sometimes in the night. Whereupon I told her if she did so, I believed she would be bigger bellied and greater bodied whether she were with child or not. Besides eating so much would make her sick if she were not with child. She answered that women with child might eat anything and as much as they would or could and it would do them no harm. But I have observed, that generally women take more pleasure when they are with child than when they are not with child, not only in eating more and feeding more luxuriously, but taking a pride in their great bellies, although it be a natural effect of a natural cause. For like as women take a greater pride in their beauty than pleasure or content in their virtue, so they take more pride in being with child than in having a child, for when they are brought to bed and up from their lying in, they seem nothing so well pleased nor so proud as when they were great with child. And to prove they are prouder and take more pleasure in being with child and in lying in than in having a child is their care, pains, and cost in getting, making, and buying fine and costly childbed linen, swaddling clothes, mantles, and the like. As also fine beds, cradles, baskets, and other furniture for their chambers, as hangings, cabinets, plates, artificial flowers, looking-glasses, screens, and many such like things of great cost and charge, besides their banquets of sweet meats and other junkets, as cakes, wafers, biscuits, jellies, and the like as also such strong drinks, as methinks the very smell should put a childbed wife

---

19. Cavendish was childless. A few years years after their marriage, her husband arranged for her to meet with the fashionable physician Sir Theodore Mayerne, who argued that she was better off not trying to bear children, since her health was poor. Her husband ignored this advice and instead acquired a "Receipt for the Sterillitie" from another physician, Richard Farrer. Cavendish felt no responsibility to have children, since her husband already had several offspring.
20. In an odd usage, "breeding" here seems to mean "trying to conceive."

into a fever, as hippocras[21] and burnt wine, with hot spices, mulled sack, strong and high-colored ale, well spiced, and stuffed with toasts of cake, and the like, all which is more chargeable than to bring up a child when it is born. Nay, they will rather want portions for their children when they are grown to be men or women or want sufficiency of means to pay for their learning and education than want these extravagancies of luxury and vanity at their birth. And their children being christened are like some brides and bridegrooms that are so fine on their wedding day as they are forced to go in rags all their lives after, which methinks is very strange that for the vanity and show of one day they will spend so much as to be beggars all their lives after. But, as I said, this proves that women take a greater pride and pleasure in being with child than in having children well bred and well bestowed or maintained when grown to years. And that which makes me wonder more is that wise men will suffer their foolish wives to be so foolishly and imprudently expensive. Wherefore such men are worthy to be impoverished that will suffer their wives to be so vain. For it shows them to be better husbands than fathers, kinder to their wives than careful of their children. Also it shows them fonder husbands than loving children, because they ruin their forefathers' posterity by impoverishing their own succession and that only to please their wives' humors and to expend for their wives' vanities. But leaving the Lady S.M. to her breeding pride or pride of breeding, to her sick pleasure or pleasurable sickness, to her luxurious feeding and vain providing, and wishing her a good gossiping, I rest,

Madam,

Your faithful friend
and servant.

Letter 54

Madam,

The other day the Lady D.C. and the Lady G.B. came to visit me, and being both met together as visitants, they fell into a discourse of history and so of former times and persons of both sexes. At last they fell into a discourse of married wives giving their opinions of good and bad wives that had lived in former ages, and the Lady D.C. said that Lucretia[22] was the best wife that ever history mentioned in that she killed herself to save her husband's honor, being a dishonor for a husband to have an abused, as a ravished wife. For though her husband was not a cuckold through her free consent, yet was he a cuckold through her enforcement, which was a dishonor in the second degree. The Lady G.B. said that though she did believe Lucretia was a very chaste woman and a

21. Hippocras was a cordial.
22. The Roman historian Livy describes how Lucretia, after being raped by Sextus Tarquinius, summoned her husband and her father to exact an oath of vengeance and then stabbed herself to death.

virtuous and loving wife, yet whether she killed herself to save her husband's honor or her own, she could not judge unless she had the effect of a god to know the minds and thoughts of human creatures.[23] For perchance Lucretia might know or verily believe that when her husband should come to know the dishonorable abuse that was done unto her, he would have killed her himself, not so much through a jealous mistrust of her, but for the dishonor or disgrace of the abuse. And if so, then the cause of Lucretia's killing herself was as much through prudence and wisdom as through virtue, for in killing herself she gained an immortal fame. For by dying by her own hand she seemed innocent, whereas had she died by her husband's hand or command the world being censorious would have thought her a criminal. Wherefore since Lucretia must die, she chose the best way, to die by her own voluntary act. "But had Lucretia been unmarried," said she, "and had been so abused, she had been a fool to have killed herself before she had endeavored to have killed her abuser. For it would be more justice to have killed the murderer of her honor than to have murdered her innocent self, only the revenge ought in honor to have been executed in some public place and assembly, and then the private abuse declared, if it had not been known already." But these two ladies arguing whether Lucretia killed herself for her husband's honor or for her own at last grew so earnest in their discourse as they fell to quarrel with each other, and in such a fury they were as they were ready to beat one another. Nay, I was afraid they would have killed each other, and for fear of that mischief I was forced to be a defender of both, standing between them and making orations to the one and then to the other. At last I intreated them to temper their passions and to allay their anger. "And give me leave ladies," said I, "to ask you what Lucretia was to either of you? Was she of your acquaintance or kindred or friend or neighbor or nation? And if she was none of these, as it was very probable she was not, living and dying in an age so long afore this, nay, so long as the truth might rationally be questioned, if not of the person, yet of the manner of the action, for perchance the clear truth was never recorded, falsehood having been written in histories of much later times than that of Lucretia. Therefore allay your passions. For why should you two ladies fall out and become enemies for Lucretia's sake whom you never knew or heard of, but as in an old wife's tale which is an old history. But howsoever, good ladies," said I, "leave Lucretia to live and die in history and be you two friends in present life. Abuse not yourselves with rage concerning Tarquin's abusing Lucretia with lust." Thus talking to them, at last I calmed their passions and made them friends again. But making peace between them, I spent more breath and spirits than the peace of two foolish, at least choleric, ladies was worth, for although

---

23. In *The Worlds Olio*, Cavendish says Lucretia is praiseworthy, but the husband is to blame for her rape. Elsewhere in *Sociable Letters*, Cavendish alters the usual interpretations of various stories of virtue in classical women. Portia is foolish to commit suicide, and Penelope enjoyed the flattery of the suitors.

there is an old saying, "Happy is the peacemaker," yet I am happy I am quit at this present of their company, and that I can subscribe myself,
Madam,

Your faithful friend
and servant.

Letter 56

Madam,

In your last letter, you writ how much the Lord N.O. doth admire Mrs. B.U. and what addresses he makes to her, for he being in years hath seen much of the world and many and different beauties, and hath conversed with many and different wits, and hath found and observed many and different humors, and hath made many and different courtships to many and different women. Yet I have observed that men in years would seem lovers and admirers but are not. And young men are lovers and admirers and would not seem so. Men in years praise all the young women they meet withal but think not of them when they are out of their companies, but young men praise some particulars and when absent are more fond and deeper in love than when they are personally present. And it is to be observed that the chiefest employment of the most part of men is to make love, not that they are really in love, but feignedly make themselves so. And amorous courtships are the most general actions in the world and the most general employments of the thoughts in men's minds. And the same is also amongst women. So that most of mankind are amorous lovers, for love is the subject of their thoughts and courtly addresses the action of their time and the chief business of their lives. But if it were a noble love, it were commendable, for then their time, industry, and actions of their lives would be employed in acts of charity, friendship, humanity, magnificence, generosity, and the like, but being amorous lovers their time is idly wasted in adorning, fashioning, flattering, protesting and forswearing. Besides, amorous lovers are inconstant, prodigal, fantastical, and the like. But leaving them to their complimental addresses, I rest,
Madam,

Your faithful friend
and Servant.

Letter 68

Madam,

I am sorry that Sir C.A. is killed and as sorry that V.A. hath killed him, for by report they were both worthy and right honorable persons, which causes me to wonder how such two persons could fall out.[24] For

24. This letter may contain a fictionalized retelling of an actual incident. In 1652, William Cavendish was asked by Edward Hyde to stop a duel between Aubrey de Vere, the earl of Oxford, and a Colonel Slinger (*HMC* Portland, 2:140.). V.A. works well as an anagram for Aubrey de Vere, and C. could stand for "Colonel." Unfortunately, there is no evidence to link Slinger with the letter *a*. The two were dissuaded from the duel, and nobody was killed.

surely they were such men as would be as unwilling to give an offense as to take an affront, and if the offence was unwillingly given as by chance they being men of honor and merit would not be grieved, at least not angry at or for it. But many times a third man will make a quarrel betwixt two others and leave them to fight it out. You may say that sometimes quarrels cannot be avoided, although they be betwixt two noble persons, as for example two dukes about the preeminence of place, none knowing which of them had the first place, and neither yielding must needs fight to decide it. But such cases are not often put to the trial or ought not to be, for heralds are for that purpose judges. But these two noble persons which you mentioned in your last letter, whatsoever their quarrel was, the one is killed, the other banished. And now to speak of such quarrels as generally cause duels between private persons, they are either about words, or women, or hawks, or dogs, or whores, or about cards or dice, or such frivolous, idle, or base causes. I do not say all quarrels but most, for some are more honorable. But of all sorts or causes of quarrels, drunken quarrels are the most senseless. As for the manner or fashion of fighting, duels in my opinion are not proper, for in this age in most nations they fight private duels somewhat after the manner of a public battle, as three against three, or at least two against two. Also they fight with pistols and swords with their doublets on, which serves instead of an armor and for the most part a horseback. First, they shoot off their pistols at each other, and then they come to the sword if they be not shot dead before their time comes to fight. For shooting is not a direct fighting because they must stand at some distance to take aim, which in my opinion appears cowardly to pelt at each other, as if they were afraid to come near each other. Besides, a child may have so much skill and courage as to shoot off a pistol and may chance to kill a man, but a child cannot tell how to use a sword or manage a horse. Also a peasant or such mean bred persons can shoot off pistols or carbines or muskets, but they have no skill to use a sword, nor know not how to manage an horse, unless a cart horse and that better in a cart than when astride. 'Tis true, peasants or common soldiers will fight with force and fury like as beasts and kill their enemy with mere strength but not with pure valor, for they fight as in an uproar and will knock one another down with their staves or butt ends of their muskets, which is more a club or clown-fighting.[25] And if they have swords, they fight with the pummel, not with the point, for they know not how to use it. Neither is it fit they should, wherefore the gentlemen are too strong for them, for the gentleman's point of his sword hath the advantage of the clown's club. And the only grief to gallant, valiant gentlemen in the day of battle or duel is the fear they should be killed with a bullet, against which they can show no active

---

25. "Clown": an uneducated rustic. Although Cavendish may seem to have little sympathy for the lower classes, she defends their depiction in the plays of Shakespeare. See letter 123.

valor or well-bred skill. The last observation concerning fighting duels in this age is in choosing of seconds. And the right use of seconds in all ages that I have heard of, unless these later, is to be overseers, witnesses and judges, wherefore they ought to be upright, honest, judicious, and skillful men and worthy and honorable persons, for they are to judge whether their quarrel requires blood and may not be passed over without dishonor. Also they are to see that each man may be equally armed and that there be no untimely advantages taken of each other. Also they are to help or assist them when they are wounded, as to bind up their wounds, and they are to witness to the world how they fought. But in this age, the seconds are so far from being judges, overseers, witnesses, or helpful friends, as they become duellers themselves, fighting for company, not for injury or wrong done to each other, and for fashion's sake, which is an unjust, irrational, inhuman, and wicked fashion or practice. Neither is it manly or noble, but base and beastly, as to fight without reason or injury, wherefore pistols and fighting seconds ought not to be. But, madam, if any should read this letter besides yourself, I should be found fault with, it being not fit nor proper for a woman to discourse or write of duels or wars, nor of horses or swords or the like. But pray if you hear any say so, tell him, that I have a greater privilege than other women in this discourse, for my husband hath been a general of an army of 30,000 men and hath fought battles. Also he is master of those two arts, the use of the sword and the manage of the horse, as there is not any man, nor hath never been, so well known, skillful and practiced as he, so that he is the best horseman and swordman in the world.[26] Also two of my three brothers were soldiers or commanders in war and well experienced in that profession. And my father was a swordman, who was banished for a time for killing a gentleman in a duel of honor.[27] Thus have I been born, bred, lived, and married, all with swordmen and to my greater honor all valiant men. And so leaving this discourse, I rest,

Madam,

Your faithful Fr. and S.

Letter 113

Madam,

In your last letter, you were pleased to tell me you were invited to a meeting where many ladies and gentlemen were, and amongst their

---

26. Ben Jonson wrote a poem on the horsemanship of William Cavendish, who both owned a riding school (recently reopened) and published on the subject of training horses.
27. Margaret Cavendish did have several family members who were swordsmen. Thomas Lucas, her father, was banished during the reign of Elizabeth for killing a man in a duel. Although Cavendish defends his valor, his exile caused hardship for her mother, who gave birth to a son out of wedlock. Sir Charles Lucas, brother to Margaret Cavendish, became a royalist martyr when he was executed after the battle of Colchester.

several discourses the Lady M.L. spoke of me, saying I lived a dull, unprofitable, unhappy life, employing my time only in building castles in the air.[28] Indeed if I were of her ladyship's humor, I should be unhappy, but as I am, I would not change the course of my life with her ladyship, might I have the years of Methusalem to boot. And as for the mind's architecture as castles in the air or airy castles, which are poetical conceptions and solitary contemplations which produce poems, songs, plays, masks, elegies, epigrams, anagrams, and the like, they will be more lasting than castles of wood, brick, or stone. And their architecture if well designed and built will be more famous and their fame spread farther than those of stone, *viz.* to the view and prospect of diverse nations, if translated into diverse languages. Whereas castles of timber, brick, or stone, cannot be removed nor translated if built upon the ground, neither is the mind's architecture and castles subject to ruin as castles of stone, which are subject to time, accidents, and the rage of wars by which they are destroyed or moulder to dust and are buried in oblivion, whenas poetical castles are set in fame's palace. Neither doth the building of poetical castles impoverish and ruin the builders' families as corporeal castles of timber, brick, or stone for the most part do, wasting their worldly wealth so much as they leave nothing for their posterity, but leave them to poverty. Which poverty forces them many times to act dishonorably, so that what fame they get by building brave and sumptuous castles, houses, tombs, and the like, they lose by their children's base, sharking, cheating, robbing, and wicked actions and so instead of fame get infamy. At best, those builders are accounted but vain and prodigal, whenas the architecture of the mind, which she names castles in the air, give a reputation not only to the building, but to the builder's temporal posterity. Neither doth the builder need any other monument or tomb than his own airy works, which if curiously composed and adorned with fancies, similitudes, metaphors, and the like and carefully written and printed, are more glorious, stately, and durable, than tombs or monuments of marble, costly gilt, and carved, nay more lasting than the tomb of Mausolus. For Homer's works live and are public to the view, whereas that famous monument is consumed and only mentioned there was such a thing. And yet it was one of the corporeal wonders of the world. The like of the great Colossus, and what is become of the Egyptian pyramids? By this we see that poetical castles are both profitable and lasting, and will be remembered when the Lady M.L. is forgotten. But as much as she slights poetical castles, she would be well pleased to have an epigram made in her commendation, and she will crowd hard and sit so long in a masking room upon a scaffold as to be incommoded in her seat and benumbed

28. As with letter 34, M.L. is a comic choice of initials, since Cavendish was M.L. (Margaret Lucas) before her marriage. Here, however, M.L.'s characterization does not parallel the life of Cavendish. It is, instead, the narrator who is like her creator. John Wilkins, author of *The Discovery of a World in the Moone,* is said to have told Cavendish that she built "castles in the air."

with sitting to see a masque. And she will be at the charge to give money to see a play and will sit two or three hours as a spectator and weep or laugh as the poet pleases to have her. Also she will be as amorous as any lover the poet can make. Indeed, the poet doth make her an amorous lover. His wit moves her mind to love and courtships or loving courtships. But though she delights in the poet's works, yet she dislikes the poet's life and wants a poet's wit to build poetical castles. And so leaving her to her little wit and many words, to her gossiping life and her light heels,[29] I rest,

Madam,

Your faithful friend
and servant.

Letter 123

Madam,

I wonder how that person you mention in your letter could either have the conscience or confidence to dispraise Shakespeare's plays, as to say they were made up only with clowns, fools, watchmen, and the like.[30] But to answer that person, though Shakespeare's wit will answer for himself, I say that it seems by his judging or censuring he understands not plays or wit. For to express properly, rightly, usually, and naturally a clown's or fool's humor, expressions, phrases, garbs, manners, actions, words, and course of life is as witty, wise, judicious, ingenious, and observing as to write and express the expressions, phrases, garbs, manners, actions, words, and course of life of kings and princes. And [it is equally so] to express naturally to the life a mean country wench [as well] as a great lady, a courtesan [as well] as a chaste woman, a mad man [as well] as a man in his right reason and senses, a drunkard [as well] as a sober man, a knave [as well] as an honest man, and so a clown [as well] as a well-bred man, and a fool [as well as] as a wise man. Nay, it expresses and declares a greater wit to express and deliver to posterity the extravagancies of madness, the subtlety of knaves, the ignorance of clowns, and the simplicity of naturals,[31] or the craft of feigned fools, than to express regularities, plain honesty, courtly garbs, or sensible discourses. For tis harder to express nonsense than sense and ordinary conversations, than that which is unusual. And tis harder and requires more wit to express a jester than a grave statesman. Yet Shakespeare did not want wit to express to the life all sorts of persons of what quality, profession, degree, breeding, or birth soever. Nor did he want wit to express the divers, and different humours, or natures, or several passions in mankind. And so well he hath expressed in his plays

29. *Light-heeled* meant "unchaste."
30. F. E. Halliday in *The Cult of Shakespeare* (London: G. Duckworth, 1957) discusses the Restoration distaste for Shakespeare's lower-class characters.
31. Persons naturally deficient in intellect.

all sorts of persons as one would think he had been transformed into everyone of those persons he hath described. And as sometimes one would think he was really himself the clown or jester he feigns, so one would think he was also the king and privy counselor. Also as one would think he were really the coward he feigns, so one would think he were the most valiant and experienced soldier. Who would not think he had been such a man as his Sir John Falstaff? And who would not think he had been Harry the Fifth? And certainly Julius Caesar, Augustus Caesar, and Antonius did never really act their parts better, if so well, as he hath described them. And I believe that Antonius and Brutus did not speak better to the people than he hath feigned them. Nay, one would think that he had been metamorphosed from a man to a woman, for who could describe Cleopatra better than he hath done and many other females of his own creating, as Nan Page, Mrs. Page, Mrs. Ford, the Doctor's Maid, Be[a]trice, Mrs. Quickly, Doll Tearsheet, and others, too many to relate? And in his tragic vein, he presents passions so naturally and misfortunes so probably, as he pierces the souls of his readers with such a true sense and feeling thereof, that it forces tears through their eyes and almost persuades them they are really actors or at least present at those tragedies. Who would not swear he had been a noble lover that could woo so well? And there is not any person he hath described in his book but his readers might think they were well acquainted with them. Indeed Shakespeare had a clear judgment, a quick wit, a spreading fancy, a subtle observation, a deep apprehension, and a most eloquent elocution. Truly, he was a natural orator as well as a natural poet, and he was not an orator to speak well only on some subjects, as lawyers who can make eloquent orations at the bar and plead subtly and wittily in law cases, or divines that can preach eloquent sermons or dispute subtly and wittily in theology. But take them from that and put them to other subjects, and they will be to seek. But Shakespeare's wit and eloquence was general, for and upon all subjects he rather wanted subjects for his wit and eloquence to work on, for which he was forced to take some of his plots out of history, where he only took the bare designs, the wit and language being all his own. And so much he had above others that those who writ after him were forced to borrow of him or rather to steal from him. I could mention divers places that others of our famous poets have borrowed or stolen, but lest I should discover[32] the persons I will not mention the places or parts but leave it to those that read his plays and others to find them out. I should not have needed to write this to you, for his works would have declared the same truth. But I believe those that dispraised his plays dispraised them more out of envy than simplicity or ignorance, for those that could read his plays could not be so foolish to condemn them. Only the excellency of them caused an envy to them. By this we may perceive envy doth not leave a man in the grave. It follows him

32. Identify.

after death unless a man be buried in oblivion, but if he leave anything
to be remembered, envy and malice will be still throwing aspersion
upon it or striving to pull it down by detraction. But leaving Shakespeare's works to their own defense, and his detractors to their envy,
and you to your better employments than reading my letter, I rest,
    Madam,

Your faithful friend
and humble servant.

Letter 164

Madam,

In your last letter, you writ that your employment was to read the
history of King Charles the First written by S.A. Give me leave to tell
you, madam, you lose your time in reading that history, for it is only a
number of weekly gazettes compiled into a history, wherein are more
falsehoods than truth.[33] For he being mean and poor had not wealth
nor power to inform himself truly of every particular action, much less
of their designs. But you tell me he mentions an entertainment my lord
made the king, where he says it cost 5,000 pounds or thereabout,
condemning another writer of the same subject for saying it cost
more.[34] Let me tell you, madam, that neither of them was my lord's
steward nor treasurer to know the expenses, but only what they have
heard reported. And therefore in this I cannot say S.A. writes false nor
true, for it is a mistake. For when the king went into Scotland to be
crowned, in the way he was pleased to take a dinner at one of my lord's
houses, namely Welbeck, which cost between four and five thousand
pounds, and the next summer following, as I heard my lord say, the
king sent him word, that he and the queen would make a progress into
the northern parts. And liking his former entertainment, he desired my
lord should do the like, which he obeyed. For, whenas the king came
with his queen thither, my lord, to show his love, duty, and loyalty,
made them an entertainment, as one dinner and a banquet that cost
fifteen thousand pounds sterling at his house at Bolsover, which is five
miles from the former house called Welbeck. Which entertainment it
seems S.A. mistook, setting down the first for the last or for both. But
this is not the only mistake in his history, for there are many and not
only gross mistakes, but very false relations which I can prove. As for
example concerning the wars in the northern parts, I know every particular from the chief actor, which was my lord, and he is a most true
speaker as being both a noble person and a just and honest man, which

---

33. S.A. is Sir William Sanderson, and his biography is *A Compleat History of the Life and Raigne of King Charles* (1658). According to the *DNB*, Sanderson relied heavily on newspaper accounts and was frequently inaccurate.
34. Edward Hyde, earl of Clarendon, felt the expense was excessive *(History of the Rebellion)*, but it is important to remember that Hyde and William Cavendish were long-term political rivals. Ben Jonson wrote short pieces to be acted for each occasion, and the two houses, Welbeck and Bolsover, still stand. Bolsover is open to the public.

all that know him must, if conscience speaks, witness for him. But, madam, you desire me to ask my lord concerning his army, *viz.* the number and by what power he raised so many men, as also of the several successes and how many several armies were against him. I desire you will pardon me if I do not send you a relation, by reason I intend to write the history of my lord's life, if I live and he pleases to inform me, as he hath promised he will.[35] In which history, I intend to write all the several passages and particular actions of the wars in those parts, where my lord was the chief for the king as being general to command all the kingdom of that side, and I will write it truly, honestly, and uprightly without any aggravation or feigned illustration. For my lord and I believe that the chief principle of religion, honor, and honesty is speaking truth and doing justly in all our actions, and I take heaven to witness that I have observed in him and found in myself not so much as an inclination to do otherwise, but always a delight and pleasure in truth and right. But, madam, to return to speak of general histories, they are for the most part mere fables, and it is almost impossible they should be otherwise unless every particular author do write his own story. Nay, those may be false through vainglory and self-partiality, unless they be such noble and worthy persons as make justice, honor, and honesty the ground and foundation of their relations upon which they build their story. And, madam, by reason you desire some particular passages and affairs concerning my lord's actions, I shall be the more earnest with him to set some time apart to declare them to me. In the meantime, I rest,

Madam,

Your faithful friend
and servant.

Letter 173

Madam,
You were pleased in your last letter to express how the Lady C.D. did read some of M.N.'s plays and that she read the passionate sad parts so whiningly that where it should have moved compassion it caused an aversion.[36] Truly, madam, women for the most part spoil all good writing with ill reading, and not only women but most men. For I heard a man who was a great scholar and a learned man, having read much and one that pretended to be a good poet and eloquent orator, read Mr. W.N.'s excellent works quite out of tune and time, neither humoring the sense nor words, but always persisting in the same tune, which was dull and flat and made my sense of hearing as dull as his reading. But yet

35. Cavendish did publish a life of her husband in 1667. It was ridiculed by Samuel Pepys and imitated by Lucy Hutchinson. Although Cavendish is rarely credited as a source, information from her life of her husband has been used by many historians, beginning with John Rushworth.
36. M.N. is, of course, Margaret Cavendish, duchess of Newcastle. Below, W.N. is William, duke of Newcastle, and "Mr." is a little joke, since his various titles of nobility took precedence.

it was better than if he had made a greater noise in his reading, for that would have put me beyond all patience, grating or wounding my ears, which would have discomposed my thoughts extremely. For my thoughts live so peaceably and silently and take such delight therein as they hate a noise. But in truth I never heard any man read well but my husband, and have heard him say he never heard any man read well but B.J., and yet he hath heard many in his time.[37] But I know my husband reads so well that he is like skillful masters of music, which can sing and play their parts at the first sight. So my husband at the first reading will so humor the sense and words of the work, as if he himself had made and writ it. Nay, I have heard him read some works that have been but mean and plain pieces so well as to give a grace to the author and to make his work sound harmoniously like as an ill instrument well played on, whereas others put rare instruments out of tune. Wherefore knowing the difference, as what harmony or discord reading makes, I am so affected with fear of unskillful readers for my poor works, as when I look upon them, I cannot choose but mourn for their danger of disreputation. Yet to pacify my grief, I imagine that every several person likes his own way of reading best and so will not dislike my writing for want of well reading. But for fear I should anger your patience to read so long a letter, I take my leave, and rest,

Madam,

Your faithful friend
and servant.

TEXTUAL NOTES

Copy-text: Huntington Library copy of *CCXI Sociable Letters, Written by the Thrice Noble, Illustrious and Excellent Princess, The Lady Marchioness of Newcastle* (1664). All abbreviated verb forms have been expanded. Cavendish's extremely long sentences with multiple clauses have been subdivided, and quotation marks have been added to mark direct discourse.

BIBLIOGRAPHY

Editions

Ferguson, Moira, ed. "Margaret Cavendish: A 'Wise, Wittie and Learned Lady.'" In *Women Writers of the Seventeenth Century.* Ed. Katharina M. Wilson and Frank J. Warnke. Athens: Univ. of Georgia Press, 1989. 302–40.

Grant, Douglas, ed. *The Phanseys of William Cavendish Marquis of Newcastle Addressed to Margaret Lucas and Her Letters in Reply.* London: Nonesuch Press, 1956.

Lilley, Kate, ed. *The Description of a New World, Called the Blazing World and Other Writings.* New York: New York Univ. Press, 1992. Rpt. London: Penguin, 1994.

---

37. B.J. is Ben Jonson, who composed the entertainments performed before Charles I at Welbeck and Bolsover. These entertainments are also mentioned in letter 164.

Lower, M. A., ed. *Lives of William Cavendish, Duke of Newcastle, and His Wife Margaret.* London: J. R. Smith, 1872.

Salzman, Paul, ed. *The Blazing World.* In *An Anthology of Seventeenth-Century Fiction.* New York: Oxford Univ. Press, 1991. 251–348.

Secondary Works

Blaydes, Sophia B. "Nature Is a Woman: The Duchess of Newcastle and Seventeenth-Century Philosophy." In *Man, God, and Nature in the Enlightenment.* Ed. Donald C. Mell Jr., Theodore E. D. Braun, and Lucia M. Porter. East Lansing, Mich.: Colleagues Press, 1988. 51–64.

———. "The Poetry of the Duchess of Newcastle: A Pyramid of Praise." *Bulletin of the West Virginia Association of College Teachers of English* 6 (1981): 26–34.

Bowerbank, Sylvia. "The Spider's Delight: Margaret Cavendish and the 'Female' Imagination." *English Literary Renaissance* 14 (1984): 392–408.

Findley, Sandra, and Elaine Hobby. "Seventeenth-Century Women's Autobiography." In *1642: Literature and Power in the Seventeenth Century.* Ed. Francis Barker, Jay Bernstein, John Coombes, Peter Hulme, Jennifer Stone, and Jon Stratton. Colchester: Univ. of Essex, 1981. 11–36.

Fitzmaurice, James. "Fancy and the Family: Self-Characterizations of Margaret Cavendish." *Huntington Library Quarterly* 53 (1990): 198–209.

———. "Margaret Cavendish on Her Own Writing; Evidence from Revision and Handmade Correction." *Papers of the Bibliographical Society of America* 85 (1991): 297–307.

———. "Some Problems in Editing Margaret Cavendish." In *New Ways of Looking at Old Texts: Papers of the Renaissance English Text Society, 1985–1991.* Ed. W. Speed Hill. Binghamton, N. Y.: Medieval and Renaissance Texts and Studies, 1993. 253–61.

Gagen, Jean. "Honor and Fame in the Works of the Duchess of Newcastle." *Studies in Philology* 56 (1959): 519–38.

Gallagher, Catherine. "Embracing the Absolute: The Politics of the Female Subject in Seventeenth-Century England." *Genders* 1 (1988): 24–29.

Goulding, Richard William. *Margaret (Lucas) Cavendish, Duchess of Newcastle.* London: Lincolnshire Chronicle, 1925.

Grant, Douglas. *Margaret the First: A Biography of Margaret Cavendish, Duchess of Newcastle.* London: Rupert Hatt-Davis, 1957.

Jones, Kathleen. *A Glorious Fame: The Life of Margaret Cavendish, Duchess of Newcastle, 1623–1673.* London: Bloomsbury, 1988.

Khanna, Lee Cullen. "Margaret Cavendish and Her Blazing World." In *Utopian and Science Fiction by Women.* Ed. Jane L. Donawerth. Syracuse, N.Y.: Syracuse Univ. Press, 1994. 15–34.

Kramer, Annette. "'Thus by the Musick of a Ladyes Tongue': Margaret Cavendish's Dramatic Innovations in Women's Education." *Women's History Review* 2 (1993): 57–80.

Lamb, Charles. "Mackery End." In *Elia: Essays which Have Appeared under that Signature in the London Magazine.* London: Printed for Taylor and Hessey, 1823. 173–74.

McGuire, Mary Ann. "Margaret Cavendish, Duchess of Newcastle, on the Nature and Status of Women." *International Journal of Women's Studies* 1, no. 2: 193–206.

Mendelson, Sara Heller. *The Mental World of Stuart Women: Three Studies.* Amherst: Univ. of Massachusetts Press, 1987.

Mintz, Samuel I. "The Duchess of Newcastle's Visit to the Royal Society." *JEGP* 51 (1952): 168–76.

Paloma, Delores. "Margaret Cavendish: Defining the Female Self." *Women's Studies* 7 (1980): 55–66.

Payne, Linda R. "Dramatic Dreamscape: Women's Dreams and Utopian Vision in the Works of Margaret Cavendish, Duchess of Newcastle." In *Curtain Calls: British and American Women and the Theater, 1660–1820.* Ed. Mary Anne Schofield and Cecilia Macheski. Athens: Ohio Univ. Press, 1991. 18–33.

Pearson, Jacqueline. "'Women May Discourse . . . as Well as Men': Speaking and Silent Women in the Plays of Margaret Cavendish, Duchess of Newcastle." *Tulsa Studies in Women's Literature* 4 (1985): 33–45.

Pepys, Samuel. *The Diary of Samuel Pepys,* 11 vols. Ed. Robert Latham and William Mathews. Berkeley and Los Angeles: Univ. of California Press, 1970–83.

Perry, Henry Ten Eyck. *The First Duchess of Newcastle and Her Husband as Figures in Literary History.* Boston: Ginn and Company, 1918.

Rose, Mary Beth. "Gender, Genre, and History: Seventeenth-Century English Women and the Art of Autobiography." In *Women in the Middle Ages and the Renaissance: Literary and Historical Perspectives.* Ed. Mary Beth Rose. Syracuse, N.Y.: Syracuse Univ. Press, 1986. 245–78.

Salzman, Paul. *English Prose Fiction, 1558–1700.* Oxford: Oxford Univ. Press, 1985.

Sarasohn, Lisa T. "A Science Turned Upside Down: Feminism and the Natural Philosophy of Margaret Cavendish." *Huntington Library Quarterly* 47 (1984): 289–307.

Sherman, Sandra. "Trembling Texts: Margaret Cavendish and the Dialectic of Authorship." *English Literary Renaissance* 24 (1994): 184–210.

Smith, Hilda. *Reason's Disciples: Seventeenth-Century English Feminists.* Urbana: Univ. of Illinois Press, 1982.

Smith, Sidonie. *A Poetics of Women's Autobiography.* Bloomington: Indiana Univ. Press, 1987.

Todd, Janet. *The Sign of Angellica: Women, Writing, and Fiction, 1660–1800.* London: Virago Press, 1989.

Tomlinson, Sophie. "'My Brain the Stage': Margaret Cavendish and the Fantasy of Female Performance." In *Women, Texts, and Histories, 1575–1760.* Ed. Clare Brant and Diane Purkiss. London: Routledge, 1992. 134–63.

Trubowitz, Rachel. "The Re-enchantment of Utopia and the Female Monarchical Self: Margaret Cavendish's *Blazing World.*" *Tulsa Studies in Women's Literature* 11 (1992): 229–46.

Turberville, Arthur Stanley. *A History of Welbeck Abbey and Its Owners,* 2 vols. London: Faber and Faber, 1938–39.

Walpole, Horace. *A Catalogue of the Royal and Noble Authors of England, Scotland, and Ireland.* Vol. 3. London, 1806. 144–55.

Wiseman, Susan. "Gender and Status in Dramatic Discourse: Margaret Cavendish, Duchess of Newcastle." In *Women, Writing, History: 1640–1740.* Ed. Isobel Grundy and Susan Wiseman. London: B. T. Batsford, 1992. 161–77.

Woolf, Virginia. *The Common Reader.* London: Hogarth Press, 1925.

———. *A Room of One's Own.* London: Hogarth Press, 1929.

KATHERINE PHILIPS
(1632–1664)

INTRODUCTION

Katherine Philips is now best known for her celebration of female friendship, but her contemporaries praised her as "The Matchless Orinda," the author of elegant and learned poems. Her male contemporaries Abraham Cowley, Henry Vaughan, Jeremy Taylor, and John Dryden paid tribute to her verse, as did such women writers as Aphra Behn, Ephelia, Anne Killigrew, and Anne Finch. In the years after her death (at the age of thirty-two), she became enshrined as the model of the woman poet, both for the refined quality of her verse, as well as her spotless personal reputation. She was often contrasted with Behn, whose unconventional private life tarnished her literary stature, but Behn herself wished to be remembered alongside of Philips and Sappho, the greatest woman poet of antiquity.

> Let me with *Sappho* and *Orinda* be
> Oh ever sacred Nymph, adorn'd by thee;
> And give my Verses Immortality.
> (From Behn's translation of Cowley's Latin poem "Of Plants")

Philips was most likely born on New Year's Day, 1632, to James Fowler, a London cloth merchant, and Katherine (Oxenbridge), and baptized at Saint Mary Woolchurch in London. According to John Aubrey, her initial education was at home, where a cousin named Blackett taught her to read. At around eight years of age she was enrolled in Mrs. Salmon's Presbyterian school for girls, where she was first introduced to the concept of friendship that she would extol in her later poetry. Aubrey further reports that she was intelligent, a devout Presbyterian, and a poet at age ten. In her school years Philips read works by William Cartwright, James Shirley, Beaumont and Fletcher, and others who would influence the direction of her later writing. During her early school years she became friends with Mary Aubrey, cousin of the biographer John Aubrey, and later the "Rosania" in her coterie circle. Philips's father died in 1642, leaving behind a widow, a son Joshua, and Katherine. In 1646 Philips's mother married Sir Richard Phillips of Picton Castle in Pembrokeshire. In 1648, at the age of sixteen, Katherine married James Philips, who was then fifty-four, a relative of her stepfather, a strong Puritan, and a staunch supporter of Parliament. They made their new home at Cardigan Priory, Wales, where in 1655 she gave birth to a son, Hector, who lived less than two weeks. A daughter, Katherine, was born in 1656. Except for an occasional trip to London, most likely with her husband for Parliamentary terms, and a trip to Ireland, Philips spent her adult life in the Welsh countryside. Although reared as a Puritan and married to a Parliamentarian, Philips was a staunch royalist and later celebrated the return of the monarchy as a revival of a pastoral paradise.

Katherine Philips. Frontispiece portrait from *Poems. By the Most Deservedly Admired Mrs. Katherine Philips* (1667). (Reproduced by permission of the Folger Shakespeare Library, Washington, D.C.)

During the early years of her marriage when Philips accompanied her husband to London, she was introduced to royalist intellectual circles and friends who would later become part of her own coterie. During this period she met Henry Lawes, Sir Edward Dering, John Berkenhead, and other intellectuals and writers who seemed to have encouraged and supported her literary endeavors. In their various ways these royalists attempted to preserve older values, including the Neoplatonic concepts of love and friendship that had been fashionable in the waning years of Queen Henrietta Maria's court and expressed in masques, plays, and verse. The growing neoclassicism, the aesthetic preciosity, and the rituals of courtly and Neoplatonic friendship that were central features of Cavalier literature during the reign of Charles I and Henrietta Maria were carried over into the Interregnum and appear to have exerted a strong influence on Philips, who would transform them into a unique feminine style and voice.

During the Parliamentary years James Philips was quite successful, becoming a leading political force in Wales. Serving as high sheriff of Cardiganshire and as member of Parliament from 1653 until 1662, he was appointed to the High Court of Justice and sentenced a prominent royalist, Colonel John Gerrard, to death in 1654. Because of his activities as a prosecutor, he found at the beginning of the Restoration his power, wealth, and perhaps even his life were threatened, so that his wife and her royalist friends had to come to his defense.

At home in Wales, Philips created an intimate circle of friendship. The "Society of Friendship" most likely existed through correspondence except for the few persons who lived in her immediate area, such as Anne Owen ("Lucasia"), to whom Philips wrote some twenty poems. Whether or not the Society actually met to discuss literary, intellectual, or political matters, we do know that it consisted of a social set of men and women who all shared certain royalist and Cavalier values. Identities have been established for many of the sobriquets Orinda gave to members of her coterie: "Antenor" (James Philips), "Lucasia" (Anne Owen), "Palaemon" (Francis Finch), "Silvander" (Sir Edward Dering), "Cratander" (John Berkenhead), "Poliarchus" (Sir Charles Cotterell), and "Philoclea" (Mallet Steadman). Aware of the male tradition of friendship, especially through Francis Finch's *Friendship* (1654) and Jeremy Taylor's *Discourse on Friendship* (1657), and the employment of the concept by displaced Cavaliers, Philips transformed those conventions into a series of poems on female friendship that earned her the praise of her contemporaries as a modern Sappho. From within the confines of a patriarchal literary system that privileged male subjectivity—what Donne called the "masculine persuasive force" of language—Philips created a voice to articulate her experience, especially one in which the woman speaker initiates both speech and desire. Her poems on female friendship exhibit the romantic and witty qualities found in Donne's verse, which influenced her own sense of the conceit. Philips's coterie world provided her with numerous subjects—visits, courtships, partings, marriages, quarrels, betrayals, and deaths—to which she brought a distinctive feminine perspective. Although many of her amatory and friendship poems contain allusions to Donne and other male poets, Philips transforms those allusions into unique metaphors expressing the ideals of female friendship. Moreover, Philips employs themes that were central in the Cavalier mode, while also developing the traits of the new neoclassical aesthetic. For example, in poems that imitate the Horatian motif of country retirement, she brings together concepts of the return to a golden age with friendship in order to make personal statements about politics and life.

Philips wrote in a wide range of genres, represented in the selection of poems included here. She composed political poems ("Upon the Double Murder of King Charles I," "To Antenor, on a Paper of mine which J. J. threatens to publish to prejudice him"). Philips probably did not express her royalist sympathies publicly until the return of Charles II was a near certainty, but her elegy "In Memory of Mr. Cartwright" makes her allegiances clear. Philips frequently wrote in classical genres, such as the epitaph ("Wiston Vault," "Epitaph On her Son H.P. at St. Syth's Church, where her body also lies Interred"), the epithalamion ("To My Dear Sister Mrs. C. P. on Her Marriage), and the pastoral invitation ("Invitation to the Country"). She subtly adapts the classical forms to her own purposes, as in the epithalamion where she rejects conventional garlands and altars to celebrate a companionate marriage. Another important genre is the poem of parting ("To my dearest Antenor, on his parting," "Friendship's Mystery"), in which Philips self-consciously responds to the verse of her predecessors. Finally, an example of her religious poems ("To His Grace Gilbert Lord Arch-Bishop of Canterbury") is important as an expression of her Anglican faith, as well as a reference to the unauthorized publication of her verse.

At the Restoration, Orinda began a friendship with Sir Charles Cotterell, master of ceremonies first to Charles I and then to Charles II. She sent him verses to edit and engaged in correspondence with him. In turn, Cotterell showed Philips's verses to members of the royal family, who praised them. Cotterell had courted Anne Owen and shared literary interests with Philips, who also wrote to him to aid her husband with the new Restoration Parliament. In 1662 Philips went to Dublin with Anne Owen, who had rejected Cotterell's suit and married Marcus Trevor ("Memnon"). While in Dublin, she met Roger Boyle, the earl of Orrery, who saw parts of her translation of Corneille's *La Mort de Pompée* and encouraged her to complete the work. When Philips finished it, Orrery had it produced in Dublin on February 10, 1663, and subsequently published in April of that year. The play may have been produced in London, because there was a subsequent parody of it in the fifth act of Sir William Davenant's *The Play-house to be Lett* (1673). Nevertheless, the Dublin production of *Pompey* and its publication earned Philips substantial praise. Her success inspired her to begin a translation of Corneille's *Horace,* which she did not live to complete.

In 1664, Richard Marriot published a pirated edition of 116 of Philips's poems. Although she denied responsibility for the edition, its publication brought her both fame and criticism. She had the pirated edition recalled, and with her husband's permission went to London in March 1664 to oversee an authorized edition. While in London she met with her friends, including Lady Cork and Abraham Cowley, who had previously praised her work. In June of that year Philips contracted smallpox and died. Her death was mourned by her friends, and numerous elegies and eulogies were written in her honor. Sir Charles Cotterell probably assisted in compiling the authorized edition of her poems, published in 1667 and reprinted in 1669, 1678, and 1710, as testimony to her success and fame as a writer.

Many of Philips's poems exist both in manuscript and printed versions. Although the text printed here is based on the 1667 folio of her works, the footnotes call attention to variant readings found in the manuscripts, which circulated among her friends. A complete list of variants follows in the textual notes. The following abbreviations are used for the manuscript and printed texts:

Manuscripts

024	Orielton Estate MSS Parcel 24, National Library of Wales
107	Ms 2.1073, Cardiff City Library
151	MS 151 pre-1700, Harry Ranson Humanities Center, University of Texas
775	MS 775 B, National Library of Wales
776	MS 776 B, National Library of Wales

Printed Texts

51	William Cartwright, *Comedies, Tragi-Comedies, with Other Poems* (1651)
55	Henry Lawes, *Second Book of Ayres and Dialogues* (1655)
64	Katherine Philips, *Poems* (1664)
67	Katharine Philips, *Poems* (1667)
69	Katherine Philips, *Poems* (1669)
78	Katherine Philips, *Poems* (1678)

SELECTED POEMS

[Untitled Juvenilia][1]

No blooming youth shall ever make me err,
I will the beauty of the mind prefer.
If Hymen's[2] rites shall call me hence,
It shall be with some man of sense:
Not with the great, but with a good estate   5
Not too well read nor yet illiterate.
In all his actions moderate, grave, and wise,
Readier to bear than offer injuries;
And in good works a constant doer,
Faithful in promise and liberal to the poor.   10
He thus being qualified is always seen
Ready to serve his friend, his country, and his king.
Such men as these you'll say there are but few,
They're hard to find, and I must grant it too.

---

1. This manuscript poem was written before 1648, when Philips was about fifteen or sixteen. Given that Philips is reported to have read the complete Bible at an early age, this poem may reflect the description of the ideal male found in Song of Songs 5:10–16 and may have been composed in anticipation of her impending marriage to Col. James Philips. The poem shows Philips's early proficiency with heroic couplets.
2. Hymen is the god of marriage.

But if I ever hap to change my life,   15
It's only such a man shall call me wife.
         Humbly dedicated to Mistress Anne Barlow[3]
                        C. Fowler

Upon the Double Murder of King Charles I.
In Answer to a Libelous Copy of Rimes by
Vavasor Powell

I think not on the state, nor am concern'd[1]
Which way soever the great helm[2] is turn'd:
But as that son whose father's danger nigh
Did force his native dumbness, and untie
The fetter'd organs; so this is[3] a cause   5
That will excuse the breach of Nature's laws.[4]
Silence were now a sin,[5] nay passion now
Wise men themselves for merit would allow.
What noble[6] eye could see (and careless pass)
The dying lion kick'd by every ass?[7]   10
Has[8] Charles so broke God's laws, he must not have
A quiet crown, nor yet a quiet grave?
Tombs have been sanctuaries; thieves lie there[9]
Secure from all their penalty and fear.
Great Charles his double misery was this,   15
Unfaithful friends, ignoble enemies.
Had any heathen been this Prince's foe,
He would have wept to see him injur'd so.
His title was his crime, they'd reason good
To quarrel at the right they had withstood.   20
He broke God's laws, and therefore he must die;
And what shall then become of thee[10] and I?
Slander must follow treason; but yet stay,
Take not our reason with our King away.

3. Anne Barlow's father, John, was a staunch royalist.
1. Vavasor Powell (1617–70), an itinerant Welsh preacher, was a strong sympathizer with the Fifth Monarchists and believed in the imminent coming of Christ. Apparently Powell had attempted to justify the execution of Charles I in one of his sermons or poems with the argument that the king had usurped God's powers. As a royalist, Philips responds by stating that Christ, the Prince of Peace, would never approve of violence. Philips's royalist sympathies in this and other poems may have caused her Parliamentarian husband some difficulties before the Restoration.
2. Philips employs the traditonal metaphor of the ship of state, but with the implication that a woman may not steer it.
3. "here's a fair" in 107 and 151.
4. Philips may be referring to the patriarchal idea that women should not speak on public events as well as to the king's execution as a violation of nature's laws.
5. "criminal" in 776.
6. "human" in 776.
7. Possible allusion to Plato, *Phaedrus*, bk. I.
8. "Hath" in 107, 151, 776.
9. "here" in 107, 151.
10. "you" in 776.

Though you have seiz'd upon all our defense,   25
Yet do not sequester our common sense.
[But I admire not at this new supply:
No bounds will hold those who at scepters fly.][11]
Christ will be King,[12] but I ne're understood
His subjects built his Kingdom up with blood,   30
Except their own; or[13] that he would dispense
With his commands, though for his own defense.
Oh! to what height of horror are they come,
Who dare pull down a crown, tear up a tomb?

To the Noble Palaemon, on His Incomparable Discourse of Friendship[1]

We had been still undone, wrapt in disguise,
Secure, not happy; cunning, and[2] not wise;
War had been our design, interest our trade;
We had not dwelt in safety, but in shade,
Hadst thou[3] not hung out light more welcome far   5
Than wand'ring sea-men think the northern star;
To show, lest we our happiness should miss,
'Tis plac'd in friendship, men's and angels' bliss.
Friendship, which had a scorn or mask been made,
And still had been derided or betray'd;   10
At which the great physician[4] still had laugh'd,
The soldier stormed, and the gallant scoff'd;
Or worn not as a passion, but a plot,
At first pretended, and at last forgot;
Hadst thou[5] not been her great deliverer,   15
At first discover'd, and then rescu'd her,
And raising what rude malice had flung down,
Unveil'd her face, and then restor'd her crown.
By so august an[6] action to convince,

11. These lines are omitted in 1667. They are supplied on the basis of 151, 776, 64.
12. Prior to Charles I's execution, royalists portrayed the king as a Christlike martyr.
13. "nor" in 776.
1. "Palaemon" is Sir Francis Finch, whose *Friendship* (1654) is addressed to "D. Noble Lucasia-Orinda." Philips praises Finch's concept of Platonic friendship as the basis of a stable society. Friendship in this context was a popular Cavalier theme used to hold together the remnants of courtly culture during the Interregnum. The sobriquet alludes to Chaucer's "Knight's Tale," Shakespeare's *Two Noble Kinsmen*, Spenser's *Faerie Queene* (IV.xi.13), Honoré D'Urfé's *L'Astrée*, and Saint-Amant's "La Solitude," which Philips translated.
2. "but" in 775.
3. "Had you" in 776.
4. "politician" in 151, 775, 776. Thomas suggests a tenuous allusion to Dr. William Harvey, whom Finch and possibly Philips knew.
5. "Had you" in 776.
6. "that transcendent" in 776.

'Tis greater[7] to support than be a prince.   20
Oh for a voice which[8] loud[9] as thunder were,
That all mankind thy[10] conqu'ring truths might hear!
Sure the litigious as amaz'd would stand,
As fairy knights touch'd with[11] Cambina's wand,[12]
Drawn by thy softer, and yet stronger charms,   25
Nations and armies[13] would lay down[14] their arms.
And what more honor can on thee be hurl'd,
Than to protect a virtue, save a world?[15]
But while great friendship thou hast copied out,
Thou'st drawn thyself so well, that we may doubt   30
Which most appears, thy candor or thy art,
Whether we owe more to thy brain or heart.
But this we know without thy own consent,
Thou'st rais'd thyself a glorious monument;[16]
[And that so lasting that all fate forbids,   35
And will outlive Egyptian pyramids.][17]
Temples and statues time will eat away,
And tombs (like their inhabitants) decay;
      But there[18] Palaemon lives, and so he must,
      When marbles crumble to forgotten dust.   40

To Mr. Henry Lawes[1]

Nature, which is the vast creation's soul,
That steady curious agent[2] in the whole,
The art of heaven, the order of this frame,
Is only number in another name.[3]
For as some king conqu'ring what was his own,   5

---

7. "better" in 151, 775, 776, 64.
8. "as" in 776.
9. "big" in 151, 775, 776, 64.
10. "these" in 776.
11. "by" in 776.
12. In Spenser's *Faerie Queene* (IV.iii.48) Cambina brings peace to two knights fighting over Canace.
13. "people" in 151, 775, 776.
14. "let fall" in 151, 775, 776.
15. These lines are omitted in 776.
16. Possible allusion to Horace's famous ode, "Exegi monumentum aere perennius" (3.30).
17. These lines are omitted in 1667, but appear in 775, 1664.
18. "here" in 776.
1. Henry Lawes (1596–1662) was one of the major musicians and composers in the seventeenth century. He was appointed a Gentleman of the Chapel Royal in 1626 and a member of the King's Private Musick in 1630. Lawes was instrumental in keeping alive the courtly culture of Charles I and Henrietta Maria during the Interregnum. Philips most likely met Lawes through her friend, Mary, Lady Dering. In turn, Lawes probably introduced Philips into his intellectual and literary circles. Later, Lawes would set some of Philips's poems to music; this poem was first published in Lawes's *Second Book of Ayres and Dialogues* (1655).
2. "curious": careful, particular, skilful; "agent": efficient cause.
3. Philips employs the traditional topos of universal musical harmony both as a means of praising Lawes and as a metaphor for the political condition of England. "Number": conformity in music or verse to a regular beat or measure.

Hath choice of several titles to his crown;
So harmony on this score now, that then,
Yet still is all that takes and governs men.
Beauty is but composure,[4] and we find
Content is but the concord[5] of the mind,   10
Friendship the unison[6] of well-tun'd hearts,
Honor[7] the chorus of the noblest parts
And all the world on which we can reflect
Music to th' ear, or to the intellect.
If then each man a little world must be,[8]   15
How many worlds are copied out in thee,
Who art so richly formed, so complete
T'epitomize all that is good and great;
Whose stars this brave advantage did impart,
Thy nature's[9] as harmonious as thy art?   20
Thou dost above the poets' praises live,
Who fetch from thee th'eternity they give.
And as true reason triumphs over sense,
Yet is subjected to intelligence:
So poets on the lower world look down,   25
But Lawes on them; his height is all his own.
For, like divinity itself, his lyre
Rewards the wit it did at first inspire.[10]
And thus by double right poets allow
His and their laurel should adorn his brow.   30
Live then, great soul of nature, to assuage
The savage dullness of this sullen age.[11]
Charm us to sense; for though experience fail
And reason too, thy numbers may prevail.
Then, like those ancients, strike, and so command   35
All nature to obey thy gen'rous hand.
None will resist but such who needs will be
More stupid than a stone, a fish, a tree.[12]
Be it thy care our age to new-create:
What built a world may sure repair a state.   40

4. Literary, musical, or artistic composition.
5. "accord" in 776, 64.
6. "union" in 776, 64.
7. "Honour's" in 775, 64, 55.
8. Philips employs a musical version of the traditional Renaissance concept of the macro-microcosm.
9. "nature" in 776.
10. Philips here uses the traditional topos of music and poetry as sister arts as a means of praising Lawes, the master of both.
11. Philips is probably comparing the Cavalier love of music with the Puritan dislike and condemnation of the arts.
12. As a means of praise Philips compares Lawes to ancient musicians, such as Orpheus, Amphion, and Arion, whose musical powers possessed magical and lifesaving qualities. Lawes was a strong supporter of monarchy. Within her conceit of musical harmony as political harmony, Philips also articulates her own wish for a return to royalist rule brought about by the power of Lawes's music.

A Sea-Voyage from Tenby to Bristol, begun Sept. 5, 1652.
Sent From Bristol to Lucasia, Sept. 8, 1652[1]

Hoise up the sail, cry'd they who understand
No word that carries kindness for the land:
Such sons of clamor, that I wonder not
They love the sea, whom sure some storm begot.
Had he who doubted motion[2] these men seen,   5
Or heard their tongues, he had convinced been.
For had our bark mov'd half as fast as they,
We had not need cast anchor by the way.
One of the rest pretending to more wit,
Some small Italian spoke, but murder'd it;   10
For I (thanks to Saburra's[3] letters) knew
How to distinguish 'twixt the false and true.
But t' oppose these as mad a thing would be
As 'tis to contradict a Presbyt'ry.
'Tis Spanish though, (quoth I) e'en what you please: 15
For him that spoke it 'tmight be bread and cheese.[4]
So softly moves the[5] bark which none controls,
As are the meetings of agreeing souls;[6]
And the moon-beams did on the water play,
As if at midnight 'twould create a day.   20
The amorous wave that shar'd in such[7] dispense,
Exprest at once delight and reverence.
Such trepidation we in lovers spye,
Under th'oppression of a mistress eye.[8]
But then the wind so high did rise and roar,   25
Some vow'd they'd never trust the traitor more.
Behold the fate that all our glories[9] sweep,
Writ in the dangerous wonders of the deep:
And yet behold man's easy folly more,
How soon we curse what erst we did adore.   30

1. Philips sent this poem to Anne Owen, an early member of the Society of Friendship, whose friendship with Philips is recorded in numerous poems and letters. The poem imitates elements of the classical journey poem found in Horace, Propertius, and Ausonius, and may also allude to Donne's verse letters, "The Storme" and "The Calm," where the voyage and storm serve as metaphors for mental, political, and amatory states.
2. Zeno's paradox of motion stated that if an arrow were in flight, then, at any given instant, it would be somewhere, occupying a space equal to its dimensions. But anything occupying a space is at rest, and anything at rest is not in motion. Hence, an arrow in flight could not move.
3. Unidentified person.
4. Lines 13–16 are omitted in 776.
5. "our" in 151, 775.
6. Philips's veiled allusion to the controversy over a Presbyterian system of church government and the lack of control over the ship of state shows that she is very much aware of current political events.
7. "that" in 776.
8. The shift here to an amatory theme within the metaphor indicates the influence of Donne and other metaphysical poets on Philips.
9. "that doth all glory" in 776.

Sure he that first himself did thus convey,
Had some strong passion that he would obey.
The bark wrought hard, but found it was in vain
To make its party good against the main,
Toss'd and retreated, till at last we see   35
She must be fast if ere she should[10] be free.
We gravely anchor cast, and patiently
Lie prisoners to the weather's cruelty.
We had nor wind nor tide, nor ought but grief,
Till a kind spring-tide was our first relief.   40
Then we float merrily, forgetting quite
The sad confinement of the stormy night.
Ere we had lost these thoughts, we ran aground,
And then how vain to be secure we found.
Now they were all surpris'd. Well, if we must,   45
Yet none shall say that dust is gone to dust.
But we are off now, and the civil tide
Assisted us the tempests[11] to out-ride.
But what most pleas'd my mind upon the way,
Was the ship's posture that in harbor lay: 50
Which to a rocky grove so close[12] were fix'd,
That the tree's branches with the tackling mix'd.
One would have thought it was, as then it stood,
A growing navy, or floating wood.
But I have done at last, and do confess   55
My voyage taught me so much tediousness.
In short, the heav'ns must needs propitious be,
Because Lucasia was concern'd in[13] me.

Friendship's Mysteries, To My Dearest Lucasia[1]

1.

Come, my Lucasia, since we see
    That miracles men's faith do move,
By wonder and by prodigy
    To the dull angry world let's prove
There's a religion in our love.[2]   5

10. "would" in 151, 775.
11. "tempest" in 151, 775, 776.
12. "so close to a rocky grove" in 151, 775, 776.
13. "for" in 151, 775.
 1. Of the several poems by Philips set to music by Lawes, this is the only one to survive. It was published as "Mutual Affection between *Orinda* and *Lucatia*" in Lawes's *The Second Book of Ayres and Dialogues* (1655). During the Interregnum, Lawes continued to give concerts in his London home, thereby providing a social center for displaced Cavaliers.
 2. The opening conceit may be a conflated allusion to Donne's "The Good-morrow" and "The Canonization."

2.

For though we were design'd t'agree,
    That fate no liberty destroys,
But our election[3] is as free
    As angels, who with greedy choice
    Are yet determin'd to their joys.[4]   10

3.

Our hearts are doubled by the loss,
    Here mixture is addition grown;
We both diffuse, and both ingross:[5]
    And we whose minds are so much one,
    Never, yet ever are alone.   15

4.

We court our own captivity
    Than Thrones[6] more great and innocent:
'Twere banishment to be set free,
    Since we wear fetters whose intent
    Not bondage is, but ornament.   20

5.

Divided joys are tedious found,
    And griefs united easier grow:
We are ourselves but by rebound,
    And all our titles shuffled so,
    Both princes, and both subjects too.[7]   25

6.

Our hearts are mutual victims laid,
    While they (such power in friendship lies)
Are altars, priests, and off'rings made:
    And each heart which thus kindly[8] dies,
    Grows deathless by the sacrifice.   30

Content, to my Dearest Lucasia[1]

1.

Content, the false world's best disguise,
The search and faction of the wise,
Is so abstruse and hid in night,

---

3. The Protestant doctrine of election.
4. Philips argues that she and Lucasia have been "elected" to this friendship, just as angels seek to fulfill their fate. She is perhaps echoing and modifying Donne in these lines.
5. These are alchemical terms for spreading out and collecting material. There are perhaps echoes of Henry Vaughan here.
6. The third choir of the first hierarchy of angels, who support the throne of God and represent divine justice.
7. Perhaps an allusion to Donne's "The Sunne Rising," l. 21.
8. Naturally; generously.
1. Philips's poem analyzes the favorite Cavalier theme of seeking contentment in bad times.

That, like that Fairy Red-cross Knight,[2]
Who treacherous falsehood for clear truth had got,   5
Men think they have it when they have it not.

2.
For courts content would gladly own,
But she ne'er dwelt about a throne:
And to be flatter'd, rich, and great,
Are things that do men's senses cheat.   10
But grave experience long since this did see,
Ambition and content would[3] ne'er agree.

3.
Some vainer would content expect
From what their bright outsides reflect:
But sure content is more divine   15
Than to be digg'd from rock or mine:
And they that[4] know her beauties will confess,
She needs no luster from a glittering dress.

4.
In mirth some place her, but she scorns
Th'assistance of such crackling thorns,   20
Nor owes herself to such thin sport,
That is so sharp and yet so short:
And painters tell us they the same strokes place,
To make a laughing and a weeping face.

5.
Others there are that place content   25
In liberty from government:
But whomsoe'er passions deprave,
Though free from shackles, he's a slave.
Content and bondage differ only then,
When we are chain'd by vices, not by men.   30

6.
Some think the camp content does know,
And that she sits o' th' victor's brow:
But in his laurel there is seen
Often a cypress-bough[5] between.
Nor will content herself in that place give,   35
Where noise and tumult and destruction live.

7.
But yet the most discreet believe

---

2. Philips alludes to *The Faerie Queene* (I.iv), where the Redcross Knight mistakenly protects Duessa, disguised as Fidessa.
3. "could" in 151, 775, 776.
4. "who" in 776.
5. The cypress was a traditional symbol of death and mourning.

The schools this jewel do receive,
And thus far's true without dispute,
Knowledge is still the sweetest fruit. 40
But whilst men seek for truth they lose their peace;
And who heaps knowledge, sorrow doth increase.⁶

8.

But now some sullen hermit smiles,
And thinks he all the world beguiles,
And that his cell and dish contain 45
What all mankind wish for in vain.
But yet his pleasure's follow'd with a groan,
For man was never born to be alone.⁷

9.

Content her self best comprehends
Betwixt two souls, and they two friends, 50
Whose either joys in both are fix'd,
And multiply'd by being mix'd:
Whose minds and interests are so the same;
Their griefs, when once imparted, lose that name.

10.

These far remov'd from all bold noise, 55
And (what is worse) all hollow joys,
Who never had a mean design,
Whose flame is serious and divine,
And calm, and even, must contented be,
For they've both union and society.⁸ 60

11.

Then, my Lucasia, we who have
Whatever love can give or crave;
Who can with pitying scorn survey
The trifles which the most betray;
With innocence and perfect friendship fir'd 65
By virtue join'd, and by our choice retir'd.

12.

Whose mirrors are the crystal brooks,
Or else each other's hearts and looks;
Who cannot wish for other things
Than privacy and friendship brings: 70
Whose thoughts and persons chang'd and mixt are one,
Enjoy content, or else the world hath none.

6. Ecclesiastes 1:18.
7. Genesis 2:18.
8. Lines 55–60 are omitted in 776.

To My Dear Sister Mrs. C. P. on her Marriage[1]

1.

We will not like those men our offerings pay
Who crown the cup, then think they crown the day.[2]
We make no garlands, nor an altar build,
Which help not joy, but ostentation yield.
Where mirth is justly grounded, these wild toys   5
Are but a troublesome, and empty noise.

2.

But these shall be my great solemnities,
Orinda's wishes for Cassandra's[3] bliss.
May her content be as unmix'd and pure
As my affection, and like that endure;   10
And that strong happiness may she still find
Not owing to her fortune, but her mind.

3.

May her content and duty be the same,
And may she know no grief but in the name.
May his and her pleasure and love be so   15
Involv'd and growing, that we may not know
Who most affection or most peace engrost;
Whose love is strongest, or whose bliss is most.

4.

May nothing accidental e're appear
But what shall with new bonds their souls endear;   20
And may they count the hours as they pass,
By their own joys, and not by sun or glass:
While every day like this may sacred prove
To friendship, gratitude, and strictest love.

A Retir'd Friendship. To Ardelia[1]

1.

Come, my Ardelia, to this bower,
     Where kindly mingling souls awhile,
Let's innocently spend an hour,
     And at all serious follies smile.

---

1. Thomas identifies C.P. as Philips's sister-in-law, Cicely Philips, who married John Lloyd of Kilr-hewy. However, Lucy Brashear identifies her as Catherine Darcye, who married Erasmus Phillipps. Philips modifies the conventions of the epithalamion in order to convey a private message on marriage to her new sister-in-law, while urging her to find happiness within.
2. Philips plays upon multiple meanings of "crown": to fill to overflowing, and to bless, amplify or endow with honor, dignity, plenty, with the further implication of rule.
3. Cassandra may be the name given to Cicely Philips and may allude to the Trojan prophetess and seer Cassandra.
1. Ardelia has not been identified.

2.

Here is no quarreling for crowns,   5
   Nor fear of changes in our fate;
No trembling at the great ones' frowns,
   Nor any slavery of state.

3.

Here's no disguise nor treachery,
   Nor any deep conceal'd design;   10
From blood and[2] plots this place is free,
   And calm as are those looks of thine.[3]

4.

Here let us sit and bless our stars,
   Who did such happy quiet give,
As that remov'd from noise of wars   15
   In one another's hearts we live.

5.

Why should we entertain a fear?
   Love cares not how the world is turn'd:
If crowds of dangers should appear,
   Yet friendship can be[4] unconcern'd.   20

6.

We wear about us such a charm,
   No horror can be our offense;
For mischief's self can do no harm
   To friendship or to innocence.

7.

Let's mark how soon Apollo's[5] beams   25
   Command the flocks to quit their meat,
And not entreat the neighboring streams
   To quench their thirst, but cool their heat.

8.

In such a scorching age as this
   Who would not ever seek a shade,   30
Deserve their happiness to miss,
   As having their own peace betray'd.

9.

But we (of one another's mind
   Assur'd) the boisterous world disdain;[6]

2. "bloody" in 776.
3. Philips invokes the topos of the golden age, as she does in other poems. The golden age of friendship contrasts with the "scorching Age" of the present and was a popular theme for Cavalier poets. Her employment of this theme may owe something to Donne's "The Extasie." However, Philips modifies this Cavalier convention to suggest the contentment found in female friendship.
4. "Our harmless souls are" in 776.
5. Apollo is the classical god of the sun.
6. Philips echoes Donne's "A Valediction Forbidding Mourning," ll. 18–20.

With quiet souls and unconfin'd   35
Enjoy what princes wish in vain.

To the Excellent Mrs. Anne Owen, upon her receiving the Name of Lucasia, and Adoption into Our Society, December 28, 1651[1]

We are complete, and fate hath now
No greater blessing to bestow:
Nay, the dull world must now confess,
We have all worth, all happiness.
Annals of state are trifles to our fame,   5
Now 'tis made sacred by Lucasia's name.

But as though through a burning-glass[2]
The sun more vigorous doth pass,
Yet still with general freedom shines;
For that contracts, but not confines: 10
So though by this her beams are fixed here,
Yet she diffuses glory everywhere.

Her mind is so entirely bright,
The splendor would but wound our sight,
And must to some disguise submit,   15
Or we could never worship it.
And we by this relation are allow'd
Luster enough to be Lucasia's cloud.

Nations will own us now to be
A temple of divinity;   20
And pilgrims shall ten ages hence
Approach our tombs with reverence.
May then that time which did such bliss convey,
Be kept by us perpetual holy-day.[3]

1. Philips may have taken the name "Lucasia" for Anne Lewis, who married John Owen, from William Cartwright's play, *The Lady Errant*, but she may also have been inspired by a poem by John Berkenhead, a royalist propagandist, to whom Philips wrote "To Mr. J. B. the Noble Cratander, upon a composition of his, which he was not willing to own publiquely." John Owen's sobriquet was "Charistus." Anne married Marcus Trevor, Lord Dungannon, after Owen died in 1655. Trevor's name was "Memnon," after the protagonist in Beaumont and Fletcher's *The Mad Lover* (1647).
2. Philips is alluding to the image of a burning glass and the sun that Jeremy Taylor used to depict "Christian charity" in *A Discourse of the Nature and Offices of Friendship. In a Letter to the Most Ingenious and Excellent M[istress] K[atherine] P[hilips]* (1657).
3. These lines may allude to Donne's "The Canonization" and to Marvell's "To His Coy Mistress."

Wiston Vault[1]

And why this vault and tomb? alike we must
Put off distinction, and put on our dust.
Nor can the stateliest fabric help to save
From the corruptions of a common grave;
Nor for the Resurrection more prepare,   5
Than if the dust were scatter'd into[2] air.
What then? th'ambition's just, say some, that we
May thus perpetuate our memory.
Ah false vain task of art! ah poor weak man!
Whose monument does more than's merit can: 10
Who[3] by his friend's best care and love's[4] abus'd,
And in his very epitaph accus'd:
For did they not suspect his name would fall,
There would not need an epitaph at all.
But after death too I would be alive,   15
And shall, if my Lucasia do, survive.
I quit these pomps[5] of death, and am content,
Having her heart to be my monument:
Though ne'er stone to me, 'twill stone for me prove,
By the peculiar miracle of love.   20
There I'll inscription have, which no tomb gives,
Not, "Here Orinda lies," but, "Here she lives."[6]

Friendship in Emblem, or the Seal. To My Dearest Lucasia[1]

1.

The hearts thus intermixed speak[2]
A love that no bold shock can break;
For join'd and growing both in one,
Neither can be disturb'd alone.

2.

That means a mutual knowledge too;   5
For what is't either heart can do,

1. Philips's mother-in-law was Anne, daughter of Sir William Wogan of Wiston. Philips seems to have had close contact with various members of the Wogan family. The poem is a variation on the epitaph that Philips turns into a personal statement about her friendship with Lucasia and her own poetry.
2. "in the" in 151, 775, 776.
3. "Who's" in 151, 775, 776.
4. "love" in 151, 775, 776.
5. "this pomp" in 151, 775, 776.
6. Thomas suggests that the major conceit alludes to and plays upon Herrick's "His Poetrie his Pillar."
1. This poem describes what may have been the emblem or seal for the Society of Friendship.
2. An emblem of three interlaced hearts appears in Mildmay Fane's *Otia Sacra* (1648). The union of hearts was also a theme in the *schola cordis* tradition.

Which by its panting sentinel
It does not to the other tell?

3.

That friendship hearts so much refines,
It nothing but itself designs: 10
The hearts are free from lower ends,
For each point to the other tends.

4.

They flame, 'tis true, and several ways,
But still those flames do so much raise,
That while to either they incline   15
They yet are noble and divine.[3]

5.

From smoke or hurt those flames are free,
From grossness or mortality:
The heart (like Moses' bush presum'd)[4]
Warm'd and enlightened, not consum'd.   20

6.

The compasses that stand above,[5]
Express this great immortal love;
For friends, like them, can prove this true,
They are, and yet they are not, two.

7.

And in their posture is exprest   25
Friendship's exalted interest:
Each follows where the other leans,
And what each does, this other means.

8.

And as when one foot does stand fast,
And t'other circles seeks to cast,   30
The steady part does regulate
And make the wand'rer's motion straight:

9.

So friends are only two in this,
T'reclaim each other when they miss:
For whosoe'er will grossly fall,   35
Can never be a friend at all.

3. George Wither's *A Collection of Emblemes* (1635) connects the flaming heart to friendship in two emblems.
4. Exodus 3:2. "Presum'd": to proceed on the basis of right or permission.
5. Philips plays upon the famous compass conceit in Donne's "A Valediction Forbidding Mourning," but she turns the image into a conceit expressing the constancy and equality in female friendship, in contrast to relationships of male dominance.

10.

And as that useful instrument
For even lines was ever meant;
So friendship from good angels springs,
To teach the world heroic things.   40

11.

As these are found out in design
To rule and measure every line;
So friendship governs actions best,
Prescribing unto all the rest.

12.

And as in nature nothing's set   45
So just as lines in number met;
So compasses for these be'ing made,
Do friendship's harmony persuade.

13.

And like to them, so friends may own
Extension, not division: 50
Their points, like bodies, separate;
But head, like souls, knows no such fate.

14.

And as each part so well is knit,
That their embraces ever fit:
So friends are such by destiny,   55
And no third can the place supply.

15.

There needs no motto to the seal:
But that we may the mind reveal
To the dull eye, it was thought fit
That friendship only should be writ.   60

16.

But as there are degrees of bliss,
So there's no friendship meant by this,
But such as will transmit to fame
Lucasia[6] and Orinda's name.

6. "Lucasia's" in 151, 775.

To Antenor, on a Paper of mine which J. J. threatens to publish to prejudice him[1]

Must then my crimes become[2] thy scandal too?
Why, sure the devil hath not much to do.
The weakness of the other charge is clear,
When such a trifle must bring up the rear.
But this is mad design, for who before   5
Lost his repute upon another's score?
My love and life I must confess are thine,
But not my errors, they are only mine.
And if my faults must be for thine allow'd,
It will be hard to dissipate the cloud.[3]   10
But Eve's rebellion did not Adam blast,
Until himself forbidden fruit did taste.[4]
'Tis possible this magazine of Hell
(Whose name would turn a verse into a spell,
Whose mischief is congenial to his life)   15
May yet enjoy an honorable wife.
Nor let his ill be reckoned as her blame,
Nor let my follies blast Antenor's name.[5]
But if those lines a punishment could call,
Lasting and great as this dark lanthorn's[6] gall;   20
Alone I'd court the torments with content,
To testify that thou art innocent.
So if my ink through malice prov'd a stain,
My blood should justly wash it off again.
But since that mint of slander could invent   25
To make so dull a rhyme his instrument,
Let verse revenge the quarrel. But he's worse
Than wishes, and below a poet's curse;
And more than this wit knows not how to give,
Let him be still himself, and let him live.   30

1. The circumstances occasioning this poem and "To (the truly competent Judge of Honor) Lucasia, upon a scandalous libel made by J. Jones" are an attack made upon Philips and her husband because of the poet's Cavalier sympathies and poems defending and praising the royal family. Thomas identifies J. Jones as Jenkin Jones, a close associate of Vavasor Powell. Apparently a copy of one of Philips's proroyalist poems, most likely her poem against Vavasor Powell, fell into his hands, and he used it to attack Philips and her husband. Philips gave her husband the name "Antenor" after the elderly Trojan counselor who had attempted to make peace between the Trojans and the Greeks. James Philips was a moderate supporter of Cromwell, and thus open to attack by more radical parties, such as the Fifth Monarchists.
2. "folly's be" in 776.
3. Although Philips apologizes for causing her husband difficulties because of her publications, she uses the poem to state her independence.
4. Genesis 3:12-19. Philips invokes the Fall to assert her belief that women and men should be autonomous.
5. Lines 13-18 are omitted in 776.
6. "lanthorn": lantern.

To Regina Collier, on her cruelty to Philaster[1]

Triumphant queen of scorn! how ill doth sit
In all that sweetness, such injurious wit?
Unjust and cruel! what can be your prize,
To make one heart a double sacrifice?
Where[2] such ingenious rigor you do show,   5
To break his heart, you break his[3] image too;
And by a tyranny that's strange and new,
You murder him because he worships you.
No pride can raise you, or can make him start,
Since love and honor do enrich his heart.   10
Be wise and good, lest when fate will be just,
She should o'erthrow those glories in the dust,
Rifle your beauties, and you thus forlorn
Make a cheap victim to another's scorn;
And in those fetters which you do upbraid,   15
Yourself a wretched captive may be made.
Redeem the poison'd age, let it be seen
There's no such freedom as to serve a queen.[4]
But you I see are lately Round-head grown,[5]
And whom you vanquish you insult upon.   20

To Mrs. Mary Awbrey[1]

Soul of my soul, my joy, my crown, my friend,
A name which all the rest doth comprehend;
How happy are we now, whose souls are grown,
By an incomparable[2] mixture, one:
Whose well-acquainted minds are now as near   5
As love, or vows, or friendship can endear?
I have no thought but what's to thee reveal'd,
Nor thou desire that is from me conceal'd.
Thy heart locks up my secrets richly set,
And my breast is thy private cabinet.   10
Thou shed'st no tear but what my moisture lent,

---

1. Regina Collier was an early member of Orinda's society. After Collier's husband died in 1649, John Jeffreys ("Philaster") sought her hand but was rejected. Her rejection of Jeffreys seems to have occasioned a quarrel with Philips, who devotes several poems to the incident. Possibly, Philips acted as Philaster's advocate.
2. "When" in 776.
3. "your" in 776.
4. Philips consistently links themes of love and friendship with the politically troubled times.
5. "Round-head": a Parliamentarian; the name derives from the custom of wearing short hair. Philips criticizes Collier for acting as a "Round-head" or Parliamentarian in rejecting a suitor (Jeffreys) who was a royalist.
1. Mary Aubrey was one of Orinda's earliest friends and is known as "Rosania," a name taken from James Shirley's *The Doubtful Heir* (1652). This is another poem in which Philips articulates her concepts of feminine friendship.
2. "indissoluable" in 776.

And if I sigh, it is thy breath is spent.
United thus, what horror can appear
Worthy our sorrow, anger, or our fear?
Let the dull world alone to talk and fight,   15
And with their vast ambitions nature fright;[3]
Let them despise so innocent a flame,
While envy, pride, and faction play their game:
But we by love sublim'd so high shall rise,
To pity kings, and conquerors despise,   20
Since we that sacred union have engrost,
Which they and all the factious world have lost.

In Memory of Mr. Cartwright[1]

Stay, prince of fancy, stay, we are not fit
To welcome or admire thy raptures yet:
Such horrid ignorance benights the times,
That wit and honor are become our crimes.
But when those happy pow'rs which guard thy dust   5
To us, and to thy mem'ry shall be just,
And by a flame from thy blest genius lent,
Rescue us from our dull imprisonment,
Unsequester our fancies, and create
A worth that may upon thy glories wait: 10
We then shall understand thee, and descry
The splendor of restored poetry.
Till when let no bold hand profane thy shrine,
'Tis high wit-treason to debase thy coin.[2]

To My Dearest Antenor, on his parting[1]

Though it be just to grieve when I must part
With him that is the guardian of my heart;
Yet by a[2] happy change[3] the loss of mine
Is with advantage paid in having thine.
And I (by that dear guest instructed) find   5

3. Philips employs the Cavalier theme of contrasting true friendship with a troubled society, allowing one to weather the political storm.
1. William Cartwright, the royalist poet and playwright, died of camp fever during the siege of Oxford in 1643 when Orinda was only eleven years old. Philips was familiar with and influenced by Cartwright's works and political sympathies. This poem, the first of Philips's works to appear in print, was included in the 1651 memorial edition of Cartwright's works. He was celebrated as an ideal Cavalier in contrast to the rake image created by Puritans.
2. Debasing coinage was a crime declared to be high treason.
1. Addressed to Philips's husband, James, this poem treats marriage as a form of friendship. However, in the several poems she addresses to her husband, Philips does not speak with the same fervor or enthusiasm as in the poems to women friends.
2. Emended on the basis of 151, 775, 776. 1667 has "an."
3. "chance" in 776.

Absence can do no hurt to souls combin'd.
As we were born to love, brought to agree
By the impressions of Divine Decree:
So when united nearer we became,
It did not weaken, but increase, our flame.   10
Unlike to those who distant joys admire,
But slight them when possest of their desire.
Each of our souls did its own temper fit,
And in the other's mould so fashion'd it,
That now our inclinations both are grown,[4]   15
Like to[5] our interests and persons, one;
And souls whom such an union fortifies,
Passion can ne'er betray, nor fate surprise.[6]
 Now as in watches, though we do not know
When the hand moves, we find it still doth go: 20
So I, by secret sympathy inclin'd,
Will absent meet, and understand thy mind;
And thou at thy return shalt find thy heart
Still safe, with all the love thou did'st impart.
For though that treasure I have ne'er deserv'd,   25
It shall with strong religion be preserv'd.
And besides this thou shalt in me survey
Thyself reflected while thou art away.
For what some forward arts do undertake,
The images of absent friends to make,   30
And represent their actions in a glass,
Friendship itself can only bring to pass,
That magic which both fate and time beguiles,
And in a moment runs a thousand miles.
So in my breast thy picture drawn shall be,   35
My guide, life, object, friend, and destiny:
And none shall know, though they employ their wit,
Which is the right Antenor, thou, or it.

Invitation to the Country

Be kind, my dear Rosania,[1] though 'tis true
Thy friendship will become thy penance too;
Though there be nothing can reward the pain,
Nothing to satisfy or entertain;

4. Another allusion to Donne's "A Valediction Forbidding Mourning" and the compass conceit.
5. "As well as" in 776.
6. Lines 17–18 are omitted in 776.
1. "Rosania," or Mary Aubrey, had privately married William Montagu in 1652. Orinda apparently was not invited and did not learn of the wedding until later, causing her to feel a sense of betrayal. She writes several poems on the topic in which she attempts to reconcile her friendship with the marriage. This poem treats that subject within the conventions of the country retirement poem, which had, following classical precedents, become a popular Cavalier genre.

Though all be empty, wild, and like to me,   5
Who make new troubles in my company:
Yet is the action more obliging great;
'Tis hardship only makes desert complete.
But yet to prove mixtures all things compound,
There may in this be some advantage found;   10
For a retirement from the noise of towns,
Is that for which some kings have left their crowns:
And conquerors, whose laurel prest the brow,
Have chang'd it for the quiet myrtle-bough.[2]
For titles, honors, and the world's address,   15
Are things too cheap to make up happiness;
The easy tribute of a giddy race,
And paid less to the person than the place.
So false reflected and so short content
Is that which fortune and opinion lent,   20
That who most tried it have of fate complain'd,
With titles burden'd and to greatness chain'd.
For they alone enjoy'd what they possest,
Who relisht most and understood it best.
And yet that understanding made them know   25
The empty swift dispatch of all below.
So that what most can outward things endear,
Is the best means to make them disappear:
And even that tyrant (sense) doth these destroy,
As more officious to our grief than joy.   30
Thus all the glittering world is but a cheat,
Obtruding on our sense things gross for great.
But he that can inquire and undisguise,
Will soon perceive the sting that hidden lies;
And find no joys merit esteem but those   35
Whose scene lies only at our own dispose.
Man unconcern'd without himself may be
His own both prospect and security.
Kings may be slaves by their own passions hurl'd,
But who commands himself commands the world.[3]   40
A country life assists this study best,
Where no distractions do the soul arrest:
There heav'n and earth lie open to our view,
There we search nature and its Author too;
Possest with freedom and a real state   45
Look down on vice, and vanity, and fate.
There (my Rosania) will we, mingling souls,

2. The myrtle was sacred to Venus and a popular marriage symbol. Philips's concept of retirement
may be compared to Lanyer's "A Description of Cookham" and Marvell's "The Garden."
3. Philips invokes the popular Cavalier theme of stoicism in the face of outward political or personal
turmoil. Her idea of inward retreat may also allude to the concept as developed by Henry Vaughan
in "The World" and other poems.

Pity the folly which the world controls;
And all those grandeurs[4] which the world do[5] prize
We either can enjoy, or will despise.   50

On Rosania's Apostacy, and
Lucasia's Friendship[1]

Great soul of friendship, whither art thou fled,
Where dost thou now choose to repose thy head?
Or art thou nothing but voice, air and name,
Found out to put souls in pursuit of fame?
Thy flames being thought immortal, we may doubt   5
Whether they e'er did burn that see them out.

Go, weary'd soul, find out thy wonted rest,
In the safe harbor of Orinda's breast:
There all unknown adventures thou hast found
In thy late transmigrations expound;[2]   10
That so Rosania's darkness may be known
To be her want of luster, not thy own.

Then to the great Lucasia have recourse,
There gather up new excellence and force,
Till by a free unbias'd clear commerce,   15
Endearments which no tongue can e'er rehearse,
Lucasia and Orinda shall thee give
Eternity, and make even friendship live.

Hail, great Lucasia, thou shalt doubly shine,
What was Rosania's own is now twice thine;   20
Thou saw'st Rosania's chariot and her flight,[3]
And so the double portion is thy right:
Though 'twas Rosania's spirit be content,
Since 'twas at first from thy Orinda sent.

---

4. "splendors" in 776.
5. "most do" in 775; "vulgar" in 776.
1. Following the rift caused by Rosania's private marriage, Philips transferred her affections to Lucasia, who became her closest friend.
2. Philips alludes to the Pythagorean and Platonic concept of the transmigration of souls. Here the poet transfers her soul to Lucasia.
3. 2 Kings 3:9–11, where Elijah is carried up to heaven in a chariot of fire, and a double portion of his spirit passes down to his successor, Elisha. Thus, Lucasia takes up the mantle of friendship left by Rosania's parting.

Epitaph
On Her Son H. P. at St. Syth's Church, where
her body also lies Interred[1]

What on earth deserves our trust?
Youth and beauty both are dust.
Long we gathering are with pain,
What one moment calls again.
Seven years childless, marriage past,   5
A son, a son is born at last:
So exactly limb'd and fair,
Full of good spirits, mien, and air,
As a long life promised,
Yet, in less than six weeks dead.   10
Too promising, too great a mind
In so small room to be confin'd:
Therefore, as fit in heav'n to dwell,
He quickly broke the prison shell.
So the subtle alchemist,   15
Can't with Hermes' seal resist[2]
The powerful spirit's subtler flight,
But 'twill bid him long good night.
And so the sun if it arise
Half so glorious as his eyes,   20
Like this infant, takes a shroud,
Buried in a morning cloud.

Upon the Graving of her Name upon a Tree in
Barn-Elms' Walks[1]

Alas, how barbarous are we,
Thus to reward[2] the courteous tree,
Who its broad shade affording us,
Deserves not to be wounded thus!
See how the yielding bark complies   5
With our ungrateful injuries!
And seeing this, say how much then

1. Philips's only son, Hector, was born on April 23, 1655 and died on May 2. He was buried in the church of St. Benet-Sherehog on Syth's Lane in London, where the poet was also buried.
2. Hermes Trismegistus is the legendary author of works about magic, astronomy, and alchemy. It was believed that Hermes invented a magic seal to keep vessels airtight.
1. Philips employs within this country retreat poem the classical topos of carving one's mistress' name on a tree. She transforms a traditional male perspective into a female one. For the topos see Eugene R. Cunnar, "Names on Trees, the Hermaphrodite, and 'The Garden'," in *Celebrated and Neglected Poems of Andrew Marvell*, ed. Claude J. Summers and Ted-Larry Pebworth (Columbia: Univ. of Missouri Press, 1992), 121–38. Marvell alludes to Philips's use of this topos in "The Garden," ll. 19–24, thereby complimenting the poet; see Allan Pritchard, "Marvell's 'The Garden': A Restoration Poem?," *Studies in English Literature* 23 (1983): 371–88.
2. "requite" in 776.

Trees are more generous than men,
Who by a nobleness so pure,
Can first oblige, and then endure.   10

Against Love[1]

Hence Cupid with your cheating toys,
Your real griefs, and painted joys,
Your pleasure which itself destroys.
    Lovers like men in fevers burn and rave,[2]
    And only what will injure them do crave.   5
Men's weakness makes love so severe,
They give him power by their fear,
And make the shackles which they wear.
    Who to another does his heart submit,
    Makes his own idol, and then worships it.   10
Him whose heart is all his own,
Peace and liberty does crown,
He apprehends no killing frown.
    He feels no raptures which are joys diseas'd,
    And is not much transported, but still pleas'd.   15

To the Countess of Roscommon,
with a Copy of Pompey[1]

Great Pompey's fame from Egypt made escape,
And flies to you for succor in this shape:
A shape, which, I assur'd him, would appear,
Nor fit for you to see, nor him to wear.
Yet he says, Madam, he's resolv'd to come,   5
And run a hazard of a second doom:
But still he hopes to bribe you, by that trust
You may be kind, but cannot be unjust;
Each of whose favors will delight him more
Than all the laurels that his temples wore: 10
Yet if his name and his misfortunes fail,
He thinks my intercession will prevail;
And whilst my numbers would relate his end,
Not like a judge you'll listen, but a friend;

1. Compare this poem against love with Wroth's sonnets to Cupid in *Pamphilia to Amphilanthus.*
The male Cavalier poets, including Suckling, Cowley, and Waller, also addressed a similar topic.
2. Perhaps an allusion to Donne's "The Fever."
1. Frances, eldest daughter of Richard Boyle, earl of Cork and Burlington, was married to the poet
Wentworth Dillon, earl of Roscommon. One of Sir Edward Dering's letters reveals that she was
given the name of "Amestris" in Philips's circle. Probably through Sir Charles Cotterell, Philips
arranged to send the countess a copy of her *Pompey,* printed in Dublin by John Crooke. During the
1660s Philips increasingly attempted to court various members of the aristocracy and royal family.

For how can either of us fear your frown,   15
Since he and I are both so much your own.
    But when you wonder at my bold design,
Remember who did that high task enjoin;
Th'illustrious Orrery,[2] whose least command,
You would more wonder if I could withstand: 20
Of him I cannot which is hardest tell,
Or not to praise him, or to praise him well;
Who on that height from whence true glory came,
Does there possess and thence distribute fame;
Where all their lyres the willing muses bring,   25
To learn of him whatever they shall sing;
Since all must yield, whilst there are books or men,
The universal empire to his pen;
Oh! had that powerful genius but inspir'd
The feeble hand, whose service he requir'd,   30
It had your justice then, not mercy pray'd,
Had pleas'd you more, and better him obey'd.

To Celimena[1]

Forbear, fond heart, (say I) torment no more
That Celimena whom thou dost adore;
For since so many of her chains are proud,
How canst thou be distinguish'd in the crowd?
But say, bold trifler, what dost thou pretend?   5
Wouldst thou depose thy saint into thy friend?
Equality in friendship is requir'd,
Which here were criminal to be desir'd.

An Answer to Another Persuading a Lady to Marriage[1]

1.

Forbear, bold youth, all's heaven here,
And what you do aver,

---

2. Roger Boyle, earl of Orrery (1621–79), was at the center of cultural life in Restoration Dublin. As one of the initiators of the new heroic drama, he encouraged Philips to complete her play, *Pompey*, and contributed a commendatory poem to the published edition (1667). Orrery had been a royalist, then served Cromwell, and at the Restoration served Charles II in Ireland.

1. "Celimena" was the name given to Lady Elizabeth Boyle, whom Philips met in Dublin in 1662–63; she addressed another poem to her, "To My Lady Elizabeth Boyle, Singing," written in imitation of Edmund Waller's "To a Lady Singing a Song of His Composing." Boyle was married to Nicholas Tufton, earl of Thanet. In this poem Philips makes clear how difference in social rank (the Boyles were aristocrats) hinders ideal friendship.

1. Thomas suggests that Philips may have written this poem to dissuade Lucasia from marrying Marcus Trevor.

To others courtship may appear,
  'Tis sacrilege to her.

2.

She is a public deity,
  And were't not very odd   5
She should dispose herself to be
  A petty household god?

3.

First make the sun in private shine,
  And bid the world adieu,
That so he may his beams confine   10
  In complement to you.[2]

4.

But if of that you do despair,
  Think how you did amiss,
To strive to fix her beams which are   15
  More bright and large than this.[3]

To Mr. Sam. Cooper, having taken Lucasia's Picture given December 14, 1660[1]

1.

If noble things can noble thoughts infuse,
Your art might ev'n in me create a muse,
And what you did inspire, you would excuse.

2.

But if such a miracle could do,
That muse would not return you half your due,   5
Since 'twould my thanks, but not the praise pursue.

3.

To praise your art is then itself more hard,
Nor would it the endeavor much regard,
Since it and virtue, are their own reward.

4.

A pencil from an angel newly caught,   10
And colors in the morning's bosom sought,
Would make no picture, if by you not wrought.

---

2. Elizabeth H. Hageman points to the use of the impossibility topos in this stanza, which had appeared in earlier anti-feminist literature: *Women Writers of the Renaissance and Reformation,* ed. Katharina M. Wilson (Athens: Univ. of Georgia Press, 1987), 607. See Susan Schibanoff, "Creseyde's 'Impossible' Aubes," *JEGP* 76 (1977): 326–33.
3. The lady casts her eye beams on more men than the sun; hence the young man will not be able keep the woman to himself. This conceit may have been imitated by Pope in his *The Rape of the Lock.*
1. Samuel Cooper (1609–72) was one of the finest miniaturists at the time. Although his portrait of Lucasia has not been identified, it may be among his surviving works, many of whose subjects are unknown. The poem reveals Philips's awareness of another popular Restoration genre, the advice-to-the-painter poem, such as practiced by Marvell and Waller.

5.

But done by you it does no more admit
Of an encomium from the highest wit,
Than that another hand should equal it.   15

6.

Yet whilst you with creating power vie,
Command the very spirit of the eye,
And then reward it with eternity.

7.

Whilst your each touch does life and air convey,
Fetch the soul out, like overcoming day,   20
And I my friend repeated here survey.

8.

I by a passive way may do you right,
Wearing in that what none could e're endite,
Your panegyric, and my own delight.

To His Grace Gilbert Lord Archbishop of Canterbury, July 10, 1664[1]

That private shade, wherein my muse was bred,
She always hop'd might hide her humble head;
Believing the retirement she had chose
Might yield her, if not pardon, yet repose;
Nor other repetitions did expect,   5
Than what our echoes from the rocks reflect.
But hurried from her cave with wild affright,
And dragg'd maliciously into the light.
(Which makes her like the Hebrew virgin mourn
When from her face her vail was rudely torn)[2]   10
To you (my Lord) she now for succor calls,
And at your feet, with just confusion falls.
But she will thank the wrong deserv'd her hate,
If it procure her that auspicious fate,
That the same wing may over her be cast,   15
Where the best church of all the world is plac'd,
And under which, when she is once retir'd,
She really may come to be inspir'd.

1. This was one of the last poems Orinda wrote, probably near the time of her final trip to London, and is addressed to Gilbert Sheldon, who was made archbishop of Canterbury in August 1663. The poem refers to the pirated edition of Philips's poems as well as reveals her knowledge of the religious conflicts of the time. The title date is wrong, in that Philips died on June 22, but she may have been planning to present the poem to Sheldon on July 10.
2. Philips alludes to 2 Samuel 13:1–20, the narrative of Tamar's rape.

And by the wonders which she there shall view,
May raise her self to such a theme as you,   20
Who were preserv'd to govern and restore
That church whose confessor you were before;[3]
And show by your unwearied present care,
Your suff'rings are not ended, though hers are:
For whilst your crosier her defense secures,   25
You purchase her rest with the loss of yours,
And heav'n who first refin'd your worth, and then,
Gave it so large and eminent a scene,
Hath paid you what was many ways your due,
And done itself a greater right than you.   30
For after such a rough and tedious storm[4]
Had torn the church, and done her so much harm;
And (though at length rebuk'd, yet) left behind
Such angry reliques, in the wave and wind;
No pilot could, whose skill and faith were less,   35
Manage the shatter'd vessel with success.
The piety of the apostles' times,
And courage to resist this age's crimes,
Majestic sweetness, temper'd and refin'd,
In a polite, and comprehensive mind,   40
Were all requir'd her ruins to repair,
And all united in her primate are.
In your aspect so candid and serene,
The conscience of such virtue may be seen,
As makes the sullen schismatic consent,   45
A church-man may be great and innocent.
This shall those men reproach, if not reduce,
And take away their fault or their excuse,
Whilst in your life and government appear
All that the pious wish and factious fear.   50
Since the prevailing cross her ensigns spread,
And pagan gods from Christian bishops fled,
Time's curious eye till now hath never spy'd
The church's helm so happily supply'd.
Merit and providence so fitly met,   55
The worthiest prelate in the highest seat.
     If noble things can noble thoughts infuse,
Your life (my Lord) may, ev'n in me, produce
Such raptures, that of their rich fury proud,
I may, perhaps, dare to proclaim aloud;   60
Assur'd, the world that ardor will excuse,
Applaud the subject, and forgive the muse.

3. Sheldon had been expelled from his position as warden of All Souls, Oxford in 1648 by the Parliamentary Visitation and ejected from his living in 1650.
4. Philips refers to the Civil War and the toll it took upon the Anglican Church.

TEXTUAL NOTES

Copy-text: Except for the untitled juvenilia, the copy-text for the poems is the 1667 edition, probably edited by Sir Charles Cotterell. Spelling, punctuation, and capitalization have been modernized. Rebecca Tate prepared the textual notes comparing the manuscript and printed sources.

"Upon the Double Murder": Copy-text: 1667. Variants: Title: On the double Murther of the King (In answer to a libellous paper written by V. Powell, at my house) These verses were those mention'd in the precedent copy. (776); Upon the double murther of K. Charles the First In answeare to a libellous rime made by V.P. (151); Upon the double Murther of K. Charles I. in Answer to a Libellous Copy of Rimes made by Vavasor Powell. (1664). 2 the] that (776, 151); 5 this] here (151); this is a] here's a fair (1664); 7 now a sin] criminal (776); 8 would] will (776); 9 noble] humane (776); 11 Has] Hath (776, 151); 12 Crown] Scepter (776); yet] *omitted* (776); 13 there] heere (107); 20 the] a (776); 22 thee] you (776); 24 Reason] Judgment (776); between 26 and 27: But I admire not at the new supply:] No bounds will hold those who at Scepters fly (776, 1664); the] this (776, 151); 29 or] nor (776); 30 own] *omitted* (776); 32 pull] teare (107).

"To the Noble Palaemon": Copy-text: 1667. Variants: Title: To Palaemon on his discourse of friendship (776); To the incomparable Palaemon on his noble discourse of friendship (151); 2 and] but (775, 776); Secure not happy been, cunning not wise (151); 5 Hadst thou] Had you (776); our Light] out light (775); out lights (151); 9 mask] mark (1664); 11 the great Physician] the Politician (775, 776, 151); 12 The] These (151); 14 and] or 775, 776, 1664); last] least (1664); 15 Hadst thou] Had you (776); her] our (1664); 16 At] And (775); 19 so august an] that transcendent (776); so] such (1664); 20 greater] better (776); 21 which] as (776); loud] big (775, 776, 151, 1664); 22 thy] these (776); 22 truths] truth (775); 24 with] by (776, 151); 25–26 reversed (775, 776, 151); 25 thy] your (775, 776), replaced by line of stars (1664); 26 Armies] People (775, 776, 151); lay down] let fall (775, 776, 151); 27–28 omitted (776); 27 can] could (775); 29 while] whilst (776); thou] you (776); hast] have (776); 30 Thou'st] Y'have (776); thy] your (776); 31 thy] your (776); thy] your (776); 32 Whether] Or (775, 776, 151, 1664); to] unto (775, 776, 151, 1664); thy] your (776); 33 thine] thy (775, 151); your (776); 34 Thou'st rais'd] Th'hast rear'd (775); Thou'st] Y'have (776); thy] your (776); Between 34 and 35: And that so lasting that all Fate forbids,] And will outlive Egyptian Pyramids (775, 1664); And that so solid as all Fate forbids,] And will outlast Egyptian Pyramids (776); And that so lasting as all fate forbids,] And will outlive Egyptian Pyramids (151); 37 there] here (776)

"To Mr. Henry Lawes": Copy-text: 1667. Variants: Title: To the truly noble Mr. Henry Lawes (775, 776, 1664); To Mr Henry Lawes (151); To the much honoured Mr. HENRY LAWES, On his Excellent Composition in Musick (1655); 2 That] The (151); in] through (151); 4 Number] Musick (1655); 5 For] And (1655); 10 Concord] accord (776, 1664); 11 Unison] Union (1664); 12 Honour] Honour's (775, 776, 1655, 1664); 17 formed] furnished (1655); 18 and] or (775, 1655); 20 Nature's] Nature (776); as] more (775); as] then (775); 30 His and their] Their and His (1655); 30 Laurel] Laurells (775, 151,

1655); 33 for] and (775, 151); 34 may] will (775); can (1655); 38 Stone, a Fish] Fish a Stone (1655).

"A Sea-Voyage": Copy-text: 1667: Variants: Title: A sea voyage from Tenby to Bristoll 5 of September 1652. Sent to Lucasia 8th September. 1652 (151); A Sea Voyage from Tenby to Bristol (1651, 776); A Sea-voyage from Tenby to Bristoll begun Sept. 5. 1652. sent from Bristoll to Lucasia Sept. 8. 1652 (64–78). No word] Nothing (776); 7 as] so (776); 11 I] It (151); to Saburras] o Saburra's (64); Lines 13–16 omitted in 776; 13 t'oppose] to oppose (151, 775), these] them there (151, 775); 14 'tis to contradict] contradicting (151, 775); 15 'Tis Spanish though,] Let it be Dutch (151, 775); 16 'tmight] might (151, 775); 17 the] our (151, 775); 21 such] this (776); 27 all] doth (151, 775), does (776), our] all (151, 775, 776), Glories] Glory (776); 30 erst] late (151, 775); convey] obey (151); should] would (151, 775, 776); these] those (151, 775), ran] run (151, 775); 48 Tempests] Tempest (151, 775, 776); 49 the] our (776); 50 that] which (151, 775), when't (1664); 51 to a rocky grove so close] so close to a rocky grove (151, 775, 776, 1664), were] was (1664); 57 Heav'ns] Star's (776); 58 in] for (151, 775).

"Friendship's Mysteries": Copy-text: 1667. Variants: Title: Friendships Mysterys to my dearest Lucasia. (Set by Mr H Lawes) (775); Friendships mystery set by Mr. Lawes (776); Freindships mystery to my Dearest Lucasia: Set by Mr H Lawes (151); Mutuall Affection between Orinda and Lucatia (1655); Friendship's Mystery, To my dearest Lucasia. Set by Mr. Henry Lawes (1664); 3 wonder] wonders (1664); 4 dull angry] enraged (776); dull] fierce (1655); 6 t'agree] tá Agree (151); 11 the] their (775, 776, 151, 1655); 16 court] count (1664); 17 Thrones more great and] Greatest thrones more (1664); 19 Since] While (151); Which (1655); 30 Grows] Graces (1655).

"Content, to my Dearest Lucasia": Copy-text: 1667. Variants: Title: To Lucasia. of Content (151); Content to my dearest Lucasia (775); Content (776); Content. To my dearest Lucasia (64–78). 4 that] the (776), Red-cross] red-rose (151); 9 and] or (151, 775, 776), 10 which] that (151, 775, 776), Mens] mans (151, 775, 776); 12 would] could (151, 775, 776); 17 that] who (776); 18 no] not borrow (776); 21 sport] sprot (1664); 22 That is so sharp and yet] Which is so empty, and (776); 24 make] draw (151); 27 whomsoe're Passions] who his passions doe (151, 775, 776, 1664); 28 he's] is (151, 775, 776, 1664); 29 differ only then] only differ, when (776); 30 When we are chain'd by] We are enslav'd to (776), by] to (776); 31 does] doth (151); 32 sits] crowns (776), o'the Victor's] on th'victors (151); the Conquerours (776); 34 Cypress-bow] Cypress-brow (78); 37 yet the] the (151, 775); 39 far's] far (151, 775, 776); 41 whilst] while (64–78); 42 doth] does (776); 46 wish for] doth wish for (151), do wish (775, 776); 48 For man was never] It is not good for (776), born] made (151); Whose] either (151), Where (776), either] whose (151), eithers (775, 776, 64); 52 by] in (776); 53 so] still (64); 54 Griefs] very griefs (151, 775, 776), when once] imparted (151), 775), united (776), that] their (64); Lines 55–60 omitted in 776; 61 who have] have (151, 64); 63 Who can with pitying scorn] With scorn, or pitty ca (151, 775, 64; 72 the] this (776), hath] has (775, 776, 64).

"To My Dear Sister": Copy-text: 1667. Variants: Title: Marriage] nuptials (775); Nuptial (1664). 3 We] Wee'l (775, 151); 3 garlands] garland (775); 6 omitted (776); Do but disturb, and not adorn our Joys (775, 151); replaced by line of stars (1664); 20 new] the (151); bonds] bands (775, 151); 21 they pass] they doe pass (775, 151); 24 Gratitude, and strictest] duty, gratitude and (775, 151).

"A Retir'd Friendship": Copy-text: 1667. Variants: Title: A retir'd friendship to Ardelia. 23d. Aug. 1651 (775, 151); A retir'd friendship, to Ardelia 1651 (776). 2 Souls] thoughts (776); 4 all] omitted (776); 7 frowns] frowne (776); 11 blood and] bloody (776); 20 Yet friendship can be] Our harmless souls are (776); 22 be our] give us (776); 23 For mischief's] Mischief it (776); 24 or] and 775, 776, 151); 27 neighbouring streams] neighbour-streams (775, 776, 151); neighbouring Springs (1664); 30 Who would not ever] Who ever would not (775, 776, 151); 35 With quiet Souls and unconfin'd] And here can quiet be, and kind (776); 36 Enjoy what Princes] With princes wish, but (776).

"To the Excellent Mrs. Anne Owen": Copy-text: 1667. Variants: Title: To the excellent Lucasia on her taking that name and adoption into our societie 29 Decembr 1651 (151); To the excellent Mrs. A. O. upon receiving the name of Lucasia, and adoption into our society. 29 Decemb. 1651 (775); To the Excellent Mrs Anne Owne, upon receiving the name of Lucasia, and Adoption into our Society, Decr. 28. 1651 (776); To the excellent Mrs. Ann Owen, upon her receiving the name of Lucasia, and Adoption into our Society, Decemb. 28. 1651 (64–78). 3 Nay] No (64); 9 Yet] It (151, 775); 11 are] be (151); 12 diffuses] diffuseth (151), glory] glorys (151, 775); 14 our] the (151); 24 by] with (151, 775, 776), Holy-day] Holiday (776).

"Wiston Vault": Copy-text: 1667. Variants: Title: Wiston Vault (151); Wiston=Vault (775); Wiston Vault (776); Wiston Vault (64–78). 2 off] of (151), Distinction] distinctions (775), our Dust] Dust (64); 6 into] in the (151, 775, 776); 10 does] do's (151); 11 Who] Who's (151, 775, 776), love's] love (151, 775, 776); 12 Epitaph] epitaphs (775, 776), accus'd] misused (64); 17 these] this (151, 775, 776), pomps] pomp (151, 775, 776); 19 Stone] so (151); 20 miracles] miracle (775, 776).

"Friendship in Emblem": Copy-text: 1667. Variants: Title: To my dearest Lucasi, friendship in Emblem or the seale (151); Friendship in Emblem, or the Seale to my dearest Lucasia (775); Friendship in Embleme Or the Seal, to my dearest Lucasia (776); Friendship in Embleme, or the Seal. To my dearest Lucasia (64–78). 4 Neither] None (69–78); 8 does] doth (151); 19 Heart] hearts (151, 775); 28 does] doth (151, this] the (151, 775, each (776, 64); 29 does] doth (151); 30 t'other] 'tother (775); 31 does] doth (151); 34 T'reclaime] To reclaime (151); 44 unto] Law to (151, 775); 46 in] and (151, 775), number] numbers (151, 775); 54 ever] even (151, 775); 58 mind] Mine (151, 775); 61 are] is (775); 64 Lucasia] Lucasia's (151, 775).

"To Antenor": Copy-text: 1667. Variants: Title: To Antenor on a paper of mine which J. Jones threatens to publish to his preiudice (151); To Antenor On a paper of mine, which an unworthy Adversry of his, threatened to publish, to pregiudice him, in Cromwels time (776); To Antenor, on a Paper of Mine which J. Jones threatens to publish to prejudice him (64); To Antenor, on a paper of mine which J.J. threatens to publish to prejudice him (67–78). 1 Crimes become] folly's, be (776), thy] his (64); 9 must] should (776); 11 For] But (151, 776); Lines 13–18 omitted in 776; 14 verse] Virge (64); 25 that] the (776); 26 so dull a] that triviall (776); 27 Let Verse] Verse should (776).

"To Regina Collier": Copy-text: 1667. Variants: Title: For Regina (151); For the Queen of Hearts (107); To Regina Collier, on her cruelty to Philaster

(64–78) 4 one] on (776); 5 Where] When (776), ingenious] ingenous (64), shew] show (107, 151); 6 his] your (107, 776); 12 dust] missing (107).

"To Mrs. Mary Awbrey": Copy-text: 1667. Variants: Title: 6. April. 1651. L'amitie': To Mrs Mary Awbrey (151); 6ᵗ Aprill 1651. L'amitie: To Mrs M. Awbrey (775); To Rosania L'Amitie. 1651 (776); L'Amitie. To Mrs. Mary Awbrey (64); To Mrs. Mary Awbrey (67–78). 2 doth] does (776); 4 incomparable] indissoluble (776); 5 Minds] mines (151); 6 Friendship] secrets (775, 776); 16 Ambitions] ambition (151, 776); 22 factious] sullen (151, 775, 776, 64).

"In Memory of Mr. Cartwright": Copy-text: 1667. Variants: Title: In Memory of Mr Cartwright at the Edition of his Poems (107); In Memory of Mr William Cartwright (151); In memory of Mr Cartwright (775, 776); To the memory of the most Ingenious and Vertuous Gentleman Mr. Wil: Cartwright, my much valued Friend (51); In Memory of Mr. cartwright (64–78). 3 the] our (151, 51); 4 That] Love (107), become our] the onely (107); 5 which] that (107, 151, 775, 51); 7 from] by (107); 8 Rescue] Shall rescue 951), our] this (107, 51); 9 Fancies] fancy (151); 10 Glories] glorie (151); 11 We then] Then wee (107, 51); 13 when] then (105, 151), let no bold hand profane thy shrine] tis Treason to debase thy Coyne (107); 14 'Tis high Wit-Treason to debase thy coin.] And with unhallowed hands to touch thy Shrine (107).

"To My Dearest Antenor": Copy-text: 1667. Variants: Title: on his] At (776); To Antenor parting (151); 3 an] a (775, 776, 151); change] chance (776); 7 As] And (775, 776, 151); 10 our] the (776); 13 its own] in its (1664); 16 Like to our] As well as (776); 17–18 omitted (776); 17 a] an (775, 151); 18 destroy] betray (775, 151); 20 we find it still doth] and yet we find they (776); 25 For] And (776); 27 And] But (775); besides this thou shalt in me] that Deare Spy, shall in my heart (776); 28 while] when (151); art] wert (776); 29 what] though (776); 32 Friendship it self can only bring] Nothing but kindness, can bring this (776); 35 So] Thus (776); 36 Life, Object, Friend, and] My Guide, my object, and my (776).

"Invitation to the Country": Copy-text: 1667. Variants: Title: Invitation to the countrey (151); Invitation to the Countrey (775); Invitation of Rosania to Wales (776); Invitation to the Country (64–78). 3 the] thy (151); 5 empty, wild, and] wild, and empty (776); 13 Laurel] Laurells (775), prest] hurt (776), the] their (151); 18 the] their (776); 21 Fate] it (64); 28 means] mean (151, 776); 33 he] they (776); 34 sting] thing (64); 36 lies only] ly's wholly 151, 775), is wholly (776); 39 by their own] and by their (776); 42 Where] When (151, 775), do] doth (775); 43 our] the (151); 44 its] her (776); 45 Possest] And fill'd (776); 46 and] on (151, 775, 776); 49 Grandeurs] splendours (776), World do] most do (775); vulgar (776); 50 can] will (776), will] can (776, 64).

"On Rosania's Apostacy": Copy-text: 1667. No substantive variants.

"Epitaph": Copy-text: 1667. Variants: Title: EPITAPH ON HECTOR PHILLIPS at St. Sith's Church (776); On her son H. P. at St. Syth's Church where her body also lies Interred (67–78). 13 as fit] fit (776); 14 He quickly] Quickly (776); 19 And so] So (776).

"Upon the Graving of her Name": Copy-text: 1667. Variants: Title: Upon the engraving: K: P; on a Tree in the short walke at Barn=Elms (776); Upon the graving of her name upon a tree in Barnelemes Walks (67–78). 2 reward] requite (776); 4 Deserves] Deseru'd (776); 6 ungrateful] ingratefull (776).

"Against Love": Copy-text: 1667. This is the earliest known version of this poem.

"To the Countess of Roscommon": Copy-text: 1667. This is the earliest known version of this poem.

"To Celimena": Copy-text: 1667. This is the earliest known version of this poem. 7 in] of 1678.

"An Answer to Another": Copy-text: 1667. This is the earliest known version of this poem.

"To Mr. Sam. Cooper": Copy-text: 1667. This is the earliest known version of this poem.

"To His Grace Gilbert Lord Archbishop of Canterbury": Copy-text: 1667. Variants: Title: To my Lord Arch-bishop of Canterbury his Grace 1664 (776); To his Grace Gilbert Lord Arch-Bishop of Canterbury, June 10. 1664 (67–78). 9 the Hebrew] Hebrew (78); 35 and] or (776); 45 makes] from (776), consent] gains consent (776); 60 proclaim] repeat (776).

BIBLIOGRAPHY

Editions

Beal, Peter. "Orinda to Silvander: A New Letter by Katherine Philips." *English Manuscript Studies* 4 (1993): 281–86.

Greer, Germaine, Jeslyn Medoff, Melinda Sansone, and Susan Hastings, eds. *Kissing the Rod: An Anthology of Seventeenth-Century Women's Verse.* London: Virago Press, 1988. 186–203.

Hageman, Elizabeth H., ed. "Katherine Philips." In *Writers of the Renaissance and Reformation.* Ed. Katharina M. Wilson. Athens: Univ. of Georgia Press, 1987. 566–608.

Limbert, Claudia, ed. "Two Poems and a Prose Receipt: The Unpublished Juvenilia of Katherine Philips (text)." *English Literary Renaissance* 16 (1986): 383–90.

Saintsbury, George, ed. "Katherine Philips." In *Minor Poets of the Caroline Period.* Oxford: Clarendon Press, 1905. 1:485–612.

Sant, Patricia M. "Two Unpublished Poems by Katherine Philips." *English Literary Renaissance* 24 (1994): 211–28.

Thomas, Patrick, ed. *The Collected Works of Katherine Philips, the Matchless Orinda. Vol. 1: The Poems.* Stump Cross, Essex: Stump Cross Press, 1990.

Secondary Works

Adam, Michel. "Katherine Philips, traductrice du théâtre de Pierre Corneille." *Revue d'Histoire littéraire de la France* 85 (1985): 841–51.

Alspach, R. K. "The Matchless Orinda." *Modern Language Notes* 52 (1937): 116–17.

Andreadis, Harriette. "The Sapphic-Platonics of Katherine Philips, 1632–1664." *Signs* 15 (1989): 34–60.

Aubrey, John. *Brief Lives.* Ed. Andrew Clark. 2 vols. Oxford: Clarendon Press, 1898.

Barash, Carol. *English Women's Poetry, 1649–1714: Politics, Community, and*

Linguistic Authority. Oxford: Clarendon Press, 1996.

Brashear, Lucy. "The Forgotten Legacy of the 'Matchless Orinda.'" *Anglo-Welsh Review* 65 (1979): 68–79.

———. "Gleanings from the Orinda Holograph." *American Notes and Queries* 23 (1985): 100–102.

———. "The 'Matchless Orinda's' Missing Sister: Mrs. C. P." *Restoration* 10 (1986): 76–81.

Cotton, Nancy. *Women Playwrights in England, c. 1363–1750.* Lewisburg, Pa.: Bucknell Univ. Press, 1980.

Easton, Celia A. "Excusing the Breach of Nature's Laws: The Discourse of Denial and Disguise in Katherine Philips' Friendship Poetry." *Restoration* 14 (1990): 1–14.

Elmen, Paul. "Some Manuscript Poems by the Matchless Orinda." *Philological Quarterly* 30 (1951): 53–57.

Faderman, Lillian. *Surpassing the Love of Men: Female Romantic Friendships from the Renaissance to the Present.* New York: Morrow, 1981.

Hageman, Elizabeth H. "Katherine Philips." *Dictionary of Literary Biography.* Ed. M. Thomas Hester. Vol. 131, *Seventeenth-Century British Nondramatic Poets.* Columbia, S.C.: Bruccoli Clark Layman, 1993. 202–14.

———. "Making a Good Impression: Early Texts of Poems and Letters by Katherine Philips, the 'Matchless Orinda.'" *South Central Review* 11 (1994): 39–65.

Hageman, Elizabeth H., and Andrea Sununu. "New Manuscript Texts of Katherine Philips, the 'Matchless Orinda.'" *English Manuscript Studies* 4 (1993): 174–216.

Hiscock, W. G. "Friendship: Francis Finch's Discourse and the Circle of the Matchless Orinda." *Review of English Studies* 15 (1939): 466–68.

Hobby, Elaine. "Katherine Philips: Seventeenth-Century Lesbian Poet." In *What Lesbians Do in Books.* Ed. Elaine Hobby and Chris White. London: Women's Press, 1991. 183–204.

———. *Virtue of Necessity: English Women's Writing, 1649–88.* Ann Arbor: Univ. of Michigan Press, 1989.

Kelliher, Hilton. "Cowley and 'Orinda': Autograph Fair Copies." *British Library Journal* 2 (1976): 102–8.

Libertin, Mary. "Female Friendship in Women's Verse: Toward a New Theory of Female Poetics." *Women's Studies* 9 (1982): 291–308.

Lilley, Kate. "True State Within: Women's Elegy 1640–1700." In *Women, Writing, History, 1640–1740.* Ed. Isobel Grundy and Susan Wiseman. Athens: Univ. of Georgia Press, 1992. 72–92.

Limbert, Claudia. "Katherine Philips: Another Step-Father and Another Sibling, 'Mrs C:P.,' and 'Polex.'" *Restoration* 13 (1989): 2–6.

———. "Katherine Philips: Controlling a Life and Reputation." *South Atlantic Review* 56 (1991): 27–42.

———. "Katherine Philips' Friend Regina Collyer." *Restoration* 13 (1989): 62–67.

———. "The Poetry of Katherine Philips: Holographs, Manuscripts, and Early Printed Texts." *Philological Quarterly* 70 (1991): 181–98.

———. "'The Unison of Well-Tun'd Hearts': Katherine Philips' Friendships with Male Writers." *English Language Notes* 29 (1991): 25–37.

Loscocco, Paula. " 'Manly Sweetness': Katherine Philips among the Neoclassicals." *Huntington Library Quarterly* 56 (1993): 259–79.

Lund, Roger D. "Bibliotecha and 'the British Dames': An Early Critique of the Female Wits of the Restoration." *Restoration* 12 (1988): 96–105.

MacLean, Gerald M. "What Is a Restoration Poem? Editing a Discourse, Not an Author." *Text* 3 (1987): 319–46.

Mambretti, Catherine Cole. " 'Fugitive Papers': A New Orinda Poem and Problems in Her Canon." *Papers of the Bibliographical Society of America* 71 (1977): 443–52.

———. "Orinda on the Restoration Stage." *Comparative Literature* 37 (1985): 233–51.

Mermin, Dorothy. "Women Becoming Poets: Katherine Philips, Aphra Behn, Anne Finch." *ELH* 57 (1990): 335–55.

Miner, Earl. *The Cavalier Mode from Jonson to Cotton*. Princeton: Princeton Univ. Press, 1971.

Moody, Ellen. "Orinda, Rosania, Lucasia, *et aliae:* Towards a New Edition of the Works of Katherine Philips." *Philological Quarterly* 66 (1987): 325–54.

Morgan, Fidelis. *The Female Wits: Women Playwrights on the London Stage 1660–1720*. London: Virago Press, 1981.

Mulvihill, Maureen E. "A Feminist Link in the Old Boys' Network: The Cosseting of Katherine Philips." In *Curtain Calls: British and American Women and the Theater, 1660–1820*. Ed. Mary Anne Schofield and Cecilia Macheski. Athens: Ohio Univ. Press, 1991. 71–104.

Pearson, Jacqueline. *The Prostituted Muse: Images of Women and Women Dramatists, 1642–1737*. New York: St. Martin's Press, 1988.

Price, Curtis A. "The Songs for Katherine Philips' *Pompey (1663)*." *Theater Notebook* 33 (1979): 61–66.

Pritchard, Allan. "Marvell's 'The Garden': A Restoration Poem?" *Studies in English Literature* 23 (1983): 371–88.

Radzinowicz, Mary Ann. "Reading Paired Poems Nowadays." *Literature, Interpretation, Theory* 1 (1990): 275–90.

Roberts, William. "The Dating of Orinda's French Translations." *Philological Quarterly* 49 (1970): 56–67.

———. "Saint-Amant, Orinda, and Dryden's Miscellany." *English Language Notes* 1 (1964): 191–96.

———. "Sir William Temple on Orinda: Neglected Publications." *Papers of the Bibliographical Society of America* 57 (1963): 328–36.

Røstvig, Maren-Sofie. *The Happy Man: Studies in the Metamorphosis of a Classical Ideal, 1600–1700*. Oxford: Blackwell, 1954.

Souers, Philip Webster. *The Matchless Orinda*. Cambridge: Harvard Univ. Press, 1931.

Stiebel, Arlene. "Not since Sappho: The Erotic in Poems of Katherine Philips and Aphra Behn." In *Homosexuality in Renaissance and Enlightenment England: Literary Representations in Historical Context*. Ed. Claude J. Summers. New York: Haworth Press, 1992. 153–71.

———. "Subversive Sexuality: Masking the Erotic in Poems by Katherine Philips and Aphra Behn." In *Renaissance Discourses of Desire*. Ed. Claude J. Summers and Ted-Larry Pebworth. Columbia: Univ. of Missouri Press, 1993. 223–36.

Thomas, Patrick. "Orinda, Vaughan, and Watkyns: Anglo-Welsh Literary Relationships during the Interregnum." *Anglo-Welsh Review* 26 (1976): 96–102.

Turner, James. *The Politics of Landscape: Rural Scenery and Society in English Poetry, 1630–1660.* Cambridge: Harvard Univ. Press, 1979.

Wheatley, Christopher J. "'Our Fetter'd Muse': The Reception of Katherine Philips's *Pompey.*" *Restoration and 18th-Century Theatre Research* 7 (1992): 18–28.

APHRA BEHN
(1640?–1689)

INTRODUCTION

Aphra Behn was the first of the major women writers of seventeenth-century England to receive scholarly attention. But her life and works have long been a source of discussion and controversy. A brief biography, placed in front of the third edition of her prose works (1698), identifies Behn as "a Gentlewoman by Birth, of a good Family in the City of Canterbury in Kent; her Father's name was Johnson." This early life, "written by one of the Fair Sex," was most likely composed by Charles Gildon, who knew Behn personally and may have also written two earlier biographical sketches. According to some accounts, her father was appointed to a government post in Surinam, West Indies, but died on the voyage over, leaving her on a plantation in Surinam for an extended period of time. Following her return to London, she may have married a tradesman and shipowner of Dutch ancestry, John Behn, who died of the plague in 1665. She went on to become a spy in Antwerp for King Charles II, but needed to borrow money to cover her expenses in Holland and was imprisoned for debt in 1668 when the court failed to pay her for her work.

Behn became a force in the world of the theater in the early 1670s. For the Duke's Company (one of the two dramatic troupes licensed by the king shortly after the Restoration), she wrote thirteen of the seventeen plays later printed with her name; two additional plays have been attributed to her. When *The Rover* was first published in 1677, Behn's name did not appear on the first two issues, but it was added to the third. The play was so successful that Behn later composed a sequel, *The Second Part of the Rover* (c. 1681). By her death in 1689, she had written at least seventeen plays, poetry enough to fill a substantial volume, and fiction for two volumes. Unlike women who wrote before her, she made her living by her pen and earned the admiration of Virginia Woolf on this account. She was an ardent Tory, and much of her writing reflects her political positions at a time when partisan politics served very much as a legitimate topic for imaginative literature. Many of her plays were popular in her own day, and they continued to be performed in altered texts for a hundred years after her death. More recently it has been possible to see on stage the bawdy original versions.

Witty and entertaining, *The Rover* places the women characters—Hellena, Florinda, Lucetta, and Angellica—at the center of the action. In the opening scene Hellena rebels against her family's plans to send her to a convent, but argues that an arranged marriage would be even more distasteful. Through the medium of disguise, the devious and chaste Hellena seeks out the husband of her own choice and is even willing to cross gender lines to accomplish her desire. Ironically, the courtesan Angellica maintains a high moral position in the play and suffers a great deal of pain because she believes that love should necessarily bring commitment. In the original production of *The Rover* in

THE

ROVER;

OR, THE

Banish'd Cavaliers.

A

COMEDY,

As it is Now Acted by His
MAJESTY's Servants.

Written by Mrs. BEHN.

LONDON,

Printed for JOHN DARBY, ARTHUR BETTESWORTH, and
FRANCIS CLAY, in Truſt for RICHARD, JAMES, and
BETHEL WELLINGTON. M.DCC.XXIX. (Price 1s.)

Title page of Aphra Behn's *The Rover* (1729). (Reproduced by
permission of the Special Collections Library, University of
Michigan.)

March 1677, the famous actress Elizabeth Barry performed the role of the virgin Hellena, but over the years as her acting abilities developed, she assumed the more demanding part of the passionate Angellica.

The title character, Willmore, is a typical gallant, at once a lovable little boy and a self-centered rakehell, or womanizer. Behn contrasts him with the upright Belvile, who disapproves of Willmore's interest in every passing female, and the lustful country squire, Blunt, a good-natured fool who mindlessly pursues his carnal interests. Lacking Willmore's brilliance, energy, and wit, Blunt travels through the sewer, both literally and figuratively. His fate is set in opposition to that of Willmore, who finally meets his match in Hellena. The character of the rover may be based partly on the dashing, sophisticated earl of Rochester, as well as Behn's bisexual lover, John Hoyle, a lawyer and a notorious ladies' man.

When regulation of the theater increased after Monmouth's Rebellion and it became harder to produce plays in London, Behn turned to writing poetry and fiction. She wrote virtually every type of poem common in the Restoration—translations and paraphrases of others' works, political poems, and bawdy lyrics, as well as numerous satires, songs, and verse dialogues with the major male poets of her time. One contemporary poem called her the "female laureate" and compared her work favorably to that of poet laureate John Dryden, who was England's first poet laureate. Behn oversaw the publication of *Poems Upon Several Occasions* (1684), her first volume of poems. She also edited several poetic miscellanies, in which she encouraged other women poets into print.

In marked contrast to Katherine Philips, Behn openly resisted prevailing ideals of women's honor and chastity. The themes and problems central to her poetry are similar to those found in *The Rover*: the constraints imposed by codes about women's "honor," women's economic dependence, and especially the sexual appeal of witty language. Like Hellena (and Angellica Bianca, whose initials are the same as the author's), Behn's poetic speakers often flaunt their sexual desire, making love a linguistic game that the witty woman can sometimes win. "To the Fair Clarinda" emphasizes the appeal of sexual ambiguity and cross-dressing; "On Desire" claims that women's sexual desire is a story that cannot be officially told.

The poems included here represent the wide range of poetic forms used by Behn. Often she works against the very forms she inherits from other poets, revealing the hidden assumptions of literary convention. In "The Disappointment," for instance, Behn takes on the classical poem of "imperfect enjoyment" (or premature ejaculation) and retells it from the woman's point of view. "The Willing Mistress" was written two ways, telling a story of seduction first from the male and then from the female point of view. And in the poems to and about male writers—"On the Death of Rochester" and "To Mr. Creech"—Behn emphasizes the limited range of poetic stock a woman writer begins with and then reveals the authority she can generate by resisting her linguistic dependence on men. Although written under extreme duress to pay the bills from Behn's last illness, the "Congratulatory Poem" to Mary II remains a subversive, almost treasonous poem. Behn seems at first to praise the new queen, but subtly undercuts both the queen's authority and the assumptions of political panegyric at the heart of so much Restoration poetry.

Although Behn was unquestionably the most important woman writer of

the Restoration—respected and encouraged by her male contemporaries—
most of her poetry was too threatening to withstand the increased moral
regulation of the later eighteenth and nineteenth centuries; and, with the exception of Montague Summers's edition of 1915, it is not until our own time that
editions of Behn's works have begun to work their way back into print.

THE ROVER, OR THE BANISHED CAVALIERS

Prologue

Wits, like physicians, never can agree,
When of a different society.
And Rabel's drops[1] were never more cried down
By all the learned doctors of the town
Than a new play whose author is unknown.   5
Nor can those doctors with more malice sue
(And powerful purses) the dissenting few,
Than those with an insulting pride do rail
At all who are not of their own cabal.
 If a young poet hit your humor[2] right   10
You judge him then out of revenge and spite.
So amongst men there are ridiculous elves,
Who monkeys hate for being too like themselves.
So that the reason of the grand debate,
Why wit so oft is damn'd, when good plays take,   15
Is that you censure as you love or hate.
 Thus like a learned conclave poets sit,
Catholic judges both of sense and wit,
And damn or save, as they themselves think fit.
Yet those who to others' faults are so severe,   20
Are not so perfect but themselves may err.
 Some write correct indeed, but then the whole,
Bating[3] their own dull stuff i'th' play, is stole.
As bees do suck from flowers their honey dew,
So they rob others striving to please you.   25
 Some write their characters gentle and fine,
But then they do so toil for every line
That what to you does easy seem and plain
Is the hard issue of their laboring brain.
And some th'effects of all their pains we see,   30
Is but to mimic good extempore.
Others by long converse about the town
Have wit enough to write a lewd lampoon,

---

1. A patent medicine.
2. "Humor" here means "individual inclination or oddity."
3. Subtracting.

But their chief skill lies in a bawdy song.
In short, the only wit that's now in fashion   35
Is but the gleanings of good conversation.
As for the author of this coming play,
I ask'd him[4] what he thought fit I should say
In thanks for your good company today.
He call'd me fool and said it was well known   40
You came not here for our sakes but your own.
New plays are stuff'd with wits and with debauches
That crowd and sweat like cits in May-Day Coaches.[5]

Written By a Person of Quality

The Actors' Names

Mr. Jevon	Don Antonio, the viceroy's son
Mr. Medbourne	Don Pedro, a noble Spaniard and his friend
Mr. Betterton	Belvile, an English colonel in love with Forinda
Mr. Smith	Willmore, the Rover
Mr. Crosby	Frederick, an English gentleman and friend to Belv. and [Blunt][6]
Mr. Underhill	Blunt, an English country gentleman
Mr. Richards	Stephano, servant to Don Pedro
Mr. Percival	Philippo, Lucetta's gallant
Mr. John Lee	Sancho, pimp to Lucetta
	Biskey and Sebastian, two bravos to Angellica
	[Diego,] page to Don Antonio
	Officers and soldiers

Women

Mrs. Betterton	Florinda, sister to Don Pedro
Mrs. Barry	Hellena, a gay young woman designed[7] for a nun and sister to Florinda
Mrs. Hughes	Valeria, a kinswoman to Florinda
Mrs. Quin	Angellica Bianca, a famous courtesan
Mrs. Leigh	Moretta, her woman
Mrs. Norris	Callis, governess to Florinda and Hellena
Mrs. Gillow	Lucetta, a jilting wench

4. Behn's name did not appear on the title page until the third issue of the 1677 first quarto.
5. Cits were persons living in the city as opposed to the country. On May Day, many people went to Hyde Park to see and be seen. Samuel Pepys, for instance, spent the whole of a day in 1667 trying to catch a glimpse of Margaret Cavendish in her coach.
6. "Fred.," an obvious error in the copy-text, is corrected to "Blunt" here and in the second quarto (1697).
7. Intended. "Gay" means something like "quick-witted and sassy."

Servants, other masqueraders, men, and women

The scene: Naples in carnival time

Act the First

Scene the First. *A chamber.*

Enter Florinda and Hellena.

Flor. What an impertinent thing is a young girl bred in a nunnery. How full of questions. Prithee, no more Hellena. I have told thee more than thou understandst already.

Hell. The more's my grief. I would fain know as much as you, which makes me so inquisitive. Nor is't enough I know you're a lover, unless you tell me, too, who 'tis you sigh for.

Flor. When you're a lover, I'll think you fit for a secret of that nature.

Hell. 'Tis true. I never was a lover yet. But I begin to have a shrewd guess, what 'tis to be so, and fancy it very pretty to sigh and sing, and blush and wish, and dream and wish, and long and wish to see the man. And when I do, look pale and tremble, just as you did when my brother brought home the fine English colonel to see you. What do you call him, Don Belvile?

Flor. Fie, Hellena.

Hell. That blush betrays you. I'm sure 'tis so. Or is it Don Antonio the viceroy's son? Or, perhaps, the rich old Don Vincentio, whom my father designs you for a husband? Why do you blush again?

Flor. With indignation, and how near soever my father thinks I am to marrying that hated object, I shall let him see I understand better what's due to my beauty, birth, and fortune—and more, to my soul—than to obey those unjust commands.

Hell. Now hang me if I don't love thee for that dear disobedience. I love mischief strangely,[8] as most of our sex do who are come to love nothing else. But tell me Florinda, don't you love that fine *Anglese?* For I vow, next to loving him myself, 'twill please me most that you do so, for he is so gay and so handsome.

Flor. Hellena, a maid designed for a nun ought not to be so curious in a discourse of love.

Hell. And dost thou think that ever I'll be a nun? Or at least till I'm so old I'm fit for nothing else? Faith no, sister, and that which makes me long to know whether you love Belvile is because I hope he has some mad companion or other that will spoil my devotion. Nay, I'm resolved to provide myself this carnival, if there be e'er a handsome proper fellow of my humor above ground, though I ask first.

Flor. Prithee, be not so wild.

Hell. Now you have provided yourself of a man, you take no care of poor me. Prithee tell me, what dost thou see about me that is unfit

8. Very greatly.

for love? Have I not a world of youth, a humor gay, a beauty pass-
able, a vigor desirable, [a body] well shaped, clean limbed, sweet
breathed, and sense enough to know how all these ought to be
employed to the best advantage? Yes, I do and will. And therefore
lay aside your hopes of my fortune by my being a devote,[9] and tell
me how you came acquainted with this Belvile, for I perceive you
knew him before he came to Naples.

Flor. Yes, I knew him at the siege of Pamplona. He was then a colonel of
French horse, who when the town was ransacked, nobly treated my
brother and myself, preserving us from all insolences. And I must
own (besides great obligations), I have I know not what that pleads
kindly for him about my heart, and will suffer no other to enter. But
see my brother.

Enter Pedro, Steph. with a masquing habit, and Call.

Pedro. Good morrow, sister. Pray, when saw you your lover, Don
Vincentio?

Flor. I know not sir. Callis, when was he here? For I consider it so little, I
know not when it was.

Pedro. I have a command from my father here to tell you, you ought
not to despise him, a man of so vast a fortune and such a passion for
you. Stephano, my things.

(Puts on his masquing habit.)

Flor. A passion for me? 'Tis more than ere I saw or he had a desire
should be known. I hate Vincentio, sir, and I would not have a man
so dear to me as my brother follow the ill customs of our country
and make a slave of his sister. And, sir, my father's will I'm sure you
may divert.

Pedro. I know not how dear I am to you, but I wish only to be ranked in
your esteem equal with the English colonel Belvile. Why do you
frown and blush? Is there any guilt belongs to the name of that
cavalier?

Flor. I'll not deny I value Belvile. When I was exposed to such dangers
as the licensed lust of common soldiers threatened (when rage and
conquest flew through the city), then Belvile (this criminal for my
sake) threw himself into all dangers to save my honor, and will you
not allow him my esteem?

Pedro. Yes, pay him what you will in honor. But you must consider Don
Vincentio's fortune and the jointure[10] he'll make you.

Flor. Let him consider my youth, beauty, and fortune, which ought not
to be thrown away on his age and jointure.

Pedro. 'Tis true he's not so young and fine a gentleman as that Belvile,
but what jewels will that cavalier present you with—those of his
eyes and heart?

9. Nun.
10. A jointure was the amount due a widow from her husband's estate. Later in the play, Blunt thinks
    he can take advantage of what he sees as Lucetta's innocence and give her a paltry jointure after he
    has murdered her supposed husband.

Hell. And are not those better than any Don Vincentio has brought from the Indies?

Pedro. Why how now! Has your nunnery breeding taught you to understand the value of hearts and eyes?

Hell. Better than to believe Vincentio's deserve value from any woman. He may perhaps increase her bags but not her family.

Pedro. This is fine. Go. Up to your devotion. You are not designed for the conversation of lovers.

Hell. (Aside.) Nor saints yet awhile, I hope. [*To Pedro.*] Is't not enough you make a nun of me, but you must cast my sister away, too? Exposing her to a worse confinement than a religious life.

Pedro. The girl's mad. It is a confinement to be carried into the country to an ancient villa belonging to the family of the Vincentios these five hundred years and have no other prospect than that pleasing one of seeing all her own that meets her eyes—a fine air, large fields and gardens where she may walk and gather flowers.

Hell. When? By moonlight? For I am sure she dares not encounter with the heat of the sun. That were a task only for Don Vincentio and his Indian breeding, who loves it in the dog days.[11] And if these be her daily divertissements,[12] what are those of the night—to lie in a wide moth-eaten bed chamber with furniture in fashion in the reign of King Sancho the first, the bed that which his forefathers lived and died in?

Pedro. Very well.

Hell. This apartment (new furbished and fitted out for the young wife) he (out of freedom) makes his dressing room. And being a frugal and a jealous coxcomb,[13] instead of a valet to uncase his feeble carcass, he desires you to do that office—signs of favor I'll assure you, and such as you must not hope for unless your woman be out of the way.

Pedro. Have you done yet?

Hell. That honor being past, the giant stretches itself, yawns and sighs a belch or two loud as a musket, throws himself into bed, and expects you in his foul sheets, and ere you can get yourself undrest, calls you with a snore or two. And are not these fine blessings to a young lady?

Pedro. Have you done yet?

Hell. And this man you must kiss. Nay, you must kiss none but him, too, and nuzzle through his beard to find his lips. And this you must submit to for threescore years, and all for a jointure.

Pedro. For all your character of Don Vincentio, she is as like to marry him as she was before.

Hell. Marry Don Vincentio! Hang me! Such a wedlock would be worse than adultery with another man. I had rather see her in the *Hostel de*

11. Dog days occurred in the hottest part of summer.
12. Entertainments.
13. A coxcomb was literally a fool's cap intended to resemble a rooster's comb. Figuratively, a coxcomb was the fool himself.

Dieu[14] to waste her youth there in vows and be a handmaid to lazars and cripples than to lose it in such a marriage.

Pedro. You have considered, sister, that Belvile has no fortune to bring you to: banished his country, despised at home, and pitied abroad?

Hell. What then? The viceroy's son is better than that old Sir Fifty. Don Vincentio! Don Indian! He thinks he's trading to Gambia still and would barter himself (that bell and bauble) for your youth and fortune.

Pedro. Callis, take her hence and lock her up all this carnival. And at Lent she shall begin her everlasting penance in a monastery.

Hell. I care not. I had rather be a nun than be obliged to marry as you would have me if I were designed for't.

Pedro. Do not fear the blessing of that choice. You shall be a nun.

Hell. Shall I so? You may chance to be mistaken in my way of devotion. *(Aside.)* A nun! Yes, I am like to make a fine nun! I have an excellent humor for a grate.[15] No, I'll have a saint of my own to pray to shortly, if I like any that dares venture on me.

Pedro. Callis, make it your business to watch this wildcat. As for you, Florinda, I've only tried you all this while and urged my father's will. But, mine is that you would love Antonio. He is brave and young and all that can complete the happiness of a gallant maid. This absence of my father will give us opportunity to free you from Vincentio by marrying here, which you must do tomorrow.

Flor. Tomorrow!

Pedro. Tomorrow, or 'twill be too late. 'Tis not my friendship to Antonio which makes me urge this, but love to thee and hatred to Vincentio. Therefore resolve upon tomorrow.

Flor. Sir, I shall strive to do as shall become your sister.

Pedro. I'll both believe and trust you. Adieu.

   (Exeunt Pedro. and Steph.)

Hell. As becomes his sister! That is to be as resolved your way as he is his.

   Hell. goes to Call.

Flor.

  I ne'er till now perceived my ruin near.
  I've no defense against Antonio's love,
  For he has all the advantages of nature,
  The moving arguments of youth and fortune.

Hell. But hark you, Callis. You will not be so cruel to lock me up indeed, will you?

Call. I must obey the commands I have. Besides, do you consider what a life you are going to lead?

Hell. Yes, Callis, that of a nun. And till then I'll be indebted a world of prayers to you if you'll let me now see what I never did—the divertissements of a carnival.

14. Literally, "hospital of God."
15. Lattice covering a convent window.

Call. What, go in a masquerade? 'Twill be a fine farewell to the world, I take it. Pray, what would you do there?

Hell. That which all the world does, as I am told, be as mad as the rest, and take all innocent freedoms. Sister, you'll go, too, will you not? Come, prithee, be not sad. We'll outwit twenty brothers if you'll be ruled by me. Come put off this dull humor with your clothes, and assume one as gay and as fantastic as the dress my cousin Valeria and I have provided, and let's ramble.

Flor. Callis, will you give us leave to go?

Call. *(Aside.)* I have a youthful itch myself. *[To Flor.]* Madam, if I thought your brother might not know it, and I might wait on you, for by my troth I'll not trust young girls alone.

Flor. Thou seest my brother's gone already, and thou shalt attend and watch us.

Enter Steph.

Steph. Madam? The habits are come, and your cousin Valeria is drest and stays for you.

Flor. 'Tis well. I'll write a note, and if I chance to see Belvile and want an opportunity to speak to him, that shall let him know what I've resolved in favor of him.

Hell. Come, let's in and dress us.

    (Exeunt.)

Scene ii. *A Long Street.*

Enter Belv., melancholy, Blunt, and Fred.

Fred. Why, what the devil ails the colonel? In a time when all the world is gay, to look like mere Lent thus? Hadst thou been long enough in Naples to have been in love, I should have sworn some such judgment had befallen thee.

Belv. No, I have made no new amours since I came to Naples.

Fred. You have left none behind you in Paris?

Belv. Neither.

Fred. I cannot divine the cause then, unless the old cause—the want of money.

Blunt. And another old cause—the want of a wench. Would not that revive you?

Belv. You are mistaken, Ned.

Blunt. Nay, 'Sheartlikins,[16] then thou'rt past cure.

Fred. I have found it out. Thou hast renewed thy acquaintance with the lady that cost thee so many sighs at the siege of Pamplona. Pox on't, what d'ye call her? Her brother's a noble Spaniard, nephew to the dead general. Florinda. Aye, Florinda. And will nothing serve thy turn but that damned virtuous woman, whom on my conscience

---

16. A mild curse literally meaning "by God's little heart."

thou lovest in spite, too, because thou seest little or no possibility of gaining her?

Belv. Thou art mistaken. I have interest enough in that lovely virgin's heart to make me proud and vain, were it not abated by the severity of a brother, who perceiving my happiness . . .

Fred. Has civilly forbid thee the house?

Belv. 'Tis so, to make way for a powerful rival, the viceroy's son, who has the advantage of me in being a man of fortune, a Spaniard, and her brother's friend; which gives him liberty to court, whilst I have recourse only to letters and distant looks from her window, which [looks] are as soft and kind as those which heaven sends down on penitents.

Blunt. Heyday! 'Sheartlikins, simile! By this light, the man is quite spoiled. Fred, what the devil are we made of that we [can] be thus concerned for a wench?[17] 'Sheartlikins, our Cupids are like the cooks of the camp. They can roast or boil a woman, but they have none of the fine tricks to set 'em off, no hogoes[18] to make the sauce pleasant and the stomach sharp.

Fred. I dare swear I have had a hundred as young, kind,[19] and handsome as this Florinda. And, dogs eat me, if they were not as troublesome to me i'the morning as they were welcome o'er night.

Blunt. And yet I warrant he would not [hesitate to] touch another woman if he might have her for nothing.

Belv. That's thy joy—a cheap whore.

Blunt. Whe,[20] I. 'Sheartlikins, I love a frank soul. When did you ever hear of an honest woman that took a man's money? I warrant 'em good ones. But, gentlemen, you may be free. You have been kept so poor with Parliaments and Protectors that the little stock you have is not worth preserving.[21] But I thank my stars I had more grace than to forfeit my estate by cavaliering.

Belv. Methinks only following the court should be sufficient to entitle 'em to that.[22]

Blunt. 'Sheartlikins, they know I follow it to do it no good, unless they pick a hole in my coat for lending you money now and then, which is a greater crime to my conscience, gentlemen, than to the commonwealth.

Enter Willmore.

Will. Ha! Dear Belvile! Noble Colonel!

---

17. The copy-text reads "cannot be," but the passage makes better sense in the affirmative.
18. Fancy or elegant food.
19. Throughout the play, the word *kind* in various forms provides the basis for punning. In addition to "caring and understanding," it meant "affectionate," "according to nature," and, during the Restoration, "willing to sleep with."
20. "Whe," a word now obsolete, works as a male-oriented interjection in the play.
21. Belvile and Fredrick, as Cavaliers, sided with the king against the Parliament during the English civil wars (1642–1648). Because the royalists lost and Oliver Cromwell became Protector, the two Cavaliers suffered financially.
22. Belvile suggests that Blunt is hypocritical for following the court in exile, while staying in favor with the Parliament at home.

Belv. Willmore! Welcome ashore, my dear rover! What happy wind blew us this good fortune?

Will. Let me salute my dear Fred, and then command me. How is't honest lad?

Fred. Faith, sir, the old compliment. Infinitely the better to see my dear mad Willmore again. Prithee why camest thou ashore? And where's the prince?[23]

Will. He's well and reigns still lord of the watery element. I must aboard again within a day or two, and my business ashore was only to enjoy myself a little this carnival.

Belv. Pray know our new friend, sir; he's but bashful, a raw traveler, but honest, stout,[24] and one of us.

([Will.] embraces Blunt.)

Will. That you esteem him gives him an interest here.

Blunt. Your servant, sir.

Will. But well. Faith, I'm glad to meet you again in a warm climate, where the kind sun has its god-like power still over the wine and women. Love and mirth are my business in Naples, and if I mistake not the place, here's an excellent market for chapmen of my humor!

Belv. See, here be those kind merchants of love you look for.

Enter several men in masquing habits, some playing on music,[25] others dancing after; women drest like courtesans with papers pinned on their breasts and baskets of flowers in their hands.

Blunt. 'Sheartlikins, what have we here?

Fred. Now the game begins.

Will. Fine pretty creatures! May a stranger have leave to look and love? What's here? *(Reads the papers.)* Roses for every month?

Blunt. Roses for every month? What means that?

Belv. They are or would have you think they're courtesans, who here in Naples are to be hired by the month.

Will. Kind and obliging to inform us. Pray, where do these roses grow? I would fain plant some of 'em in a bed of mine.

Wom. Beware such roses, sir.

Will. A pox of fear. I'll be baked with thee between a pair of sheets and that's thy proper still, so I might but strew such roses over me and under me.[26] Fair one, would you give me leave to gather at your bush this idle month, I would go near to make somebody smell of it all the year after.

Belv. And thou hast need of such a remedy, for thou stinkst of tar and ropes' ends like a dock or pesthouse.[27]

The woman puts herself into the hands of a man and exits.

Will. Nay, nay. You shall not leave me so.

---

23. The prince was the exiled Charles II, legally king of England in the view of the royalists.
24. Resolute, brave.
25. Musical instruments.
26. Willmore alludes a treatment for venereal disease that involved heat and sweating.
27. A hospital for plague victims.

Belv. By all means use no violence here.

Will. Death![28] Just as I was going to be damnably in love, to have her led off! I could pluck that rose out of his hand and even kiss the bed the bush grew in.

Fred. No friend to love like a long voyage at sea.

Blunt. Except a nunnery, Fred.

Will. Death! But will they not be kind? Quickly be kind? Thou knowest I am no tame sigher, but a rampant lion of the forest.

> *(Advances from the farther end of the scenes two men drest all over with horns[29] of several sorts making grimaces at one another, with papers pinned on their backs.)*

Belv. Oh the fantastical rogues, how they are drest! 'Tis a satire against the whole sex.

Will. Is this a fruit that grows in this warm country?

Belv. Yes. 'Tis pretty to see these Italians start, swell, and stab at the word "cuckold," and yet stumble at horns on every threshold.

Will. See what's on their back? *(Reads.)* "Flowers of every night." Ah, Rogue! And more sweet than roses of every month! This is a gardener of Adam's own breeding.

> *(They dance.)*[30]

Belv. What think you of these grave people? Is a wake in Essex half so mad or extravagant?

Will. I like their sober grave way. 'Tis a kind of legal, authorized fornication, where the men are not chid for't, nor the women despised as amongst our dull English. Even the monsieurs want that part of good manners.

Belv. But here in Italy, a monsieur is the humblest best bred gentleman. Duels are so baffled by bravos that an age shows not one but between an Frenchman and a hangman, who is as much too hard for him on the Piazza as they are for a Dutchman on the New Bridge.[31] But see, another crew.

Enter Flor., Hell., and Val. drest like gypsies. Call. and Steph., Lucett., Phil., and San. in masquerade.

Hell. Sister, there's your Englishman and with him a handsome, proper fellow. I'll to him, and instead of telling him his fortune, try my own.

Will. Gypsies, on my life. Sure these will prattle if a man cross their hands. *(Goes to Hell.)* Dear, pretty, and (I hope) young devil, will you tell an amorous stranger what luck he's like to have?

---

28. A mild curse derived from "by God's death."
29. Horns signified cuckoldry.
30. Probably the Englishmen merely observe the Italians dancing.
31. Strictly speaking, bravos were assassins, but their function here seems to be less sinister. "Piazza": market square. The reference to the battle of New Bridge is obscure, but it is possible that Behn has in mind the Battle of Nieuport (literally "New Port") in mind. Hoping to demonstrate their resolve and gain English intervention by attacking the Spanish at Nieuport, the Dutch were ill prepared and badly defeated: Geoffrey Parker, *The Dutch Revolt* (Ithaca: Cornell Univ. Press, 1977), 234.

Hell. Have a care how you venture with me, sir, lest I pick your pocket, which will more vex your English humor than an Italian fortune will please you.

Will. How the devil camest thou to know my country and humor?

Hell. The first I guess by a certain forward impudence, which does not displease me at this time, and the loss of your money will vex you because I hope[32] you have but very little to lose.

Will. Egad, child, thou'rt i'th' right. It is so little I dare not offer it to thee for a kindness. But cannot you divine what other things of more value I have about me that I would more willingly part with.

Hell. Indeed no, that's the business of a witch, and I am but a gypsy yet. Yet without looking in your hand, I have a parlous[33] guess, 'tis some foolish heart you mean—an inconstant English heart as little worth stealing as your purse.

Will. Nay, then thou dost deal with the devil, that's certain. Thou hast guessed as right as if thou hadst been one of that number it has languisht for. I find you'll be better acquainted with it, nor can you take it in a better time, for I am come from sea, child. And, Venus not being propitious to me in her own element, I have a world of love in store. Would you be good natured and take some on't off my hands?

Hell. Whe. I could be inclined that way, but for a foolish vow I am going to make to die a maid.

Will. Then thou art damned without redemption, and, as I am a good Christian, I ought in charity to divert so wicked a design. Therefore prithee, dear creature, let me know quickly when and where I shall begin to set a helping hand to so good a work.

Hell. If you should prevail with my tender heart ([*aside*] as I begin to fear you will, for you have horrible loving eyes), there will be difficulty in't that you'll hardly undergo for my sake.

Will. Faith, child, I have been bred in dangers and wear a sword that has been employed in a worse cause than for a handsome, kind woman. Name the danger. Let it be anything but a long siege, and I'll undertake it.

Hell. Can you storm?

Will. Oh most furiously.

Hell. What think you of a nunnery wall? For he that wins me must gain that first.

Will. A nun! Oh now I love thee for't! There's no sinner like a young saint. Nay, now there's no denying me. The old law had no curse (to a woman) like dying a maid. Witness Jeptha's daughter.[34]

32. Expect.
33. Dangerous.
34. Jeptha's daughter was an Old Testament figure who, learning that she was to die a virgin, asked to be given two months to "bewail" the fact. Judges 11:31–40.

Hell. A very good text this, if well handled. And I perceive, Father Captain, you would impose no severe penance on her who were inclined to console herself before she took orders.

Will. If she be young and handsome.

Hell. Aye, there's it. But if she be not . . .

Will. By this hand, child, I have an implicit faith and dare venture on thee with all faults. Besides it is more meritorious to leave the world when thou hast tasted and proved the pleasure on't. Then 'twill be a virtue in thee, which now will be pure ignorance.

Hell. I perceive, good Father Captain, you design only to make me fit for heaven. But if on the contrary you should quite divert me from it and bring me back to the world again, I should have a new man to seek, I find. And what a grief that will be, for when I begin, I fancy I shall love like anything I never tried yet.

Will. Egad and that's kind. Prithee, dear creature, give me credit for a heart, for faith I'm a very honest fellow. Oh, I long to come first to the banquet of love! And such a swingeing³⁵ appetite I bring! Oh, I'm impatient. Thy lodging, sweetheart, thy lodging, or I'm a dead man!

Hell. Why must we be either guilty of fornication or murder if we converse with you men? And is there no difference between "leave to love me" and "leave to lie with me"?

Will. Faith, child, they were made to go together.

Lucett. (Pointing to Blunt.) Are you sure this is the man?

San. When did I mistake your game?

Lucett. This is a stranger. I know by his gazing. If he be brisk, he'll venture to follow me, and then if I understand my trade he's mine. He's English, too, and they say that's a good natured loving people and have generally so kind an opinion of themselves that a woman with any wit may flatter 'em into any sort of fool she pleases.

(She often passes by Blunt and gazes on him. He struts and cocks and walks and gazes on her.)

Blunt. 'Tis so. She is taken. I have beauties which my false glass at home did not discover.

Flor. [Aside.] This woman watches me so, I shall get no opportunity to discover myself to him and so miss the intent of my coming.

([To Belv.] looking in his hand.)

But as I was saying, sir, by this line you should be a lover.

Belv. I thought how right you guessed. All men are in love or pretend to be so. Come let me go; I'm weary of this fooling.

(Walks away. She holds him, he strives to get from her.)

Flor. I will not, till you have confessed whether the passion that you have vowed Florinda be true or false.

([He] turns quick towards her.)

Belv. Florinda!

35. Powerful. The verb *swinge*, to beat or flog, is now obsolete.

Flor. Softly.

Belv. Thou hast named one will fix me here forever.

Flor. She'll be disappointed then, who expects you this night at the garden gate, and, if you fail not (as let me see the other hand: you will go near to do), she vows to die or to make you happy.

>   *(Looks on Call., who observes 'em.)*

Belv. What canst thou mean?

Flor. That which I say. Farewell.

>   *(Offers to go.)*

Belv. Oh charming sybil, stay. Complete that joy which as it is will turn into distraction! Where must I be? At the garden gate? I know it. At night, you say? I'll sooner forfeit heaven than disobey.

Enter Pedro and other masquers and pass over the stage.

Call. Madam, your brother's here.

Flor. Take this to instruct you further.

>   *(Gives him a letter and goes off.)*

Fred. Have a care, sir, what you promise. This may be a trap laid by her brother to ruin you.

Belv. Do not disturb my happiness with doubts.

>   *(Opens the letter.)*

Will. My dear pretty creature, a thousand blessings on thee! Still in this habit you say? And after dinner at this place?

Hell. Yes, if you will swear to keep your heart and not bestow it between this and that.

Will. By all the little gods of love, I swear. I'll leave it with you, and if you run away with it, those deities of justice will revenge me.

>   *(Exeunt all the women [except Lucett.].)*

Fred. Do you know the hand?

Belv. 'Tis Florinda's.

All blessings fall upon the virtuous maid.

Fred. Nay, no idolatry. A sober sacrifice I'll allow you.

Belv. Oh friends, the welcomest news! The softest letter! Nay, you shall all see it! And could you now be serious, I might be made the happiest man the sun shines on!

Will. The reason of this mighty joy?

Belv. See how kindly she invites me to deliver her from the threatened violence of her brother. Will you not assist me?

Will. I know not what thou meanst, but I'll make one at any mischief where a woman's concerned. But she'll be grateful to us for the favor, will she not?

Belv. How mean you?

Will. How should I mean? Thou knowst there's but one way for a woman to olige me.

Belv. Do not profane. The maid is nicely[36] virtuous.

---

36. Strictly. In the next speech "who" from the copy-text is emended and becomes "whe," the interjection discussed in note 20.

Will. [Whe,] pox. Then she's fit for nothing but a husband. Let her e'n go, Colonel.

Fred. Peace. She's the colonel's mistress,[37] sir.

Will. Let her be the devil. If she be thy mistress, I'll serve her. Name the way.

Belv. Read here this postscript.

(Gives him a letter.)

Will. *(Reads.)* "At ten at night at the garden gate of which, if I cannot get the key, I will contrive a way over the wall. Come attended with a friend or two." Kind heart, if we three cannot weave a string to let her down a garden wall, 'twere pity but the hangman wove one for us all.

Fred. Let her alone for that. Your woman's wit! Your fair kind woman will out-trick a broker or a Jew and contrive like a Jesuit in chains. But see, Ned Blunt is stolen out after the lure of a damsel.

(Exeunt Blunt and Lucett.)

Belv. So. He'll scarce find his way home again unless we get him cried by the bellman in the market place, and 'twould sound prettily—"A lost English boy of thirty."

Fred. I hope 'tis some common crafty sinner, one that will fit him. It may be she'll sell him for Peru. The rogue's sturdy and would work well in a mine. At least I hope she'll dress him for our mirth, cheat him of all, then have him well-favoredly banged, and turned out naked at midnight.

Will. Prithee, what humor is he of, that you wish him so well?

Belv. Why of an English elder brother's humor—educated in a nursery with a maid to tend him till fifteen and lies with his grandmother till he's of age. One that knows no pleasure beyond riding to the next fair, or going up to London with his right worshipful father in Parliament time, wearing gay clothes, or making honorable love to[38] his lady mother's laundry maid. [He] gets drunk at a hunting match and ten to one then gives some sort of proofs of his prowess. A pox on him. He's our banker, and has all our cash about him, and if he fail, we are all broke.

Fred. Oh let him alone for that matter. He's of a damned stingy quality that will secure our stock. I know not in what danger it were indeed if the jilt should pretend she's in love with him, for 'tis a kind, believing coxcomb. Otherwise, if he part with more than a piece of eight, geld him. For which offer he may chance to be beaten if she be a whore of the first rank.

Belv. Nay, the rogue will not be easily beaten. He's stout enough. Perhaps if they talk beyond his capacity he may chance to exercise his courage upon some of them, else I'm sure they'll find it as difficult to beat as to please him.

---

37. Beloved. Frederick does not imply sexual involvement in this particular case. Either the platonic or physical lover of a mistress was generally called a "servant."
38. Talking of love to.

Will. 'Tis a lucky devil to light upon so kind a wench!

Fred. Thou hadst a great deal of talk with thy little gypsy. Couldst thou do no good upon her? For mine was hard hearted.

Will. Hang her. She was some damned honest person of quality, I'm sure, she was so very free and witty. If her face be but answerable to her wit and humor, I would be bound to constancy this month to gain her. In the meantime, have you made no kind acquaintance since you came to town? You do not use to be honest so long, gentlemen.

Fred. Faith, love has kept us honest. We have been all fired with a beauty newly come to town—the famous Paduana, Angellica Bianca.[39]

Will. What? The mistress of the dead Spanish general?

Belv. Yes, she's now the only adored beauty of all the youth in Naples, who put on all their charms to appear lovely in her sight. Their coaches, liveries, and themselves all gay as on a monarch's birthday to attract the eyes of this fair charmer, while she has the pleasure to behold all languish for her that see her.

Fred. 'Tis pretty to see with how much love the men regard her, and how much envy the women.

Will. What gallant has she?

Belv. None, she's exposed to sale, and four days in the week she's yours for so much a month.

Will. The very thought of it quenches all manner of fire in me. Yet prithee, let's see her.

Belv. Let's first to dinner, and after that we'll pass the day as you please. But at night ye must be at my devotion.

Will. I will not fail you.

The End of the First Act.

Act II

Scene i. *The Long Street.*

Enter Belv. and Fred. in masquing habits, and Will. in his own clothes with a vizard in his hand.

Will. But why thus disguised and muzzled?

Belv. Because whatever extravagances we commit in these faces, our own may not be obliged to answer 'em.

Will. I should have changed my eternal buff,[40] too. But no matter, my little gypsy would not have found me out then. For if she should change hers, it is impossible I should know her, unless I should hear her prattle. A pox on't. I cannot get her out of my head. Pray heaven, if ever I do see her again, she prove damnably ugly, that I may fortify myself against her tongue.

39. Angellica is from Padua.
40. Leather uniform.

Belv. Have a care of love, for o' my conscience she was not of a quality to give thee any hopes.

Will. Pox on 'em. Why do they draw a man in then? She has played with my heart so, that 'twill never lie still till I have met with some kind wench that will play the game out with me. Oh for my arms full of soft, white, kind—woman! Such as I fancy Angellica.

Belv. This is her house, if you were but in stock to get admittance. They have not dined yet. I perceive the picture is not out.⁴¹

Enter Blunt.

Will. I long to see the shadow of the fair substance. A man may gaze on that for nothing.

Blunt. Colonel, thy hand, and thine, Fred. I have been an ass, a deluded fool, a very coxcomb from my birth till this hour, and heartily repent my little faith.

Belv. What the devil's the matter with thee, Ned?

[Blunt.] Oh, such a mistress, Fred. Such a girl.

Will. Ha! Where?

Fred. Aye where?⁴²

[Blunt.] So fond, so amorous, so toying, and so fine! And all for sheer love, ye rogue! Oh how she looked and kissed! And soothed my heart from my bosom. I cannot think I was awake, and yet methinks I see and feel her charms still. Fred, try if she have not left the taste of her balmy kisses upon my lips.
(Kisses him.)

Belv. Ha! Ha! Ha!

Will. Death, man, where is she?

[Blunt.] What a dog I was to stay in dull England so long. How have I laught at the colonel when he sighed for love! But now the little archer has revenged him! And by this one dart, I can guess at all his joys, which then I took for fancies, mere dreams and fables. Well, I am resolved to sell all in Essex and plant here forever.

Belv. What a blessing 'tis thou hast a mistress thou darest boast of, for I know thy humor is rather to have proclaimed clap than a secret amour.

Will. Dost know her name?

Blunt. Her name? No, 'sheartlikins. What care I for names. She's fair! Young! Brisk and kind! Even to ravishment! And what a pox care I for knowing her by any other title?

Will. Didst give her anything?

Blunt. Give her? Ha, ha, ha! Whe! She's a person of quality. That's a good one, give her! 'Sheartlikins, dost think such creatures are to be bought? Or are we provided for such a purchase? Give her, quoth ye? Why she presented me with this bracelet for the toy of a dia-

---

41. The picture acted as a sign indicating that Angellica was ready to receive prospective clients.
42. The copy-text runs Frederick's speech into the same line as Willmore's, but it is emended here.

mond I used to wear. No, gentlemen, Ned Blunt is not everybody.
She expects me again tonight.

Will. Egad, that's well. We'll all go.

Blunt. Not a soul. No, gentlemen, you are wits. I am a dull country
rogue, I.

Fred. Well, sir, for all your person of quality, I shall be very glad to
understand your purse be secure. 'Tis our whole estate at present,
which we are loath to hazard in one bottom. Come, sir, unlade.⁴³

Blunt. Take the necessary trifle useless now to me, that am beloved by
such a gentlewoman. 'Sheartlikins, money! Here, take mine too.

Fred. No, keep that to be cozened, that we may laugh.

Will. Cozened! Death! Would I could meet with one that would cozen
me of all the love I could spare tonight.

Fred. Pox, 'tis some common whore upon my life.

Blunt. A whore! Yes with such clothes! Such fine jewels! Such a house!
Such furniture and so attended! A whore!

Belv. Why, yes, sir, they are whores, though they'll neither entertain you
with drinking, swearing, or bawdry, are whores in all those gay
clothes and right jewels, are whores with those great houses richly
furnisht with velvet beds, store of plate, handsome attendance and
fine coaches, are whores and arrant ones.⁴⁴

Will. Pox on't. Where do these fine whores live?

Belv. Where no rogues in office ycleped⁴⁵ constables dare give 'em laws
nor the wine inspired bullies of the town break their windows. Yet
they are whores though this Essex calf believe 'em persons of quality.

Blunt. 'Sheartlikins, y'are all fools. There are things about this Essex
calf that shall take with the ladies beyond all your wit and parts.⁴⁶
This shape and size gentlemen are not to be despised—my waist,
too, tolerably long, with other inviting signs that shall be nameless.

Will. Egad, I believe he may have met with some person of quality that
may be kind to him.

Belv. Dost thou perceive any such tempting things about him that
should make a fine woman and of quality pick him out from all
mankind to throw away her youth and beauty upon—nay and her
heart too! No, no, Angellica has raised the price too high.

Will. May she languish for mankind till she die, and be damned for that
one sin alone.

*Enter two bravos and hang up a great picture of Angellica against the
balcony, and two little ones at each side of the door.*

43. Frederick's sexual puns involve nautical terminology and recall Thomas Carew's "A Rapture."
"Bottom": ship. "Unlade": unload a ship.
44. "Plate": silver or gold cups, plates, salt and pepper shapers, utensils. Other editors have let
"errant" (wandering) from the copy-text stand. "Arrant," as "notorious and unmitigated," more
accurately describes Lucetta, who does not travel. In all other cases where *errant* is found, it
carries the force of *arrant* and is so spelled.
45. An obsolete and hence comic way of saying "named."
46. Physical good looks.

Belv. See there the fair sign to the inn where many a man may lodge that's fool enough to give her price.

    (Will. gazes on the picture.)

Blunt. 'Sheartlikins, gentlemen, what's this?

Belv. A famous courtesan, that's to be sold.

Blunt. How? To be sold? Nay, then I have nothing to say to her. Sold! What impudence is practiced in this country? With what order and decency whoring's establisht here by virtue of the Inquisition. Come, let's be gone. I'm sure we're no chapmen for this commodity.

Fred. Thou art none, I'm sure, unless thou couldst have her in thy bed at a price of a coach in the street.

Will. How wondrous fair she is. A thousand crowns a month. By heaven, as many kingdoms were too little. A plague of this poverty of which I ne'er complain but when it hinders my approach to beauty which virtue ne'er could purchase.

    (Turns from the picture.)

Blunt. What's this? *(Reads.)* "A thousand crowns a month"! 'Sheartlikins, here's a sum. Sure 'tis a mistake. Hark you friend, does she take or give so much by the month?

Fred. A thousand crowns! Why 'tis a portion for the infanta.[47]

Blunt. Hark ye, friends, won't she trust?

Brav. This is a trade, sir, that cannot live by credit.

Enter Pedro in masquerade, followed by Steph.

Belv. See, here's more company. Let's walk off a while.

    (Exit English. Pedro Reads.)

Enter Ang. and Morett. in the Balcony and draw a silk Curtain.

Ped. Fetch me a thousand crowns. I never wisht to buy this beauty at an easier rate.

    (Passes off.)

Ang. Prithee, what said those fellows to thee?

Brav. Madam, the first were admirers of beauty only, but no purchasers. They were merry with your price and picture, laught at the sum, and so passed off.

Ang. No matter. I'm not displeased with their rallying. Their wonder feeds my vanity, and he that wishes but to buy gives me more pride than he that gives my price can make my pleasure.

Brav. Madam, the last I knew through all his disguises to be Don Pedro, nephew to the general, and who was with him in Pamplona.

Ang. Don Pedro! My old gallant's nephew. When his uncle died, he left him a vast sum of money. It is he who was so in love with me at Padua and who used to make the general so jealous.

Morett. Is this he that used to prance before our window and take such care to show himself an amorous ass? If I am not mistaken, he is the likeliest man to give your price.

47. Daughter of the king of Spain.

Ang. The man is brave and generous, but of an humor so uneasy and inconstant that the victory over his heart is as soon lost as won. [He is] a slave that can add little to the triumph of the conquerer. But inconstancy's the sin of all mankind. Therefore, I'm resolved that nothing but gold shall charm my heart.

Morett. I'm glad on't. 'Tis only interest that women of our profession ought to consider. Though I wonder what has kept you from that general disease of our sex so long—I mean that of being in love.

Ang. A kind but sullen star under which I had the happiness to be born. Yet I have had no time for love. The bravest and noblest of mankind have purchast my favors at so dear a rate, as if no coin but gold were current with our trade. But here's Don Pedro again. Fetch me my lute, for 'tis for him or Don Antonio, the viceroy's son, that I have spread my nets.

Enter at one door Pedro, Steph. Ant. at the other door with people following him in masquerade, antically attired—some with music. They both go up to the picture.

Ant. A thousand crowns! Had not the painter flattered her, I should not think it dear.

Pedro. Flattered her! By heaven, he cannot. I have seen the original, nor is there one charm here more than adorns her face and eyes. All this soft and sweet, with a certain languishing air that no artist can represent.

Ant. What I heard of her beauty before had fired my soul, but this confirmation of it has blown it to a flame.

Pedro. Ha!

[*Diego. (To Ant.)*] Sir, I have known you throw away a thousand crowns on a worse face, and though y'are near your marriage, you may venture a little love here. Florinda will not miss it.

Pedro. (Aside.) Ha! Florinda! Sure 'tis Antonio.

Ant. Florinda! Name not those distant joys. There's not one thought of her will check my passion here.

(A noise of a lute above.)

Pedro. Florinda scorned! And all my hopes defeated of the possession of Angellica. *(Ant. gazes up.)* Her injuries, by heaven, he shall not boast of.

(Song to a lute above.)

Song

[I.]
When Damon first began to love
He languisht in a soft desire
And knew not how the gods to move,
To lessen or increase his fire.

For Caelia in her charming eyes
Wore all love's sweets, and all his cruelties.

II.

But as beneath a shade he lay,
Weaving of flowers for Caelia's hair
She chanc't to lead her flock that way
And saw the am'rous shepherd there.
She gaz'd around upon the place,
And saw the grove (resembling night),
To all the joys of love invite,
Whilst guilty smiles and blushes drest her face.
At this the bashful youth all transport grew,
And with kind force he taught the virgin how
To yield what all his sighs could never do.

(Ang. throws open the curtains and bows to Ant., who pulls off his vizard and bows and blows up kisses. Pedro, unseen, looks in's face.)

Ant. By heaven, she's charming fair!
Pedro. [*Aside.*] 'Tis he, the false Antonio.
Ant. *(To the bravo.)*
Friend, where must I pay my offering of love?
My thousand crowns, I mean.
Pedro.
That off'ring I have design'd to make.
And yours will come too late.
Ant.
Prithee, begone. I shall grow angry else.
And then thou art not safe.
Pedro.
My anger may be fatal, sir, as yours,
And he that enters here may prove this truth.
Ant. I know not who thou art, but I am sure thou'rt worth my killing
for aiming at Angellica.

(They draw and fight.)

Enter Will. and Blunt, who draw and part 'em.
Blunt. 'Sheartlikins, here's fine doings.
Will. Tilting for the wench, I'm sure. Nay, gad if that would win her, I
have as good a sword as the best of ye. Put up. Put up, and another
time and place, for this is designed for lovers only.

(They all put up.)

Pedro. We are prevented. Dare you meet me tomorrow on the Molo?[48]
For I've a title to a better quarrel,
That of Florinda in whose credulous heart
Thou'st made an int'rest and destroy'd my hopes.

48. A quay or wharf at the port of Naples, where Il Molo, a castle, is found.

Ant. Dare!

I'll meet thee there as early as the day.

Pedro. We will come thus disguised that whosoever chance to get the better, he may escape unknown.[49]

(*Exeunt Pedro and Steph.*)

Ant. It shall be so. Who should this rival be, unless the English colonel, of whom I've often heard Don Pedro speak. It must be he, and time he were removed who lays a claim to all my happiness.

(*Will. having gazed all this while on the picture, pulls down a little one.*)

Will.

This posture's loose and negligent,

The sight on't would beget a warm desire,

In souls whom impotence and age had chilled.

This must along with me.

Brav. What means this rudeness, sir? Restore the picture.

Ant. Ha! Rudeness committed to the fair Angellica! Restore the picture, sir.

Will. Indeed I will not, sir.

Ant. By heaven, but you shall.

Will. Nay, do not show your sword. If you do, by this dear beauty, I will show mine, too.

Ant. What right can you pretend to't?

Will. That of possession, which I will maintain. You perhaps have a thousand crowns to give for the original.

Ant. No matter, sir. You shall restore the picture . . .

Ang. (*Ang. and Morett. above.*) Oh, Moretta! What's the matter?

Ant. Or leave your life behind.

Will. Death! You lie. I will do neither.

Ang. Hold, I command you, if for me you fight.

(*They fight, the Spaniards join with Ant. Blunt laying on like mad. [Upon hearing Ang.,] they leave off and bow [to her].*)

Will. How heavenly fair she is! Ah plague of her price.

Ang. You, sir, in buff, you that appear a soldier, that first began this insolence . . .

Will. 'Tis true I did so, if you call it insolence for a man to preserve himself. I saw your charming picture and was wounded. Quite through my soul each pointed beauty ran, and, wanting a thousand crowns to procure my remedy, I laid this little picture to my bosom, which if you cannot allow me I'll resign.

Ang. No, you may keep the trifle.

Ant. You shall first ask me leave, and this.[50]

(*They fight again as before.*)

---

49. Dueling was illegal, so the victorious party would need to hide from the law.
50. "This" presumably refers to Antonio's sword.

Enter Belv. and Fred., who join with the English.

Ang. Hold! Will you ruin me? Biskey, Sebastian. Part, 'em.
    (The Spaniards are beaten off.)

Morett. Oh madam, we're undone. A pox upon that rude fellow. He's set on to ruin us. We shall never see good days till all these fighting poor rogues are sent to the galleys.

Enter Belv., Blunt., Fred., and Will. with his shirt bloody.

Blunt. 'Sheartlikins, beat me at this sport, and I'll ne'er wear sword more.

Belv. The devil's in thee for a mad fellow, and thou art always one at an unlucky adventure. Come, let's be gone whilst we're safe, and remember these are Spaniards, a sort of people that know how to revenge an affront.

Fred. (To Will.) You bleed! I hope you are not wounded.

Will. Not much. A plague on your dons. If they fight no better, they'll ne'er recover Flanders. What the devil was't to them that I took down the picture?

Blunt. Took it? 'Sheartlikins, we'll have the great one, too. 'Tis ours by conquest. Prithee, help me up and I'll pull it down.

Ang. Stay, sir, and ere you affront me farther, let me know how you durst commit this outrage. To you I speak, sir, for you appear a gentleman.

Will. To me, madam? Gentlemen, your servant.
    ([Will. moves towards Ang.'s house and] Belv. stays him.)

Belv. Is the devil in thee? Dost thou know the danger of entering the house of an incensed courtesan?

Will. I thank you for your care, but there are other matters in hand. There are, though we have no great temptation. Death! Let me go.

Fred. Yes, to your lodging if you will, but not in here. Damn these gay harlots. By this hand, I'll have as sound and handsome a whore for a patacoon.[51] Death, man, she'll murder thee.

Will. Oh! Fear me not. Shall I not venture where a beauty calls? A lovely, charming beauty? For fear of danger? When by heaven there's none so great as to long for her, whilst I want mo[ney] to purchase her.

Pedro. Therefore 'tis loss of time unless you had the thousand crowns to pay.

Will. It may be she may give a favor. At least I shall have the pleasure of saluting her when I enter and when I depart.

Belv. Pox. She'll as soon lie with thee as kiss thee—and sooner stab than do either. You shall not go.

Ang. Fear not, sir. All I have to wound you with is my eyes.

Blunt. Let him go. 'Sheartlikins, I believe the gentlewoman means well.

---

51. A Spanish silver coin worth four shillings and sixpence in the seventeenth century.

Belv. Well, take thy fortune. We'll expect you in the next street. Farewell, fool, farewell.

Will. 'Bye, Colonel.

(Goes in.)

Fred. The rogue's stark mad for a wench.

(Exeunt.)

Scene [ii.] A fine chamber.

Enter Will., Ang. and Morett.

Ang. Insolent sir, how durst you pull down my picture?

Will. Rather, how durst you set it up to tempt poor amorous mortals with so much excellence, which I find you have but too well consulted by the unmerciful price you set upon't. Is all this heaven of beauty shown to move despair in those that cannot buy? And can you think th'effects of that despair should be less extravagant than I have shown?

Ang. I sent for you to ask my pardon, sir, not to aggravate your crime. I thought I should have seen you at my feet imploring it.

Will. You are deceived. I came to rail at you and rail such truths, too, as shall let you see the vanity of that pride which taught you how to set such price on sin. For such it is whilst that which is love's due is meanly bartered for.

Ang. Ha! Ha! Ha! Alas, good Captain, what pity 'tis your edifying doctrine will do no good upon me. Moretta! Fetch the gentleman a glass, and let him survey himself to see what charms he has. *(Aside in a softer tone.)* And guess my business.

Morett. He knows himself of old. I believe those breeches and he have been acquainted ever since he was beaten at Worcester.[52]

Ang. Nay, do not abuse the poor creature.

Morett. Good weatherbeaten corporal, will you march off? We have no need of your doctrine, though you have of our charity. But at present we have no scraps. We can afford no kindness for God's sake. In fine, sirrah, the price is too high i'th' mouth for you. Therefore, troop, I say.

Will. Here good forewoman of the shop, serve me and I'll be gone.

[Will. offers Morett. a pistole.][53]

Morett. Keep it to pay your laundress. Your linen stinks of the gun room. For here's no selling by retail.

Will. Thou hast sold plenty of thy stale ware at a cheap rate.

Morett. Aye, the silly,[54] kind heart I. But this is an age wherein beauty is at higher rates. In fine, you know the price of this.

Will. I grant you 'tis here set down, a thousand crowns a month. Pray, how much may come to my share for a pistole? Bawd, take your

---

52. The supporters of Charles II were defeated at the battle of Worcester in 1651.
53. "Pistole": any one of a number of foreign gold coins.
54. Innocent.

black lead and sum it up, that I may have a pistole's worth of this vain, gay [thing],[55] and I'll trouble you no more.

Morett. Pox on him. He'll fret me to death. Abominable fellow, I tell thee we only sell by the whole piece.

Will. 'Tis very hard. The whole cargo or nothing. Faith madam, my stock will not reach it. I cannot be your chapman. Yet I have countrymen in town, merchants of love like me. I'll see if they'll put in for a share. We cannot lose much by it, and what we have no use for, we'll sell upon the Friday's mart at "Who gives more?" I am studying, madam, how to purchase you, though at present I am unprovided of money.

Ang. [*Aside.*] Sure this from any other man would anger me. Nor shall he know the conquest he has made. [*To Will.*] Poor angry man, how I despise this railing.

Will.
Yes, I am poor, but I'm a gentleman.
And one that scorns this baseness which you practice.
Poor as I am, I would not sell myself,
No, not to gain your charming high priz'd person.
Though I admire you strangely for your beauty,
Yet I condemn your mind.
—And yet I would at any rate enjoy you.
At your own rate, but cannot. See here
The only sum I can command on earth.
I know not where to eat when this is gone.
Yet such a slave I am to love and beauty
This last reserve I'll sacrifice to enjoy you.
—Nay, do not frown. I know you're to be bought
And would be bought by me, by me,
For a mean trifling sum if I could pay it down,
Which happy knowledge I will still repeat,
And lay it to my heart. It has virtue in't,
And soon will cure those wounds your eyes have made.
And yet, there's something so divinely powerful there.
Nay, I will gaze to let you see my strength.
      (*Holds her, looks on her, and pauses and sighs.*)
By heaven, bright creature, I would not for the world
Thy fame were half so fair as is thy face.
      (*Turns her away from him.*)

Ang. (*Aside.*) His words go through me to the very soul.
[*To Will.*] If you have nothing else to say to me—

Will.
Yes, you shall hear how infamous you are,
For which I do not hate thee,
But that secures my heart, and all the flames it feels

55. The third quarto emends "things" to "thing."

Are but so many lusts.
I know it by their sudden bold intrusion.
The fire's impatient and betrays, 'tis false,
For had it been the purer flame of love,
I should have pined and languisht at your feet
Ere found the impudence to have discover'd it.
I now dare stand your scorn and your denial.

[*Morett.*] Sure she's bewicht that she can stand thus tamely and hear his saucy railing. Sirrah, will you be gone?

Ang. (*To Morett.*) How dare you take this liberty? Withdraw. [*To Will.*] Pray tell me, sir, are not you guilty of the same mercenary crime? When a lady is proposed to you for a wife, you never ask how fair, discreet, or virtuous she is, but what's her fortune. Which if but small you cry, "She will not do my business," and basely leave her, though she languish for you. Say, is not this as poor?

Will. It is a barbarous custom, which I will scorn to defend in our sex and do despise in yours.

Ang.
Thou'rt a brave fellow! Put up thy gold and know
That were thy fortune large as is thy soul,
Thou shouldst not buy my love
Couldst thou forget those mean effects of vanity
Which set me out to sale
And, as a lover, prize my yielding joys?
Canst thou believe they'll be entirely thine,
Without considering they were mercenary?

Will. I cannot tell. I must bethink me first. (*Aside.*) Ha, death, I'm going to believe her.

Ang. Prithee confirm that faith, or if thou canst not, flatter me a little. 'Twill please me from thy mouth.

Will. (*Aside.*)
Curse on thy charming tongue! Dost thou return
My feigned contempt with so much charming subtlety?
        [*To Ang.*]
Thou'st found the easiest way into my heart,
And yet I know that all thou sayst is false.
        (*Turning from her in rage.*)

Ang.
By all that's good 'tis real,
I never lov'd before, though oft a mistress.
Shall my first vows be slighted?

Will. (*Aside.*)
What can she mean?

Ang. (*In an angry tone.*)
I find you cannot credit me.

Will.
I know you take me for an arrant ass,

An ass that may be sooth'd into belief
And then be used at pleasure.
But, madam, I have been so often cheated
By perjur'd soft deluding hypocrites,
That I've no faith left for the cozening sex,
Especially for women of your trade.

Ang.

The low esteem you have of me, perhaps
May bring my heart again,
For I have pride, that yet surmounts my love.
　　　　　(She turns. With pride he holds her.)

Will.

Throw off this pride, this enemy to bliss,
And show the pow'r of love. 'Tis with those arms
I can be only vanquisht, made a slave.

Ang.

Is all thy mighty expectation vanisht?
No, I will not hear thee talk. Thou hast a charm
In every word that draws my heart away.
And all the thousand trophies I design'd
Thou hast undone. Why art thou soft?
Thy looks are bravely rough and meant for war.
Couldst thou not storm on still?
I then, perhaps, had been as free as thou.

Will. (Aside.)

Death, how she throws her fire about my soul! *[To Ang.]*
Take heed, fair creature, how you raise my hopes,
Which, once assum'd, pretends to all dominion.
There's not a joy thou hast in store,
I shall not then command.
For which I'll pay you back my soul! My life!
Come, let's begin th'account this happy minute!

Ang.

And will you pay me then the price I ask?

Will.

Oh, why dost thou draw me from an awful worship,
By showing thou art no divinity?
Conceal the fiend, and show me all the angel!
Keep me but ignorant, and I'll be devout
And pay my vows forever at this shrine.
　　　　　(Kneels and kisses her hand.)

Ang.

The pay, I mean, is but thy love for mine.
Can you give that?

Will. Entirely. Come, let's withdraw where I'll renew my vows and
breathe 'em with such ardor thou shalt not doubt my zeal!

Ang. Thou hast a pow'r too strong to be resisted.

(Exeunt Will and Ang.)

Morett. Now my curse go with you. Is all our project fallen to this? To love the only enemy to our trade? Nay, to love such a shameroon,[56] a very beggar, nay a pirate beggar, whose business is to rifle and be gone? A no purchase, no pay tatterdemalion and English picaroon?[57] A rogue that fights for daily drink and takes a pride in being loyally lousy? Oh, I could curse now, if I durst. This is the fate of most whores.

Trophies, which from believing fops we win,
Are spoils to those who cozen us again.

The End of the Second Act.

Act III.

Scene i. *A street.*

Enter Flor., Val., Hell. in antic,[58] different dresses from what they were before. Call. attending.

Flor. I wonder what should make my brother in so ill a humor? I hope he has not found out our ramble this morning.

Hell. No, if he had, we should have heard on't at both ears and have been mewed up this afternoon, which I would not for the world should have happened. Hey ho, I'm as sad as a lover's lute.

Val. Well, methinks we have learnt this trade of gypsies as readily as if we had been bred upon the road to Loretto.[59] And yet I did so fumble when I told the stranger his fortune that I was afraid I should have told my own and yours by mistake. But, methinks, Hellena has been very serious ever since.

Flor. I would give my garters she were in love, to be revenged upon her for abusing me. How is't, Hellena?

Hell. Ah, would I had never seen my mad monsieur, and, yet for all your laughing, I am not in love. And yet this small acquaintance, o' my conscience, will never out of my head.

Val. Ha, ha, ha. I laugh to think how thou art fitted with a lover, a fellow that I warrant loves every new face he sees.

Hell. Hum, he has not kept his word with me here, and may be taken up. That thought is not very pleasant to me. What the deuce should this be now that I feel?

Val. What is it like?

Hell. Nay, the Lord knows. But if I should be hanged, I cannot choose but be angry and afraid when I think that mad fellow should be in love with anybody but me. What to think of myself, I know not.

---

56. The context and spelling will support either "shameful person" or, better, "person who is a sham."
57. A tatterdemalion is one who wears worn-out clothing, and a picaroon is a pirate.
58. Absurd.
59. Loretto was a shrine to the Virgin Mary. The road to the shrine apparently drew people trying to sell fortunes to the pilgrims.

Would I could meet with some true damned gypsy that I might know my fortune.

Val. Know it! Why there's nothing so easy. Thou wilt love this wandering inconstant till thou findst thyself hanged about his neck, and then be as mad to get free again.

Flor. Yes, Valeria, we shall see her bestride his baggage horse and follow him to the campaign.

Hell. So, so. Now you are provided for, there's no care taken of poor me. But since you have set my heart a wishing, I am resolved to know for what. I will not die of the pip,[60] so I will not.

Flor. Art thou mad to talk so? Who will like thee well enough to have thee, that hears what a mad wench thou art?

Hell. Like me! I don't intend every he that likes me shall have me, but he that I like. I should have stayed in the nunnery still if I had liked my lady abbess as well as she liked me. No, I came thence not (as my wise brother imagines) to take an eternal farewell of the world, but to love and to be beloved, and I will be beloved, or I'll get one of your men, so I will.

Val. Am I put into the number of lovers?

Hell. You? Why, coz, I know thou'rt too good natured to leave us in any design. Thou wouldst venture a cast though thou comest off a loser, especially with such a gamester. I observe your man, and your willing ear incline that way. And if you are not a lover, 'tis an art soon learnt. That I find. *(Sighs.)*

Flor. I wonder how you learnt to love so easily. I had a thousand charms to meet my eyes and ears ere I could yield, and 'twas the knowledge of Belvile's merit, not the surprising person, took my soul. Thou art too rash, to give a heart at first sight.

Hell. Hang your considering lover. I never thought beyond the fancy that 'twas a very pretty, idle, silly, kind of pleasure to pass one's time with—to write little soft nonsensical billets and with great difficulty and danger receive answers, in which I shall have my beauty praised, my wit admired (though little or none), and have the vanity and power to know I am desirable. Then I have the more inclination that way because I am to be a nun, and so shall not be suspected to have any such earthly thoughts about me. But when I walk thus and sigh thus, they'll think my mind's upon my monastery and cry, "How happy 'tis she's so resolved." But not a word of man.

Flor. What a mad creature is this?

Hell. I'll warrant if my brother hears either of you sigh, he cries gravely, "I fear you have the indiscretion to be in love. But take heed of the honor of our house and your own unspotted fame." And so he conjures on till he has laid the soft-winged god in your hearts or broke the bird's nest. But see, here comes your lover. But where's my inconstant? Let's step aside, and we may learn something.

---

60. A disease of poultry sometimes attributed to people for comic effect.

(Go aside.)

Enter Bel., Fred, and Blunt.
Belv. What means this! The picture's taken in.
Blunt. It may be the wench is good natured and will be kind gratis.
Your friend's a proper handsome fellow.
Belv. I rather think she has cut his throat and is fled. I am mad he should
throw himself into dangers. Pox on't. I shall want him, too, at night.
Let's knock and ask for him.
Hell. My heart goes a pit a pat, for fear 'tis my man they talk of.
(Knock. Morett. above.)
Morett. What would you have!
Bel. Tell the stranger that entered here about two hours ago that his
friends stay here for him.
Morett. A curse upon him for Moretta. Would he were at the devil, but
he's coming to you.

[Enter Will.]
Hell. I, I,[61] 'tis he! Oh how this vexes me.
Bel. And how and how, dear lad, has fortune smiled? Are we to break
her windows or raise up altars to her? Ha!
Will. Does not my fortune sit triumphant on my brow! Dost not see the
little wanton god there all gay and smiling? Have I not an air about
my face and eyes that distinguish[es] me from the crowd of common
lovers? By heaven, Cupid's quiver has not half so many darts as her
eyes! Oh, such a *bona roba!*[62] To sleep in her arms is lying in *fresco,*
all perfumed air about me.
Hell. (Aside.) Here's a fine encouragement for me to fool on.
Will. Harkee, where didst thou purchase that rich canary we drank
today? Tell me that I may adore the spigot and sacrifice to the butt.
The juice was divine, into which I must dip my rosary, and then bless
all things that I would have bold or fortunate.
Belv. Well, sir, let's go take a bottle and hear the story of your success.
Fred. Would not French wine do better?
Will. Damn the hungry balderdash![63] Cheerful sack has a generous
virtue in't inspiring a successful confidence, gives eloquence to the
tongue and vigor to the soul, and has in a few hours completed all
my hopes and wishes! There's nothing left to raise a new desire in
me. Come, let's be gay and wanton. And, gentlemen study; study
what you want, for here are friends *[shows them coins]* that will
supply gentlemen. Hark, what a charming sound they make. 'Tis

61. "I, I" probably means "Aye, aye." Such was certainly the case a hundred years before, and in
1711 Greenwood says in his *English Grammar* that "I" may be used for "yes" in a "hasty, merry
way" (quoted from *OED*).
62. Literally, "good stuff." The *OED* quotes Florio, "a good, wholesome, plum-cheeked wench." In
The Alchemist, a well-dressed courtesan.
63. Balderdash was an odd mixture for drinking, for instance beer and buttermilk. The word also had
come to mean "nonsense" by the time the play was written.

[the] he and [the she] gold[64] whilst here, and shall beget new pleasures every moment.

Blunt. But harkee, sir, you are not married are you?

Will. All the honey of matrimony, but none of the sting, friend.

Blunt. 'Sheartlikins. Thou'rt a fortunate rogue!

Will. I am so, sir. Let these inform you! Ha! How sweetly they chime!
Pox of poverty. It makes a man a slave, and makes wit and honor
sneak. My soul grew lean and rusty for want of credit.

Blunt. 'Sheartlikins. This I like well. It looks like my lucky bargain. Oh,
how I long for the approach of my squire that is to conduct me to her
house again. Whe, here's two[65] provided for.

Fred. By this light, y'are happy men.

Blunt. Fortune is pleased to smile on us, gentlemen, to smile on us.

Enter San. and pulls Blunt by the sleeve.

Sancho. Sir, my lady expects you. *(They go aside.)* She has removed all
that might oppose your will and pleasure, and is impatient till you
come.

Blunt. Sir, I'll attend you—oh the happiest rogue! I'll take no leave, lest
they either dog me or stay me.

    Exit with San.

Belv. But then the little gypsy is not forgot?

Will. A mischief on thee for putting her into my thoughts. I had quite
forgot her else, and this night's debauch had drunk her quite down.

Hell. Had it so, good Captain?

    (Claps him on the back.)

Will. (Aside.) Ha! I hope she did not hear me.

Hell. What? Afraid of such a champion?

Will. Oh! You're a fine lady of your word, are you not? To make a man
languish a whole day?

Hell. In tedious search of me.

Will. Egad, child, thou'rt in the right. Hadst thou seen what a melancholy dog I have been ever since I was a lover, how I have walkt the
streets like a capuchin,[66] with my hands in my sleeves, faith sweetheart, thou wouldst pity me.

Hell. [Aside.] Now if I should be hanged I can't be angry with him. He
dissembles so heartily. *[To Will.]* Alas, good captain, what pains you
have taken. Now were I ungrateful not to reward so true a servant.

Will. Poor soul! That's kindly said. I see thou barest a conscience. Come
then, for a beginning show me thy dear face.

Hell. I'm afraid, my small acquaintance, you have been staying that
swinging stomach you boasted of this morning. I then remember my

---

64. Copy-text: "he and the gold." The emendation used in the present text follows the 1709 quarto.
65. Stage directions a few lines below specify Sancho as one of the two; the other is not mentioned.
66. Monk.

little collation would have gone down with you without the sauce of a handsome face.[67] Is your stomach so queasy now?

Will. Faith, long-fasting, child, spoils a man's appetite. Yet if you would durst treat, I could so lay about me still.

Hell. And would you fall to before a priest says grace?

Will. Oh, fie, fie. What an old out-of-fashioned thing hast thou named? Thou couldst not dash me more out of countenance shouldst thou show me an ugly face.

> *(Whilst he is seemingly courting Hell., enter Ang., Morett., Bisk., and Sebast. all in masquerade. Ang. sees Will. and stares.)*

Ang. Heavens 'tis he! And passionately fond to see another woman.

Morett. What could you less expect from such a swaggerer?

Ang.
Expect! As much as I paid him. A heart entire,
Which I had pride enough to think when ere I gave
It would have raised the man above the vulgar.
Made him all soul! And that all soft and constant.

Hell. You see, Captain, how willing I am to be friends with you, till time and ill luck make us lovers, and [to] ask you the question first rather than put your modesty to the blush by asking me. For, alas, I know you captains are such strict men and such severe observers of your vows to chastity that 'twill be hard to prevail with your tender conscience to marry a young, willing maid.

Will. Do not abuse me, for fear I should take thee at thy word and marry thee indeed, which, I'm sure, would be revenge sufficient.

Hell. O' my conscience, that will be our destiny, because we are both of one humor.[68] I am as inconstant as you, for I have considered, Captain, that a handsome woman has a great deal to do whilst her face is good. For then is our harvest time to gather friends, and, should I in these days of my youth catch a fit of foolish constancy, I were undone. 'Tis loitering by daylight in our great journey. Therefore, I declare, I'll allow but one year for love, one year for indifference, and one year for hate. And then go hang yourself, for I profess myself the gay, the kind, and the inconstant. The devil's in't, if this won't please you.

Will. Oh, most damnably. I have a heart with a hole quite through it, too. No prison mine, to keep a mistress in.

Ang. (Aside.) Perjured man! How I believe thee now.

Hell. Well, I see our business as well as humors are alike. Yours to cozen as many maids as will trust you, and I as many men as have faith. See if I have not as desperate a lying look as you have for the heart of you. *(Pulls off her vizard. He starts.)* How do you like it, Captain?

---

67. Hellena's puns involve *stayed*, meaning "comforted," and *collation*, meaning "light meal" or "lunch." She also plays on *swing* and *swinge*.

68. Medical theory of the time categorized personality according to "humor," or bodily fluid. Hellena suggests that she and Willmore share a personality type because they have the same balance of humors. See also note 2 for another use of the word.

Will. Like it! By heaven, I never saw so much beauty! Oh, the charms of those sprightly black eyes! That strangely fair face, full of smiles and dimples! Those soft, round, melting cherry lips! And small, even white teeth! Not to be expressed, but silently adored! Oh, one look more! And strike me dumb, or I shall repeat nothing else till I'm mad.

(He seems to court her to pull off her vizard. She refuses.)

Ang. I can endure no more. Nor is it fit to interrupt him for if I do, my jealousy has so destroyed my reason, I shall undo him. Therefore, I'll retire, and *(to one of her bravos)*, you Sebastian, follow that woman and learn who 'tis, while *(to the other bravo)* you tell the fugitive I would speak to him instantly.

(Exit. This while Flor. is talking to Bel., who stands sullenly. Fred. courting Val.)

Val. Prithee, dear stranger. Be not so sullen, for though you have lost your love, you see my friend frankly offers you hers to play with in the meantime.

Belv. Faith, madam, I am sorry I can't play at her game.

Fred. Pray, leave your intercession, and mind your own affair. They'll better agree apart. He's a modest sigher in company, but alone no woman scapes him.

Flor. [Aside.] Sure he does but rally. Yet if it should be true, I'll tempt him further. *[Aside.]* Believe me, noble stranger, I'm no common mistress. And for proof on it, wear this jewel. Nay, take it, sir, 'tis right, and bills of exchange may sometimes miscarry.⁶⁹

Belv. Madam, why am I chose out of all mankind to be the object of your bounty?

Val. There's another civil question askt.

Fred. Pox of 's modesty. It spoils his own markets and hinders mine.

Flor. Sir, from my window I have often seen you, and women of my quality have so few opportunities for love that we ought to lose none.

Fred. Aye, this is something! Here's a woman! *[To Val.]* When shall I be blest with so much kindness from your mouth? *(Aside to Belv.)* Take the jewel, fool.

Belv. You tempt me strangely, madam, every way.

Flor. (Aside.) So if I find him false, my whole repose is gone.

Belv. And but for a vow I've made to a very fair lady, this goodness had subdued me.

Fred. Pox on't. Be kind. In pity to me, be kind, for I am to thrive here but as you treat her friend.

Hell. Tell me what you did in yonder house, and I'll unmask.

Will. Yonder house? Oh . . . I went to . . . a . . . to . . . why there's a friend of mine lives there.

---

69. The jewel has cash value lacking in "bills of exchange," or promissory notes. Many exiled Englishmen lived on what could be bought with such promissory notes, which tradesmen did not want to take.

Hell. What? A she or a he friend?

Will. A man, upon honor! A man. A she friend? No, no, madam, you have done my business, I thank you.

Hell. And wast your man friend that had more darts in's eyes than Cupid carries in's whole budget of arrows?

Will. So . . .

Hell. "Ah, such *bona roba!* To be in her arms is lying *in fresco,* all perfumed air about me." Was this your man friend, too?

Will. So . . .

Hell. That gave you the he and the she gold, that begets young pleasures?

Will. Well, well, madam. Then you see there are ladies in the world that will not be cruel. There are, madam, there are.

Hell. And there be men, too, as fine, wild, inconstant fellows as yourself. There be captains, there be, if you go to that now. Therefore, I am resolved . . .

Will. Oh.

Hell. To see your face no more.

Will. Oh!

Hell. Till tomorrow.

Will. Egad, you frightened me.

Hell. Nor then neither, unless you'll swear never to see that lady more.

Will. See her! Whe, never to think of womankind again.

Hell. Kneel and swear.

> *(Kneels. She gives him her hand.)*

Will. I do, never to think, to see, to love, nor lie, with any but thyself.

Hell. Kiss the book.

Will. *(Kisses her hand.)* Oh, most religiously.

Hell. Now what a wicked creature am I, to damn a proper fellow.

Call. *(To Flor.)* Madam, I'll stay no longer. 'Tis e'en dark.

Flor. *[To Belv.]* However, sir, I'll leave this with you, that, when I'm gone, you may repent the opportunity you have lost by your modesty.

> *(Gives him the jewel, which is her picture, and exits. He gazes after her.)*

Will. 'Twill be an age till tomorrow. And till then I will most impatiently expect you. Adieu, my dear pretty angel.

> *(Exeunt all the women.)*

Belv. Ha! Florinda's picture. 'Twas she herself. What a dull dog was I? I would have given the world for one minute's discourse with her.

Fred. This comes of your modesty! Ah, pox o' your vow. 'Twas ten to one we had lost the jewel by't.

Belv. Willmore! The blessedest opportunity lost! Florinda! Friends! Florinda!

Will. Ah rogue! Such black eyes! Such a face! Such a mouth! Such teeth! And so much wit!

Belv. All, all, and a thousand charms besides.

Will. Why, dost thou know her?

Belv. Know her! Aye, aye, and a pox take me with all my heart for being so modest.

Will. But harkee, friend of mine. Are you my rival? And have I been only beating the bush all this while?

Belv. I understand thee not. I'm mad. See here.
(Shows the picture.)

Will. Ha! Whose picture's this? 'Tis a fine wench!

Fred. The colonel's mistress, sir.

Will. Oh, oh, here. I thought 't had been another prize. Come, come. A bottle will set thee right again.
(Gives the picture back.)

Belv. I am content to try, and by that time 'twill be late enough for our design.

Will. Agreed.

Love does all day the soul's great empire keep,
But wine at night lulls the soft god asleep.
(Exeunt.)

Scene ii. *Lucett.'s house*

Enter Blunt and Lucett., with a light.

Lucett. Now we are safe and free. No fears of the coming home of my old jealous husband, which made me a little thoughtful when you came in first. But now love is all the business of my soul.

Blunt. (Aside.) I am transported! Pox on't. That I had but some fine things to say to her such as lovers use. I was a fool not to learn of Fred a little by heart before I came. Something I must say. *[To Lucett.]* 'Sheartlikins, sweet soul! I am not used to compliment, but I'm an honest gentleman and thy humble servant.

Lucett. I have nothing to pay for so great a favor, but such a love as cannot but be great, since at first sight of that sweet face and shape it made me your absolute captive.

Blunt. (Aside.) Kind heart! How prettily she talks! Egad, I'll show her husband a Spanish trick. Send him out of the world and marry her. She's damnedably in love with me and will ne're mind settlements, and so there's that saved.

Lucett. Well, sir, I'll go and undress me, and be with you instantly.

Blunt. Make haste then, for 'adsheartlikins, dear soul, thou canst not guess at the pain of a longing lover, when his joys are drawn within the compass of a few minutes.

Lucett. You speak my sense, and I'll make haste to prove it.
(Exit.)

Blunt. 'Tis a rare girl! And this one night's enjoyment with her will be worth all the days I ever passed in Essex. Would she would go with me into England. Though, to say truth, there's plenty of whores already. But a pox on 'em. They are such mercenary, prodigal whores, that they want such a one as this, that's free and generous, to give 'em good examples. Whe, what a house she has, how rich and fine!

Enter San.

San. Sir, my lady has sent me to conduct you to her chamber.

Blunt. Sir, I shall be proud to follow. Here's one of her servants, too! 'Sheartlikins, by this garb and gravity, he might be a justice of peace in Essex, and is but a pimp here.
　　　(Exeunt.)

[Scene iii.] *The scene changes to a chamber with an alcove bed in't, a table, etc. Lucett. in bed.*

Enter San. and Blunt, who takes the candle of San. at the door.

San. Sir, my commission reaches no farther.

Blunt. Sir, I'll excuse your compliment. *[Exit San.]* What? In bed, my sweet mistress?

Lucett. You see, I still outdo you in kindness.

Blunt. And thou shalt see what haste I'll make to quit[70] scores. Oh, the luckiest rogue.
　　　(He undresses himself.)

Lucett. Should you be false or cruel now . . .

Blunt. False! 'Sheartlikins, what dost thou take me for? A Jew? An insensible heathen? A pox of thy old jealous husband. An' he were dead, egad, sweet soul, it should be none of my fault if I did not marry thee.

Lucett. It never should be mine.

Blunt. Good soul! I'm the fortunatest dog!

Lucett. Are you not undrest yet?

Blunt. As much as my impatience will permit.
　　　(Goes towards the bed in his shirt, drawers, etc.)

Lucett. Hold, sir, put out the light. It may betray us else.

Blunt. Anything. I need no other light but that of thine eyes. 'Sheartlikins, there I think I had it.
　　　(Puts out the candle, the bed descends, he gropes about to find it.)

Blunt. Whe, whe. Where am I got? What? Not yet? Where are you, sweetest? Ah, the rogue's silent now. A pretty love trick this. How she'll laugh at me anon! You need not, my dear rogue! You need not! I'm on fire already. Come, come, now call me in pity. Sure I'm enchanted! I have been round the chamber and can find neither woman nor bed. I lockt the door. I'm sure she cannot go that way. Or if she could, the bed could not. Enough, enough, my pretty wanton. Do not carry the jest too far. Ha! Betrayed! Dogs! Rogues! Pimps! Help! Help!

---

70. Literally, requite or pay back. In this case he intends "even up."

(Lights on a trap [door] and is let down.)

Enter Lucett., Phil, and San. with a light.

Phil. Ha, ha, ha. He's dispatch[ed] finely.

Lucett. Now, sir, had I been coy, we had mist of this booty.

Phil. Nay, when I saw 'twas a substantial fool, I was mollifed. But when
you dote upon a serenading coxcomb, upon a face, fine clothes, and
a lute, it makes me rage.

Lucett. You know I was never guilty of that fine folly, my dear Philippo,
but with yourself. But come, let's see what we have got by this.

Phil. A rich coat! Sword and hat. These breeches, too, are well lined.
See here, a gold watch. A purse. Ha! Gold. At least two hundred
pistoles! A bunch of diamond rings. And one with the family arms!
A gold box with a medal of his king and his lady mother's picture!
These were sacred relics, believe me! See, the waistband of his
breeches have a mine of gold—old Queen Bess's. We have a quarrel
to her ever since eighty-eight[71] and may therefore justify the theft.
The Inquisition might have committed it.

Lucett. See, a bracelet of bowed gold! These his sisters tied about his
arm at parting. But well, for all this, I fear his being a stranger may
make a noise and hinder our trade with them hereafter.

Phil. That's our security. He is not only a stranger to us, but to the
country, too. The common shore[72] to which he is descended thou
knowest conducts him into another street, which this light will
hinder him from ever finding again. He knows neither your name,
nor that of the street where your house is. Nay, nor the way to his
own lodgings.

Lucett. And art not thou an unmerciful rogue not to afford him one
night for all this? I should not have been such a Jew.

Phil. Blame me not, Lucetta, to keep as much of thee as I can to myself.
Come, that thought makes me wanton! Let's to bed. Sancho, lock up
these.
This is the fleece which fools do bear,
Designed for witty men to shear.
(Exeunt.)

[Scene iv.] *The scene changes and discovers[73] Blunt creeping out of a
common shore, his face, etc., all dirty.*

Blunt. (Climbing up.) Oh, Lord! I am got out at last, and, which is a
miracle, without a clue. And now to damning and cursing! But if
that would ease me, where shall I begin? With my fortune, myself, or
the quean that cozened me? What a dog I was to believe in woman.

71. In 1588, Queen Elizabeth's forces defeated the Spanish Armada.
72. Sewer.
73. Scene changes may have been accomplished with shutters running on grooves. Shutters painted to
resemble Lucetta's bedroom could have been pulled back to reveal Blunt in front of another set,
painted to show a sewer. The sewer shutters, then, could have been pulled back to reveal the
garden scene.

Oh, coxcomb! Ignorant, conceited coxcomb! To fancy she could be enamored with my person, at first sight enamored. Oh, I'm a cursed puppy! 'Tis plain, "Fool" was writ upon my forehead! She perceived it! Saw "The Essex Calf" there, for what allurements could there be in this countenance? Which I can endure because I am acquainted with it. Oh, dull, silly dog! To be thus soothed into a cozening! Had I been drunk, I might fondly have credited the young quean! But, as I was in my right wits, to be thus cheated confirms it: I am a dull, believing English country fop. But my comrades, death and the devil! There's the worst of all. Then a ballad will be sung tomorrow on the Prado[74] to a lousy tune of the enchanted squire and the annihilated damsel. But Fred and that rogue and the colonel will abuse me beyond all Christian patience. Had she left me my clothes, I have a bill of exchange at home would have saved my credit.[75] But now all hope is taken from me. Well, I'll home (if I can find the way) with this consolation, that I'm not the first kind, believing coxcomb. *[To the audience.]* But there are, gallants, many such good natures amongst ye.
And though you've better arts to hide your follies,
'Adsheartlikins y'are all as arrant cullies.

[Scene v.] *Scene, the garden in the night.*

Enter Florinda in an undress,[76] with a key and a little box.
Flor. Well, thus far I'm in my way to happiness. I have got myself free from Callis. My brother, too, I find by yonder light is got into his cabinet[77] and thinks not of me. I have by good fortune got the key of the garden back door. I'll open it to prevent Belvile's knocking. A little noise will now alarm my brother. Now am I as fearful as a young thief. *(Unlocks the door.)* Hark. What noise is that? Oh, 'twas the wind that played amongst the boughs. Belvile stays long, methinks. It's time. Stay,[78] for fear of a surprise, I'll hide these jewels in yonder jasmine.
(She goes to lay down the box. Enter Will. drunk.)
Will. What the devil is become of these fellows Belvile and Frederick? They promised to stay at the next corner for me, but who the devil knows the corner of a full moon? Now, whereabouts am I? Ha, what have we here? A garden. A very convenient place to sleep in. Ha! What has God sent us here? A female. By this light, a woman. I'm a dog if it be not a very wench!
Flor. He's come! Ha, who's there?
Will. Sweet soul! Let me salute thy shoestring.

74. The Prado was a park in Spain, but the word came to mean any promenade.
75. The loss of Blunt's clothes means that he cannot borrow on the basis of his personal appearance and a promissory note. Also below, "cullies": dupes, gulls.
76. An "undress" was any informal clothing.
77. Room.
78. Wait.

Flor. [Aside.] 'Tis not my Belvile. Good heavens! I know him not. *[To Will.]* Who are you and from whence come you?

Will. Prithee, prithee, child. Not so many hard questions. Let it suffice I am here, child. Come, come kiss me.

Flor. Good gods! What luck is mine?

Will. Only good luck, child, parlous good luck. Come hither. 'Tis a delicate, shining wench. By this hand, she's perfumed and smells like a nosegay. Prithee, dear soul, let's not play the fool and lose time— precious time—for, as Gad shall save me, I'm as honest a fellow as breathes, though I'm a little disguised at present. Come, I say. Whe. Thou mayst be free with me. I'll be very secret. I'll not boast who 'twas obliged me. Not I, for hang me if I know thy name.

Flor. Heavens! What a filthy beast is this?

Will. I am so, and thou oughtst the sooner to lie with me for that reason. For, look you child, there will be no sin in't, because 'twas neither designed nor premeditated. 'Tis pure accident on both sides. That's a certain thing, now. Indeed, should I make love to you, and you vow fidelity and swear and lie till you believed and yielded— that were to make wilful fornication, the crying sin of the nation. Thou art, therefore, as thou art a good Christian, obliged in conscience to deny me nothing. Now, come be kind without any more idle prating.

Flor. Oh, I am ruined. Wicked man, unhand me.

Will. Wicked! Egad, child, a judge were he young and vigorous and saw those eyes of thine, would know 'twas they gave the first blow, the first provocation. Come, prithee, let's lose no time, I say. This is a fine, convenient place.

Flor. Sir, let me go, I conjure you, or I'll call out.

Will. Aye, aye, you were best to call witness to see how finely you treat me. Do.

Flor. I'll cry, "Murder!" "Rape!" or anything, if you do not instantly let me go.

Will. A rape! Come, come, you lie, you baggage, you lie. What, I'll warrant you would fain have the world believe now that you are not so forward as I. No, not you. Why at this time of night was your cobweb door set open, dear spider, but to catch flies? Ha. Come or I shall be damnably angry. Whe. What a coil[79] is here.

Flor. Sir, can you think . . .

Will. That you would do't for nothing? Oh, oh. I find what you would be at. Look here. Here's a pistole for you. Here's a work indeed. Here, take it, I say.

Flor. For heaven's sake, sir, as you are a gentleman.

Will. So now, now, she would be wheedling me for more. What? You will not take it then? You are resolved you will not? Come, come, take it, or I will put it up again. For look ye, I never give more. Whe,

---

79. Noisy disturbance.

how now, mistress, are you so high i'th' mouth a pistole won't down with you? Ha. Whe, what a work's here. In good time! Come, no struggling to be gone. But, an y'are good at a dumb wrestle, I'm for ye. Look ye, I'm for ye.

(She struggles with him. Enter Belv. and Fred.)

Belv. The door is open. A pox of this mad fellow. I'm angry that we have lost him. I durst have sworn he had followed us.

Fred. But you were so hasty, Colonel, to be gone.

Flor. Help! Help! Murder! Help! Oh, I'm ruined.

Belv. (Comes up to them.) Ha! Sure that's Florinda's voice. A man! Villain, let go that lady.

(A noise. Will turns and draws. Fred. interposes.)

Flor. Belvile! Heavens! My brother is coming, and 'twill be impossible to escape. Belvile, I conjure you to walk under my chamber window, from whence I'll give you some instructions what to do. This rude man has undone us.

(Exit.)

Will. Belvile!

Enter Pedro, Steph., and other servants with lights.

Pedro. I'm betrayed! Run, Stephano, and see if Florinda be safe.

(Exit Steph.)

(They fight and Pedro's party beats 'em out.)

Pedro. So, who ere they be, all is not well. I'll to Florinda's chamber.

(Going out meets Steph.)

Steph. You need not, sir; the poor lady's fast asleep and thinks no harm. I would not awake her, sir, for fear of frighting her with your danger.

Pedro. I'm glad she's there. Rascals, how came the garden door open?

Steph. That question comes too late, sir. Some of my fellow servants masquerading, I'll warrant.

Pedro. Masquerading! A lewd custom to debauch our youth. There is something more in this than I imagine.

(Exeunt.)

[Scene vi.] *Scene changes to the street.*

Enter Belv. in a rage. Fred holding him and Will. melancholy.

Will. How the devil should I know Florinda?

Belv. Ah plague of your ignorance! If it had not been Florinda, must you be a beast? A brute? A senseless swine?

Will. Well, sir, you see I am endued with patience. I can bear, though, egad, y'are very free with me, methinks. I was in good hopes the quarrel would have been on my side, for so uncivilly interrupting me.

Belv. Peace, brute, whilst thou'rt safe. Oh, I'm distracted.

Will. Nay, nay, I'm an unlucky dog, that's certain.

Belv. Ah, curse upon the star that ruled my birth! Or whatsoever other influence that makes me still so wretched.

Will. Thou breakst my heart with these complaints. There is no star in fault, no influence but sack, the cursed sack I drunk.

Fred. Whe, how the devil came you so drunk?

Will. Whe, how the devil came you so sober?

Belv. A curse upon his thin skull. He was always beforehand that way.

Fred. Prithee, dear Colonel, forgive him. He's sorry for his fault.

Belv. He's always so after he has done a mischief. A plague on all such brutes.

Will. By this light, I took her for an arrant harlot.

Belv. Damn your debaucht opinion! Tell me, sot, hadst thou so much sense and light about thee to distinguish her woman, and couldst not see something about her face and person to strike an awful reverence into thy soul?

Will. Faith no, I considered her as mere a woman as I could wish.

Belv. 'Sdeath. I have no patience. Draw, or I'll kill you.

Will. Let that alone till tomorrow, and if I set not all right again, use your pleasure.

Belv. Tomorrow, damn it.
The spiteful light will lead me to no happiness.
Tomorrow is Antonio's and perhaps
Guides him to my undoing. Oh, that I could meet
This rival! This pow'rful fortunate!

Will. What then?

Belv. Let thy own reason, or my rage, instruct thee.

Will. I shall be finely informed then, no doubt. Hear me, Colonel, hear me. Show me the man, and I'll do his business.

Belv. I know him no more than thou, or if I did I should not need thy aid.

Will. This, you say, is Angellica's house. I promised the kind baggage to lie with her tonight.
(Offers to go in.)

Enter Ant. and his page [Diego]. Ant. knocks on the hilt of his sword.

Ant. You paid the thousand crowns I directed?

[Diego.] To the lady's old woman, sir, I did.

Will. Who the devil have we here?

Belv. I'll now plant myself under Florinda's window and, if I find no comfort there, I'll die.
(Exit Belv. and Fred.)

Enter Morett.

Morett. Page!

[Diego.] Here's my lord.

Will. How is this? A picaroon going to board my frigate? Here's one
    chase gun[80] for you.
>*(Drawing his sword, jostles Ant., who turns and draws.
>They fight. Ant. falls.)*

Morett. Oh bless us! We're all undone.
>*(Runs in and shuts the door.)*

Page. Help! Murder!
>*(Belv. returns at the noise of fighting.)*

Belv. Ha! The mad rogue's engaged in some unlucky adventure again.

Enter two or three masqueraders.
Masq. Ha! A man killed!
Will. How! A man killed! Then I'll go home to sleep.
>*(Puts up and reels out.)*
>*(Exeunt Masq. another way.)*

Belv. Who should it be! Pray heaven the rogue is safe, for all my quarrel
    to him.

As Bel. is groping about, enter an officer and six soldiers.
Sold. Who's there?
Offic. So, here's one dispatcht. Secure the murderer.
Belv. Do not mistake my charity for murder! I came to his assistance.
>*(Soldiers seize on Belv.)*

Offic. That shall be tried, sir. St. Jago,[81] swords drawn in the carnival
    time.
>*(Goes to Ant.)*

Ant. Thy hand, prithee.
Offic. Ha! Don Antonio! Look well to the villain there. How is it, sir?
Ant. I'm hurt.
Belv. Has my humanity made me a criminal?
Offic. Away with him.
Belv. What a curst chance is this.
>*(Exeunt soldiers with Belv.)*

Ant. *(To the Offic.)* This is the man that has set upon me twice. Carry
    him to my apartment till you have further orders from me.
>*(Exit Ant. led.)*

The End of the Third Act.

Act IV.

Scene i. *A fine room. Discovers Belv. as by dark alone.*

Belv. When shall I be weary of railing on fortune, who is resolved never
    to turn with smiles upon me? Two such defeats in one night none but

---

80. Chase guns could be moved to the front or back of a ship.
81. St. James of Compostella, a saint with a shrine in Spain.

the devil and that mad rogue could have contrived to have plagued
me with. I am here a prisoner, but where? Heaven knows, and if
there be murder done, I can soon decide the fate of a stranger in a
nation without mercy. Yet, this is nothing to the torture my soul
bows with when I think of losing my fair, my dear Florinda. Hark.
My door opens. A light, a man, and seems of quality. Armed, too!
Now shall I die like a dog, without defense.

Enter Ant. in a nightgown, with a light. His arm in a scarf, and a sword
under his arm. He sets the candle on the table.

Ant. Sir, I come to know what injuries I have done you, that could
provoke you to so mean an action as to attack me basely without
allowing time for my defense.

Belv. Sir, for a man in my circumstances to plead innocence would look
like fear. But view me well, and you will find no marks of coward on
me, nor anything that betrays that brutality you accuse me with.

Ant.
In vain, sir, you impose upon my sense.
You are not only he who drew on me last night,
But yesterday before the same house, that of Angellica.
Yet, there is something in your face and mien
That makes me wish I were mistaken.

Belv. I own I fought today in the defense of a friend of mine, with whom
you (if you're the same) and your party were first engaged.
Perhaps you think this crime enough to kill me,
But if you do, I cannot fear you'll do it basely.

Ant. No, sir, I'll make you fit for a defense with this.
(Gives him the sword.)

Belv. This gallantry surprises me, nor know I how to use this present,
sir, against a man so brave.

Ant.
You shall not need.
For know, I come to snatch you from a danger
That is decreed against you:
Perhaps your life or long imprisonment.
And 'twas with so much courage you offended,
I cannot see you punisht.

Belv. How shall I pay this generosity?

Ant.
It had been safer to kill'd another
Than have attempted me.
To show your danger, sir, I'll let you know my quality,
And 'tis the viceroy's son whom you have wounded.

Belv. The viceroy's son.
(Aside.)
Death and confusion! Was this plague reserv'd
To complete all the rest? Obliged by him!

The man of all the world I would destroy.

Ant. You seem disordered, sir.

Belv.

Yes, trust me, sir, I am and 'tis with pain
That man receives such bounties,
Who wants the pow'r to pay 'em back again.

Ant.

To gallant spirits 'tis indeed uneasy.
But you may quickly overpay me, sir.

Belv.

Then I am well, kind heaven! *(Aside.)* But set us even
That I may fight with him and keep my honor safe.
[To Ant.] Oh, I'm impatient, sir, to be discounting
The mighty debt I owe you. Command me quickly.

Ant.

I have a quarrel with a rival, sir,
About the maid we love.

Belv.

*(Aside.)*Death, 'tis Florinda he means.
That thought destroys my reason,
And I shall kill him.

Ant.

My rival, sir,
Is one has all the virtues man can boast of.

Belv.

(Aside.) Death! Who should this be?

[Ant.]

He challeng'd me to meet him on the Molo,
As soon as day appear'd, but last night's quarrel
Has made my arm unfit to guide a sword.[82]

Belv.

I apprehend you, sir, you'd have me kill the man
That lays a claim to the maid you speak of.
I'll do't. I'll fly to do't!

Ant. Sir, do you know her?

Belv. No, sir, but 'tis enough she is admired by you.

Ant.

Sir, I shall rob you of the glory on't,
For you must fight under my name and dress.

Belv.

That opinion must be strangely obliging that makes
You think I can personate the brave Antonio,
Whom I can but strive to imitate.

Ant.

You say too much to my advantage.

---

82. The copy-text assigns this speech to Belvile. It is corrected in the 1709 and 1724 editions.

Come sir, the day appears that calls you forth.
Within, sir, is the habit.
            (Exit Ant.)
Belv.
    Fantastic fortune, thou deceitful light
    That cheats the wearied traveler by night,
    Though on a precipice each step you tread,
    I am resolv'd to follow where you lead.
            (Exit.)

Scene [ii.] *The Molo.*

Enter Flor. and Call. in masks with Steph.
Flor. (Aside.) I'm dying with my fears. Belvile's not coming as I ex-
    pected under my window makes me believe that all those fears are
    true. *[To Steph.]* Canst thou not tell with whom my brother fights?
Steph. No, madam, they both were in masquerade. I was by when they
    challenged one another, and they had decided the quarrel then, but
    were prevented by some cavaliers, which made 'em put it off till now.
    But I am sure 'tis about you they fight.
Flor. (Aside.) Nay, then 'tis with Belvile, for what other lover have I that
    dares to fight for me except Antonio, and he is too much in favor
    with my brother. If it be he, for whom shall I direct my prayers to
    heaven?
Steph. Madam, I must leave you, for if my master see me, I shall be
    hanged for being your conductor. [I] escaped narrowly for the ex-
    cuse I made for you last night i'th' garden.
Flor. And I'll reward thee for't. Prithee, no more.
            (Exit Steph.)

Enter Don Pedro in his masquing habit.
Pedro. Antonio's late today. The place will fill, and we may be
    prevented.
            (Walks about.)
Flor.
    (Aside.) Antonio? Sure I heard amiss.
Pedro.
    But who will not excuse a happy lover
    When soft fair arms confine the yielding neck,
    And the kind whisper languishingly breathes,
    "Must you be gone so soon?"
    Sure I had dwelt forever on her bosom.
    But, stay, he's here.

Enter Belv. drest in Ant.'s clothes.
Flor. 'Tis not Belvile. Half my fears are vanisht.
Pedro. Antonio!

Belv. (Aside.) This must be he. *[To Pedro.]* You're early, sir, I do not use
to be outdone this way.

Pedro.

The wretched, sir, are watchful, and 'tis enough
You've the advantage of me in Angellica.

Belv. (Aside.) Angellica! Or I've mistook my man, or else Antonio.
Can he forget his interest in Florinda,
And fight for common prize?

Pedro. Come, sir, you know our terms.

Belv. (Aside.) By heaven, not I. *[To Pedro.]* No talking. I am ready, sir.
(Offers to fight. Flor. runs in.)

Flor. Oh, hold! Who ere you be, I do conjure you hold! *(To Belv.)* If you
strike, here *[points to Pedro.]* I die.

Pedro. Florinda!

Belv. Florinda imploring for my rival!

Pedro. Away. This kindness is unseasonable.
*(Puts her by. They fight. She runs in just as Belv. disarms
Pedro.)*

Flor. Who are you, sir, that dares deny my prayers?

Belv. Thy prayers destroy him. If thou wouldst preserve him, do that
thou'rt unacquainted with, and curse him.
(She holds him.)

Flor. By all you hold most dear, by her you love, I conjure you touch
him not.

Belv. By her I love!
See, I obey and at your feet resign
The useless trophy of my victory.
(Lays his sword at her feet.)

Pedro. Antonio, you've done enough to prove you love Florinda.

Belv. Love Florinda! Does heaven love adoration, prayer, or penitence!
Love her! Here, sir, your sword again. *(Snatches up the sword and
gives it him.)* Upon this truth I'll fight my life away.

Pedro. No, you've redeemed my sister and my friendship!
*(He gives him Flor. and pulls of his vizard to show his face,
and puts it on again.)*

Belv. Don Pedro!

Pedro.

Can you resign your claims to other women,
And give your heart entirely to Florinda?

Belv.

Entire! As dying saints' confessions are!
I can delay my happiness no longer.
This minute, let me make Florinda mine.

Pedro.

This minute let it be. No time so proper.
This night my father will arrive from Rome,
And possibly may hinder what we purpose.

Flor. Oh Heavens! This minute!

Enter masqueraders and pass over.
Belv. Oh, do not ruin me!
Pedro. The place begins to fill, and that we may not be observed, do
  you walk off to St. Peter's Church, where I will meet you and con-
  clude your happiness.
Belv. I'll meet you there. *(Aside.)* If there be no more saints' churches in
  Naples.
Flor.
  Oh stay, sir, and recall your hasty doom!
  Alas, I have not yet prepared my heart
  To entertain so strange a guest.
Pedro. Away, this silly modesty is assumed too late.
Belv. Heaven, madam! What do you do?
Flor.
  Do? Despise the man that lays a tyrant's claim
  To what he ought to conquer by submission.
Belv. You do not know me. Move a little this way.
            (Draws her aside.)
Flor.
  Yes, you may force me even to the altar,
  But not the holy man that offers there
  Shall force me to be thine.
            (Pedro talks to Call. this while.)
Belv.
  Oh, do not lose so blest an opportunity!
  See, 'tis your Belvile. Not Antonio,
  Whom your mistaken scorn and anger ruins.
            (Pulls off his vizard.)
Flor. Belvile!
  Where was my soul it could not meet thy voice,
  And take this knowledge in!

As they are talking, enter Will. finely drest and Fred.
Will. No intelligence, no news of Belvile yet? Well, I am the most
  unlucky rascal in nature. Ha! Am I deceived or is it he? Look, Fred.
  'Tis he, my dear Belvile.
            (Runs and embraces him. Belv.'s vizard falls out on's hand.)
Belv. Hell and confusion seize thee!
Pedro. Ha! Belvile! I beg you pardon, sir.
            (Takes Flor. from him.)
Belv.
  Nay touch her not. She's mine by conquest, sir;
  I won her by my sword.
Will. Didst thou so, and egad child, we'll keep her by the sword.
            (Draws on Pedro. Belv. goes between.)

Belv. Stand off.

Thou'rt so profanely lewd, so curst by heaven,

All quarrels thou espousest must be fatal.

Will. Nay, an you be so hot, my valor's coy and shall be courted when
you want it next.

> *(Puts up his sword.)*

Belv. (To Pedro.)

You know I ought to claim a victor's right,

But you're the brother to divine Florinda,

To whom I'm such a slave. To purchase her

I durst not hurt the man she holds so dear.

Pedro.

'Twas by Antonio's, not by Belvile's sword

This question should have been decided, sir.

I must confess much to your bravery's due,

Both now and when I met you last in arms,

But I am nicely punctual in my word,

As men of honor ought, and beg your pardon

For this mistake: another time shall clear.

> *(Aside to Flor. as they are going out. Belv. looks after her
> and begins to walk up and down in rage.)*

This was some plot between you and Belvile,

But I'll prevent you.

Will. Do not be modest now and lose the woman, but if we shall fetch
her back so . . .

Belv. Do not speak to me.

Will. Not speak to you? Egad, I'll speak to you, and will be answered,
too.

Belv. Will you, sir?

Will. I know I've done some mischief, but I'm so dull a puppy that I am
a son of a whore if I know how or where. Prithee, inform my
understanding.

Belv. Leave me, I say, and leave me instantly.

Will. I will not leave you in this humor, nor till I know my crime.

Belv. Death, I'll tell you, sir.

> *(Draws and runs at Will. He runs out, Belv. after him. Fred.
> interposes.)*

Enter Ang., Morett., and Sebast.

Ang. Ha, Sebastian. Is that not Willmore? Haste! Haste and bring him
back.

> *[Exit Sebast.]*

Fred. The colonel's mad. I never saw him thus before. I'll after 'em lest
he do some mischief, for I am sure Willmore will not draw on him.

> *(Exit.)*

Ang.

I am all rage! My first desires defeated!

For one for aught he knows that has no
Other merit than her quality,
Her being Don Pedro's sister, he loves her!
I know 'tis so: dull, dull, insensible.
He will not see me now, though oft invited
And broke his word last night. False, perjur'd man!
He that but yesterday fought for my favors
And would have made his life a sacrifice
To've gained one night with me
Must now be hir'd[83] and courted to my arms.

Morett. I told you what would come on't, but Moretta's an old doting
fool. Why did you give him five hundred crowns, but to set him out
for other lovers! You shouldst have kept him poor if you had meant
to have had any good from him.

Ang. Oh, name not such mean trifles; Had I given him all
My youth has earn'd from sin,
I had not lost a thought nor sigh upon't.
But I have given him my eternal rest,
My whole repose, my future joys, my heart!
My virgin heart, Moretta! Oh, 'tis gone!

Morett.
Curse on him. Here he comes.
How fine[84] she has made him, too.

Enter Will. and Sebast., Ang. turns and walks away.
Will.
How, now. Turned shadow![85]
Fly when I pursue! And follow when I fly.
   (Sings.)
Stay gentle shadow of my dove,
   And tell me ere I go,
Whether the substance may not prove
   A fleeting thing like you.
There's a soft kind look remaining yet.
   (As she turns, she looks on him.)

Ang. Well, sir, you may be gay. All happiness, all joys pursue you still.
Fortune's your slave, and gives you every hour choice of new hearts
and beauties till you are cloyed with the repeated bliss which others
vainly languish for. *(Turns away in a rage.)* But know, false man, that
I shall be revenged.

Will. So, Gad, there are of those faint-hearted lovers, whom such a
sharp lesson next their hearts would make as impotent as fourscore.
Pox o' this whining. My business is to laugh and love. A pox on't. I

83. Bribed.
84. Well-dressed.
85. An old comparison and one treated by Ben Jonson in "That Women Are but Men's Shadows."

hate your sullen lover; a man shall lose as much time to put you in humor now as would serve to gain a new woman.

Ang.
I scorn to cool that fire I cannot raise.
Or do the drudgery of your virtuous mistress.

Will. A virtuous mistress! Death, what a thing thou hast found out for me! Why, what the devil should I do with a virtuous woman? A sort of ill-natured creatures that take pride to torment a lover. Virtue is but an infirmity in woman, a disease that renders even the handsome ungrateful, whilst the ill-favored, for want of solicitations and address, only fancy themselves so. I have lain with a woman of quality, who has all the while been railing at whores.

Ang.
I will not answer for your mistress's virtue,
Though she be young enough to know no guilt.
And I could wish you would persuade my heart
'Twas the two hundred thousand crowns you courted.

Will. Two hundred thousand crowns! What story's this? What trick? What woman? Ha!

Ang. How strange you make it. Have you forgot the creature you entertained on the Piazzo last night?

Will. (Aside.) Ha! My gypsy worth two hundred thousand crowns! Oh, how I long to be with her. Pox, I knew she was of quality.

Ang.
False man! I see my ruin in thy face.
How many vows you breath'd upon my bosom
Never to be unjust. Have you forgot so soon?

Will. Faith no, I was just coming to repeat 'em. (Aside.) But here's a humor indeed would make a man a saint. Would she would be angry enough to leave me, and command me not to wait on her.

Enter Hell. drest in man's clothes.
Hell. [Aside.] This must be Angellica! I know it by her mumping[86] matron here. Aye, aye, 'tis she! My mad captain's with her, too, for all his swearing. How this unconstant humor makes me love him! [To Morett.] Pray good grave gentlewoman, is not this Angellica?
Morett. My too young sir, it is. I hope 'tis one from Don Antonio.
(Goes to Ang.)
Hell. (Aside.) Well, something I'll do to vex him for this.
Ang. I will not speak with him. Am I in humor to receive a lover?
Will. Not speak with him! Whe, I'll be gone and wait your idler minutes. Can I show less obedience to the thing I love so fondly?
(Offers to go.)
Ang. A fine excuse, this. Stay.

86. Grimacing.

Will. And hinder your advantage! Should I repay your bounties so
ungratefully?

Ang. [To Hell.]
Come hither, boy, that I may let *[To Will.]* you see
How much above the advantages you name
I prize one minute's joy with you.

Will. Oh, you destroy me with this endearment. *(Impatient to be gone.)*
[Aside.] Death! How shall I get away? *[To Ang.]* Madam, 'twill not
be fit I should be seen with you. Besides, it will not be convenient,
and I've a friend that's dangerously sick.

Ang. I see you're impatient. Yet you shall stay.

Will. *(Aside and walks about impatiently.)* And miss my assignation
with my gypsy.

     (Morett. brings Hell., who addresses herself to Ang.)

Hell. Madam,
You'll hardly pardon my instrusion,
When you shall know my business!
And I'm too young to tell my tale with art,
But there must be a wondrous store of goodness
Where so much beauty dwells.

Ang.
A pretty advocate, whoever sent thee.
Prithee, proceed.
     (To Will., who is stealing off.)
Nay, sir, you shall not go.

Will. *(Aside.)*
Then I shall lose my dear gypsy forever.
Pox on't. She stays me out of spite.

[Hell.]
I am related to a lady, madam,
Young, rich, and nobly born, but has the fate
To be in love with a young English gentleman.
Strangely she loves him. At first sight she loved him,
But did adore him when she heard him speak,
For he, she said, had charms in every word
That failed not to surprise, to wound, and conquer.

Will. *(Aside.)* Ha! Egad, I hope this concerns me.

Ang. [Aside.]
'Tis my false man, he means. Would he were gone.
This praise will raise his pride and ruin me.
     (To Will.)
               Well,
Since you are so impatient to be gone,
I will release you, sir.

Will. *(Aside.)*
Nay, then I'm sure 'twas me he spoke of
This cannot be the effects of kindness in her.

[To Ang.] No, madam, I've consider'd better on't,
And will not give you cause of jealousy.
Ang. But, sir, I've business that . . .
Will. This shall not do. I know 'tis but to try me.
Ang. Well, to your story, boy,
      (Aside.)
                Though 'twill undo me.
Hell.
  With this addition to his other beauties,
  He won her unresisting, tender heart.
  He vow'd, and sigh't, and swore he lov'd her dearly.
  And she believ'd the cunning flatterer,
  And thought herself the happiest maid alive.
  Today was the appointed time by both
  To consummate their bliss.
  The virgin, altar, and the priest were drest,
  And whilst she languisht for th'expected bridegroom,
  She heard he paid his broken vows to you.
Will. *[Aside.]* So this is some dear rogue that's in love with me, and this
  way lets me know it. Or if it be not me, he[87] means some one whose
  place I may supply.
Ang. Now, I perceive
  The cause of thy impatience to be gone
  And all the business of this glorious dress.
Will. Damn the young prater.[88] I know not what he means.
Hell. Madam,
  In your fair eyes I read too much concern
  To tell my further business.
Ang.
  Prithee, sweet youth, talk on. Thou mayst, perhaps,
  Raise here a storm that may undo my passion,
  And then I'll grant thee anything.
Hell.
  Madam, 'tis to intreat you (oh unreasonable),
  You would not see this stranger,
  For if you do, she vows you are undone,
  Though nature never made a man so excellent,
  And sure he 'ad been a god but for inconstancy.
Will. *(Aside.)* Ah, rogue, how finely he's instructed!
  'Tis plain, some woman that has seen me *en passant.*[89]
Ang. Oh, I shall burst with jealousy! Do you know the man you speak
  of?
Hell. Yes, madam, he used to be in buff and scarlet.
Ang. *(To Will.)* Thou, false as hell, what canst thou say to this?

---

87. "he" in the third quarto, but "she" in the first two quartos.
88. Talker.
89. In passing.

Will. By heaven . . .

Ang. Hold, do not damn thyself.

Hell. Nor hope to be believed.

> *(He walks about. They follow.)*

Ang. Oh, perjured man!

Is't thus you pay my generous passion back?

Hell. Why would you, sir, abuse my lady's faith?

Ang. And use me so unhumanely.

Hell. A maid so young, so innocent.

Will. Ah, young devil.

Ang. Dost thou not know thy life is [in] my power?

Hell. Or think my lady cannot be revenged?

Will. *(Aside.)* So, so. The storm comes finely on.

Ang.

Now thou art silent. Guilt has struck thee dumb.

Or hadst thou still been so, I'd liv'd in safety.

> *(She turns away and weeps.)*

Will. *(Aside to Hell.)* Sweetheart, the lady's name and house. Quickly,

I'm impatient to be with her.

> *(Looks towards Ang. to watch her turning, and as she*
> *comes towards them, he meets her.)*

Hell. *(Aside.)* So, now he's for another woman.

Will.

The impudent'st young thing in nature.

I cannot persuade him out of his error, madam.

Ang.

I know he's in the right, yet thou'st a tongue

That would persuade him to deny his faith.

> *(In rage walks away.)*

Will. *(Said softly to Hell.)* Her name, her name, dear boy.

Hell. Have you forgot it, sir?

Will. *(Aside.)* Oh, I perceive he's not to know I am a stranger to his lady.

[To Hell.] Yes, yes. I do know, but have forgot the . . . *([To] Ang.*

[who] turns.) By heaven, such early confidence I never saw.

Ang.

Did I not charge you with this mistress, sir,

Which you deny'd, though I beheld your perjury.

This little generosity of thine has rendered back my heart.

> *(Walks away.)*

Will. So, you have made sweet work here, my little mischief. Look your
lady be kind and good natured now, or I shall have but a cursed
bargain on't.

> *(Ang. turns towards them.)*

The rogue's bred up to mischief.

Art thou so great a fool to credit him?

Ang.

Yes, I do, and you in vain impose upon me.

Come hither, boy. Is not this not he you spake of?

Hell. I think it is. I cannot swear, but I vow he has just such another lying lover's look.

> (*Hell. looks into his face. He gazes on her.*)

Will. (Aside.)

Ha! Do I not know that face.

By heaven, my little gypsy. What a dull dog was I.

Had I but lookt that way, I'd known her.

Are all my hopes of a new woman banisht?

Egad, if I do not fit[90] thee for this, hang me.

[To Ang.] Madam, I have found out the plot.

Hell. (Aside.) Oh Lord, what does he say? Am I discovered now?

Will. Do you see this young spark here?

Hell. [Aside.] He'll tell her who I am.

Will. Who do you think this is?

Hell. [Aside.] Aye, aye. He does know me. *[Aside to Will.]* Nay, dear Captain! I am undone if you discover me.

Will. [Aside to Hell.] Nay, nay. No cogging.[91] She shall know what a precious mistress I have.

Hell. [Aside to Will.] Will you be such a devil?

Will. [Aside to Hell.] Nay, nay. I'll teach you to spoil sport you will not make. *[To Ang.]* This small ambassador comes not from a person of quality, as you imagine and he says, but from a very arrant gypsy— the talkingest, pratingest, cantingest little animal thou ever sawst.

Ang. What news you tell me! That's the thing I mean.

Hell. (Aside.) Would I were well off the place. If ever I go a captain hunting again . . .

Will. Mean that thing? That gypsy thing? Thou mayst as well be jealous of thy monkey or parrot as of her. A German motion[92] were worth a dozen of her and a dream were better enjoyment, a creature of constitution fitter for heaven than man.

Hell. (Aside.) Though I'm sure he lies, yet this vexes me.

Ang.

You are mistaken. She's a Spanish woman,

Made up of no such dull materials.

Will. Materials? Egad, and she be made of any that will either dispense or admit of love, I'll be bound to continence.

Hell. (Aside to him.) Unreasonable man, do you think so?

[Will.] You may return, my little brazen head, and tell your lady, that till she be handsome enough to be beloved, or I dull enough to be religious, there will be small hopes of me.

Ang. Did you not promise then to marry her?

Will. Not I, by heaven.

---

90. Punish.
91. Cheating, as at dice.
92. Puppet show.

Ang. You cannot undeceive my fears and torments, till you have vowed
you will not marry her.

Hell. (Aside.) If he swears that, he'll be revenged on me indeed for all
my rogueries.

Ang. I know what arguments you'll bring against me—fortune and
honor.

Will. Honor, I tell you, I hate it in your sex, and those that fancy
themselves possest of that foppery are the most impertinently troublesome of all womankind, and will transgress nine commandments
to keep one. And to satisfy your jealousy, I swear . . .

Hell. (Aside.) Oh, no swearing, dear Captain.

Will. If it were possible, I should ever be inclined to marry, it should be
some kind young sinner. One that has generosity enough to give a
favor handsomely to one that can ask for it discreetly, one that has
wit enough to manage an intrigue of love. Oh, how civil such a
wench is to a man that does her the honor to marry her.

Ang. By heaven, there's no faith in anything he says.

Enter Sebast.

Sebast. Madam, Don Antonio . . .

Ang. Come hither.

Hell. [Aside.] Ha! Antonio. He may be coming hither, and he'll certainly discover me. I'll therefore retire without a ceremony.
    (Exit Hell.)

Ang. I'll see him. Get my coach ready.

Sebast. It waits you, madam.

Will. This is lucky. What madam, now I may be gone and leave you to
the enjoyment of my rival?

Ang.
    Dull man, that canst not see how ill, how poor,
    That false dissimulation looks—be gone,
    And never let me see thy cozening face again.
    Lest I relapse and kill thee.

Will. Yes you can spare me now. Farewell, till you're in better humor.
[Aside.] I'm glad of this release.
    Now for my gypsy,
    For though to worse we change, yet still we find
    New joys, new charms in a new mistress that's kind.
    (Exit Will.)

Ang.
    He's gone and in this ague of my soul
    The shivering fit returns.
    Oh, with what willing haste he took his leave,
    As if the long'd for minute were arriv'd
    Of some blest assignation.
    In vain I have consulted all my charms,
    In vain this beauty priz'd, in vain believ'd

My eyes could kindle any lasting fires.
I had forgot my name, my infamy
And the reproach that honor lays on those
That dare pretend a sober passion here.
Nice[93] reputation, though it leave behind
More virtues than inhabit where that dwells,
Yet that once gone, those virtues shine no more.
Then since I am not fit to be belov'd,
I am resolv'd to think on a revenge
On him that soothed me thus to my undoing.
    (Exeunt.)

Scene the Third[.] *A street.*

Enter Flor. and Val. in habits different from what they have been seen in.

Flor. We're happily escaped, and yet I tremble still.

Val. A lover and fear? Whe, I am but half an one, and yet I have courage for any attempt. Would Hellena were here. I would fain have had her as deep in this mischief as we. She'll fare but ill else, I doubt.

Flor. She pretended a visit to the Augustine nuns, but I believe some other design carried her out. Pray Heaven we light on her. Prithee, what didst do with Callis?

Val. When I saw no reason would do good on her, I followed her into the wardrobe, and as she was looking for something in the great chest, I toppled her in by the heels, snatcht the key of the apartment where you were confined, locked her in, and left her bawling for help.

Flor. 'Tis well you resolve to follow my fortunes, for thou darest never appear at home again after such an action.

Val. That's according as the young stranger and I shall agree. But to our business. I delivered your letter, your note, to Belvile. When I got out under pretense of going to mass, I found him at his lodging, and believe me it came seasonably, for never was man in so desperate condition. I told him of your resolution of making your escape today, if your brother would be absent long enough to permit you. If not, to die rather than be Antonio's.

Flor. Thou shouldst have told him I was confined to my chamber upon my brother's suspicion that the business on the Molo was a plot laid between him and I.

Val. I said all this, and told him your brother was now gone to his devotion; and he resolves to visit every church till he find him, and not only undeceive him in that, but caress him so as shall delay his return home.

Flor. Oh heavens! He's here, and Belvile with him, too.

---

93. Difficult to please. Reputation "leaves behind" virtues associated with passion, but those virtues without reputation do not "shine."

(They put on their vizards.)

Enter Don Pedro, Belv., Will. Belv. and Pedro seeming in serious discourse.

Val. Walk boldly by them, and I'll come at distance, lest he suspect us.
(She [Flor.] walks by them and looks back on them.)

Will. Ha! A woman, and of excellent mien.

Pedro. She throws a kind look back on you.

Will. Death, 'tis a likely wench, and that kind look shall not be cast away. I'll follow her.

Belv. Prithee, do not.

Will. Do not? By heavens, to the antipodes[94] with such an invitation.
(She goes out and Will. follows her.)

Belv. 'Tis a mad fellow for a wench.

Enter Fred.

Fred. Oh Colonel, such news!

Belv. Prithee, what?

Fred. News that will make you laugh in spite of fortune.

Belv. What, Blunt has some damned trick put upon him? Cheated, banged, or clapt?

Fred. Cheated, sir, rarely cheated of all but his shirt and drawers. The unconscionable whore, too, turned him out before consummation, so that traversing the streets at midnight, the watch found him in this *fresco* and conducted him home. By heaven, 'tis such a sight, and yet I durst as well been hanged as laught at him or pity him. He beats all that do but ask him a question, and is in such an humor.

Pedro. Who is't has met with this ill usage, sir?

Belv. A friend of ours whom you must see for mirth's sake. *(Aside.)* I'll employ him to give Florinda time for an escape.

Pedro. What is he?

Belv. A young countryman of ours, one that has been educated at so plentiful a rate he yet ne'er knew the want of money, and 'twill be a great jest to see how simply he'll look without it. For my part, I'll lend him none, and the rogue know not how to put on a borrowing face and ask first. I'll let him see how good 'tis to play our parts whilst I play his. Prithee, Fred, do you go home and keep him in that posture till we come.
(Exeunt.)

Enter Flor. from the farther end of the scene, looking behind her.

Flor. I am followed still. Ha! My brother, too, advancing this way. Good heavens defend me from being seen by him.
(She goes off.)

Enter Will. and after him Val. at a little distance.

94. Opposite side of the earth.

Will. Ah! There she sails. She looks back as she were willing to be boarded. I'll warrant her prize.
> *(He goes out, Val. following.)*

Enter Hell., just as he goes out, with a page.
Hell. Ha! Is not that my captain that has a women in chase? 'Tis not Angellica. Boy, follow those people at a distance and bring me an account where they go in. I'll find his haunts and plague him everywhere. Ha! My brother.
> *(Exit page.)*

Belv., Will., Pedro cross the stage. Hell runs off.

[Scene iv.] *Scene changes to another street.*

Enter Flor.
Flor.
What shall I do? My brother now pursues me.
Will no kind pow'r protect me from his tyranny?
Ha! Here's a door open. I'll venture in, since nothing can be worse than to fall into his hands. My life and honor are at stake, and my necessity has no choice.
> *(She goes in.)*

Enter Val. and Hell.'s page peeping after Flor.
Page. Here she went in. I shall remember this house.
> *(Exit boy.)*

Val. This is Belvile's lodging. She's gone in as readily as if she knew it. Ha! Here's that mad fellow again. I dare not venture in. I'll watch my opportunity.
> *(Goes aside.)*

Enter Will. gazing about him.
Will. I have lost her hereabouts. Pox on't, she must not escape me so.
> *(Goes out.)*

[Scene v.] *Scene changes to Blunt's chamber, discovers him sitting on a couch in his shirt and drawers, reading.*

Blunt. So, now my mind's a little at peace, since I have resolved revenge. A pox on this tailor, though, for not bringing home the clothes I bespoke.[95] And a pox of all cavaliers. A man can never keep a spare suit for 'em. And I shall have these rogues come in and find me naked, and then I'm undone, but I'm resolved to arm myself. The rascals shall not insult over me too much. *(Puts on old rusty sword and buff belt.)* Now, how like a morris dancer I am equipt.[96] A fine

---

95. Arranged for.
96. A morris dance was performed in fanciful costume.

lady-like whore to cheat me thus without affording me kindness for my money. A pox light on her. I shall never be reconciled to the sex more. She has made me as faithless as a physician, as uncharitable as a churchman, and as ill natured as a poet. Oh how I'll use all womankind hereafter! What would I give to have one of 'em within my reach now! Any mortal thing in petticoats, kind fortune, send me, and I'll forgive thy last night's malice. Here's a cursed book, too (a warning to all young travelers), that can instruct me how to prevent such mischiefs now 'tis too late. Well, 'tis a rare convenient thing to read a little now and then, as well as hawk and hunt.

(Sits down and reads.)

Enter to him Flor.

Flor. This house is haunted sure. 'Tis well furnished and no living thing inhabits it. Ha! A man. Heavens how he's attired! Sure 'tis some rope dancer or fencing master. I tremble now for fear, and yet I must venture now to speak to him. Sir, if I may not interrupt your meditations . . .

([He] starts up and gazes.)[97]

Blunt. Ha! What's here? Are my wishes granted? And is not that a she creature? 'Adsheartlikins, 'tis. What wretched thing art thou? Ha!

Flor. Charitable sir, you've told yourself already what I am, a very wretched maid, forced by strange, unlucky accident to seek a safety here. And must be ruined if you do not grant it.

Blunt. Ruined! Is there any ruin so inevitable as that which now threatens thee? Dost thou know, miserable woman, into what den of mischiefs thou art fallen? What abyss of confusion? Ha! Dost not see something in my looks that frights thy guilty soul, and makes thee wish to change that shape of woman for any humble animal or devil? For, those were safer for thee, and less mischievous.

Flor. Alas, what mean you, sir? I must confess your looks have something in 'em makes me fear, but I beseech you, as you seem a gentleman, pity a harmless virgin that takes your house for sanctuary.

Blunt. Talk on, talk on, and weep, too, till my faith return. Do, flatter me out of my senses again. A harmless virgin with a pox—as much one as t'other, 'adsheartlikins. Whe, what the devil, can I not be safe in my house for you, not in my chamber, nay, not even being naked, too, cannot secure me? This is an impudence greater than has invaded me yet. Come, no resistance.

(Pulls her rudely.)

Flor. Dare you be so cruel?

Blunt. Cruel? 'Adsheartlikins, as a galley-slave or a Spanish whore. Cruel? Yes, I will kiss and beat thee all over, kiss and see thee all over. Thou shalt lie with me, too, not that I care for the enjoyment, but to let thee see that I have ta'en deliberate malice to thee, and will be

97. "She" in the copy-text, corrected to "he" in 1709 quarto.

revenged on one whore for the sins of another. I will smile and deceive thee, flatter thee and beat thee, embrace thee and rob thee, as she did me, fawn on thee, and strip thee stark naked; then hang thee out at my window by the heels, with a paper of scurvy verses fastened to thy breast in praise of damnable women. Come, come along.

Flor. Alas, sir, must I be sacrificed for the crimes of the most infamous of my sex? I never understood the sins you name.

Blunt. Do persuade the fool you love him, or that one of you can be just or honest. Tell me I was not an easy coxcomb, or any strange impossible tale. It will be believed sooner than thy false showers or protestations. A generation of damned hypocrites! To flatter my very clothes from my back! Dissembling witches! Are these the returns you make an honest gentleman that trusts, believes, and loves you? But if I be not even with you . . . Come along or I shall . . .

(Pulls her again.)

Enter Fred.

Fred. Ha! What's here to do?

Blunt. 'Adsheartlikins, Fred. I am glad thou art come, to be a witness of my dire revenge.

Fred. What's this? A person of quality, too, who is upon the ramble to supply the defects of some grave impotent husband?

Blunt. No, this has another pretense. Some very unfortunate accident brought her hither, to save a life pursued by I know not who or why, and forced [her] to take sanctuary here at fool's haven. 'Adsheartlikins, to me of all mankind for protection? Is the ass to be cajoled again, think ye? No, young one, no prayers or tears shall mitigate my rage. Therefore prepare for both my pleasures of enjoyment and revenge, for I am resolved to make up my loss here on thy body. I'll take it out in kindness and in beating.

Fred. Now, mistress of mine, what do you think of this?

Flor. I think he will not, dares not, be so barbarous.

Fred. Have a care, Blunt, she fetcht a deep sigh. She is enamored with thy shirt and drawers. She'll strip thee even of that. There are of her calling such unconscionable baggages and such dexterous thieves, they'll flay a man and he shall ne'er miss his skin till he feels the cold. There was a countryman of ours robbed of a row of teeth whilst he was sleeping, which the jilt made him buy again when he waked. You see, lady, how little reason we have to trust you.

Blunt. 'Adsheartlikins. Whe, this is most abominable.

Flor. Some such devils there may be, but by all that's holy, I am none such. I entered here to save a life in danger.

Blunt. For no goodness, I'll warrant her.

Fred. Faith, damsel, you had e'en confessed the plain truth, for we are fellows not to be caught twice in the same trap. Look on that wreck. A tight vessel when he set out of haven, well trimmed and laden, and see how a female picaroon of this island of rogues has shattered him, and canst thou hope for any mercy?

Blunt. No, no, gentlewoman. Come along. 'Adsheartlikins, we must be better acquainted. We'll both lie with her, and then let me alone to bang her.

Fred. I'm ready to serve you in matters of revenge. That has a double pleasure in't.

Blunt. Well said. You hear, little one, how you are condemned by public vote to the bed within. There's no resisting your destiny, sweetheart.
(*Pulls her.*)

Flor. Stay, sir, I have seen you with Belvile, an English cavalier. For his sake, use me kindly. You know him, sir.

Blunt. Belvile, whe, yes, sweeting, we do know Belvile, and wish he were with us now. He's a cormorant at whore and bacon. He'd have a limb or two of thee, my virgin pullet. But 'tis no matter. We'll leave him the bones to pick.

Flor. Sir, if you have any esteem for that Belvile, I conjure you to treat me with more gentleness. He'll thank you for the justice.

Fred. Harkee, Blunt. I doubt we are mistaken in this matter.

Flor. Sir, if you find me not worth Belvile's care, use me as you please, and that you may think I merit better treatment than you threaten, pray take this present.
(*Gives him a ring. He looks on it.*)

Blunt. Hum. A diamond! Whe, 'tis a wonderful virtue now that lies in this ring. A mollifying virtue. 'Adsheartlikins, there's more persuasive rhetoric in't than all her sex can utter.

Fred. I begin to suspect something, and 'twould anger us vilely to be trussed up for a rape upon a maid of quality, when we only believe we ruffle a harlot.

Blunt. Thou art a credulous fellow, but, 'adsheartlikins, I have no faith yet. Whe, my saint prattled as parlously as this does. She gave me a bracelet, too. A devil on her, but I sent my man to sell it today for necessaries, and it proved as counterfeit as her vows of love.

Fred. However, let it reprieve her till we see Belvile.

Blunt. That's hard, yet I will grant it.

Enter a servant.

Serv. Oh, sir, the colonel is just come in with his new friend and a Spaniard of quality, and talks of having you to dinner with 'em.

Blunt. 'Adsheartlikins, I'm undone. I would not see 'em for the world. Harkee, Fred. Lock up the wench in your chamber.

Fred. Fear nothing, madam, what e'er he threatens, you are safe whilst in my hands.
(*Exeunt Fred. and Flor.*)

Blunt. And, sirrah, upon your life, say I am not at home or that I am asleep or anything. Away. I'll prevent their coming this way.
(*Locks the door and exeunt.*)

The End of the Fourth Act.

Act V.

Scene i. *Blunt's chamber.*

After a great knocking as at his chamber door, enter Blunt softly crossing the stage, in his shirt and drawers as before.
Call within. Ned, Ned Blunt. Ned Blunt.
Blunt. The rogues are up in arms. 'Sheartlikins, this villainous Frederick has betrayed me. They have heard of my blessed fortune. *[Call within.]* Ned Blunt, Ned, Ned. *(And knocking within.)*
Belv. [Within.] Whe, he's dead, sir, without dispute dead. He has not been seen today. Let's break open the door. Here, boy.
Blunt. Ha, break open the door? 'Adsheartlikins, that mad fellow will be as good as his word.
Belv. [Within.] Boy, bring something to force the door.
 A great noise within at the door again.
Blunt. So now must I speak in my own defense. I'll try what rhetoric will do. Hold, hold. What you do you mean, gentlemen, what do you mean?
Belv. (Within.) Oh rogue, art alive? Prithee open the door and convince us.
Blunt. Yes, I am alive, gentlemen, but at present a little busy.
Belv. (Within.) How? Blunt grown a man of business? Come, come. Open and let's see this miracle.
Blunt. No. No. No. No. Gentlemen, 'tis no great business, but I am at my devotion. 'Adsheartlikins, will you not allow a man time to pray?
Belv. (Within.) Turned religious! A greater wonder than the first. Therefore open quickly, or we shall unhinge. We shall.
Blunt. This won't do. Whe, harkee, Colonel, to tell you the plain truth, I am about a necessary affair of life. I have a wench with me. Do you apprehend me? *(Aside.)* The devil's in't if they be so uncivil as to disturb me now.
Will. [Within.] How a wench! Nay, then we must enter and partake. No resistance, unless it be your lady of quality, and then we'll keep our distance.
Blunt. So, the business is out.
Will. [Within.] Come, come. Lend's more hands to the door. Now heave all together. *(Breaks open the door.)* So, well done, my boys.

Enter Belv., Will., Fred., and Pedro. Blunt looks simply, they all laugh at him; he lays his hand on his sword and comes up to Will.
Blunt. Harkee, sir, laugh out your laugh quickly, d'ye hear, and be gone. I shall spoil your sport else, 'adsheartlikins, sir, I shall. The jest has been carried on too long. *(Aside.)* A plague upon my tailor.
Will. 'Sdeath, how the whore has drest him. Faith, sir, I'm sorry.

Blunt. Are you so, sir? Keep't to yourself, then, sir, I advise you, d'ye hear? For I can as little endure your pity as his mirth.

(Lays his hand on's sword.)

Belv. Indeed, Willmore, thou wert a little too rough with Ned Blunt's mistress. Call a person of quality a whore? And one so young, so handsome, and so eloquent? Ha. Ha. He.

Blunt. Harkee, sir, you know me, and know I can be angry. Have a care, for 'adsheartlikins, I can fight, too. I can, sir. Do you mark me? No more.

Belv. Why so peevish, good Ned? Some disappointments, I'll warrant? What, did the jealous count, her husband, return just in the nick?

Blunt. Or, the devil, sir. D'ye laugh? *(They laugh.)* Look ye settle me a good sober countenance and that quickly, too, or you shall know Ned Blunt is not . . .

Belv. Not everybody. We know that.

Blunt. Not an ass to be laught at, sir.

Will. Unconscionable sinner. To bring a lover so near his happiness, a vigorous passionate lover, and then not only cheat him of his movables, but his very desires, too.

Belv. Ah! Sir, a mistress is a trifle with Blunt. He'll have a dozen the next time he looks abroad. His eyes have charms not to be resisted. There needs no more than to expose that taking person to the view of the fair, and he leads 'em all in triumph.

Pedro. Sir, though I'm a stranger to you, I am ashamed at the rudeness of my nation, and could you learn who did it, would assist you to make an example of 'em.

Blunt. Whe, aye. There's one speaks sense now and handsomely, and let me tell you, gentlemen, I should not have showed myself like a Jack Pudding[98] thus to have made you mirth, but that I have revenge within my power. For know, I have got into my possession a female, who had better have fallen under any curse than the ruin I design her. 'Adsheartlikins, she assaulted me here in my own lodgings, and had doubtless committed a rape upon me, had not this sword defended me.

Fred. I know not that, but, o' my conscience, thou had ravisht her, had she not redeemed herself with a ring. Let's see't, Blunt.

(Blunt shows the ring.)

Belv. [Aside.] Ha! The ring I gave Florinda when we exchange[d][99] our vows. Harkee, Blunt.

(Goes to whisper to him.)

Will. No whispering, good Colonel. There's a woman in the case, no whispering.

Belv. Harkee, fool. Be advised and conceal both the ring and the story for your reputation's sake. Do not let people know what despised

98. Buffoon or clown.
99. "Exchange" in the copy-text is corrected to "exchang'd" in the 1709 quarto.

cullies we English are, to be cheated and abused by one whore. And another rather bribe thee than be kind to thee is an infamy to our nation.

Will. Come, come. Where's the wench? We'll see her; let her be what she will. We'll see her.

Pedro. Aye, aye. Let us see her. I can soon discover whether she be of quality or for your diversion.

Blunt. She's in Fred's custody.

Will. Come, come the key.

(To Fred. who gives him the key [as] they are going.)

Belv. Death, what shall I do? Stay, gentlemen. Yet, if I hinder 'em, I shall discover all. Let's go one at once.[100] Give me the key.

Will. Nay, hold there, Colonel. I'll go first.

Fred. Nay, no dispute. Ned and I have the propriety[101] of her.

Will. Damn propriety. Then we'll draw cuts. *(Belv. goes to whisper [to] Will.)* Nay, no corruption, good Colonel. Come, the longest sword carries her.

(They all draw, forgetting Don Pedro, being a Spaniard, had the longest.)

Blunt. I yield up my interest to you, gentlemen, and that will be revenge sufficient.

Will. (To Pedro.) The wench is yours. Pox of his Toledo. I had forgot that.

Fred. Come, sir, I'll conduct you to the lady.

(Exeunt Fred. and Pedro.)

Belv. (Aside.) To hinder him will certainly discover her. *([To] Will, [who is] walking up and down out of humor)* Dost know, dull beast, what mischief thou hast done?

Will. Aye, aye, to trust our fortunes to lots. A devil on't. 'Twas madness. That's the truth on't.

Belv. Oh, intolerable sot . . .

Enter Florinda running masked. Pedro after her. Will gazing around her.

Flor. (Aside.) Good heaven, defend me from discovery.

Pedro. 'Tis but in vain to fly me. You're fallen to my lot.

Belv. Sure she's undiscovered yet, but now I fear there is no way to bring her off.

Will. Whe, what a pox. Is not this my woman, the same I followed but now?

(Pedro. talking to Flor., who walks up and down.)

Pedro. As if I did not know ye, and your business here.

Flor. (Aside.) Good heaven, I fear he does indeed.

Pedro. Come, pray be kind. I know you meant to be so when you entered here, for these are proper gentlemen.

---

100. "one at once": let's go together right now.
101. The copy-text reads "gropriety," and a pun could have been intended.

Will. But, sir, perhaps the lady will not be imposed upon. She'll choose her man.

Pedro. I am better bred than not to leave her choice free.

Enter Val., and is surprised at the sight of Don Pedro.

Val. (Aside.) Don Pedro here! There is no avoiding him.

Flor. (Aside.) Valeria! Then I'm undone.

Val. (To Pedro, running to him.) Oh, I have found you, sir. The strangest accident—if I had breath to tell it.

Pedro. Speak. Is Florinda safe? Hellena well?

Val. Aye, aye, sir. Florinda is safe from any fears of you.

Pedro. Why, where's Florinda? Speak.

Val. Aye, where, indeed sir, I wish I could inform you, but to hold you no longer in doubt . . .

Flor. (Aside.) Oh, what will she say?

Val. She's fled away in the habit of one of her pages, sir. But Callis thinks you may retrieve her yet, if you make haste away. She'll tell you, sir, the rest *(aside)* if you can find her out.

Pedro. Dishonorable girl. She has undone my aim. Sir, you see my necessity of leaving you, and [I] hope you'll pardon it. My sister, I know, will make her flight to you; and if she do, I shall expect she should be rendered back.

Belv. I shall consult my love and honor, sir.

　　　(Exit Pedro.)

Flor. (To Val.) My dear preserver, let me embrace thee.

Will. What the devil's all this?

Blunt. Mystery, by this light.

Val. Come, come. Make haste and get yourselves married quickly, for your brother will return again.

Belv. I am so surprised with fears and joys, so amazed to find you here in safety, I can scarce persuade my heart into a faith of what I see.

Will. Harkee, Colonel. Is this that mistress who has cost you so many sighs, and me so many quarrels with you?

Belv. (To Flor.) It is. Pray give him the honor of your hand.

Will. Thus it must be received, then. *(Kneels and kisses her hand.)* And with it give your pardon, too.

Flor. The friend to Belvile may command me anything.

Will. (Aside.) Death, would I might. 'Tis a surprising beauty.

Belv. Boy, run and fetch a father instantly.

　　　(Exit boy.)

Fred. So, now do I stand like a dog and have not a syllable to plead my own cause with? By this hand, madam, I was never thoroughly confounded before, nor shall I ever more dare look up with confidence, till you are pleased to pardon me.

Flor. Sir, I'll be reconciled to you on one condition—that you'll follow the example of your friend in marrying a maid that does not hate you, and whose fortune (I believe) will not be unwelcome to you.

Fred. Madam, had I no inclinations that way, I should obey your kind commands.

Belv. Who, Fred marry? He has so few inclinations for womankind that, had he been possest of paradise, he might have continued there to this day, if no crime but love could have disinherited him.

Fred. Oh, I do not use to boast of my intrigues.

Belv. Boast, whe, thou dost nothing but boast. And I dare swear, wert thou as innocent from the sin of the grape as thou art from the apple, thou mightst yet claim that right in Eden which our first parents lost by too much loving.

Fred. I wish this lady would think me so modest a man.

Val. She would be sorry then, and not like you half so well. And I should be loath to break my word with you, which was that if your friend and mine agreed, it should be a match between you and I.
(She gives him her hand.)

Fred. Bear witness, Colonel, 'tis a bargain.
(Kisses her hand.)

Blunt. *(To Flor.)* I have a pardon to beg, too, but, 'adsheartlikins, I am so out of countenance that I'm a dog if I can say anything to the purpose.

Flor. Sir, I heartily forgive you all.

Blunt. That's nobly said, sweet lady. Belvile, prithee present her her ring again, for I find I have not courage to approach her myself.
(Gives him the ring. He gives [it] to Flor.)

Enter boy.

Boy. Sir, I have brought the father that you sent for.

Belv. 'Tis well, and now my dear Florinda, let's fly to complete that mighty joy we have so long wisht and sighed for. Come Fred. Will you follow?

Fred. Your example, sir, 'twas ever my ambition in war, and must be so in love.

Will. And must not I see this juggling[102] knot be tied?

Belv. No, thou shalt do us better service and be our guard, lest Don Pedro's sudden return interrupt the ceremony.

Will. Content. I'll secure this pass.
(Exeunt Belv., Flor., Fred., and Val.)

Enter boy.

Boy. *(To Will.)* Sir, there's a lady without would speak to you.

Will. Conduct her in. I dare not quit my post.

Boy. *[To Blunt.]* And, sir, your tailor waits you in your chamber.

Blunt. Some comfort yet. I shall not dance naked at the wedding.
(Exeunt Blunt and boy.)

102. Cheating.

*Enter again the boy, conducting in Ang. in a masquing habit and a
vizard. Will. runs to her.*

Will. *[Aside.]* This can be none but my pretty gypsy. *[To Ang.]* Oh, I see
you can follow as well as fly. Come, confess thyself the most malicious devil in nature. You think you have done my business with
Angellica.

Ang. Stand off, base villain.

> *(She draws a pistol and holds [it] to his breast.)*

Will. Ha. 'Tis not she. Who art thou? And what's thy business?

Ang. One thou hast injured, and who comes to kill thee for't.

Will. What the devil canst thou mean?

Ang. By all my hopes to kill thee . . .

> *(Holds still the pistol to his breast, he going back, she fol-
lowing still.)*

Will. Prithee, on what acquaintance? For I know thee not.

Ang.
Behold this face so lost to thy remembrance
> *(Pulls off her vizard.)*
And then call all thy sins about thy soul,
And let 'em die with thee.

Will. Angellica!

Ang. Yes, tailor,[103]
Does not the guilty blood run shivering through thy veins?
Hast thou no horror at this sight that tells thee
Thou hast not long to boast thy shameful conquest?

Will. Faith, no child. My blood keeps its old ebbs and flows still and
that usual heat, too, that could oblige thee with a kindness, had I but
opportunity.

Ang. Devil! Dost wanton with my pain? Have at[104] thy heart.

Will. Hold, dear virago! Hold thy hand a little. I am not now at leisure
to be killed. Hold and hear me. *(Aside.)* Death, I think she is in
earnest.

Ang. *(Aside, turning from him.)*
Oh, if I take not heed,
My coward heart will leave me to his mercy
[To Will.] What have you, sir, to say? But should I hear thee,
Thoudst talk away all that is brave about me.
> *(Follows him with the pistol to his breast.)*
And I have vowed thy death by all that's sacred.

Will.
Whe, then there's an end of a proper handsome fellow,
That might have lived to have done good service yet.
That's all I can say to't.

Ang. Yet, I would give thee time for penitence

---

103. "Taylor" in the copy-text is corrected to "Traytor" in the 1697 and 1709 quartos. Tailors,
however, had a reputation for theft, so "Taylor" may be the correct reading.
104. "Have at": "I will attack."

(pausingly.)

Will.

Faith, child. I thank God I have ever took care to lead
A good, sober, hopeful life, and am of a religion
That teaches me to believe I shall depart in peace.

Ang.

So will the devil! Tell me,
How many poor believing fools hast thou undone?
How many hearts thou hast betray'd to ruin?
Yet these are little mischiefs to the ills
Thoust taught mine to commit: thoust taught it love!

Will. Egad. 'Twas shrewdly hurt the while.

Ang.

Love, that has robb'd it of its unconcern
Of all that pride that taught me how to value it.
And in its room
A mean submissive passion was convey'd
That made me humbly bow, which I ne'er did
To anything but heaven.
Thou, perjur'd man, didst this, and with thy oaths,
Which on thy knees thou didst devoutly make,
Soften'd my yielding heart. And then I was a slave,
Yet still had been content to've worn my chains,
Worn 'em with vanity and joy forever,
Hadst thou not broke those vows that put them on.
'Twas then I was undone.

(All this while follows him with the pistol to his breast.)

Will.

Broke my vows! Whe, where hast thou lived?
Amongst the gods? For I never heard of mortal man
That has not broke a thousand vows.

Ang. Oh, impudence!

Will.

Angellica! That beauty has been too long tempting
Not to have made a thousand lovers languish
Who in the amorous favor no doubt have sworn
Like me. Did they all die in that faith? Still adoring?
I do not think they did.

Ang. No, faithless man. Had I repaid their vows, as I did thine, I would
have killed the ingrateful that had abandoned me.

Will. This old general has quite spoiled thee. Nothing makes a woman
so vain as being flattered. Your old lover ever supplies the defects
of age with intolerable dotage, vast charge,[105] and that which you
call constancy. And attributing all this to your own merits, you

105. Expense.

domineer and throw your favors in's teeth, upbraiding him still with
the defects of age, and cuckold him as often as he deceives your
expectations. But the gay, young, brisk lover that brings his equal
fires and can give you dart for dart, [will][106] be as nice as you
sometimes.

Ang.
All this thoust made me know, for which I hate thee.
Had I remain'd in innocent security,
I should have thought all men were born my slaves,
And worn my pow'r like lightning in my eyes
To have destroy'd at pleasure when offended.
But when love held the mirror, the undeceiving glass
Reflected all the weakness of my soul, and made me know
My richest treasure being lost, my honor,
All the remaining spoil could not be worth
The conqueror's care or value.
Oh how I fell, like a long-worshipt idol,
Discovering all the cheat.
Would not the incense and rich sacrifice
Which blind devotion offer'd at my altars
Have fall'n to thee?
Why wouldst thou then destroy my fancy'd pow'r?

Will.
By heaven, thou'rt brave, and I admire thee strangely.
I wish I were that dull, that constant thing
Which thou wouldst have, and nature never meant me.
I must, like cheerful birds, sing in all groves
And perch on every bough,
Billing the next kind she that flies to meet me.
Yet, after all, would build my nest with thee,
Thither repairing when I'd lov'd my round,
And still reserve a tributary flame.
To gain your credit, I'll pay you back your charity,
And be oblig'd for nothing but for love.
(Offers her a purse of gold.)

Ang.
Oh, that thou wert in earnest!
So mean a thought of me,
Would turn my rage to scorn, and I should pity thee,
And give thee leave to live,
Which for the public safety of our sex,
And my own private injuries, I dare not do.
(Follows still as before.)
Prepare. I will be no more tempted with replies.

106. The copy-text reads "you'l will be as nice." It is emended in the 1709 quarto by the omission of
"you'l," and that change is followed here.

Will. Sure . . .

Ang. Another word will damn thee! I've heard thee talk too long.

Will. Ha! Angellica!

> *(She follows him with the pistol ready to shoot. He retires still amazed. Enter Don Ant., his arm in a scarf, and lays hold on the pistol.)*

Ang. Antonio! What devil brought thee hither?

Ant. Love and curoisity, seeing your coach at door. Let me disarm you of this unbecoming instrument of death. *(Takes away the pistol.)* Amongst the number of your slaves was there not one worthy the honor to have fought your quarrel?
[*To Will.*] Who are you, sir, that are so very wretched
To merit death from her?

Will. One, sir, that could have made a better end of an amorous quarrel without you, than with you.

Ant. Sure it is some rival. Ha! The very man took down her picture yesterday. The very same that set on me last night. Blest opportunity.
> *(Offers to shoot him.)*

Ang. Hold! You're mistaken, sir.

Ant.
By heaven, the very same!
Sir, what pretensions have you to this lady?

Will. Sir, I do not use to be examined, and am ill at disputes but this
(Draws.)
> *(Ant. offers to shoot.)*

Ang.
Oh, hold! *(To Will.)* You see he's arm'd with certain death.
And, you, Antonio, I command you hold,
By all the passion you've so lately vow'd me.

Enter Pedro, sees Ant., and stays.

Pedro. (Aside.) Ha! Antonio! And Angellica!

Ant.
When I refuse obedience to your will,
May you destroy me with your mortal hate.
By all that's holy, I adore you so,
That even my rival, who has charms enough
To make him fall a victim to my jealousy,
Shall live; nay, and have leave to love on still.

Pedro. (Aside.) What's this I hear?

Ang. (Pointing to Will.)
Ah thus! 'Twas thus he talkt, and I believ'd.
Antonio, yesterday
I'd not have sold my interest in his heart
For all the sword has won and lost in battle,
[*To Will.*] But now to show my utmost of contempt,

I give thee life, which if thou wouldst preserve,
Live where my eyes may never see thee more.
Live to undo someone whose soul may prove
So bravely constant to revenge my love.
        (Goes out. Ant. follows, but Pedro pulls him back.)
Pedro. Antonio, stay.
Ant. Don Pedro . . .
Pedro.

What coward fear was that prevented thee
From meeting me this morning on the Molo?
Ant. Meet thee?
Pedro.

Yes, me. I was the man that dar'd thee to't.
Ant.

Hast thou so often seen me fight in war
To find no better cause to excuse my absence?
I sent my sword and one to do thee right,
Finding myself uncapable to use a sword.
Pedro.

But 'twas Florinda's quarrel that we fought,
And you to show how little you esteem'd her,
Sent me your rival, giving him your interest.
But I have found the cause of this affront,
And when I meet you fit for the dispute,
I'll tell you my resentment.
Ant. I shall be ready, sir, ere long to do you reason.
        (Exit Ant.)
Pedro. If I could find Florinda, now whilst my anger's high, I think I
    should be kind, and give her to Belvile in revenge.
Will. Faith, sir, I know not what you would do, but I believe the priest
    within has been so kind.
Pedro. How? My sister married?
Will. I hope by this time he is and bedded, too, or he has not my
    longings about him.
Pedro. Dares he do this! Does he not fear my pow'r?
Will. Faith, not at all. If you will go in and thank him for the favor he
    has done your sister, so. If not, sir, my power's greater in this house
    than yours. I have a damned surly crew here that will keep you till
    the next tide, and then clap you on board for prize. My ship lies but a
    league off the Molo, and we shall show your donship a damned
    Tramontana[107] rover's trick.

Enter Belvile.
Belv. This rogue's in some new mischief. Ha, Pedro returned!
Pedro. Colonel Belvile, I hear you have married my sister.

---

107. North wind. Willmore suggests that he is the cold wind from beyond the Alps.

Belv. You have heard truth, then, sir.

Pedro. Have I so? Then, sir, I wish you joy.

Belv. How?

Pedro. By this embrace I do, and I am glad on't.

Belv. Are you in earnest?

Pedro. By our long friendship and my obligations to thee, I am. The sudden change I'll give you reasons for anon. Come, lead me to my sister, that she may know I now approve her choice.

(Exit Belv. with Pedro. Will. goes to follow them.)

Enter Hell. as before in boy's clothes, and pulls him back.

Will. Ha! My gypsy. Now a thousand blessings on thee for this kindness. Egad, child, I was e'en in despair of ever seeing thee again. My friends are all provided for within, each man his kind woman.

Hell. Ha! I thought they had served me some such trick!

Will. And I was e'en resolved to go aboard, and condemn myself to my lone cabin and the thoughts of thee.

Hell. And could you have left me behind? Would you have been so ill natured?

Will. Whe, 'twould have broke my heart, child. But since we are met again, I defy foul weather to part us.

Hell. And would you be a faithful friend now, if a maid should trust you?

Will. For a friend I cannot promise. Thou art of a form so excellent, a face and humor too good for cold, dull friendship. I am parlously afraid of being in love, child, and you have not forgot how severely you have used me?

Hell. That's all one. Such usage you must still look for: To find out all your haunts, to rail at you to all that love you, till I have made you love only me in your own defense because nobody else will love [you].[108]

Will. But hast thou no better quality to recommend thyself by?

Hell. Faith, none, Captain. Whe, 'twill be the greater charity to take me for thy mistress. I am a lone child, a kind of orphan lover, and why I should die a maid, and in a captain's hands, too, I do not understand.

Will. Egad, I was never clawed away with broadsides from any female before. Thou hast one virtue I adore, good nature. I hate a coy, demure mistress: she's as troublesome as a colt. I'll break none. No, give me a mad mistress when mewed,[109] and in flying, one I dare trust upon the wing, that whilst she's kind will come to the lure.

Hell. Nay, as kind as you will, good Captain, whilst it lasts. But let's lose no time.

---

108. "You" omitted from copy-text, added in 1709 quarto.
109. "Mewed" and, below, "lure" both are terms from falconry. A mew was a cage used during molting, and a lure was a device for recalling a bird of prey.

Will. My time's as precious to me as thine can be. Therefore, dear creature, since we are so well agreed, let's retire to my chamber. And if ever thou wert treated with such savory love, come. My bed's prepared for such a guest—all clean and sweet as thy fair self. I love to steal a dish and a bottle with a friend, and hate long graces. Come, let's retire and fall to.

Hell. 'Tis but getting my consent, and the business is soon done. Let but old gaffer Hymen[110] and his priest say amen to't, and I dare lay my mother's daughter by as proper a fellow as your father's son, without fear or blushing.

Will. Hold, hold. No bug[111] words, child. Priest and Hymen? Prithee, add a hangman to 'em to make up the consort. No, no. We'll have no vows but love, child, nor witness but the Lover, the kind deity.[112] Enjoin naught but Love! And enjoy! Hymen and priest wait still upon portion and jointure; love and beauty have their own ceremonies. Marriage is as certain a bane to love as lending money is to friendship. I'll neither ask nor give a vow, though I could be content to turn gypsy and become a left-handed bridegroom to have the pleasure of working that great miracle of making a maid a mother, if you durst venture. 'Tis upsy gypsy[113] that, and if I miss I'll lose my labor.

Hell. And if you do not lose, what shall I get? A cradle full of noise and mischief, with a a pack of repentance at my back? Can you teach me to weave inkle[114] to pass my time with? 'Tis upsy gypsy that, too.

Will. I can teach thee to weave a true love's knot better.

Hell. So can my dog.

Will. Well, I see we are both upon our guards, and I see there's no way to conquer good nature but by yielding. Here, give me thy hand. One kiss, and I am thine.

Hell. One kiss! How like my page he speaks. I am resolved you shall have none, for asking such a sneaking sum. He that will be satisfied with one kiss will never die of that longing, good friend. Single kiss? Is all your talking come to this? A kiss, a caudle.[115] Farewell, Captain Single Kiss.

(Going out, he stays her.)

Will. Nay, if we part so, let me die like a bird upon a bough at the sheriff's charge. By heaven, both the Indies shall not buy thee from me. I adore thy humor and will marry thee, and we are so of one humor it must be a bargain. Give me thy hand. *(Kisses her hand.)* And now let the blind ones (Love and Fortune) do their worst.

Hell. Whe, God-a-mercy, Captain!

---

110. Hymen was a Greek god associated with nuptuals. He usually was depicted as a young man, and not as a "gaffer."
111. Bugbear—an imaginary terror.
112. Willmore suggests that Hymen be replaced with the god of love, Eros (in English, "Love").
113. "upsy gypsy": in the mode of a gypsy.
114. Linen tape.
115. Thin gruel.

Will. But harkee. The bargain is now made. But is it not fit we should know each other's names? That when we have reason to curse one another hereafter (and people ask me who 'tis I gave to the devil), I may at least be able to tell what family you came of.

Hell. Good reason, Captain. And where I have cause (as I doubt not, but I shall have plentiful) that I may know at whom to throw my— blessings, I beseech ye your name.

Will. I am called Robert the Constant.

Hell. A very fine name. Pray was it your faulkner or butler that christened you? Do they not use a whistle when they call you?

Will. I hope you have a better (that a man may name without crossing himself), you are so merry with mine.

Hell. I am called Hellena the Inconstant.

Enter Pedro, Belv., Flor., Fred., Val.

Pedro. Ha! Hellena!

Flor. Hellena!

Hell. The very same. Ha! My brother! Now, Captain, show your love and courage. Stand to your arms and defend me bravely, or I am lost forever.

Pedro. (Goes roughly to her.) What's this I hear! False girl, how came you hither, and what's your business? Speak.

Will. (Puts himself between.) Hold off, sir. You have leave to parly only.

Hell. I had e'en as good tell it, as you guess it. Faith brother, my business is the same with all living creatures of my age—to love and be beloved, and here's the man.

Pedro. Perfidious maid, hast thou deceived me, too; deceived thyself and heaven?

Hell.
'Tis time enough to make my peace with that,
Be you but kind. Let me alone with heaven.

Pedro. Belvile, I did not expect this false play from you. Was't not enough you'd gain Florinda (which I pardoned), but your lewd friends, too, must be enricht with the spoils of a noble family?

Belv. Faith, sir, I am as much surprised at this as you can be. Yet, sir, my friends are gentlemen, and ought to be esteemed for their misfortunes, since they have the glory to suffer with the best of men and kings. 'Tis true, he's a rover of fortune, yet a prince aboard his little wooden world.

Pedro. What's this to the maintenance of a woman of her birth and quality?

Will. Faith, sir, I can boast of nothing but a sword which does me right where ere I come, and has defended a worse cause than a woman's. And since I loved her before I either knew her birth or name, I must pursue my resolution and marry her.

Pedro. And is all your holy intent of becoming a nun debauched into a desire of man?

Hell. Whe. I have considered the matter, brother, and find the three hundred thousand crowns my uncle left me (and you cannot keep from me) will be better laid out in love than in religion, and turn to as good an account. Let most voices carry it: for heaven or the captain?

All cry. A captain? A captain?[116]

Hell. Look ye, sir. 'Tis a clear case.

Pedro. (Aside.) Oh I am mad! If I refuse, my life's in danger. *[To Will.]* Come, there's one motive induces me. Take her: I shall now be free from fears of her honor. Guard it you now, if you can. I have been a slave to't long enough.

> *(Gives her to him.)*

Will. Faith, sir, I am of a nation that are of opinion a woman's honor is not worth guarding when she has a mind to part with it.

Hell. Well said, Captain.

Pedro. (To Val.) This was your plot, mistress, but I hope you have married one that will revenge my quarrel to you.

Val. There's no altering destiny, sir.

Pedro. Sooner than a woman's will. Therefore I forgive you all, and wish you may get my father's pardon as easily, which I fear.

Enter Blunt drest in a Spanish habit, looking very ridiculously, his man adjusting his band.

Man. 'Tis very well, sir.

Blunt. Well, sir, 'adsheartlikins. I tell you 'tis damnable ill, sir. A Spanish habit. Good lord! Could the devil and my tailor devise no other punishment for me but the mode of a nation I abominate?

Belv. What's the matter, Ned?

Blunt. Pray view me round and judge.

> *(Turns round.)*

Belv. I must confess thou art a kind of an odd figure.

Blunt. In a Spanish habit with a vengeance! I had rather be in the Inquisition for Judaism than in this doublet and breeches. A pillory were an easy collar to this, three handfulls high. And these shoes, too, are worse than the stocks, with the sole an inch shorter than my foot. In fine, gentlemen, methinks I look like a bag of bays stuft full of fool's flesh.

Belv. Methinks 'tis well, and makes thee look e'n cavalier. Come, sir, settle your face and salute our friends. Lady . . .

Blunt. Ha! Sayst thou so to my little rover? *(To Hell.)* Lady, if you be one, give me leave to kiss your hand and tell you, 'adsheartlikins, for all I look so, I am your humble servant. A pox of my Spanish habit.

---

116. Copy-text: "a captain? a captain?" Other editors have emended the line to "A Captain! A Captain!" It seems that affirmation is mixed with comic disbelief.

(Music is heard to play.)

Will. Hark. What is this?

Enter boy.

Boy. Sir, as the custom is, the gay people in masquerade, who make every man's house their own, are coming up.

Enter several men and women in masquing habits with music.[117] *They put themselves in order and dance.*

Blunt. 'Adsheartlikins, would 'twere lawful to pull off their false faces, that I might see if my doxy were not amongst 'em.

Belv. *(To the masqueros.)* Ladies and gentlemen. Since you are come so apropros, you must take a small collation with us.

Will. Whilst we'll to the good man within, who stays to give us a cast[118] of his office. *(To Hell.)* Have you no trembling at the near approach?

Hell. No more than you have in an engagement or a tempest.

Will. Egad, thou'rt a brave girl, and I admire thy love and courage.
Lead on, no other dangers they can dread,
Who venture in the storms o'th' marriage bed.

    (Exeunt.)

The End

Epilogue

The banisht Cavaliers! A roving blade!
A popish carnival! A masquerade!
The devil's in't if this will please the nation,
In these our blessed times of Reformation,
When conventicling[119] is so much in fashion.
And yet—
That mutinous tribe less factions do beget,
Than your continual differing in wit.
Your judgment's (as your passion's) a disease.
Nor muse nor mistress your appetite can please.
You're grown as nice as queasy consciences,
Whose each convulsion, when the spirit moves,
Damns everything that maggot[120] disapproves.
    With canting rule you would the stage refine,
And to dull method all our sense confine.
With th'insolence of common-wealths you rule,

---

117. Musical instruments.
118. Sample, taste, touch.
119. A conventicle was a small group of religious dissenters. The government attempted to supress such groups during the Restoration.
120. Crotchet, fancy.

Where each gay fop and politic grave fool[121]
On monarch wit impose, without control.
As for the last, who seldom sees a play,
Unless it be the old Blackfriars' way,
Shaking his empty noodle o'er bamboo,
He cries, "Good faith, these plays will never do.
Ah, sir, in my young days what lofty wit,
What high strain'd scenes of fighting there were writ.
These are slight airy toys. But tell me, pray,
What has the House of Commons done today?"
Then shows his politics, to let you see
Of state affairs he'll judge as notably
As he can do of wit and poetry.
The younger sparks, who hither do resort.
Cry—
"Pox o' your gentle things. Give us more sport.
Damn me. I'm sure 'twill never please the court."
    Such fops are never pleas'd unless the play
Be stufft with fools as brisk and dull as they.
Such might the half-crown spare, and in a glass
At home behold a more accomplisht ass.
Where they may set their cravats, wigs, and faces,
And practice all their buffonry grimaces.
See how this huff becomes, this dammy-stare,
Which they at home may act because they dare,
But must with prudent caution do elsewhere.
Oh that our Nokes or Tony Leigh[122] could show
A fop but half so much to th'life as you.

Postscript

This play had been sooner in print, but for a report about the town
(made by some, either very malicious or very ignorant) that 'twas
Thomaso altered,[123] which made the booksellers fear some trouble
from the proprietor of that admirable play, which, indeed, has wit
enough to stock a poet and is not to be pieced or mended by any but the
excellent author himself. That I have stolen some hints from it may be a
proof that I valued it more than to pretend to alter it. Had I the dex-

---

121. The "politic grave fool" could be an actual person, judging from his specific attributes. He is old, leans over a bamboo cane, and insists on the importance of the House of Commons. The Blackfriars Theater operated in his youth and was no longer in use.
122. James Nokes or Noke (d. 1692) is memorable for his portrayal in *L'Ecole des Femmes* (1670) of a character ridiculing French fashion. Anthony Leigh (d. 1692) was a well-known comic actor. Both Nokes and Leigh took parts in Behn's *Sir Patient Fancy* (printed 1678). Leigh's wife apparently played the role of Moretta in *The Rover*.
123. Behn borrowed parts of the plot of *The Rover* from *Thomaso, or the Wanderer* (1664), a ten-act play written by Thomas Killigrew for a reading audience. She also borrowed from *The Novella, A Comedy* (1632) by Richard Brome.

terity of some poets, who are not more expert in stealing than in the art of concealing, and who even that way outdo the *Spartan-boys*,[124] I might have appropriated all to myself, but I, vainly proud of my judgment, hang out the sign of Angellica (the only stolen object) to give notice where a great part of the wit dwelt; though if the play of the *Novella* were as well worth remembering as *Thomaso*, they might (bating the name) have as well said I took it from thence. I will only say the plot and business,[125] not to boast on it, is my own. As for the words and characters, I leave the reader to judge and compare 'em with *Thomaso*, to whom I recommend the great entertainment of reading it, though had this succeeded ill, I should have had no need of imploring that justice from the critics, who are naturally so kind to any that pretend to usurp their dominion [especially of our sex];[126] they would doubtless have given me the whole honor on't. Therefore, I will only say in English what famous Virgil does in Latin: I make verses, and others have the fame.[127]

TEXTUAL NOTES

Copy-text: First issue of the 1677 quarto. Copy used: Huntington Library 106785 compared against Huntington Library 125975 (third issue of the 1677 quarto). Editions of 1696, 1709, 1724, 1729, 1757, *Plays* (1702), Summers, and Link used for reference.

The spelling and abbreviation of characters' names are regularized. "Fred." from the copy-text is treated as a familiar name in speeches by his friends ("Fred") and as an abbreviation ("Fred.") in stage directions. The spelling of actors' names follows the index of *The London Stage: 1660–1800*, vol. 1. Scene markings are added where missing; stage directions are regularized in their position on the page and placed in parentheses. Obvious typesetting errors are silently corrected. In the past tense, " 'd" is expanded to "ed," except in verse, where modernization would alter the number of syllables. Other contractions are reproduced as they appear in the copy-text. Occasionally in the prose passages the typesetter left blank sections, which are silently removed. The compositor mixed italic and roman first-person singular "I," which is here regularized to roman. All other emendation is indicated by notes or square brackets.

124. "The Spartan-boys" is printed in italic in the copy-text, as if it were the title of a play. If so, the play is not recorded in *The London Stage: 1660–1800*. The reference could be a parody of some sort, perhaps on the title *The Spartan Ladies* (a play by Lodowick Carlel, assigned to the King's Company in 1669).
125. A theatrical term meaning action as distinct from dialogue.
126. The phrase "especially of our sex" was omitted in the first issue of the 1677 quarto, and in some copies of the second issue.
127. Possibly an allusion to the popular motto, *sic vos non vobis mallificatis apes* (Thus you bees make honey not for yourselves). The motto was attributed to Virgil in a post-classical anecdote about a false poet, Bathyllus, who stole some of Virgil's verses.

SELECTED POEMS

The Golden Age.
A Paraphrase on a Translation out of French[1]

I.

Blest age! when ev'ry purling[2] stream
  Ran undisturb'd and clear,
When no scorn'd shepherds on your banks were seen,
Tortur'd by love, by jealousy, or fear;
When an eternal spring dressed ev'ry bough,   5
And blossoms fell, by new ones dispossest;
These their kind shade affording all below,
And those a bed where all below might rest.
The groves appear'd all dressed with wreaths of flowers,
And from their leaves dropt aromatic showers,   10
Whose fragrant heads in mystic twines above,
Exchang'd their sweets, and mix'd with thousand kisses,
    As if the willing branches strove
    To beautify and shade the grove
    Where the young wanton gods of love   15
Offer their noblest sacrifice of blisses.

II.

Calm was the air, no winds blew fierce and loud,
The sky was dark'ned with no sullen cloud;
But all the heav'ns laugh'd with continued light,
And scatter'd round their rays serenely bright.   20
    No other murmurs fill'd the ear
    But what the streams and rivers purl'd,
When silver waves o'er shining pebbles curl'd;
  Or when young Zephyrs[3] fann'd the gentle breeze,
  Gath'ring fresh sweets from balmy flow'rs and trees,   25
Then bore 'em on their wings to perfume all the air,
    While to their soft and tender play,
    The gray-plum'd natives[4] of the shades
    Unwearied sing till love invades,
Then bill, then sing again, while love and music makes the   30
day.

---

1. "The Golden Age" is a paraphrase of the chorus from the end of the first act of Torquato Tasso's *Aminta*, which was originally published in Italian in 1573.
2. Flowing with a whirling motion of particles.
3. Calm, soft winds.
4. Turtle doves.

III.

The stubborn plough had then,
Made no rude rapes[5] upon the virgin earth;
Who yielded of her own accord her plenteous[6] birth,
  Without the aids of men;
  As if within her teeming womb,   35
  All nature, and all sexes lay,[7]
  Whence new creations every day
  Into the happy world did come;
  The roses fill'd with morning dew,
  Bent down their loaded heads,   40
T'adorn the careless shepherd's grassy beds
While still young opening buds each moment grew
And as those withered, dressed his shaded couch anew;
  Beneath whose boughs the snakes securely dwelt,
  Not doing harm, nor harm from others felt;   45
  With whom the nymphs did innocently play,
  No spiteful venom in the wantons[8] lay;
But to the touch were soft, and to the sight were gay.

IV.

  Then no rough sound of wars' alarms,
  Had taught the world the needless use of arms.   50
    Monarchs were uncreated then,
    Those arbitrary rulers over men;
  Kings that made laws, first broke 'em, and the gods
By teaching us religion first, first set the world at odds.
    Till then ambition was not known,   55
  That poison to content, bane to repose;
  Each swain was lord o'er his own will alone,
  His innocence religion was, and laws;
    Nor needed any troublesome defense
    Against his neighbors' insolence.   60
Flocks, herds, and every necessary good
Which bounteous nature had design'd for food,
Whose kind increase o'er-spread the meads[9] and plains,
Was then a common sacrifice to all th'agreeing swains.[10]

V.

Right and property were words since made,   65
  When power taught mankind to invade;
When pride and avarice became a trade,
  Carri'd on by discord, noise and wars,

---

5. Invasions or violations, particularly of a sexual nature.
6. Bountiful, abundant.
7. Contrary to popular medical models of her time, Behn depicts the female earth (rather than the male seed) as the source of "nature" or essential energy of life.
8. Playful persons.
9. Meadows.
10. Shepherds, male lovers.

For which they barter'd wounds and scars;
And to inhaunce[11] the merchandise, miscall'd it *Fame*,   70
   And rapes, invasions, tyrannies,
   Was gaining of a glorious name;
Styling their savage slaughters, victories.
   Honor, the error and the cheat
   Of the ill-natur'd busy great,   75
   Nonsense, invented by the proud,
   Fond idol of the slavish crowd,
   Thou wert not known in those blest days
Thy poison was not mixt with our unbounded joys;
   Then it was glory to pursue delight,   80
And that was lawful all, that pleasure did invite,
   Then 'twas the amorous world enjoy'd its reign;
And tyrant Honor strove t'usurp in vain.

VI.

The flow'ry meads, the rivers and the groves,
Were fill'd with little gay-wing'd Loves,[12]   85
   That ever smil'd and danc'd and play'd,
   And now the woods, and now the streams invade,
   And where they came all things were gay and glad.
When in the myrtle groves the lovers sat
   Oppressed with a too fervent heat,   90
A thousand Cupids fann'd their wings aloft,
And through the boughs the yielded air would waft,
   Whose parting leaves discovered all below,
   And every god his own soft power admir'd,
   And smil'd and fann'd, and sometimes bent his bow,   95
   Where e'er he saw a shepherd uninspir'd.
The nymphs were free, no nice, no coy disdain,
Deny'd their joys, or gave the lover pain.
The yielding maid but kind resistance makes;
   Trembling and blushing are not marks of shame,   100
   But the effect of kindling flame,
   Which from the sighing, burning swain she takes,
   While she with tears all soft, and down-cast eyes,
Permits the charming conqueror to win the prize.

VII.

The lovers thus, thus uncontrol'd did meet,   105
Thus all their joys and vows of love repeat,
   Joys which were everlasting, ever new
   And every vow inviolably true,
Not kept in fear of gods, no fond religious cause,
Nor in obedience to the duller laws.   110

11. Archaic spelling of "enhance"; literally, to raise up.
12. Cupids.

Those fopperies of the gown[13] were then not known,
Those vain, those politic curbs[14] to keep man in,
Who by a fond mistake created that a sin;
Which freeborn we, by right of nature claim our own.
Who but the learned and dull moral fool 115
Could gravely have foreseen, man out to live by rule?

VIII.

Oh cursed Honor![15] thou who first didst damn
A woman to the sin of shame;
Honor! that rob'st us of our gust,[16]
Honor! that hind'red mankind first, 120
At love's eternal spring to squench his amorous thirst.
Honor! who first taught lovely eyes the art,
To wound, and not to cure the heart;
With love to invite, but to forbid with awe,
And to themselves prescribe a cruel law; 125
To veil 'em from the lookers on,
When they are sure the slave's undone,
And all the charmingst part of beauty hid;
Soft looks, consenting wishes, all deny'd.
It gathers up the flowing hair, 130
That loosely plaid[17] with wanton air,
The envious net, and stinted order hold,
The lovely curls of jet[18] and shining gold,
No more neglected on the shoulders hurl'd;
Now dressed to tempt, not gratify the world. 135
Thou, miser Honor, hoard'st the sacred store,
And starv'st thy self to keep thy votaries[19] poor.

IX.

Honor! that put'st our words that should be free
Into a set formality.
Thou base debaucher of the generous heart, 140
That teachest all our looks and actions art;
What love design'd a sacred gift,
What nature made to be possessed,
Mistaken honor, made a theft,
For glorious love should be confessed. 145
For when confin'd, all the poor lover gains,
Is broken sighs, pale looks, complaints and pains.
Thou foe to pleasure, nature's worst disease,
Thou tyrant over mighty kings,

13. "fopperies of the gown": follies of university men.
14. "politic curbs": political restraints.
15. Here, the meaning is closest to "chastity."
16. Desire.
17. Played, but also a plait of braided hair.
18. Black.
19. Worshippers.

What mak'st thou here in shepherds' cottages; 150
Why troublest thou, the quiet shades and springs?
    Be gone, and make thy fam'd resort
      To princes' palaces;
Go deal and chaffer[20] in the trading court,
That busy market for phantastick[21] things; 155
Be gone and interrupt the short retreat,
    Of the illustrious and the great;
    Go break the politician's sleep,
    Disturb the gay ambitious fool,
    That longs for scepters, crowns, and rule, 160
Which not his title, nor his wit can keep;
But let the humble honest swain go on,
In the blest paths of the first rate of man;
    That nearest were to gods allied,
And form'd for love alone, disdain'd all other pride. 165

X.

Be gone! and let the Golden Age again,
    Assume its glorious reign;
  Let the young wishing maid confess,
  What all your arts would keep conceal'd,
  The mystery will be reveal'd, 170
And she in vain denies, whilst we can guess,
She only shows the jilt[22] to teach man how,
To turn the false artillery on the cunning foe.
    Thou empty vision hence, be gone,
      And let the peaceful swain love on; 175
The swift pac'd hours of life soon steal away,
  Stint not ye gods, his short liv'd joy.
The spring decays, but when the winter's gone,
  The trees and flowers anew come on;
The sun may set, but when the night is fled, 180
    And gloomy darkness does retire,
    He rises from his wat'ry bed,
All glorious, gay, all dressed in amorous fire.
    But Sylvia when your beauties fade,
When the fresh roses on your cheeks shall die, 185
  Like flowers that wither in the shade,
Eternally they will forgotten lie,
And no kind spring their sweetness will supply,
When snow shall on those lovely tresses lie.
And your fair eyes no more shall give us pain, 190
    But shoot their pointless darts in vain.
What will your duller honor signify?

20. "chaffer": to buy and sell.
21. As spelled, punning on phantasm, phantom, and fantasy.
22. "shows the jilt": plays the role of harlot or cheat.

Go boast it then! and see what numerous store
Of lovers will your ruin'd shrine adore.
    Then let us, Sylvia, yet be wise,   195
    And the gay hasty minutes prize;
The sun and spring receive but our short light,
Once set, a sleep brings an eternal night.

On a Juniper-Tree Cut Down to Make Busks[1]

    Whilst happy I triumphant stood,
The pride and glory of the wood,
My aromatic boughs and fruit,
Did with all other trees dispute.
Had right by nature to excel,   5
In pleasing both the taste and smell,
But to the touch I much confess,
Bore an ungrateful sullenness.
My wealth, like bashful virgins, I
Yielded with some reluctancy;   10
For which my value should be more,
Not giving easily my store.
My verdant branches all the year
Did an eternal beauty wear,
Did ever young and gay appear.   15
Nor needed any tribute pay,
For bounties from the god of day;
Nor do I hold supremacy,
(In all the wood) o'er every tree,
But even those too of my own race,   20
That grow not in this happy place.
But that in which I glory most,
And do my self with reason boast,
Beneath my shade the other day,
Young Philocles and Cloris[2] lay;   25
Upon my root she lean'd her head,
And where I grew, he made their bed,
Whilst I the canopy more largely spread.
Their trembling limbs did gently press,
The kind supporting yielding grass,   30
Ne'er half so blest as now, to bear
A swain so young, a nymph so fair;
My grateful shade I kindly lent,
And every aiding bough I bent.
So low, as sometimes had the bliss,   35

1. The juniper is an evergreen with prickly leaves and pungent berries. "Busks": corset stays.
2. Philocles and Cloris: Common pastoral names.

To rob the shepherd of a kiss;
Whilst he in pleasure far above
The sense of that degree of love,
Permitted every stealth I made,
Unjealous of his rival shade. 40
I saw 'em kindle to desire,
Whilst with soft sighs they blew the fire,
Saw the approaches of their joy,
He growing more fierce, and she less coy,
Saw how they mingled melting rays, 45
Exchanging love a thousand ways.
Kind was the force on every side,
Her new desire she could not hide,
Nor would the shepherd be deny'd.
Impatient he waits no consent 50
But what she gave by languishment,
The blessed minute he pursu'd,
Whilst love, her fear, and shame subdu'd;
And now transported in his arms,
Yields to the conqueror all her charms, 55
His panting breast to hers now join'd,
They feast on raptures unconfin'd,
Vast and luxuriant, such as prove
The immortality of love.
For who but a divinity, 60
Could mingle souls to that degree,
And melt 'em into ecstasy?
Now like the Phoenix,3 both expire,
While from the ashes of their fire,
Sprung up a new, and soft desire. 65
Like charmers, thrice they did invoke,
The god! and thrice new vigor took.
Nor had the mystery ended there,
But Cloris reassum'd her fear,
And chid the swain, for having pressed, 70
What she alas would not resist;
Whilst he in whom love's sacred flame,
Before and after was the same,
Fondly implor'd she would forget
A fault, which he would yet repeat. 75
From active joys with some they haste,
To a reflection on the past;
A thousand times my covert4 bless,
That did secure their happiness;

3. Mythical bird with brilliant plumage; unable to reproduce normally, it burned itself on an aromatic
pyre to produce an offspring, and was thus reborn out of its own ashes.
4. A hidden place.

Their gratitude to every tree 80
They pay, but most to happy me;
The shepherdess my bark caressed,
Whilst he my root, love's pillow, kissed;
And did with sighs, their fate deplore,
Since I must shelter them no more; 85
And if before my joys were such,
In having heard and seen too much,
My grief must be as great and high,
When all abandon'd I shall be,
Doom'd to a silent destiny. 90
No more the charming strife to hear,
The shepherd's vows, the virgin's fear;
No more a joyful looker on,
Whilst love's soft battle's lost and won.

With grief I bow'd my murmuring head, 95
And all my christal⁵ dew I shed.
Which did in Cloris pity move
(Cloris whose soul is made of love).
She cut me down, and did translate,
My being to a happier state. 100
No martyr for religion died
With half that unconsidering pride;
My top was on that altar laid,
Where love his softest offerings paid,
And was as fragrant incense burn'd, 105
My body into busks was turn'd,
Where I still guard the sacred store,
And of love's temple keep the door.

Song¹

I led my Silvia to a grove,
Where all the boughs did shade us,
The sun itself, though it had strove,
It could not have betray'd us;
The place secur'd from humane eyes, 5
No other fear allows,
But when the winds do gently rise,
And kiss the yielding boughs.

Down there we sat upon the moss,
And did begin to play, 10

---

5. Behn's spelling of *crystal* has possible religious connotations.
1. This poem and "The Willing Mistress" tell exactly the same story, from the male and female points of view, respectively. Behn published "Song," the version with a male speaker, first (see the textual notes for additional information about the poems' publication).

A thousand wanton tricks to pass,
The heat of all the day.
A many kisses I did give,
And she return'd the same,
Which made her willing to receive,   15
That which I dare not name.

My greedy eyes no aids requir'd,
To tell their amorous tale,
On her that was already fir'd,
'Twas easy to prevail.   20
I did but kiss and clasp her round,
Whose they my thoughts expressed,[2]
And laid her gently on the ground;
Oh! who can guess the rest.

The Willing Mistress

Amyntas led me to a grove,
    Where all the trees did shade us;
The sun it self, though it had strove,
    It could not have betray'd us;
The place secur'd from human eyes,   5
    No other fear allows,
But when the winds that gently rise,
    Do kiss the yielding boughs.

Down there we sat upon the moss,
    And did begin to play   10
A thousand amorous tricks, to pass
    The heat of all the day.
A many kisses he did give,
    And I return'd the same
Which made me willing to receive   15
    That which I dare not name.

His charming eyes no aid requir'd
    To tell their soft'ning tale;
On her that was already fir'd,
    'Twas easy to prevail.   20
He did but kiss and clasp me round,
    Whilst those his thoughts expressed,
And laid me gently on the ground;
    Ah who can guess the rest?

2. "Whose they my thoughts exprest": i.e., his kisses and clasps express his thoughts to her.

Love Arm'd

Love in fantastic triumph sat,
Whilst bleeding hearts around him flow'd,
For whom fresh pains he did create,
And strange tyrannic power he show'd.
From thy bright eyes he took his fire,   5
Which round about in sport he hurl'd;
But 'twas from mine he took desire,
Enough to undo the amorous world.

From me he took his sighs and tears,
From thee his pride and cruelty;   10
From me his languishments and fears,
And every killing dart from thee.
Thus thou and I the god have arm'd,
And set him up a deity;
But my poor heart alone is harm'd,   15
Whilst thine the victor is, and free.

The Disappointment[1]

I.

One day the amorous Lysander,
By an impatient passion sway'd,
Surpris'd fair Cloris, that lov'd maid
Who could defend her self no longer.
All things did with his love conspire;   5
The gilded planet[2] of the day,
In his gay chariot drawn by fire,
Was now descending to the sea,
And left no light to guide the world,
But what from Cloris's brighter eyes was hurl'd.   10

II.

In a lone thicket made for love,
Silent as yielding maid's consent,
She with a charming languishment,
Permits his force, yet gently strove;
Her hands his bosom softly meet,   15
But not to put him back design'd,
Rather to draw 'em on inclin'd,
Whilst he lay trembling at her feet,
Resistance 'tis in vain to show,
She wants the pow'r to say—*Ah! What d'ye do?*   20

1. "The Disappointment" is Behn's interpretation of the "imperfect enjoyment" or premature-ejaculation poem, a type of bawdy poem popular in late seventeenth-century England and France.
2. The sun.

III.

Her bright eyes sweet, and yet severe,
Where love and shame confus'dly strive,
Fresh vigor to Lysander give,
And breathing faintly in his ear,
She cry'd—*Cease, cease—your vain desire,*   25
Or I'll call out—what would you do?
My dearer honor ev'n to you
I cannot, must not give—retire,
Or take this life, whose chiefest part
I gave you with the conquest of my heart.   30

IV.

But he as much unus'd to fear,
As he was capable of love,
The blessed minutes to improve,
Kisses her mouth, her neck, her hair;
Each touch her new desire alarms,   35
His burning trembling hand he pressed
Upon her swelling snowy breast,
While she lay panting in his arms.
All her unguarded beauties lie
The spoils and trophies of the enemy.   40

V.

And now without respect or fear,
He seeks the object of his vows,
(His love no modesty allows)
By swift degrees advancing—where
His daring hand that altar seiz'd,   45
Where gods of love do sacrifice,
That awful throne, that paradise
Where rage is calm'd, and anger pleas'd,
That fountain where delight still flows,
And gives the universal world repose.   50

VI.

Her balmy lips encount'ring his,
Their bodies, as their souls are join'd,
Where both in transports unconfin'd
Extend themselves upon the moss.
Cloris half dead and breathless lay,   55
Her soft eyes cast a humid light,
Such as divides the day and night,
Or falling stars, whose fires decay,
And now no signs of life she shows,
But what in short-breath'd sighs returns and goes.   60

VII.

He saw how at her length she lay,
He saw her rising bosom bare,
Her loose thin robes, through which appear
A shape design'd for love and play,
Abandon'd by her pride and shame.   65
She does her softest joys dispense,
Off'ring her virgin innocence
A victim to love's sacred flame
While the o'er-ravish'd shepherd lies
Unable to perform the sacrifice.   70

VIII.

Ready to taste a thousand joys,
The too transported hapless swain
Found the vast pleasure turn'd to pain,
Pleasure which too much love destroys.
The willing garments by he laid,   75
And heaven all open'd to his view,
Mad to possess, himself he threw
On the defenseless lovely maid.
But, Oh! what envying god conspires
To snatch his power, yet leave him the desire!   80

IX.

Nature's support (without whose aid
She can no human being give)
Itself now wants the art to live;
Faintness its slack'ned nerves invade.
In vain th' enraged youth essay'd   85
To call its fleeting vigor back,
No motion 'twill from motion take,
Excess of love his love betray'd;
In vain he toils, in vain commands,
The insensible fell weeping in his hand.   90

X.

In this so amorous cruel strife,
Where love and fate were too severe,
The poor Lysander in despair
Renounc'd his reason with his life.
Now all the brisk and active fire   95
That should the nobler part inflame,
Serv'd to increase his rage and shame,
And left no spark for new desire;
Not all her naked charms could move
Or calm that rage that had debauch'd his love.   100

XI.

Cloris returning from the trance
Which love and soft desire had bred,
Her timorous hand she gently laid
(Or guided by design or chance)
Upon that fabulous Priapus,[3]   105
That potent god, as poets feign;
But never did young shepherdess,
Gath'ring of fern upon the plain,
More nimbly draw her fingers back,
Finding beneath the verdant leaves a snake,   110

XII.

Than Cloris her fair hand withdrew,
Finding that god of her desires
Disarm'd of all his awful fires,
And cold as flow'rs bath'd in the morning dew.
Who can the nymph's confusion guess?   115
That blood forsook the hinder place,
And strew'd with blushes all her face,
Which both disdain and shame expressed,
And from Lysander's arms she fled,
Leaving him fainting on the gloomy bed.   120

XIII.

Like lightning through the grove she hies,
Or Daphne from the Delphic god,[4]
No print upon the grassy road
She leaves t' instruct pursuing eyes.
The wind that wanton'd in her hair,   125
And with her ruffled garments plaid,
Discover'd in the flying maid
All that the gods e'er made if fair.
So Venus, when her love[5] was slain,
With fear and haste flew o'er the fatal plain.   130

XIV.

The nymph's resentments none but I
Can well imagine or condole,
But none can guess Lysander's soul,
But those who sway'd his destiny.
His silent griefs swell up to storms,   135
And not one god his fury spares,
He curs'd his birth, his fate, his stars,

---

3. Greek fertility god, usually depicted with a large erect phallus.
4. Apollo. See Ovid, *Metamorphoses*, bk. 1.
5. Adonis, who was fatally wounded during a hunt.

But more the shepherdess's charms,
Whose soft bewitching influence
Had damn'd him to the hell of impotence.   140

To the Fair Clarinda, Who Made Love to Me,[1] Imagin'd More than Woman

Fair lovely maid, or if that title be
Too weak, too feminine for nobler thee,
Permit a name that more approaches truth,
And let me call thee lovely, charming youth.[2]
This last will justify my soft complaint,[3]   5
While that may serve to lessen my constraint,
And without blushes I the youth pursue,
When so much beauteous woman is in view.
Against thy charms we struggle but in vain
With thy deluding form thou giv'st us pain,   10
While the bright nymph betrays us[4] to the swain.
In pity to our sex sure thou were sent,
That we might love, and yet be innocent;[5]
For sure no crime with thee we can commit,
Or if we should—thy form excuses it.   15
For who that gathers fairest flowers believes
A snake lies hid beneath the fragrant leaves.

Thou beauteous wonder of a different kind,
Soft Cloris with the dear Alexis[6] join'd,
When e'r the manly part of thee would plead   20
Thou tempts us with the image of the maid,
While we the noblest passions do extend
The love to Hermes, Aphrodite[7] the friend.

On Desire. A Pindaric

What art thou, oh! thou new-found pain?
From what infection dost thou spring?
Tell me.—oh! tell me, thou enchanting thing,
Thy nature, and thy name;

1. To "make love" meant to play the game of love.
2. A young person, either male or female.
3. Lover's address.
4. Shows us disloyal.
5. Innocent because still chaste, and thus no "crime" is committed (l.14).
6. Cloris, Alexis: conventional pastoral names.
7. Hermes, Aphrodite: Hermes and Aphrodite are joined into the male-and-female Hermaphroditus (see Ovid, *Metamorphoses*, bk.IV).

Inform me by what subtle art,   5
    What powerful influence,
You got such vast dominion in a part
Of my unheeded, and unguarded, heart,
That fame and honor cannot drive ye thence.
Oh! mischievous usurper of my peace,   10
Oh! soft intruder on my solitude,
    Charming disturber of my ease,
    That has my nobler fate pursu'd,
And all the glories of my life subdu'd.

Thou haunt'st my inconvenient hours;   15
The business of the day, nor silence of the night,
        That should to cares and sleep invite,
    Can bid defiance to thy conquering powers.

Where hast thou been this live-long age
        That from my birth till now,   20
    Thou never couldst one thought engage,
Or charm my soul with the uneasy rage
That made it all its humble feebles¹ know?

Where wert thou, oh, malicious spright,
    When shining honor did invite?   25
    When interest called, then thou wert shy,
Nor to my aid one kind propension² brought,
    Nor would'st inspire one tender thought,
    When princes at my feet did lie.

When thou could'st mix ambition with my joy,   30
Then peevish phantom thou were nice and coy,
        Not beauty could invite thee then
        Nor all the arts of lavish men!
Not all the powerful rhetoric of the tongue
    Not sacred wit could charm thee on;   35
        Not the soft play that lovers make,
Nor sigh could fan thee to a fire,
Not pleading tears, nor vows could thee awake,
Or warm the unform'd—something—to desire.

Oft I've conjur'd thee to appear   40
    By youth, by love, by all their pow'rs,
    Have searched and sought thee everywhere,
In silent groves, in lonely bow'rs,
On flow'ry beds where lovers wishing lie,
    In sheltering woods where sighing maids   45

1. Foibles, weaknesses.
2. Propensity.

To their assigning[3] shepherds hie,
And hide their blushes in the gloom of shades.
　　Yet there, even there, tho youth assail'd,
Where beauty prostrate lay and fortune woo'd,
My heart insensible to neither bow'd,　　　　　　　　　　50
Thy lucky aid was wanting to prevail.

In courts I sought thee then, thy proper sphere
　　But thou in crowds were stifl'd there,
Int'rest did all the loving business do,
Invites the youths and wins the virgins too.　　　　　　55
Or if by chance some heart thy empire own
(Ah power ingrate!) the slave must be undone.

Tell me, thou nimble fire, that dost dilate
　　Thy mighty force through every part,
What god, or human power did thee create　　　　　　60
　　In my, till now, unfacil[4] heart?
Art thou some welcome plague sent from above
　　In this dear form, this kind disguise?
　　Or the false offspring of mistaken love,
　　Begot by some soft thought that faintly strove,　　65
With the bright piercing beauties of Lysander's[5] eyes?

　　Yes, yes, tormenter, I have found thee now,
　　And found to whom thou dost thy being owe,
　　　'Tis thou the blushes dost impart,
　　　For thee this languishment[6] I wear,　　　　　　70
　　　'Tis thou that tremblest in my heart
　　When the dear shepherd does appear,
　　I faint, I die with pleasing pain,
　　My words intruding sighing break
　　When e'er I touch the charming swain　　　　　　75
　　When e'er I gaze, when e'er I speak.
Thy conscious fire is mingl'd with my love,
　　As in the sanctifi'd abodes
　　Misguided worshippers approve
　　The mixing idol with their gods.　　　　　　　　80
　　In vain, alas! in vain I strive
With errors, which my soul do please and vex,
　　For superstition will survive,
　　Purer religion to perplex.

3. Having the power to dispose of.
4. Unwilling.
5. Behn often used the name Lysander to refer to her bisexual lover, John Hoyle.
6. Pining.

Oh! tell me you, philosophers, in love, 85
That can its burning feverish fits control,
   By what strange arts you cure the soul,
   And the fierce calenture[7]remove?

Tell me, ye fair ones, that exchange desire,
   How 'tis you hid the kindling fire. 90
   Oh! would you but confess the truth,
It is not real virtue makes you nice,
But when you do resist the pressing youth,
'Tis want of dear desire, to thaw the virgin ice.
   And while your young adorers lye 95
All languishing and hopeless at your feet,
   Raising new trophies to your chastity,
   Oh tell me, how you do remain discreet?
   How you suppress the rising sighs,
And the soft yielding soul that wishes in your eyes? 100
  While to th'admiring crowd you nice are found,
  Some dear, some secret, youth that gives the wound
  Informs you, all your virtue's but a cheat
    And honor but a false disguise,
  Your modesty a necessary bait 105
  To gain the dull repute of being wise.

Deceive the foolish world—deceive it on,
   And veil your passions in your pride,
But now I've found your feebles by my own,
From me the needful fraud you cannot hide. 110
   Though 'tis a mighty power must move
   The soul to this degree of love,
And though with virtue I the world perplex,
Lysander finds the weakness of my sex,
So Helen while from Theseus's arms she fled, 115
To charming Paris yields her heart and bed.[8]

On the Death of the Late Earl of Rochester[1]

Mourn, mourn, ye Muses, all your loss deplore,
The young, the noble Strephon[2] is no more.

---

7. Fever or burning passion.
8. Theseus attempted to rape Helen of Troy, a daughter of Zeus, when she was a young girl; Helen was later married to Menelaus and abducted by Paris, thus causing the Trojan War.
1. John Wilmot, second earl of Rochester (1647–80), poet, satirist, and libertine.
2. Rochester.

Yes, yes, he fled quick as departing light,
And ne'er shall rise from death's eternal night,
So rich a prize the Stygian gods[3] ne'er bore,   5
Such wit, such beauty, never grac'd their shore.
He was but lent this duller world t' improve
In all the charms of poetry, and love;
Both were his gift, which freely he bestow'd,
And like a god, dealt to the wond'ring crowd.   10
Scorning the little vanity of fame,
Spite of himself attain'd a glorious name.
But oh! In vain was all his peevish pride,
The sun as soon might his vast luster hide,
As piercing, pointed, and more lasting bright,   15
As suffering no vicissitudes of night.
　　Mourn, mourn, ye Muses, all your loss deplore,
　　The young, the noble Strephon is no more.

Now uninspir'd upon your banks we lye,
Unless when we would mourn his elegy;   20
His name's a genius that would wit dispense,
And give the theme a soul, the words a sense.
But all fine thought that ravished when it spoke,
With the soft youth eternal leave has took,
Uncommon wit that did the soul o'ercome,   25
Is buried all in Strephon's worship'd tomb.
Satyr[4] has lost its art, its sting is gone,
The fop and cully[5] now may be undone;
That dear instructing rage is now allay'd,
And no sharp pen dares tell 'em how they've stray'd;   30
Bold as a god was ev'ry lash he took
But kind and gentle the chastising stroke.
　　Mourn, mourn, ye youths, whom fortune has betray'd,
　　The last reproacher of your vice is dead.

Mourn, all ye beauties, put your cypress on,[6]   35
The truest swain that e'er ador'd you's gone;
Think how he lov'd, and writ, and sigh'd, and spoke,
Recall his mien, his fashion, and his look.
By what dear arts the soul he did surprise,
Soft as his voice, and charming as his eyes.   40
Bring garlands all of never-dying flow'rs,
Bedew'd with everlasting falling show'rs,
Fix your fair eyes upon your victim'd slave,
Sent gay and young to his untimely grave.[7]

3. Gods of the Styx; in Greek mythology the primary river of the underworld.
4. Satire, with a pun on *satyr*, a follower of Dionysus that was half-man, half-goat.
5. "fop": man who is foolishly attentive to his appearance; "cully": a dupe.
6. The cypress tree was associated with mourning.
7. Rochester died at age thirty-two.

See where the noble swain extended lies,   45
Too sad a triumph of your victories,
Adorn'd with all the graces heav'n e'er lent,
All that was great, soft, lovely, excellent
You've laid into his early monument.
 Mourn, mourn, ye beauties, your sad loss deplore,   50
 The young, the charming Strephon is no more.

Mourn, all ye little gods of love, whose darts
Have lost their wonted power of piercing hearts;
Lay by the gilded quiver and the bow,
The useless toys can do no mischief now,   55
Those eyes that all your arrows' points inspir'd,
Those lights that gave ye fire are now retir'd,
Cold as his tomb, pale as your mother's doves,[8]
Bewail him then oh all ye little loves,
For you the humblest votary have lost   60
That ever your divinities could boast.
Upon your hands your weeping heads decline,
And let your wings encompass round his shrine;
Instead of flow'rs your broken arrows strow,
And at his feet lay the neglected bow.   65
 Mourn, all ye little gods, your loss deplore,
 The soft, the charming Strephon is no more.

Large was his fame, but short his glorious race,
Like young Lucretius liv'd and dy'd apace.[9]
So early roses fade, so over all   70
They cast their fragrant scents, then softly fall,
While all the scatter'd perfum'd leaves declare,
How lovely 'twas when whole, how sweet, how fair.
Had he been to the Roman Empire known,
When great Augustus[10] fill'd the peaceful throne,   75
Had he the noble wond'rous poet seen,
And known his genius, and survey'd his mien,
(When wits and heroes grac'd divine abodes)
He had increas'd the number of their gods;
The royal judge[11] had temples rear'd to's name,   80
And made him as immortal as his fame;
In love and verse his Ovid[12] he'd out-done,
And all his laurels, and his Julia[13] won.
 Mourn, mourn, unhappy world, his loss deplore,
 The great, the charming Strephon is no more.   85

8. The dove was associated with Venus.
9. It was a common misconception that Lucretius lived a short and wanton life.
10. Gaius Octavius, later Octavian (63 B.C.–A.D. 14), adopted son of Julius Caesar and first of the Roman emperors.
11. Augustus.
12. Publius Ovidius Naso, Roman poet (43 B.C.–A.D. 17), author of *Amores*.
13. Augustus's daughter. She was probably not Ovid's mistress, but it was a popular legend.

To Mr. Creech (Under the Name of Daphnis) on His Excellent Translation of Lucretius[1]

Thou great young man! Permit amongst the crowd
Of those that sing thy mighty praises loud,
My humble Muse to bring its tribute too.
    Inspir'd by thy vast flight of verse,
Methinks I should some wondrous thing rehearse,   5
Worthy divine Lucretius, and diviner thou.
       But I of feebler seeds design'd,
         Whilst the slow moving atoms[2] strove,
       With careless heed to form my mind,
         Compos'd it all of softer love.   10
In gentle numbers[3] all my songs are dressed,
      And when I would thy glories sing,
   What in strong manly verse I would express,
Turns all to womanish tenderness within,
Whilst that which admiration does inspire   15
In other souls, kindles in mine a fire.
Let them admire thee on—whilst I this newer way
      Pay thee yet more than they;
For more I owe, since thou hast taught me more,
Than all the mighty bards that went before.   20
Others long since have pal'd the vast delight,
In duller Greek and Latin[4] satisfy'd the appetite,
But I unlearn'd in schools, disdain that mine
Should treated be at any feast but thine.
Till now, I cursed my birth,[5] my education,   25
And more the scanted customs of the nation,
Permitting not the female sex to tread,
The mighty paths of learned heroes dead.
The god-like Virgil,[6] and great Homer's verse,
Like divine mysteries are conceal'd from us.   30
     We are forbid all grateful themes,
      No ravishing thoughts approach our ear,
       The fulsome jingle[7] of the times,
Is all we are allow'd to understand or hear.
     But as of old, when men unthinking lay,   35
Ere gods were worshipped, or ere laws were fram'd,

1. Thomas Creech (1659–1700) was an Oxford scholar and classicist. Titus Lucretius Carus was a Roman poet (c. 99–55 B.C.) and well-known proponent of atomic theory derived from the Greeks.
2. "feebler seeds . . . slow moving atoms": Lucretius's philosophy claimed that the universe was sustained by the movement of atoms. The speaker's "seeds" are "feebler" because they are female.
3. Poetic meter.
4. Greek and Latin were standard subjects in boys' public schools, only occasionally taught to women.
5. "my birth": here both the speaker's sex and her station limit her education, and thus her ability to read Lucretius in the original.
6. Publius Vergilius Maro (70–19 B.C.) Roman poet.
7. "fulsome": cloying; "jingle": a cheap, frequently repeated phrase.

The wiser bard[8] that taught 'em first t' obey
Was next to what he taught, ador'd and fam'd;
Gentler they grew, their words and manners chang'd,
And savage now no more the woods they rang'd.   40
So thou by this translation dost advance
Our knowledge from the state of ignorance,[9]
And equals us to man: Ah how can we,
Enough adore, or sacrifice enough to thee!

The mystic terms of rough philosophy,   45
Thou dost so plain and easily express,
Yet deck'st them in so soft and gay a dress,
So intelligent to each capacity,
That they at once instruct and charm the sense,
With heights of fancy, heights of eloquence;   50
And reason over all unfetter'd plays,
Wanton and undisturb'd as summer's breeze,
        That gliding murmurs o'er the trees,
And no hard notion meets or stops its way.
        It pierces, conquers and compels,   55
Beyond poor feeble faith's dull oracles.
        Faith the despairing soul's content,
Faith the last shift of routed argument.

Hail sacred Wadham! whom the Muses grace
And from the rest of all the reverend pile,   60
Of noble palaces,[10] design'd thy space,
        Where they in soft retreat might dwell. .
They blest thy fabric, and said—Do thou,
        Our darling sons contain;
We thee our sacred nursery ordain,   65
        They said and blest, and it was so.
And if of old the fanes[11] of sylvian gods,
        Were worshipped as divine abodes,
        If courts are held as sacred things,
        For being the awful seats of kings,   70
        What veneration should be paid,
To thee that hast such wondrous poets made!
        To gods for fear devotion was design'd,
        And safety made us bow to majesty;
        Poets by nature awe and charm the mind,   75
Are born not made by dull religion or necessity.

---

8. God.
9. "state of ignorance": a pun on Dryden's *State of Innocence* (1677).
10. "Wadham . . . noble palaces": Wadham College, Oxford, from which Sprat, Creech, and Rochester all received degrees.
11. Temples.

The learned Thyrsis[12] did to thee belong,
Who Athen's plague has so divinely sung.
Thyrsis to wit, as sacred friendship true,
Paid mighty Cowley's memory its due.   80
Thyrsis who whilst a greater plague did reign,
Than that which Athens did depopulate,
Scattering rebellious fury o'er the plain,
That threatn'd ruin to the church and state,
Unmov'd he stood, and fear'd no threats of fate.   85
That loyal champion for the church and crown,
That noble ornament of the sacred gown,
Still did his sovereign's cause[13] espouse,
And was above the thanks of the mad senate-house.
Strephon[14] the great, whom last you sent abroad,   90
Who writ, and lov'd, and looked like any god;
For whom the muses mourn, the love-sick maids
Are languishing in melancholy shades.
   The Cupids flag their wings, their bows untie,
   And useless quivers hang neglected by,   95
   And scatter'd arrows all around 'em lie.
By murmuring brooks the careless deities are laid,
Weeping their rifled power now noble Strephon's dead.

   Ah sacred Wadham! should'st thou never own
   But this delight of all mankind and thine;   100
   For ages past of dullness, this alone,
      This charming hero would atone.
   And make thee glorious to succeeding time,
   But thou like nature's self disdain'st to be,
      Stinted to singularity.   105
   Even as fast as she thou dost produce,
   And over all the sacred mystery infuse.
      No sooner was fam'd Strephon's glory set,
      Strephon the soft, the lovely and the great,
      But Daphnis[15] rises like the morning-star,   110
      That guides the wand'ring traveler from afar,
      Daphnis whom every grace and muse inspires,
      Scarce Strephon's ravishing poetic fires
         So kindly warm, or so divinely cheer.

   Advance young Daphnis, as thou hast begun,   115
      So let thy mighty race be run.

12. Behn's poetic name for longtime friend Thomas Sprat (1635–1713), author of *The Plague of Athens* (1659) and a biography of Abraham Cowley.
13. "sacred gown . . . sovereign's cause": As a bishop Sprat would have worn the ecclesiastical gown; he was a staunch royalist and supporter of James II, a position that often caused his popularity to suffer in Parliament, the "mad senate-house" of l. 89.
14. John Wilmot, second earl of Rochester (1647–80); see Behn's elegy, "On the Death of the late Earl of Rochester," above.
15. Creech.

Thou in thy large poetic chase,
Begin'st where others end the race.
If now thy grateful numbers are so strong,
If they so early can such graces show,   120
Like beauty so surprising, when so young,
What Daphnis will thy riper judgment do,
When thy unbounded verse in their own streams shall flow!
   What wonder will they not produce,
      When thy immortal fancy's loose,   125
Unfetter'd, unconfin'd by any other muse!
Advance young Daphnis then,[16] and mayst thou prove
Still sacred in thy poetry and love.
May all the groves with Daphnis's songs be blessed,
Whilst every bark is with thy distichs[17] dressed.   130
May timorous maids learn how to love from thence
And the glad shepherd *arts of eloquence*.
And when to solitude thou would'st retreat,
May their tun'd pipes thy welcome celebrate.
And all the nymphs strow garlands at thy feet.   135
May all the purling streams that murmuring pass,
   The shady groves and banks of flowers,
   The kind reposing beds of grass,
   Contribute to their softer hours.
Mayst thou thy muse and mistress there caress,   140
And may one heighten t'others happiness.
And whilst thou so divinely dost converse,
We are content to know and to admire thee in thy sacred verse.

A Congratulatory Poem on Her Sacred Majesty Queen Mary[1] upon Her Arrival in England

While my sad muse the darkest covert sought,
To give a loose to melancholy thought,
Oppressed and sighing with the heavy weight
Of an unhappy dear lov'd monarch's fate,
A lone retreat, on Thames's brink she found,   5
With murmuring osiers fring'd, and bending willows crown'd,
Through the thick shade could dart no cheerful ray,
Nature dwelt here as in disdain of day.
Content, and pleas'd with nobler solitude,

---

16. In ll. 127–39 Creech is described as Pan, half-man and half-god, guardian of shepherds and flocks, an enthusiastic lover adored by both men and women; the "tun'd pipes" (l. 134) are his reed instrument.
17. Heroic couplets, the English metric form Creech used to translate Lucretius's Latin hexameters.
1. Mary II (1662–94). Mary stayed at the Hague while her husband, William Nassau, prince of Orange (later William III), led the invasion and "Glorious Revolution" that drove her father (the "dear lov'd monarch" of l. 4) from England and reestablished a Protestant monarchy. She arrived in England February 12, 1689; Behn supported the father, James II.

No wood gods, fawns, nor loves did here intrude,   10
Nor nests for wanton birds, the glade allows;
Scarce the soft winds were heard amongst the boughs.

While thus she lay resolv'd to tune no more
Her fruitless songs on Britain's faithless shore,[2]
All on a sudden through the woods there rung,   15
Loud sounds of joy that *Io Paeans*[3] sung.
Maria! Blest Maria! was the theme,
Great Britain's happy genius, and her queen.

The river nymphs their crystal courts forsake,
Curl their blue locks, and shelly trumpets take,   20
And the surprising news along the shore,
In raptur'd songs the wond'ring virgins bore,
Whilst mourning Echo[4] now forgot her sighs,
And sung the new taught anthem to the skies.

All things in nature, a new face put on,   25
Thames with harmonious purlings glides along,
And tells her ravished banks, she lately bore
A prize more great than all her hidden store,
Or all the sun itself e'er saw before.
The brooding spring, her fragrant bloom sent out,   30
Scattering her early perfumes round about;
No longer waits the lazy teeming hours,
But e'er her time produc'd her odorous flowers,
Maria's eyes anticipate the May,
And life inspired beyond the god of day.   35

The Muses all upon this theme divine,
Tun'd their best lays, the Muses all, but mine,
Sullen with stubborn loyalty she lay,
And saw the world its eager homage pay,
While heav'n and earth on the new scene looked gay.   40
But, oh! What human fortitude can be
Sufficient to resist a deity?
Even our allegiance here, too feebly pleads,
The change in so divine a form persuades;
Maria with the sun has equal force,   45
No opposition stops her glorious course,
Her pointed beams through all a passage find,
And fix their rays triumphant in the mind.

And now I wish'd among the crowds to adore,
And constant wishing did increase my power;   50
From every thought a new-born reason came

2. Britain is "faithless" because it has abandoned its king.
3. Exclamations of joy or triumph.
4. Wood nymph who pined for Narcissus.

Which fortified by bright Maria's fame,
Inspired my genius with new life and flame,

And thou, great lord,[5] of all my vows, permit
My muse who never fail'd obedience yet,   55
To pay her tribute at Maria's feet,
Maria so divine a part of you,
Let me be just—but just with honor too.

Resolv'd, she join'd her chorus with the throng,
And to the list'ning groves Maria's virtues sung,   60
Maria all enchanting, gay, and young.

All hail illustrious daughter of a king,
Shining without, and glorious all within,
Whose eyes beyond your scantier power give laws,
Command the world, and justify the cause,   65
Nor to secure your empire needs more arms
Than your resistless, and all conquering charms;
Minerva thus alone, old Troy sustain'd,
Whilst her blessed image with three gods remain'd,[6]
But, oh! your form and manner to relate,   70
The envying fair as soon may imitate,
'Tis all engaging sweet, 'tis all surprising great;
A thousand beauties triumph in your air,
Like those of soft young loves, your smiles appear,
And to th' unguarded hearts, as dangerous are.   75

All nature's charms are open'd in your face,
You look, you talk, with more than human grace;
All that is wit, all that is eloquence.
The births of finest thought and noblest sense,
Easy and natural from your language break,   80
And 'tis eternal music when you speak.
Through all no formal nicety is seen,
But free and generous your majestic mien,
In every motion, every part a queen;
All that is great and lovely in the sex,   85
Heav'n did in this one glorious wonder fix,
Apelles[7] thus to dress the queen of love,
Robb'd the whole race, a goddess to improve.

Yet if with sighs we view that lovely face,
And all the lines of your great father's trace,   90
Your virtues should forgive, while we adore

---

5. Presumably James II, to whom the poem remains loyal even as it turns reluctantly to praise his daughter. In the margin of the original, the printer has added "J. R." (i. e., Jacobus Rex, or James the King).
6. The Palladium was an ancient statue of Minerva/Athena, believed to protect the city where it was kept; in some stories it was stolen with Helen from Troy.
7. Painter to Alexander the Great, best known for his picture of Aphrodite.

That face that awes and charms our hearts the more.
But if the monarch in your looks we find,
Behold him yet more glorious in your mind;
'Tis here his god-like attributes we see,   95
A gracious sweetness, affability,
A tender mercy and true piety;
And virtues even sufficient to atone
For all the ills the ungrateful world has done,
Where several factions, several int'rests sway,   100
And that is still i'th' right who gains the day;
How e'er they differ, this they all must grant,
Your form and mind, no one perfection want,
Without all angel, and within all saint.

The murmuring world till now divided lay,   105
Vainly debating whom they should obey,
Till you great Caesar's off-spring[8] blessed our isle,
The differing multitudes to reconcile;
This stiff-necked Israel[9] in defiance stood,
Till they beheld the prophet of their god,   110
Who from the mount with dazzling brightness came,
And eyes all shining with celestial flame;
Those awful looks, dispel'd each rebel thought,
And to a just compliance, the wild nations brought.

TEXTUAL NOTES

Copy-text: *Poems Upon Several Occasions* (1684) for poems appearing in this edition, and specified variants from the first printing for those poems published earlier. The copy-text has been emended where a solid case can be made for later or variant readings having been the author's intent; all such emendations are included in the textual notes below. Spelling, punctuation, and capitalization have been modernized, except in cases where old spelling implies a range of meanings not obvious in modern English.

Editions

1684	Behn, *Poems Upon Several Occasions: With a Voyage to the Island of Love* (printed for R. Tonson and J. Tonson, 1684)
Miscellany, 1685	*Miscellany, Being a Collection of Poems by Several Hands. Together with Reflections on Morality, or Seneca Unmasqued* (printed for J. Hindmarsh, 1685), edited by Behn
Rochester	Poems included with Rochester's *Poems on Several Occasions,* 1680

8. Caesar was a name frequently used in panegyrics to the late Stuart monarchs, including James.
9. See Exodus 32–34 for the story of Moses, Aaron, and the golden calf.

Lycidus	Poems appended to *Lycidus: or the Lover in Fashion...* *Together with a Miscellany of New Poems* (printed for Joseph Knight and Francis Saunders, 1688)
Creech	Creech's translation of *Lucretius*
Abdelazer	*Abdelazer,* play, 1677
Mercury	*Muses Mercury,* 1707
CGD	*Covent Garden Drolery,* miscellany edited by Behn, 1672
Dutch Lover	*The Dutch Lover: a Comedy,* 1673
State Affairs	*Poems on Affairs of State,* 1697
Mary	*Congratulatory Poem on Her Sacred Majesty Queen Mary Upon her Arrival in England* (printed by R. E. for Bentley and Canning, 1689)

"**The Golden Age**": Copy-text: 1684. See Hagedorn for the French translations of Tasso's *Aminta* Behn was paraphrasing and reworking.

"**On a Juniper Tree, cut down to make Busks**": Copy-text: 1684. First printed in Rochester's *Poems on Several Occasions* (1680); at one time attributed to Rochester (Vieth, *Attribution in Restoration Poetry;* O'Donnell, *Bibliography,* 92).
Variants:
Juniper-Tree, cut down] Giniper-Tree now cut down (Rochester)
l.8 *ungrateful*] unwilling (Rochester)
l.21 *grow*] grew (Rochester)
l.26 *she lean'd*] he plac'd (Rochester)
l.27 *their bed*] her bed (Rochester)
l.28 not in Rochester
l.30 *grass*] moss (Rochester)
l.53 not in 1684; added from Rochester
l.63 *Now*] Where (Rochester)
l.66 Two additional lines follow in Rochester:
  And had the nymph been half so kind,
  As was the shepherd, well inclin'd
l.68 *Nor had the mystery ended there,*] The myst'ry had not ended there, (Rochester)
l.71 *alas would not*] Alas cou'd not (Rochester)
l.74 *Fondly*] Humbly (Rochester)
l.75 *A fault*] That fault (Rochester)
l.76 *with some*] with shame (Rochester)
l.78 *times my*] times the (Rochester)
l.86 *And if before*] and before (Rochester)
l.87 *In having heard, and seen too much,*] In having seen, and heard so much; (Rochester)
l.88 *grief*] griefs (Rochester)
l.89 *I shall be*] I must lye (Rochester)
l.91 *charming*] am'rous (Rochester)

"**Song: I Led My Silvia to a Grove**": Copy-text: *CGD.* "Song: I led my Silvia to a Grove" was first printed in *Covent Garden Drolery* (1672, probably edited by Behn) and printed (with extensive revisions) in *The Muses Mercury* (1707),

where the stanzas are numbered I–III. The Behn poems published in *The Muses Mercury* may derive from the papers of her lover John Hoyle; Duyfhuizen speculates that Behn's original had female homoerotic overtones.
Variants:
Title "A Song for J. H." *(Mercury)*
l.1 *a grove*] the Grove *(Mercury)*
1.2 *all the boughs did*] ev'ry Tree might *(Mercury)*
l.3 *though it had strove*] a Foe to Love *(Mercury)*
l.4 *It could not have*] Cou'd not have there *(Mercury)*
l.5 *Humane*] human *(Mercury)*
l.7 *winds do*] Zephirs *(Mercury)*
l.9 *there*] then *(Mercury)*
l.10 *did begin*] both began *(Mercury)*
l.11 *wanton tricks*] sports we found *(Mercury)*
l.12 *heat of all the*] sultry Heat of Day *(Mercury)*
l.13 *A many kisses I did*] What Kisses did the Shepherd *(Mercury)*
l.14 *she return'd the same*] what the Nymph return *(Mercury)*
ll.15–16 They lov'd so much, they scarce cou'd live,
        So much they both did burn. *(Mercury)*
l.17 *My*] His *aids*] Aid *(Mercury)*
l.19 *On her that*] Enough she *(Mercury)*
l.20 *'Twas easy to*] And he might soon *(Mercury)*
l.21 *I did but kiss and clasp*] Again he kiss'd and clasp'd *(Mercury)*
l.22 *Whose they my*] And thus his *(Mercury)*
l.23 *And laid her gently*] He sigh'd and laid her *(Mercury)*
l.24 *Oh! who can*] Let Lovers guess *(Mercury)*
    "The Willing Mistress": Copy-text: 1684. "The Willing Mistress" retells the story of "Song: I Led My Silvia to a Grove" from the woman's point of view. It first appeared as a song in Act II of *The Dutch Lover*, in 1673.
Variants:
l.11 *amorous*] wanton *(Dutch Lover)*
l.18 *soft'ning*] amorous *(Dutch Lover)*
l.22 *those*] they *(Dutch Lover)*
    "Love Arm'd": Copy-text: 1684. Originally published as opening song in *Abdelazer* (1677).
    "The Disappointment": Copy-text: 1684. First published in Rochester and long believed to be his.
Variants:
l.19 *in vain*] too late (Rochester)
l.24 *breathing faintly*] whisp'ring softly (Rochester)
l.29 *this*] that (Rochester)
l.34 *mouth*] lips (Rochester)
l.37 *swelling*] melting (Rochester)
l.48 *calm'd*] tam'd (Rochester)
l.49 *where delight still flows*] from whose trills (Rochester)
l.50 *And gives the universal world repose*] The melted soul, in liquid drops distills (Rochester)
l.52 *are*] they (Rochester)

l.56 *Her soft eyes cast a*] Her eyes appear'd like (Rochester)
l.66 *joys*] sweets (Rochester)
l.128 *if*] of (Rochester)
l.132 *or*] and (Rochester)
l.138 *more*] mere (Rochester)
    "To the fair Clarinda": Copy-text: *Lycidus*
    "On Desire": Copy-text: *Lycidus*
Variants:
l.21 *could'st*] didst *(State Affairs)*
l.25 *honor*] glory *(State Affairs)*
l.27 *to my aid one kind propension brought*] one kind aid to my assistance brought *(State Affairs)*
l.32 *could invite*] would invade *(State Affairs)*
l.39 emended from *(State Affairs)* —*something*—] something— *(Lycidus)*
l.70 Missing in *State Affairs*.
l.73 *I*] and *(State Affairs)*
l.86 *its*] these *(State Affairs)*
l.88 *fierce*] fiery *(State Affairs)*
l.89 *that exchange*] you that give *(State Affairs)*
l.98 Two additional lines follow in *State Affairs*:
    And not the passion to the throng make known,
    Which Cupid in revenge has now confin'd to one.
l.102 *that*] who *(State Affairs)*
l.105 *bait*] slight *(State Affairs)*
l.109 *feebles*] weakness *(State Affairs)*
ll.111–112 Missing in *State Affairs*.
l.113 *And*] For *(State Affairs)*
l.114 *weakness*] feeble *(State Affairs)*
l.115 *while*] though *(State Affairs)*
    "On the Death of Rochester": Copy-text: *Miscellany, 1685*.
    "To Mr. Creech": Copy-text: 1684. A substantially revised version was printed in Creech's translation of Lucretius's *De rerum natura* (1683) as "To the Unknown Daphnis on his Excellent Translation of *Lucretius*." Duffy, Greer and O'Donnell now believe the later, more atheistic version, published the following year in *Poems Upon Several Occasions* (1684), to have been Behn's intent; the less emphatic version published with Creech's translation was suggested or required by Creech's publishers, though it is unclear exactly who made the changes to Behn's poem.
Variants:
l.3 *it's tribute*] her tribute (Creech)
l.6 *diviner thou*] diviner you (Creech)
l.13 *I would*] should be (Creech)
l.25 *Birth, my*] Sex and (Creech)
l.29 *Verse*] Muse (Creech)
l.43 *Ah how can we,*] Oh how shall we (Creech)
l.56 *Beyond poor feeble faith's dull oracles*] As strong as faith's resistless oracles (Creech)
l.57 *despairing soul's*] religious soul's (Creech)

l.58 *last shift*] secure retreat (Creech)
l.76 *made by dull religion or necessity*] made or by religion or necessity. (Creech)
l.87 Missing in Creech.
l.99 *should'st*] couldst (Creech)
l.106 *Even as fast*] As fast (Creech)
l.107 *infuse*] dost infuse (Creech)
l.109 *lovely and the great*] lovely, gay and great (Creech)
l.121 *when so*] whilst so (Creech)
l.128 *sacred*] happy (Creech)
l.138 *kind*] low (Creech)
l.139 *their Softer*] thy softest (Creech)
l.142 *so divinely*] thus divinely (Creech)
l.143 *thy Sacred Verse*] thy Verse (Creech)
"**Congratulatory Poem ... Sacred Majesty Queen Mary**": Copy-text: *Mary*, 1689. O'Donnell (*Bibliography*, 149–51) lists only one edition. Greer (*Uncollected Verse*) seems, however, to be working from an edition substantially different from the one in Firestone Library, Princeton University, which is here used as copy-text.

BIBLIOGRAPHY

Editions

Duffy, Maureen, introd. *Behn: Five Plays*. London: Methuen, 1990.
Greer, Germaine, ed. *The Uncollected Verse of Aphra Behn*. Saffron Walden, Essex: Stump Cross Books, 1989.
Link, Frederick M., ed. *The Rover*. Lincoln: Univ. of Nebraska Press, 1967.
Naismith, Bill, introd. *The Rover*. London: Methuen, 1993.
O'Donnell, Mary Ann, ed. "Tory Wit and Unconventional Woman: Aphra Behn." In *Women Writers of the Seventeenth Century*. Ed. Katharina M. Wilson and Frank J. Warnke. Athens: Univ. of Georgia Press, 1989. 341–54.
Salzman, Paul, ed. *Oroonoko and Other Writings*. Oxford: Oxford Univ. Press, 1994.
Summers, Montague, ed. *The Works of Aphra Behn*. 6 vols. London: Heinemann, 1915.
Todd, Janet, ed. *Oroonoko, The Rover, and Other Works*. London: Penguin, 1992.
———. *The Poems of Aphra Behn, A Selection*. London: William Pickering, 1994.
———. *The Works of Aphra Behn*. 7 vols. Columbus: Ohio State Univ. Press, 1993–96.

Secondary Works

Aercke, Kristiaan P. "Theatrical Background in English Novels of the Seventeenth Century." *Journal of Narrative Technique* 18 (1988): 120–36.
Andrade, Susan Z. "White Skin, Black Masks: Colonialism and the Sexual

Politics of *Oroonoko.*" *Cultural Critique* 27 (1994): 189–214.

Armistead, J. M. *Four Restoration Playwrights: A Reference Guide to Thomas Shadwell, Aphra Behn, Nathaniel Lee, and Thomas Otway.* Boston: G. K. Hall, 1984.

Athey, Stephanie, and Daniel Cooper Alarcon. "*Oroonoko'*s Gendered Economies of Honor/Horror: Reframing Colonial Discourse Studies in the Americas." *American Literature* 65 (1993): 415–43.

Backscheider, Paula R. *Spectacular Politics: Theatrical Power and Mass Culture in Early Modern England.* Baltimore: Johns Hopkins Univ. Press, 1993.

Ballaster, Ros. "New Hystericism: Aphra Behn's *Oroonoko:* The Body, the Text, and the Feminist Critic." In *New Feminist Discourses: Critical Essays on Theories and Texts.* Ed. Isobel Armstrong. London: Routledge, 1992. 283–95.

———. *Seductive Forms: Women's Amatory Fiction from 1684–1740.* Oxford: Clarendon Press, 1992.

———. "Seizing the Means of Seduction: Fiction and Feminine Identity in Aphra Behn and Delarivier Manley." In *Women, Writing, History, 1640–1740.* Ed. Isobel Grundy and Susan Wiseman. London: B. T. Batsford, 1992. 93–108.

Barash, Carol. *English Women's Poetry, 1649–1714: Politics, Community, and Linguistic Authority.* Oxford: Clarendon Press, 1996.

———. "The Political Possibilities of Desire: Teaching the Erotic Poems of Aphra Behn." In *Teaching Eighteenth-Century Poetry.* Ed. Christopher Fox. New York: AMS Press, 1990. 159–76.

Boehrer, Bruce Thomas. "Behn's 'Disappointment' and Nashe's 'Choise of Valentines.'" *Essays in Literature* 16 (1989): 172–87.

Bowers, Toni O'Shaughnessy. "Sex, Lies, and Invisibility: Amatory Fiction from the Restoration to Mid-Century." In *The Columbia History of the British Novel.* Ed. John Richetti, John Bender, Diedre David, and Michael Seidel. New York: Columbia Univ. Press, 1994. 50–72.

Brinks, Ellen. "Meeting over the Map: Madeleine de Scudéry's *Carte du Pays de Tendre* and Aphra Behn's *Voyage to the Isle of Love.*" *Restoration* 17 (1993): 39–52.

Brown, Laura. *Ends of Empire: Women and Ideology in Early Eighteenth-Century English Literature.* Ithaca: Cornell Univ. Press, 1993.

———. "The Romance of Empire: *Oroonoko* and the Trade in Slaves." In *The New Eighteenth Century: Theory, Politics, English Literature.* Ed. Felicity Nussbaum and Laura Brown. New York: Methuen, 1987. 41–61.

Burnett, Mark Thornton. "Behn and Jonson." *Notes and Queries* 237 (1992): 463–64.

Cameron, William J. *New Light on Aphra Behn.* Auckland: Univ. of Auckland Press, 1961. Rpt. Darby, Pa.: Arden Library, 1978.

Chibka, Robert L. "'Oh! Do Not Fear a Woman's Invention': Truth, Falsehood, and Fiction in Aphra Behn's *Oroonoko.*" *Texas Studies in Literature and Language* 30 (1988): 510–37.

Copeland, Nancy. "'Once a Whore and Ever'? Whore and Virgin in *The Rover* and Its Antecedents." *Restoration* 16 (1992): 20–27.

———. "Re-Producing *The Rover*: John Barton's *Rover* at the Swan." *Essays in Theatre* 9 (1990): 45–59.

328 · *Aphra Behn*

Cotton, Nancy. "Aphra Behn and the Pattern Hero." In *Curtain Calls: British and American Women and the Theater, 1660–1820*. Ed. Mary Anne Schofield and Cecilia Macheski. Athens: Ohio Univ. Press, 1991. 212–19.

Craft, Catherine. "Reworking Male Models: Aphra Behn's Fair Vow-Breaker, Eliza Haywood's Fantomina, and Charlotte Lennox's Female Quixote." *Modern Language Review* 86 (1991): 821–38.

Day, Robert Adams. "Aphra Behn and the Works of the Intellect." In *Fetter'd or Free? British Women Novelists, 1670–1815*. Ed. Mary Anne Schofield and Cecilia Macheski. Athens: Ohio State Univ. Press, 1986. 372–82.

De Ritter, Jones. "The Gypsy, *The Rover*, and the Wanderer: Aphra Behn's Revision of Thomas Killigrew." *Restoration* 10 (1986): 524–26.

Diamond, Elin. "Closing No Gaps: Aphra Behn, Caryl Churchill, and Empire." In *Caryl Churchill: A Casebook*. Ed. Phyllis R. Randall. New York : Garland, 1988. 161–74.

———. "Gestus and Signature in Aphra Behn's *The Rover*." *ELH* 56 (1989): 519–41.

Doody, Margaret. *The Daring Muse: Augustan Poetry Reconsidered*. Cambridge: Cambridge Univ. Press, 1985.

Duchovnay, Gerald. "Aphra Behn's Religion," *Notes and Queries* 221 (1976): 234–36.

Duffy, Maureen. *The Passionate Shepherdess: Aphra Behn, 1640–89*. London: Jonathan Cape, 1977.

Duyfhuizen, Bernard. "'That Which I Dare Not Name': Aphra Behn's 'The Willing Mistress.'" *ELH* 58 (1991): 63–82.

Erickson, Robert A. "Mrs. A. Behn and the Myth of Oroonoko-Imoinda." *Eighteenth-Century Fiction* 5 (1993): 201–16.

Ezell, Margaret J. M. *The Patriarch's Wife: Literary Evidence and the History of the Family*. Chapel Hill: Univ. of North Carolina Press, 1987.

———. *Writing Women's Literary History*. Baltimore: Johns Hopkins Univ. Press, 1993.

Ferguson, Margaret W. "Juggling the Categories of Race, Class, and Gender: Aphra Behn's *Oroonoko*." *Women's Studies* 19 (1991): 159–81.

———. "News from the New World: Miscegenous Romance in Aphra Behn's *Oroonoko* and *The Widow Ranter*." In *The Production of English Renaissance Culture*. Ed. David Lee Miller, Sharon O'Dair, and Harold Weber. Ithaca: Cornell Univ. Press, 1994. 151–89.

Ferguson, Moira. "*Oroonoko*: Birth of a Paradigm." *New Literary History* 23 (1992): 339–59.

———. "Transmuting *Othello*: Aphra Behn's *Oroonoko*." In *Cross-Cultural Performances: Differences in Women's Re-Visions of Shakespeare*. Ed. Marianne Novy. Urbana: Univ. of Illinois Press, 1993. 15–49.

Fitzmaurice, James. "Aphra Behn and the Abraham's Sacrifice Case." *Huntington Library Quarterly* 56 (1993): 319–27.

———. "The Language of Gender and a Textual Problem in Aphra Behn's *The Rover*." *Neuphilologische Mitteilungen* 96 (1995): 283–93.

———. "The Narrator in Aphra Behn's *The Fair Jilt*." *Zeitschrift für Anglistik und Amerikanistik* 41 (1994): 131–38.

Gallagher, Catherine. *Nobody's Story: The Vanishing Acts of Women Writers in the Marketplace, 1670–1820*. Berkeley and Los Angeles: Univ. of California Press, 1994.

————. "Who Was That Masked Woman? The Prostitute and the Playwright in the Comedies of Aphra Behn." *Women's Studies* 15 (1988): 23–42.

Gardiner, Judith Kegan. "The First English Novel: Aphra Behn's Love Letters." *Tulsa Studies in Women's Literature* 8 (1989): 201–22.

Goreau, Angeline. "'Last Night's Rambles': Restoration Literature and the War between the Sexes." In *The Sexual Dimension in Literature*. Ed. Alan Bold. Totowa, N.J.: Barnes and Noble, 1982. 49–69.

————. *Reconstructing Aphra: A Social Biography of Aphra Behn.* New York: Dial, 1980.

Hagedorn, Suzanne. "Of Sexuality and Intertextuality: A Study of Aphra Behn's 'The Golden Age.'" Manuscript, 1987.

Hill, Rowland M. "Aphra Behn's Use of Setting." *Modern Language Quarterly* 7 (1946): 189–203.

Hoegberg, David E. "Caesar's Toils: Allusion and Rebellion in *Oroonoko*." *Eighteenth-Century Fiction* 7 (1995): 239–58.

Houston, Beverle. "Usurpation and Dismemberment: Oedipal Tyranny in *Oroonoko*." *Literature and Psychology* 32 (1986): 30–36.

Hutner, Heidi, ed. *Rereading Aphra Behn: History, Theory, and Criticism.* Charlottesville: Univ. of Virginia Press, 1993.

Jones, Jane, "New Light on the Background and Early Life of Aphra Behn." *Notes and Queries* 235 (1990): 288–93.

Kavenik, Frances M. "Aphra Behn: The Playwright as 'Breeches Part.'" In *Curtain Calls: British and American Women and the Theater, 1660–1820.* Ed. Mary Anne Schofield and Cecilia Macheski. Athens: Ohio Univ. Press, 1991. 177–92.

Kinney, Suzanne. "Confinement Sharpens the Invention: Aphra Behn's *The Rover* and Susanna Centlivre's *The Busie Body*." In *Look Who's Laughing: Gender and Comedy.* Ed. Gail Finney. Langhorne, Pa.: Gordon and Breach, 1994. 81–98.

Kretsch, Donna Raske. "Sisters across the Atlantic: Aphra Behn and Sor Juana Inez de la Cruz." *Women's Studies* 21 (1992): 361–79.

Langdell, Cheri Davis. "Aphra Behn and Sexual Politics: A Dramatist's Discourse with Her Audience." In *Drama, Sex, and Politics.* Ed. James Redmond. Cambridge: Cambridge Univ. Press, 1985. 109–28.

Link, Frederick M. *Aphra Behn.* Twayne English Authors Series. New York: Twayne, 1968.

Little, Roger. "*Oroonoko* and Tamango: A Parallel Episode." *French Studies* 46 (1992): 26–32.

Lund, Roger D. "Bibliotecha and 'the British Dames': An Early Critique of the Female Wits of the Restoration." *Restoration* 12 (1988): 96–105.

MacCarthy, B. G. *Women Writers: Their Contribution to the English Novel, 1621–1744.* Cork: Cork University Press; Oxford: Blackwell, 1944.

Maclean, Ian. *The Renaissance Notion of Woman: A Study in the Fortunes of Scholasticism and Medieval Science in European Intellectual Life.* Cambridge: Cambridge Univ. Press, 1980.

Markley, Robert. "'Be Impudent, Be Saucy, Forward, Bold, Touzing, and Leud': The Politics of Masculine Sexuality and Feminine Desire in Behn's Tory Comedies." In *Cultural Readings of Restoration and Eighteenth-Century English Theater.* Ed. J. Douglas Canfield and Deborah Payne. Athens: Univ. of Georgia Press, 1995. 114–40.

McKendrick, Neil, John Brewer, and J. H. Plumb. *The Birth of a Consumer Society: The Commercialization of Eighteenth-Century England*. Bloomington: Indiana Univ. Press, 1982.

McKeon, Michael. *The Origins of the English Novel*. Baltimore: John Hopkins Univ. Press, 1987.

Medoff, Jeslyn. "The Daughters of Behn and the Problem of Reputation." In *Women, Writing, History, 1640–1740*. Ed. Isobel Grundy and Susan Wiseman. London: B. T. Batsford, 1992. 33–54.

Mendelson, Sara Heller. "Aphra Behn." In *The Mental World of Stuart Women: Three Studies*. Amherst: Univ. of Massachusetts Press, 1987.

Mermin, Dorothy. "Women Becoming Poets: Katherine Philips, Aphra Behn, Anne Finch." *ELH* 57 (1990): 335–55.

Messenger, Ann. "Novel into Play: Aphra Behn and Thomas Southerne." In *His and Hers: Essays in Restoration and Eighteenth-Century Literature*. Lexington: Univ. of Kentucky Press, 1986.

Munns, Jessica. "Barton and Behn's *The Rover*: or, The Text Transpos'd." *Restoration and 18th-Century Theatre Research* 3 (1988): 11–22.

———. " 'I by a Double Right Thy Bounties Claim': Aphra Behn and Sexual Space." In *Curtain Calls: British and American Women and the Theater, 1660–1820*. Ed. Mary Anne Schofield and Cecilia Macheski. Athens: Ohio Univ. Press, 1991. 193–210.

Musser, Joseph F., Jr. " 'Imposing Nought but Constancy in Love': Aphra Behn Snares *The Rover*." *Restoration* 3 (1979): 17–25.

O'Donnell, Mary Ann. *Aphra Behn: An Annotated Bibliography of Primary and Secondary Sources*. New York: Garland, 1986.

———. "A Verse Miscellany of Aphra Behn: Bodleian Library MS Firth c.16." *English Manuscript Studies* 2 (1990): 189–227.

Payne, Deborah C. " 'And Poets Shall by Patron-Princes Live': Aphra Behn and Patronage." In *Curtain Calls: British and American Women and the Theater, 1660–1820*. Ed. Mary Anne Schofield and Cecilia Macheski. Athens: Ohio Univ. Press, 1991. 105–19.

Pearson, Jacqueline. "Gender and Narrative in the Fiction of Aphra Behn." *Review of English Studies* 42 (1991): 40–56; 179–90.

———. *The Prostituted Muse: Images of Women and Women Dramatists, 1642–1737*. New York: St. Martins Press, 1988.

Pollak, Ellen. *The Poetics of Sexual Myth: Gender and Ideology in the Verse of Swift and Pope*. Chicago: Univ. of Chicago Press, 1985.

Quaintance, Richard. "French Sources of the Restoration 'Imperfect Enjoyment' Poem." *Philological Quarterly* 442 (1963): 190–99.

Rogers, Katharine M. "Fact and Fiction in Aphra Behn's *Oroonoko*." *Studies in the Novel* 20 (1988): 1–15.

Sackville-West, Vita. *Aphra Behn: The Incomparable Astrea*. New York: Viking, 1928.

Salzman, Paul. *English Prose Fiction, 1558–1700: A Critical History*. Oxford: Oxford Univ. Press, 1985.

Shulman, Jeff. "An Ovidian Echo in Behn's *The Rover*." *Notes and Queries* 229 (1984): 345–46.

Spencer, Jane. "Aphra Behn on the Eighteenth-Century Stage." *Studies on Voltaire and the Eighteenth Century* 304 (1992): 831–34.

————. "Not Being a Historian: Women Telling Tales in Restoration and Eighteenth-Century England." In *Contexts of Pre-Novel Narrative: The European Tradition*. Ed. Roy Eriksen. Berlin: Mouten de Gruyter, 1994. 319–40.

————. *The Rise of the Woman Novelist: From Aphra Behn to Jane Austen.* Oxford: Blackwell, 1986.

Spengemann, William C. "The Earliest American Novel: Aphra Behn's *Oroonoko.*" *Nineteenth-Century Literature* 38 (1984): 384–414.

Starr, G. A. "Aphra Behn and the Genealogy of the Man of Feeling." *Modern Philology* 87 (1990): 362–72.

Stiebel, Arlene. "Not since Sappho: The Erotic in Poems of Katherine Philips and Aphra Behn." In *Homosexuality in Renaissance and Enlightenment England: Literary Representations in Historical Context*. Ed. Claude J. Summers. New York: Haworth Press, 1992. 153–71.

————. "Subversive Sexuality: Masking the Erotic in Poems by Katherine Philips and Aphra Behn." *Renaissance Discourses of Desire*. Ed. Claude J. Summers and Ted-Larry Pebworth. Columbia: Univ. of Missouri Press, 1993. 223–36.

Taetzsch, Lynne. "Romantic Love Replaces Kinship Exchange in Aphra Behn's Restoration Drama." *Restoration* 17 (1993): 30–38.

Todd, Janet. "Aphra Behn: A Female Poet." *Studies on Voltaire and the Eighteenth Century* 304 (1992): 834–37.

————. " 'Rebellions Antidote': A New Attribution to Aphra Behn." *Notes and Queries* 236 (1991): 175–77.

————. *The Sign of Angellica: Women, Writing, and Fiction, 1660–1800.* London: Virago Press, 1989.

Veith, David M. *Attribution in Restoration Poetry.* New Haven: Yale Univ. Press, 1963.

Wehrs, Donald R. "Eros, Ethics, Identity: Royalist Feminism and the Politics of Desire in Aphra Behn's Love Letters." *Studies in English Literature* 32 (1992): 461–78.

Williamson, Marilyn. *Raising Their Voices: British Women Writers, 1650–1750.* Detroit: Wayne State Univ. Press, 1990.

Winn, James. *John Dryden and His World.* New Haven: Yale Univ. Press, 1987.

————. *"When Beauty Fires the Blood": Love and Arts in the Age of Dryden.* Ann Arbor: Univ. of Michigan Press, 1992.

Woodcock, George. *The Incomparable Aphra.* London: Boardman, 1948.

Young, Elizabeth V. "Aphra Behn, Gender, and Pastoral." *Studies in English Literature* 33 (1993): 523–43.

Zimbardo, Rose. "Aphra Behn: A Dramatist in Search of the Novel." In *Curtain Calls: British and American Women and the Theater, 1660–1820*. Ed. Mary Anne Schofield and Cecilia Macheski. Athens: Ohio Univ Press, 1991. 371–82.

————. "The Late Seventeenth-Century Dilemma in Discourse: Dryden's *Don Sebastian* and Behn's *Oroonoko.*" In *Rhetorics of Order/Ordering Rhetorics in English Neoclassical Literature*. Ed. J. Douglas Canfield and J. Paul Hunter. Newark: Univ. of Delaware Press, 1989. 46–67.

Anne Finch, Countess of Winchilsea. Miniature. (Reproduced by permission of the National Portrait Gallery, London.)

ANNE FINCH
COUNTESS OF WINCHILSEA
(1661–1720)

INTRODUCTION

Unlike many of her predecessors, Anne Finch, countess of Winchilsea, was both well-known as a poet in her own lifetime and widely praised and imitated after her death. She wrote in all of the poetic forms popular in her age— pindaric odes, verse epistles, songs, satires, mock heroics, Aesopean fables, paraphrases of the Bible, and two plays—and her work was respected by her Augustan contemporaries (most notably Pope and Swift), women poets throughout the eighteenth century, as well as the major Romantics. Despite the remarkable range and quality of Finch's poetry, her intelligence and wit, she has been largely misrepresented as a poet of nature and melancholy, her poetry described by Virginia Woolf in *A Room of One's Own* as "harmless . . . rambling about the fields and dreaming." Nothing could be further from the truth.

Anne Kingsmill was born in 1661 into a prominent royalist family, loyal to the Church of England. Although her parents died before she was four, her father—also purportedly a poet—left her (as well as her younger sister) a modest inheritance at age twenty-one, whether or not she chose to marry. Her father's will also charged that Anne and her sister should be educated in a serious manner, unlike most young women of their time. After being tossed between various litigious relatives for nearly two decades, Anne became maid of honor in 1682 to Maria Beatrice of Modena, second wife to James, duke of York. In later life, Finch recalled the lavish court of James and Mary as "paradise . . . e're innocence was lost" (see "On the Death of the Queen").

Italian-born and extremely pious (tradition claims she begged her father to let her become a nun rather than marry the future king of England), Mary of Modena brought a wealth of baroque art and literature to her English court. She was also fluent in four languages and, according to contemporary sources, greatly enjoyed time spent with the young women in her retinue. Most significantly, Mary of Modena encouraged her waiting women to act in plays; to read, write, and translate classics from French and Italian; and to write their own verse. Three of the women who attended the queen—Anne Killigrew, Anne Finch, and Sarah Churchill, later duchess of Marlborough—became published writers.

After her marriage to Heneage Finch in 1684, Anne and her husband stayed near court for a time, celebrating the coronation of James II in 1685. They left London abruptly in 1688, when William III and Mary II deposed James II in the Glorious (or Bloodless) Revolution. Ardent supporters of James II and later his son, "the Old Pretender," the Finches became nonjurors, refusing to take the oath of allegiance to William of Orange as the new king. Between their exile from court in 1688 and their inheritance of the Winchilsea title and estate in 1712, the Finches stayed with various friends and relatives around Kent, living what they both described as a happy and intellectually stimulating (though anything but lavish) life of genteel poverty. Although she wrote at least some of her poems earlier, in the 1690s Finch began circulating her poems both in private manuscript collections and in poetic miscellanies published through London's booksellers. Finch seems to have envisioned these two audiences quite differently: one private, elite, and of shared political sympathies; the other public and thus politically and socially unwieldy. In many ways her works straddle Cavalier and Augustan assumptions both about the form of individual poems, and about the overall shape of a volume of poems. As a poet, Finch was deeply indebted to the unlikely triumvirate of Katherine Philips, Aphra Behn, and John Milton.

Finch named her poetic speaker "Ardelia," from a minor figure in Philips's Society of Friendship. And like Philips she addressed many poems to other women, reworking metaphysical conceits about the relationships between women and men, and between written and spoken language. Unfortunately, also like Philips's "Orinda," Finch's persona has long been read, in simplistic and condescending fashion, as continuous with the poet herself. For while Finch's speaker often *claims* to retreat to shade and silence, to leave behind the contests of this world and hope for triumph in the world-to-come, her poems return to those submerged conflicts again and again, unwilling finally to stifle their rebellious muse into obedience and submission. In order to shape this rhetorical posture of indifference and retreat, Finch often softened—or, in several cases, completely excised—the political and religious conflicts explicit in manuscript poems, when she and her husband prepared the poems for publication in *Miscellany Poems, On Several Occasions* (1713).

Like many Royalist and Jacobite women writers of the late seventeenth century, Finch was inspired by the oppositional voice of radical Protestantism—and especially Milton's epic, *Paradise Lost* (1667). Unlike Protestant mystics and prophets, however, Finch toned down her fiercest polemic for public circulation. For instance, in one of her widely anthologized poems, "The Nightingale," the lines about political conflict—"factions" and "false opinions"—found in the manuscript were excluded from every published edition. Such deletions tend to move Finch away from the satiric and narrative poetic traditions of the seventeenth century toward the lyric intensity for which she was later valued by Romantic poets such as William Wordsworth and Percy Shelley (the latter, like Alexander Pope her contemporary, recycled some of her best lines in his own verse). Yet Finch's manuscript poems, as well as letters and other primary documents, reveal a life of pain and self-doubt, both as a woman poet and as a supporter of the ousted James II.

Finch's first poem published outside a poetic miscellany was the "Poem on the Death of King James." Published cheaply (in at least two different versions) and anonymously just after James's death, the elegy contains a nearly hagiographic account of the king's youth and early military triumphs, and a call to other supporters of James to put their politically dangerous feelings into verse. The poem ends with the speaker's rhetorical "retreat" into the "solitary" life of a political outsider, a gesture Finch would use time and again when the storms of political and religious conflict placed her poetry and her life at odds with established authorities. That same year, Finch published her breathtaking pindaric "The Spleen"—with its fierce criticism of fashionable society, and another veiled attack on William III's authority—in one of publisher Charles Gildon's numerous poetic miscellanies, marking her slow but steady entrance into the urban world of London's booksellers. Other poems must have been circulating around London before they were published in *Miscellany Poems* in 1713, since Delariver Manley had copies of at least three of them and included them in her notorious *New Atalantis* (1709), a roman à clef that worked as Tory polemic against the Whigs in the election that year (Anderson 95–96).

The selections included here suggest the range of Finch's poetic output, and the ways she reworks patterns found in earlier women's poetry, particularly the friendship topos of Katherine Philips and the assertive public voice of playwright, poet, and novelist Aphra Behn. Although Finch seems at first to chastise Behn in rather predictable fashion in "The Circuit of Apollo" by claiming that she wrote "too loosely," the end of Finch's poem alludes to the conclusion of Behn's "On Desire," revealing indirectly her knowledge of and pleasure in Behn's works. The odd spellings and tangled biblical allusions in "The Introduction" suggest Finch's awareness of the ways public criticism acts to inhibit women's public writing—censure acting as self-censorship, to use Finch's own pun. "Fanscomb Barn" is an hilarious parody of *Paradise Lost*. At the same time that Finch mocks Milton's pretentious diction, she delights in his incursions into biblical texts and their authority, and like him reenters an imaginary, paradisiacal garden. Finch was acutely aware of the ways women's voices and desires—like those of Milton's Eve—were in the late seventeenth century central though stifled. And even when silenced, their works were suppressed in strikingly public ways, which ironically tended to draw more women into poetry and print.

What, finally, does Finch have to offer to the modern reader? Her poems urge women to imitate heroic models, not to be limited by the lives others might choose for them, to thrive and soar in the imagination, even when they cannot do so in public life. Her uncanny explorations of natural images, Miltonic themes, and concerns about the boundaries of public and private life, grounded in her painful experience of political exile, became a hundred years later the primary tropes of romanticism: psyche, solitude, and shade. She thus provides a crucial connection between women's poetry of the seventeenth and eighteenth centuries and between women's voices and men's, in the transformation of poetic discourse over the long eighteenth century.

SELECTED POEMS

The Introduction[1]

Did I my lines intend for public view,
How many censures[2] would their faults pursue.
Some would because such words they do affect,

---

1. This manuscript poem was not published until the twentieth century.
2. Adverse judgement or hostile criticism.

Cry they're insipid, empty, uncorrect.
And many have attain'd, dull and untaught,   5
The name of wit[3] only by finding fault.
True judges might condemn their want of wit,
And all might say, they're by a woman writ.
Alas! a woman that attempts the pen,
Such an intruder on the rights of men,   10
Such a presumptuous creature is esteem'd,
The fault can by no virtue be redeem'd.
They tell us, we mistake our sex and way;
Good breeding, fashion, dancing, dressing, play
Are the accomplishments we should desire;   15
To write, or read, or think, or to enquire
Would cloud our beauty, and exhaust our time,
And interrupt the conquests of our prime;[4]
Whilst the dull mannage[5] of a servile house
Is held by some our outmost[6] art and use.   20

Sure 'twas not ever thus; nor are we told
Fables of women that excell'd of old,
To whom, by the diffusive hand of Heaven,
Some share of wit and poetry was given.
On that glad day on which the Ark return'd,[7]   25
The holy pledge for which the land had mourn'd,
The joyful tribes attend it on the way—
The Levites[8] do the sacred charge convey,
Whilst various instruments before it play;
Here, holy virgins[9] in the consort join,   30
The louder notes to soften and refine,
And with alternate verse, complete the hymn divine.

Lo! the young poet,[10] after God's own heart,
By Him inspir'd and taught the Muses' art,
Return'd from conquest a bright chorus meets,   35
That sing his slain ten thousand in the streets.
In such loud numbers they his acts declare,
Proclaim the wonders of his early war,
That Saul upon the vast applause does frown,

3. Person of lively verbal skill.
4. "conquests of our prime": love interests, in which women were expected to spend their youth.
5. Housekeeping.
6. Utmost.
7. In ll. 25–32 Finch joins elements from several stories: the Philistines's stealing the ark of the covenant (I Samuel 5), David's triumphal procession as king of Israel (II Samuel 1–6), and the return of the ark to Jerusalem (I Kings 8).
8. The priestly class responsible for attending the ark.
9. The "holy virgins" are Finch's addition; the biblical story, in contrast, emphasizes the attraction of both women and men to the charismatic David.
10. David, supposed author of the biblical book of Psalms. David won the hand of Saul's daughter, Michal, in battle, but Saul feared David's appeal to the masses and tried to have him killed; David was saved by Michal's brother, Jonathan, who also loved him (I Samuel 18–19).

And feels its mighty thunder shake the crown.   40
What, can the threaten'd judgment now prolong?
Half of the kingdom is already gone;
The fairest half, whose influence guides the rest,
Have David's empire o're their hearts confessed.[11]
   A woman[12] here, leads fainting Israel on,   45
She fights, she wins, she triumphs with a song,
Devout, majestic, for the subject fit,
And far above her arms exalts her wit.
Then, to the peaceful, shady palm withdraws,
And rules the rescu'd nation with her laws.   50

   How are we fallen, fallen by mistaken rules?
And education's more than nature's fools,[13]
Debarr'd from all improvements of the mind,
And to be dull, expected, and design'd;
And if some one would soar above the rest,   55
With warmer fancy, and ambition pressed,
So strong, th'opposing faction still appears,
The hopes to thrive can ne'er outweigh the fears.
Be caution'd then my Muse, and still retir'd;
Nor be despis'd aiming to be admir'd;   60
Conscious of wants, still with contracted wing,
To some few friends, and to thy sorrows sing;
For groves of laurel[14] thou wert never meant;
Be dark enough thy shades,[15] and be thou there content.

On Affliction

Welcome, what e're my tender flesh may say,
   Welcome affliction, to my reason, still,
Though hard, and rugged on that rock I lay,[1]
   A sure foundation, which if rais'd with skill,
     Shall compass Babel's aim, and reach th'Almighty's hill.   5

Welcome the rod that does adoption[2] shew,

---

11. I.e., David has conquered "half the kingdom" (the women) with his charm.
12. Deborah, ruler of Israel, whose song of triumph is found in Judges 5.
13. ll. 51–52: In the final fourteen lines, Finch works against Milton's description in *Paradise Lost* of Eve as closer to nature and therefore more vulnerable to temptation. Finch claims that women are not naturally "fools," ones "deficient in judgement or sense"; in contrast, women's lack of education, their training in "mistaken rules," constitutes their fall from sense and judgment.
14. In ancient Greece, laurel wreaths were used to crown poets (the poet laureate).
15. Shadows; also spirits of the underworld.
1. God as a rock of salvation (see, e.g., Jeremiah 49:16); alluding also to Prometheus, who was chained to a rock, where his liver was perpetually eaten by an eagle, as punishment for his gift of fire to humankind. The phrase rests on the notion that affliction and redemption, to be true, must be undiluted.
2. Adoption into a community of chosen people and redemption of the body.

The cup whose wholesome dregs[3] are giv'n me here;
There is a day behind, if God be true,
    When all these clouds shall pass and heav'n be clear,
    When those whom most they shade, shall shine most   10
        glorious there.

Affliction is the line which every saint
    Is measur'd by, his stature taken right;
So much it shrinks, as they repine or faint,
    But if their faith and courage stand upright,
    By that is made the crown, and the full robe of light.[4]   15

On My Self

Good Heav'n, I thank thee, since it was design'd
I should be fram'd, but of the weaker kind,[1]
That yet my soul is loosen'd from the love
Of all those trifles, which their passions move.
Pleasures, and praise, and plenty have with me   5
But their just value; if allow'd they be,
Freely and thankfully as much I taste,
As will not reason, or religion waste.
If they're deny'd, I on my self can live,
And slight those aids unequal chance does give;   10
When in the sun, my wings can be display'd,
And in retirements, I can bless the shade.[2]

Ardelia to Melancholy

At last, my old inveterate foe,
No opposition shalt thou know,
Since I by struggling can obtain
Nothing, but increase of pain.
I will at last, no more do so,   5
Tho' I confess, I have apply'd
Sweet mirth, and music, and have try'd
A thousand other arts besides,
To drive thee from my darken'd breast,

---

3. See Isaiah 51:17–23 and Revelations 14:10; in ancient times the dregs at the bottom of the wineglass were used for divination.
4. See Revelations 6:11.
1. According to both Jewish and Christian sources, the female body was considered to be weaker than the male body and more susceptible to temptation.
2. Cf. "The Introduction," ll. 63–64.

Thou, who hast banish'd all my rest.   10
    But, though sometimes a short reprieve they gave,
Unable they and far too weak to save;
All arts to quell did but augment thy force,
As rivers check'd, break with a wilder course.

    Friendship, I to my heart have laid,   15
Friendship, th' applauded sov'rain aid,
And thought that charm, so strong would prove,
As to compel thee to remove;
And to my self I boasting said,
    Now, I a conqueror sure shall be,   20
The end of all my conflicts see,
And noble triumph, wait on me;
My dusky, sullen foe will sure
Ne'er this united charge endure.
    But leaning on this reed,[1] ev'n whilst I spoke,   25
It pierc'd my hand, and into pieces broke.
Still, some new object, or new int'rest came
And loos'd the bands, and quite dissolv'd the claim.

    These failing, I invok'd a Muse,
And poetry would often use   30
To guard me from thy tyrant pow'r,
And to oppose thee ev'ry hour
New troops of fancies did I choose.
    Alas! in vain, for all agree
To yield me captive up to thee,   35
And heav'n alone can set me free.
Thou, through my life wilt with me go,
And make the passage sad, and slow.
    All that could ere thy ill got rule invade,
Their useless arms before thy feet have laid;   40
The fort is thine, now ruin'd all within,
Whilst by decays without, thy conquest too is seen.

To the Echo.
In a Clear Night upon Astrop Walks

Say lovely Nymph,[1] where dost thou dwell?
Where is that secret, sylvan seat,
That melancholy, sweet retreat,
From whence thou dost these notes repel,

1. Cane.
1. The nymph Echo loved the vain Narcissus and pined away; when she died, only her voice remained, repeating the ends of others' words.

And moving syllables repeat?   5
Oh! lovely Nymph, our joys to swell,
Thy hollow, leafy mansion tell,
Or if thou only charm'st the ear,
And never wilt to sight appear,
But dost alone in voice excel,   10
Still with it, fix us here.

    Where Cynthia[2] lends her gentle light,
Whilst the appeas'd, expanded air,
A passage for thee does prepare,
And Strephon's[3] tuneful voice invite,   15
Thine, a soft part with him to bear.
Oh pleasure! when thou'dst take a flight
Beyond thy common mortal height,
When to thy sphere above thou'dst press,
And men like angels thou would'st bless,[4]   20
Thy season be like this, fair night,
And harmony thy dress.

A Letter to Daphnis[1] April the 2nd: 1685

This, to the crown and blessing of my life,
The much lov'd husband of a happy wife.
To him, whose constant passion found the art
To win a stubborn and ungrateful heart;
And to the world by tend'rest proof discovers   5
They err, who say that husbands can't be lovers.
With such return of passion as is due,
Daphnis I love, Daphnis my thoughts pursue;
Daphnis, my hopes, my joys, are bounded all in you.
Ev'n I, for Daphnis and my promise sake,   10
What I in women censure, undertake,
But this from love, not vanity proceeds;
You know who writes, and I who 'tis that reads.
Judge not my passion by my want of skill,
Many love well though they express it ill;   15
And I your censure could with pleasure bear,
Would you but soon return and speak it here.

---

2. The moon.
3. Strephon was a conventional pastoral name for a shepherd.
4. Ll. 19–20: the echo becoming like the music of heaven, the "sphere above."
1. Finch's pastoral name for her husband, Heneage Finch, comes from the second-century Greek
   romance *Daphnis and Chloe*, which describes the awakening of desire in two young lovers.

To Mr. F. now Earl of W.

(Who going abroad had desired Ardelia to write some Verses upon
whatever subject she thought fit, against his Return in the Evening)[1]

Written in the Year 1689.

No sooner, Flavio,[2] was you gone,
But your injunction thought upon,
   Ardelia took the pen;
Designing to perform the task,
Her Flavio did so kindly ask,   5
   Ere he returned again.

Unto Parnassus[3] straight she sent,
And bid the messenger that went
   Unto the Muses court,
Assure them, she their aid did need,   10
And begg'd they'd use their utmost speed,
   Because the time was short.

The hasty summons was allow'd;
And being well-bred, they rose and bow'd,
   And said, they'd post[4] away;   15
That well they did Ardelia know,
And that no female's voice below
   They sooner would obey.

That many of that rhyming train,
On like occasions sought in vain   20
   Their industry[5] t'excite,
But for Ardelia all they'd leave;
Thus flatt'ring can the Muse deceive,
   And wheedle us to write.

Yet, since there was such haste requir'd,   25
To know the subject 'twas desir'd,
   On which they must infuse;
That they might temper words and rules,
And with their counsel carry tools,
   As country-doctors use.   30

Wherefore to cut off all delays,
'Twas soon reply'd, a *husband*'s praise

1. Mr. F. now Earl of W.: the poet's husband, Heneage Finch, became fourth earl of Winchilsea in 1712. "abroad": out of doors, away from home. "Ardelia": the persona Finch adopted as the speaker of her poems; the name comes from Katherine Philips's Society of Friendship. "against": before.
2. Another poetic name for Finch's husband.
3. Mountain north of Delphi in Greece, sacred to Apollo and the Muses.
4. Make haste.
5. Work.

(Tho' in these looser times)
Ardelia gladly would rehearse
A *husband*'s, who indulg'd her verse,   35
And now requir'd her rhymes.

A *husband!* echo'd all around:
And to Parnassus sure that sound
    Had never yet been sent;
Amazement in each face was read,   40
In haste th' affrighted sisters[6] fled,
    And unto council went.

Erato[7] cry'd, since Grizel's[8] days,
Since Troy-Town pleas'd, and Chivey-chace,[9]
    No such design was known;   45
And 'twas their bus'ness, to take care,
It reach'd not to the public ear,
    Or got about the town;

Nor came where ev'ning beaux were met
O'er billet-doux, and chocolate,[10]   50
    Lest it destroy'd the house;
For in that place, who could dispense
(That wore his clothes with common sense)
    With mention of a *spouse?*

'Twas put unto the vote at last,   55
And in the negative it passed,
    None to her aid should move;
Yet, since Ardelia was a friend,[11]
Excuses 'twas agreed to send,
    Which plausible might prove;   60

That Pegasus[12] of late had been
So often rid thro' thick and thin,
    With neither fear nor wit;
In panegyric been so spurr'd,
He could not from the stall be stirr'd,   65
    Nor would endure the bit.

Melpomene[13] had given a bond,
By the new house alone to stand,

6. "The Muses—Erato, Melpomene, Thalia, Urania, &c." (Finch's note).
7. Muse of lyric and love poetry.
8. The story of Patient Griselda is told in Boccaccio's *Decameron* (c. 1350) and Chaucer's "Clerk's Tale."
9. "Troy-Town": Homer's *Iliad*. "Chivey-chace": "The Ballad of Chevy Chase," one of the oldest English ballads, tells of rival families and national conflict between England and Scotland.
10. In the early eighteenth century coffee (or chocolate) houses were a popular place for men—and occasionally women—to meet casually. "Beaux": suitors; "billet-doux": love letters.
11. Friend of the muses, i.e., a poet.
12. Winged horse associated with poetry.
13. Muse of tragedy.

And write of war and strife;[14]
Thalia,[15] she had taken fees,   70
And stipends from the patentees,
    And durst not for her life.[16]

Urania[17] only lik'd the choice;
Yet not to thwart the public voice,
    She whisp'ring did impart: 75
They need no foreign aid invoke,
No help to draw a moving stroke,
    Who dictate from the heart.

Enough! the pleas'd Ardelia cry'd;
And slighting ev'ry Muse beside,   80
    Consulting now her breast,
Perceiv'd that ev'ry tender thought,
Which from abroad she'd vainly sought,
    Did there in silence rest;

And should unmoved that post maintain,   85
Till in his quick return again,
    Met in some neighb'ring grove,
(Where vice nor vanity appear)
Her Flavio them alone might hear,
    In all the sounds of love.   90

For since the world does so despise
Hymen's[18] endearments and its ties,
    They should mysterious be;
Till we that pleasure too possess
(Which makes their fancy'd happiness)   95
    Of stolen secrecy.

The Tree

Fair Tree! for thy delightful shade,
'Tis just that some return be made;
Sure, some return is due from me,
To thy cool shadows, and to thee.
When thou to birds do'st shelter give,   5
Thou music do'st from them receive;
If travelers beneath thee stay,
Till storms have worn themselves away,

14. Ll. 67–69: i.e., she writes for the new government.
15. Muse of pastoral.
16. Ll. 67–72: While early in the poem the muses were "well-bred" ladies (l. 14), these lines suggest that the Revolution has lowered them to the conflicts of the political and literary marketplace.
17. "Urania is the Heavenly Muse, and suppos'd to inspire thoughts of Vertue" (Finch's note). Urania is also Milton's muse; see *Paradise Lost* VII.1–11.
18. Hymen was the ancient deity of marriage.

That time in praising thee they spend,
And thy protecting pow'r commend;   10
The shepherd here, from scorching freed,
Tunes to thy dancing leaves his reed,
Whilst his lov'd nymph in thanks bestows
Her flow'ry chaplets[1] on thy boughs.
Shall I then only silent be,   15
And no return be made by me?
No; let this wish upon thee wait,
And still to flourish be thy fate,
To future ages may'st thou stand
Untouch'd by the rash workman's hand,   20
'Till that large stock of sap is spent,
Which gives thy summer's ornament;
'Till the fierce winds that vainly strive
To shock thy greatness whilst alive,
Shall on thy lifeless hour attend,   25
Prevent the axe, and grace thy end;
Their scatter'd strength together call,
And to the clouds proclaim thy fall,
Who then their ev'ning-dews may spare,
When thou no longer art their care;   30
But shalt like ancient heroes burn,
And some bright hearth be made thy urn.[2]

Fanscomb Barn.
In Imitation of Milton.[1]

In Fanscomb Barn (who knows not Fanscomb Barn?)
Seated between the sides of rising hills,
Whose airy tops o'er-look the Gallic seas,[2]
Whilst gentle Stower[3] thy waters near them flow,
To beautify the seats that crown thy banks.   5
——————————————In this retreat,
Through ages past consign'd for harbor meet,
And place of sweet repose to wand'rers poor,[4]
The weary Strolepedon[5] felt that ease,
Which many a dangerous borough had deny'd   10

1. Garlands.
2. Ll. 31–32: i.e., may you end as firewood.
1. "Fanscomb Barn" is a burlesque of Milton's *Paradise Lost* (1667, hereafter *PL*).
2. English Channel.
3. Stour, river in Kent.
4. "Fanscomb-Barn, near Wye in Kent, is a privileg'd Retreat for Beggars" (Finch's note).
5. The characters' names are comic: "Strolepedon" is an onomatopoeia, "stroll up and down"; "Budgeta," meaning purse, refers to the couple's poverty. Their dog, "Trundle," runs off to fetch them food.

To him,[6] and his Budgeta lov'd compeer;[7]
Nor food was wanting to the happy pair,
Who with meek aspect, and precarious tone,
Well suited to their hunger and degree,
Had mov'd the hearts of hospitable dames,   15
To furnish such repast as nature crav'd.
Whilst more to please the swarthy bowl appears,
Replete with liquor, globulous to sight,
And threat'ning inundation o'er the brim;
Yet, ere it to the longing lips was rais'd   20
Of him who held it at its due desert,
And more than all entreated bounty priz'd,
Into the strong profundity he throws
The floating healths of females, blithe and young,
Who there had rendezvouz'd in past delight,   25
And to stol'n plenty added clamorous mirth,
With song and dance, and every jovial prank
Befitting buxom crew, untied by forms;[8]
Whilst kind Budgeta nam'd such sturdy youths,
As next into her tender thoughts revolv'd,   30
And now were straggling East, and West, and South,
Hoof-beating,[9] and at large, as chance directs,
Still shifting paths, lest men (tho' stil'd of peace)[10]
Should urge their calmer thoughts to iron war,
Or force them to promote coercive laws,   35
Beating that hemp which oft entraps their lives;
Or into cordage pleated, and amass'd,
Deprives unruly flesh of tempting skin.[11]
Thus kind remembrance brought the absent near
And hasten'd the return of either's pledge;   40
Brown[12] were the toasts, but not unsav'ry found,
To fancies clear'd by exercise and air,
Which the spirituous nectar[13] still improves,
And gliding now thro' ev'ry cherish'd vein,
New warmth diffus'd, new cogitations bred,   45
With self-conceit of person, and of parts.[14]
When Strolepedon (late distorted wight,[15]
Limb-wanting to the view, and all mis-shap'd)

6. Ll. 9–11: In the seventeenth century, harsh laws against vagrancy did not distinguish between indigence and crime.
7. Equal.
8. The women are playful and unresisting, not restrained by cumbersome rules or clothing.
9. Going on foot, with a hint of the devil's cloven hoof.
10. Justices of the Peace were responsible for enforcing local laws against vagrancy.
11. Ll. 36–38: One of the few types of work available to the vagrant poor was beating or processing hemp plants, in effect helping to make the cords that bind them.
12. Gloomy, serious (because about friends who have been bound and beaten by local authorities).
13. Liquor.
14. Cf. *PL* IV.801–19 and IX.598–604.
15. Warrior, but could also be a diminutive.

Permits a pinion'd arm to fill the sleeve,
Erst pendant, void, and waving with the wind, 50
The timber-leg obsequiously withdraws,
And gives to that of bone precedence due.[16]
Thus undisguis'd that form again he wears,
Which damsel fond had drawn from household toils,
And strict behests of parents, old and scorn'd; 55
Whilst farther yet his intellects confess
The boozy spell dilated and enhanc'd,
Ripe for description and set turns of speech,
Which to conjugal spouse were thus addressed:[17]
My wife (acknowledg'd such thro' maunding tribes, 60
As long as mutual love, the only law,[18]
Of hedge or barn, can bind our easy faiths)
Be thou observant of thy husband's voice,
Sole auditor of flights and figures bold;
Know, that the valley which we hence descry 65
Richly adorn'd, is Fanscomb-Bottom call'd;
But whether from these walls it takes the name,
Or they from that, let antiquaries tell,
And men, well-read in stories obsolete,
Whilst such denomination either claims, 70
As speaks affinity contiguous———
Thence let thy scatter'd sight, and oft-griev'd smell
Engulf the sweets, and colors free dispos'd
To flowers promiscuous, and redundant plants.[19]
And (if the drowsy vapor will admit, 75
Which from the bowl soon triumphs o'er thy lids,
And thee the weaker vessel still denotes)
With looks erect[20] observe the verdant slope
Of graceful hills, fertile in bush and brake,[21]
Whose height attain'd, th'expatiated[22] downs 80
Shall wider scenes display of rural glee;
Where banner'd lords, and fair escutcheon'd[23] knights,
With gentle squires, and the staff-griping clown,
Pursue the trembling prey impetuous;
Which yet escaping, when the night returns, 85
And downy beds enfold their careless limbs,
More wakeful Trundle (knapsack-bearing cur)

16. Ll. 48–52: i.e., he takes out his seemingly missing arm and takes off his false wooden leg.
17. Cf. Adam and Eve's conversation, *PL* IV.610–88.
18. Cf. *PL* III.68 and IV.750; unlike Milton, Strolepedon does not distinguish between innocent ("wedded") and fallen ("free") love.
19. Cf. *PL* IV.230–71 and IX.205–12.
20. Cf. *PL* IV.288–89 and IX.501.
21. Thicket.
22. Enlarged upon.
23. With shields bearing heraldic coats of arms; cf. *PL* I.579ff.

Follows the scent untrac'd by nobler hounds,
And brings to us the fruit of all their toil.

Thus sung the Bard, whom potent liquor rais'd,   90
Nor so contented, wish'd sublimer aid.
Ye wits! (he cry'd) ye poets! (loiterers vain,
Who like to us, in idleness and want
Consume fantastic hours) hither repair,
And tell to list'ning mendicants[24] the cause   95
Of wonders, here observ'd but not discuss'd;
   Where the white sparrow never soil'd her plumes,
   Nor the dull russet clothes the snowy mouse.[25]
To Helicon[26] you might the spring compare,
That flows near Pickersdane renowned stream,[27]   100
Which, for disport and play, the youths frequent,
Who, train'd in learned school of ancient Wye,[28]
First at this fount suck in the Muses' lore,
When mixed with product of the Indian cane,
They drink delicious draughts, and part inspir'd,   105
Fit for the banks of Isis, or of Cham.[29]
(For Cham and Isis to the Bard were known,
A servitor,[30] when young in college-hall,
Tho' vagrant liberty he early chose,
Who yet, when drunk, retain'd poetic phrase.)   110
Nor should (quoth he) that Well, o'erhung with shade,[31]
Amidst those neighb'ring trees of dateless growth,
Be left unfathom'd by your nicer skill
Who thence could extricate a thousand charms,
Or to oblivious Lethe[32] might convert   115
The stagnant waters of the sleepy pool.
But most unhappy was that Morphean[33] sound
For lull'd Budgeta, who had long desir'd
Dismission fair from tales not throughly scann'd,[34]
Thinking her love a sympathy confessed,   120
When the word *Sleepy* parted from his lips,
Sunk affable and easy to that rest,
Which straw affords to minds unvex'd with cares.

---

24. Beggars.
25. "Fanscomb-Barn is famous for Breeding White Sparrows and White Mice" (Finch's note).
26. Mountain in Greece sacred to the Muses.
27. "Pickersdane, is a Point of Wye-Downs, where there is an excellent Spring, much frequented by the Scholars of the Free-School at Wye; who meet there, to drink the Water with Sugar; which has been an ancient Custom, and a great Diversion to them" (Finch's note).
28. Ll. 90–94 and 99–110 describe Wye College.
29. Rivers on whose banks Oxford ("Isis") and Cambridge ("Cham") Universities are located.
30. Waiter.
31. "A very deep Well, within a little Wood near Fanscomb-Barn" (Finch's note).
32. River of forgetfulness in the underworld.
33. Morpheus was the Greek god of dreams.
34. Lacking perfect poetic meter.

An Elegy on the Death of King James.[1]
By a Lady.

If the possession of imperial sway,
    Thou hadst by death, unhappy Prince, resign'd,
    And to a mournful successor made way,
    Whil'st all was uncontested, all combin'd:
How had the streets? How had the palace rung,   5
    In praise of thy acknowledg'd worth?
What had our numerous writers then brought forth?
    What melancholy dirges had they sung?
        What weeping elegies prepar'd;
If not from loyal grief, yet to obtain reward?   10
Thus is that gift (which Heaven did, sure bestow
      To elevate the hearts of men,
And lead them to those blissful seats again,
Whence all harmonious sounds, and lofty numbers flow)
Now, Mammon,[2] turn'd thy slave, to dig thy mines below.   15

II.

But Royal James, tho' none shall pay this verse,
    Bred in a land not honor'd with thy hearse;
    But Royal James, who never shall return
To cheer those hearts, which did thy sorrows mourn,
Who never shall the woes, the wants repair,   20
Which for thy sake, have been thy followers' share,
    Tho' with thy latest breath such prospects fled;
And all who saw thee die, now wish themselves as dead.
      Yet shall a free disinterested Muse,
In chosen lines, perform that task,   25
Which does an abler writer ask;
    But abler writers will the work refuse:
And where, Alas! 'twill but the feather cost,
The noblest subjects for the pen, are lost.

III.

Else how would the poetic crew,   30
    Those public heralds of immortal fame,
      Unto the present times renew
All which the past, did with such wonder view,
    And down to future ages would proclaim
What future ages scarce would take for true: 35
When they describe thee on the stage of war,
      Earlier than Caesar far,[3]

---

1. James (1633–1701), duke of York and later James II, king of England from 1685 to 1688. Finch, a maid of honor to James's second wife, Mary of Modena, remained a supporter of James and Mary after the Glorious Revolution of 1688.
2. Riches.
3. "He [i.e., James] was Born 1633, and was i[n] the Battel at Edgehill, Anno 1642" (Finch's note).

And made thee, e're thy tenth accomplish'd year,
　　　　Undaunted in the lists appear,
And martial lightnings see, and martial thunder hear: 40
Which Caesar never prov'd, nor the Tenth Legion knew.[4]
　　　　Next had they shown thee in the Gallic host,[5]
Performing such stupend'ous things,
　　　　As influenc'd the fates of kings;
Whilst the best general which the world could boast,[6]   45
　　　　Tho' ready to resign his breath,
Assur'd his troops they should not feel his death,
　　If that illustrious York would fill th'important post.
　　Thus would they, thy exalted valor raise,
By Turrenne form'd, and stamped with Turrenne's praise,   50
　　O'er seas and lands (as seas and land have seen
　　Thee greatly brave) that fame had sounded been,
Which to the skies was born, in Opdam's fiery blaze:[7]
　　　　High o'er the invading fleet, the vessel rose,
By thy prevailing batt'ries driven,   55
　　Which, like a streaming meteor, dreadful shows,
Now threatning from the illuminated air,
　　To all beneath it, ruin and despair,
　　　　As heathen wits are said to have inkindled heaven,
Till down at length, the plague portended came,   60
And wrought such various deaths, that some must want a name.
Oh mighty Prince! for here thy darkned lot,
　　　　Must be in this reverse of sight forgot:

---

4. "The 10th Legion was the most Valiant and Favoured of Julius Caesar's Legions" (Finch's note).
5. France.
6. "When very young, he was in the French Service, and a Lieutenant-General under Marischal Turrenne against the Spaniards, where he behaved himself with that Valour and Conduct, that when Turrenne was so Sick, as it was thought he could not live; the King of France sending for his Advice, who should Command the Army, if he should not recover: He answered the King, That if he would have his Affairs prosper, he should make choice of that Noble, Valourous and Heroick Prince the D[uke] of York.——In that Famous Action, when Turrenne forced the Spanish Trenches altho' Defended by Condé, and relieved Arras, the Duke of York behaved himself with remarkable Bravery, and was wounded. As in the French Translation of Cardinal Mazarine's Life, written Originally in Italian by Count Gualdo" (Finch's note). Henri de la Tour d'Auvergne, vicomte de Turrenne (1611–1715) led the royalist army supporting Anne of Austria, her minor son Louis XIV and Cardinal Jules Mazarin (1602–61) in the Fronde, a series of civil wars in France roughly contemporary with the English Civil Wars. The Prince of Condé, Louis II de Bourbon (1621–86, "The Great Condé") led the opposition army. James made a stunning diplomatic victory for Turrenne in 1652 and they remained lifelong friends. James was second in command to Turrenne at the relief of Arras, in August 1654, where Turrenne was slightly wounded. When Turrenne was called away to court in September 1654 (he was not ill), he left James in command of the French army, which was not engaged in battle at the time. Finch's description draws on Galeazzo Gualdo Priorato's hagiographic biography of Mazarin, translated in French as *Histoire du ministère du cardinal Jules Mazarin* (1671) and in English as *History of the Managements of Cardinal Julio Mazarine* (1671; rep. 1691).
7. "In the first Dutch War after the Restauration, the Duke of York commanded the Fleet, beat the Dutch, blew up their Admiral Opdam in the Orange-Tree. And in an Engagement afterwards, he behaved himself with that Bravery, that he was forc'd three Times to change his Ship, and take himself to the Long-boat, on which he hois'd the Admiral['s] Flag, and braved the Fury of his Enemies, till he recovered another Ship, which he parted not with whilst she continued capable of Service. For all which Services, the Parliament, with great Commendation of his Valour and conduct, made him a Magnificent Present, as appears upon their Journals" (Finch's note).

All must be glorious, whilst thy youth we trace,
Whilst sheltering waves shall British shores embrace,   65
    Or whilst our records shall have place;
        Where thy rewards and attributes are such,
      As shew no gratitude was thought too much,
    For keeping England then superior to the Dutch:
Whilst these shall last, no envy shall deface,   70
Of that triumphant day, th' advantage and the grace.

IV.

Yet even in youth, war ne'er was thy delight,
    Nor led by thee, but in the nation's right;
    Which well asserted, and the soldier paid,
The honor rescu'd, and the gainful trade;   75
        The solid business wisely done,
        And each who shar'd the generous cause
    Possess'd too of the share that he had won,
    The warrantable spoils, the favor and applause:
Again commissions ceas'd, and arms apart were laid.   80
    So good dictators fought for ancient Rome,
And brought not single fame, but peace and plenty home:
    Nor bred new strifes to keep that ample sway,
    But to the plough return'd,[8] could cheerfully obey.
So had our Charles,[9] whilst reigning, cause to own   85
    (The power recall'd, which his great seal had
      shown[)]
    The readiest subject stood the next his throne.
Oh you who under James in fight were try'd,
    Who strove successful by that Prince's side,
Who've seen him brave the cannon's angry breath;   90
      For Britain's interest and renown,
      As if he'd courted, rather than her crown,
    (Which was his right of birth) to merit it by death.
Oh you who in his frequent dangers stood,
And fought to fence them at the expense of blood,   95
    Now let your tears a heavier tribute pay,
      Give the becoming sorrow way:
      Nor bring bad parallels upon the times,
    By seeking, thro' mistaken fears,
To curb your sighs, or to conceal your tears;   100
'Twas but in Nero's days, that sighs and tears were crimes.[10]

---

8. "to the plough return'd": a commonplace of royalist panegyric was the notion that the Stuart monarchs returned to a pastoral life when war was over.
9. Charles II (1630–85), king of England from 1660 to 1685. James was his younger brother and next in line for the throne after his death.
10. Nero (A.D.37–68), Roman emperor (A.D.54–68), notorious for his zeal in making Christians scapegoats for the fire that destroyed half of Rome in A.D.64. "Tears" thus suggest religious martyrdom as well as emotional triumph.

V.

Weep then ye realms,[11] who once his sway confessed,
Who had he been of your belief possessed,
Amongst the kings that have laid down
(As all must do) at death's cold feet, the crown,   105
Him had you sure enroll'd, and justly, with the best:
Then Alfred's piety had form'd his praise,[12]
His thoughtful nights compar'd, and his assiduous days:
Then had that providential care,
Which kept the treasury full yet not the subject bare,   110
Unto our frugal Henry[13] been preferr'd,
Applauses of that temprance had we heard;
By whose example had excluded been
What even Eliza's days brought in,[14]
The wasting foul excess, miscall'd, good-natur'd sin.   115

VI.

Weep ye attendants, who compo[s]'d his train,
And no observance spent in vain,
Nor ever, with uneasy fears,
Contracted needful debts, and doubled your arrears.
All whom his justice, or his bounty fed,   120
Now grateful weep, and mix the silent dew
(Which none will e'er suspect untrue)
With your embittered draughts, and since diminish'd bread.
You who subordinate in public cares
For his inspection, model'd the affairs,   125
Remember still, how easy your access,
No pleasures kept him from your sight,
No late debauch, no revel of the night,
No distant slothful seat e'er serv'd as a recess.
Open to all: But when the seaman came,   130
Known by his face, and greeted by his name,
Peculiar smiles and praises did impart
To all, his prowess and desert;
All had his willing hand, the sailor had his heart;
Who born an islander, by nature knew   135
Her wooden walls her strength, her guard the naval crew.

VII.

But draw the veil, nor seek to paint the grief,
Which knows no bounds, nor meditates relief;

11. Cf. Milton, *Lycidas*, l. 165.
12. "Alfred one of the Saxon Kings famous for his Piety and Application to Publick Business" (Finch's note).
13. "[Henry] VII" (Finch's note). Henry VII of England (1457–1509) founded the Tudor dynasty.
14. "Cambden saith, That the Custom of Excessive Drinking was brought amongst us out of Holland, by those Troops which Queen Elizabeth lent the States" (Finch's note). "Cambden": William Camden (1551–1623), Tudor historian; "Eliza": Elizabeth I (1533–1603), queen of England.

Maria[15] weeps, with unexhausted tears;
No look that beauteous face, but sorrow, wears: 140
    And in those eyes, where majesty was seen
    To warn admirers, and declare the Queen,
Now only reigns incurable distress,
    Which, Royal James, thy faithful consort shows,
Who, by her different grief, does too confess,   145
    That now, Alas! she the distinction knows
'Twixt weeping for thy loss, or with thee for thy woes,
    No more the diadem attracts her sight,
    Held but by reflection bright[:]
Thoughts of returning-glory move no more,   150
Nor can she e'er receive what she possess'd before:
    A grave is all, she with her James can share,
    And were it not for what he left, her care,
How soon would she descend, and be his consort, there.
Pleas'd better in that fourth and last remove,[16]   155
    Securely by thy unmolested side,
From life itself an exile to abide,
    Than in th'experienc'd former three,
Which yet she well sustain'd, accompany'd by thee:
    Strong are the bonds of death, but stronger those of love[.]   160

VII[I].

O Britain! take this wish before we cease:
May happier kings procure the[e] lasting peace;
    And having rul'd thee to thy own desire,
    On thy maternal bosom late expire,
Clos['d] in that earth where they had reigned before,   165
    'Till states and monarchies shall be no more:[17]
        Since in the day of unappealing doom,
    Or king or kingdom must declare,
What the sad chance or weighty causes were,
That forc'd them to arise from out a foreign tomb[.]   170
    O Britain! may thy days to come be fair,
    And all that shall intend thy good,
Be reverently heard, and rightly understood.
    May no intestine broils[18] thy [e]ntrails tear,
No field in the[e] be fought, or nam'd a-new in blood: 175
    May all who shield thee, due applauses have,
    Whilst for myself, like solitary Men,
        Devoted only to the pen,

15. Maria Beatrice d'Este, Mary of Modena (1658–1718), James II's second wife; Finch was one of the Catholic queen's maids of honor.
16. "The First Remove was, when she went into Flanders. The Second, when she went into Scotland with the Duke. And the Third, when she went into France" (Finch's note); i.e., the three times that James and Mary were separated for political reasons.
17. Cf. Haggai 2:7 and 2:22, which exhorted a new monarch to rebuild the temple in Jerusalem.
18. "intestine broils": domestic disputes.

I but a safe retreat amidst thee crave
Below the ambitious world, and just above my grave.   180

The Spleen.[1]
A Pindaric Poem.

What art thou, *Spleen*, which ev'ry thing dost ape?[2]
　　Thou Proteus[3] to abus'd mankind,
　　Who never yet thy real cause could find,
Or fix thee to remain in one continued shape.
　　Still varying thy perplexing form,   5
　　Now a dead sea thou'lt represent,
　　A calm of stupid discontent,
Then, dashing on the rocks wilt rage into a storm.
　　Trembling sometimes thou dost appear,
　　Dissolv'd into a panic fear;   10
　　On sleep intruding dost thy shadows spread,
　　Thy gloomy terrors round the silent bed,
And crowd with boding dreams the melancholy head;
　　Or, when the midnight hour is told,
And drooping lids thou still dost waking hold,   15
　　Thy fond delusions cheat the eyes,
　　Before them antic spectres dance,
　　Unusual fires their pointed heads advance,
　　And airy phantoms rise.
　　Such was the monstrous vision seen,   20
When Brutus (now beneath his cares oppressed,
And all Rome's fortunes rolling in his breast,
　　Before Phillipi's latest field,
Before his fate did to Octavius lead)
　　Was vanquish'd by the Spleen.[4]   25

　　Falsely, the mortal part we blame
　　Of our depressed, and pond'rous frame,
　　Which, till the first degrading sin
　　Let thee, its dull attendant, in;[5]
　　Still with the other did comply,   30
Nor clogg'd the active soul, dispos'd to fly,
And range the mansions of its native sky;[6]

---

1. Melancholy, often with violent mood swings (what we now call "manic depression"), from which
　Finch herself suffered. "Pindaric" poems, popular in Augustan England, were based on the odes of
　the Greek poet Pindar (522–442 B.C.)
2. Imitate.
3. In Homer's *Odyssey* IV.351, a minor sea-god who changes shape to avoid answering questions.
4. Shakespeare portrays the nightmares that precede Brutus's downfall at Philippi (*Julius Caesar*
　IV.iii).
5. I.e., the body should not be blamed for the spleen, since the separation of body and spirit results
　from the fall.
6. Finch is suggesting that before the fall material and spiritual understandings of sensory experience
　were not opposed.

Nor, whilst in his own heaven he dwelt,
Whilst man his paradise possessed,
His fertile garden in the fragrant East,[7]   35
And all united odors smelt,
No armed sweets, until thy reign,
Could shock the sense, or in the face
A flushed, unhandsome color[8] place.
Now the jonquille o'ercomes the feeble brain;   40
We faint beneath the aromatic pain,
Till some offensive scent thy pow'rs appease,
And pleasure we resign for short, and nauseous ease.[9]

In ev'ry one thou dost possess,
New are thy motions, and thy dress: 45
Now in some grove a list'ning friend
Thy false suggestions must attend,
Thy whisper'd griefs, thy fancy'd sorrows hear,
Breath'd in a sigh, and witness'd by a tear;
Whilst in the light, and vulgar crowd,   50
Thy slaves, more clamorous and loud,
By laughters unprovok'd, thy influence too confess.
In the imperious wife thou vapors art,
Which from o'erheated passions rise
In clouds to the attractive brain,   55
Until descending thence again,
Thro' the o'er-cast, and show'ring eyes,
Upon her husband's soften'd heart,
He the disputed point must yield,
Something resign of the contested field;   60
Till lordly man, born to imperial sway,
Compounds for peace, to make that right away,
And woman, arm'd with Spleen, does servilely obey.[10]

The fool, to imitate the wits,
Complains of thy pretended fits,   65
And dullness, born with him, would lay
Upon thy accidental sway;
Because, sometimes, thou dost presume
Into the ablest heads to come;
That, often, men of thoughts refin'd,   70
Impatient of unequal sense,
Such slow returns, where they so much dispense,
Retiring from the crowd, are to thy shades inclin'd.

7. Garden of Eden, where sensory pleasures were not overwhelming.
8. Odors make the sufferer flushed and faint.
9. "nauseous ease": like "aromatick pain," an oxymoron suggesting that the speaker is attracted to but also fears the intensity of heightened sensory experience and the blurring of boundaries brought on by spleen.
10. Ll. 53–63: the spleen makes the wife fight with her husband, who attempts to assert his authority over her, as she swings from manic "o'erheated passions" to melancholic obedience.

O'er me alas! thou dost too much prevail:
I feel thy force, whilst I against thee rail; 75
I feel my verse decay, and my cramped numbers[11] fail.
Thro' thy black jaundice[12] I all objects see,
As dark, and terrible as thee,
My lines decry'd, and my employment thought
An useless folly, or presumptuous fault; 80
Whilst in the Muses' paths I stray,
Whilst in their groves, and by their secret springs
My hand delights to trace unusual things,
And deviates from the known, and common way;
Nor will in fading silks compose 85
Faintly th'inimitable rose,
Fill up an ill-drawn bird, or paint on glass
The sov'reign's blurr'd and undistinguish'd face,
The threatning angel, and the speaking ass.[13]

Patron thou art to ev'ry gross abuse, 90
The sullen husband's feign'd excuse,
When the ill humor with his wife he spends,
And bears recruited wit, and spirits to his friends.
The son of Bacchus[14] pleads thy pow'r,
As to the glass he still repairs, 95
Pretends but to remove thy cares,
Snatch from thy shades one gay, and smiling hour,
And drown thy kingdom in a purple show'r.
When the coquette,[15] whom ev'ry fool admires,
Would in variety be fair, 100
And, changing hastily the scene
From light, impertinent, and vain,
Assumes a soft, a melancholy air,
And of her eyes rebates[16] the wand'ring fires,
The careless posture, and the head reclin'd, 105
The thoughtful, and composed face,
Proclaiming the withdrawn, the absent mind,
Allows the fop[17] more liberty to gaze,
Who gently for the tender cause inquires;
The cause, indeed, is a defect in sense, 110
Yet is the Spleen alledg'd, and still the dull pretence.

11. Poetic meter.
12. Morbid disease resulting from obstruction of black bile (one of the four humors), believed to be a cause of melancholy.
13. Ll. 85–89: i.e., the speaker will not confine herself to safe, mediocre, domestic arts; nor will she slavishly praise the "undistinguish'd" monarch (William III). "threatning angel . . . speaking ass": see Numbers 22:22–35.
14. "son of Bacchus": a drunk.
15. Flirt.
16. "Calls back": i.e., the coquette uses spleen to feign disinterest, while at the same time allowing men to gaze on her.
17. A man who is overly attentive to his own appearance.

But these are thy fantastic harms,
The tricks of thy pernicious stage,
Which do the weaker sort engage;
Worse are the dire effects of thy more pow'rful charms.   115
By thee religion, all we know,
That should enlighten here below,
Is veil'd in darkness, and perplexed
With anxious doubts, with endless scruples vexed,
And some restraint imply'd from each perverted text.   120
Whilst *touch not, taste not,* what is freely giv'n,
Is but thy niggard voice, disgracing bounteous Heav'n.
From speech restrain'd, by thy deceits abus'd,
To deserts banish'd, or in cells reclus'd,
Mistaken vot'ries to the pow'rs divine,   125
Whilst they a purer sacrifice design,
Do but the Spleen obey, and worship at thy shrine.[18]
In vain to chase thee ev'ry art we try,
In vain all remedies apply,
In vain the Indian leaf infuse,   130
Or the parch'd Eastern berry bruise;
Some pass, in vain, those bounds, and nobler liquors[19] use.
Now harmony,[20] in vain, we bring,
Inspire the flute, and touch the string.
From harmony no help is had;   135
Music but soothes thee, if too sweetly sad,
And if too light, but turns thee gayly mad.
Tho' the physician's greatest gains,
Altho' his growing wealth he sees
Daily increas'd by ladies' fees,   140
Yet dost thou baffle all his studious pains.
Not skillful Lower[21] thy source could find,
Or thro' the well-dissected body trace
The secret, the mysterious ways,
By which thou dost surprise, and prey upon the mind.   145
Tho' in the search, too deep for human thought,
With unsuccessful toil he wrought,
'Till thinking thee to've catch'd, himself by thee was caught,
Retain'd thy pris'ner, thy acknowledg'd slave,
And sunk beneath thy chain to a lamented grave.   150

18. Ll. 116–27: like Burton, Locke, and a number of seventeenth- and eighteenth-century medical writers, Finch here dismisses religious enthusiasm—and particularly the excesses of radical Protestantism—as a kind of mental illness.
19. I.e., stronger than tea and coffee, the "Indian leaf" and "Eastern berry" of ll. 130–31.
20. I.e., music.
21. Physician to Charles II.

Adam Pos'd[1]

Could our first father, at his toilsome plough,[2]
Thorns in his path, and labor on his brow,
Cloth'd only in a rude, unpolish'd skin,
Could he a vain fantastic nymph have seen,
In all her airs, in all her antic graces,   5
Her various fashions, and more various faces;
How had it pos'd that skill, which late assign'd
Just appellations to each several kind!
A right idea of the sight to frame;
T' have guessed from what new element she came;   10
T' have hit the wav'ring form, or giv'n this thing a name.

Friendship between Ephelia and Ardelia[1]

Eph. What *Friendship* is, Ardelia shew.
Ard.   'Tis to love, as I love you.
Eph. This account, so short (tho' kind)
           Suits not my enquiring mind.
           Therefore farther now repeat;   5
           What is *Friendship* when complete?
Ard.   'Tis to share all joy and grief;
           'Tis to lend all due relief
           From the tongue, the heart, and hand;
           'Tis to mortgage house and land;   10
           For a friend be sold a slave;
           'Tis to die upon a grave,
           If a friend therein do lie.
Eph. This indeed, tho' carry'd high,
           This, tho' more than e'er was done   15
           Underneath the rolling sun,
           This has all been said before.
           Can Ardelia say no more?
Ard.   Words indeed no more can shew:
           But 'tis to love, as I love you.   20

The Circuit of Apollo[1]

  Apollo, as lately, a circuit he made,
Thro' the lands of the Muses, when Kent[2] he survey'd,

---

1. "Pos'd": opposed.
2. I.e., after the fall.
1. A poem based on Katherine Philips's poems from Orinda to Lucasia; see, for instance, Philips, "Friendship's Mysteries, to My Dearest Lucasia (found on p. 187 in this volume)." "Ardelia" is Finch's poetic persona.
1. The sun's daily course across the sky.
2. Anne and Heneage Finch settled in Eastwell, Kent, in late 1690.

And saw then that poets were not very common,
But most that pretended to verse, were the women,
Resolv'd to encourage, the few that he found,   5
And she that writ best, with a wreath should be crown'd.[3]
    A summons sent out, was obey'd but by four,
When Phebus,[4] afflicted, to meet with no more,
And standing, where sadly, he now might descry,
From the banks of the Stowre, the desolate Wye,   10
He lamented for Behn, o're that place of her birth,[5]
And said amongst females was not on the earth,
Her superior in fancy, in language, or wit,
Yet own'd that a little too loosely she writ:
Since the art of the Muse, is to stir up soft thoughts,   15
Yet to make all hearts beat, without blushes, or faults.
    But now to proceed, and their merits to know,
Before he on any, the bays[6] would bestow,
He order'd them each in their several way,
To show him their papers, to sing, or to say,   20
What ere they thought best, their pretensions might prove,
When Alinda, began, with a song upon love.
So easy the verse, yet compos'd with such art,
That not one expression, fell short of the heart;
Apollo himself did their influence obey,   25
He catch'd up his lyre, and a part he would play,
Declaring, no harmony else could be found,
Fit to wait upon words, of so moving a sound.
The wreath, he reach'd out, to have plac'd on her head,
If Laura, not quickly, a paper had read,   30
Wherein she Orinda,[7] had praised so high,
He own'd it had reach'd him, while yet in the sky.
That he thought with himself, when it first struck his ear,
Who ere could write that, ought the laurel to wear.
Betwixt them he stood, in a musing suspense,   35
Till Valeria withdrew him a little from thence,
And told him as soon as she'd got him aside,
Her works, by no other, but him should be try'd;
Which so often he read, and with still new delight,
That judgment 'twas thought would not pass till 'twas night;   40
Yet at length, he restor'd them, but told her withal
If she kept it still close, he'd the talent recall.
Ardelia, came last, as expecting least praise,

3. "with a wreath should be crown'd": like the poet laureate.
4. Another name for Apollo.
5. "Mrs. [Aphra] Behn was Daughter to a Barber, who liv'd formerly in Wye, a little market Town
(now much decay'd) in Kent—though the account of her Life before her Works pretends otherwise[,] some persons now alive do testify upon their knowledge, [it] not to be her Original" (Finch's
note).
6. Laurels.
7. Orinda: Katherine Philips's poetic persona.

Who writ for her pleasure, and not for the bays.
But yet, as occasion, or fancy should sway, 45
   Would sometimes endeavor to pass a dull day,
In composing a song, or a scene of a play;[8]
Not seeking for fame, which so little does last,
That ere we can taste it, the pleasure is past;
But Apollo reply'd, tho' so careless she seem'd, 50
Yet the bays, if her share, would be highly esteem'd.

And now, he was going to make an oration,
Had thrown by one lock, with a delicate fashion,
Upon the left foot, most genteelly did stand,
Had drawn back the other, and wav'd the white hand, 55
When calling to mind, how the prize altho' given,
By Paris, to her, who was fairest in heaven,
Had pulled on the rash, inconsiderate boy,
The fall of his house, with the ruin of Troy,[9]
Since in wit, or in beauty, it never was heard 60
One female could yield, t' have another preferr'd,
He chang'd his design, and divided his praise,
And said that they all had right to the bays,
And that 'twere injustice, one brow to adorn,
With a wreath, which so fitly by each might be worn. 65
Then smil'd to himself, and applauded his art,
Who thus nicely had acted so subtle a part,
Four women to wheedle, but found 'em too many,
For who would please all, can never please any.
In vain then, he thought it, there longer to stay, 70
But told them, he now must go drive on the day,
Yet the case to Parnassus[10] should soon be referr'd,
And there in a council of Muses be heard,
Who of their own sex, best the title might try,
Since no man upon earth, nor himself in the sky, 75
Would be so imprudent, so dull, or so blind,
To lose three parts in four, from amongst womankind.

A Nocturnal Reverie

In such a night, when every louder wind
Is to its distant cavern safe confin'd;
And only gentle Zephyr[1] fans his wings,

---

8. At court in the 1680s Finch wrote two plays, *Aristomenes: Or, The Royal Shepherd* (1713) and *The Triumphs of Love and Innocence.*
9. Paris, called in to decide who among the goddesses Hera, Athena, and Aphrodite was most beautiful, chose Aphrodite, who helped him abduct Helen of Troy, thus precipitating the Trojan War.
10. Mountain sacred to the Muses.
1. The west wind.

And lonely Philomel,[2] still waking, sings;
Or from some tree, fam'd for the owl's delight,   5
She, hollowing clear, directs the wand'rer right;
In such a night, when passing clouds give place,
Or thinly veil the heav'ns' mysterious face;
When in some river, overhung with green,
The waving moon and trembling leaves are seen;   10
When freshen'd[3] grass now bears itself upright,
And makes cool banks to pleasing rest invite,
Whence springs the woodbind, and the bramble-rose,
And where the sleepy cowslip shelter'd grows;
Whilst now a paler hue the foxglove takes,   15
Yet checkers still with red the dusky brakes:[4]
When scatter'd glow-worms, but in twilight fine,
Show trivial beauties watch their hour to shine;
Whilst *Salisb'ry*[5] stands the test of every light,
In perfect charms, and perfect virtue bright: 20
When odors, which declin'd repelling day,
Thro' temp'rate air uninterrupted stray;
When darken'd groves their softest shadows wear,
And falling waters we distinctly hear;
When thro' the gloom more venerable shows   25
Some ancient fabric, awful in repose,
While sunburned hills their swarthy looks conceal,
And swelling haycocks thicken up the vale:
When the loos'd horse now, as his pasture leads,
Comes slowly grazing thro' th' adjoining meads,   30
Whose stealing pace, and lengthen'd shade we fear,
Till torn up forage in his teeth we hear:
When nibbling sheep at large pursue their food,
And unmolested kine[6] rechew the cud;
When curlews[7] cry beneath the village-walls,   35
And to her straggling brood the partridge calls;
Their shortliv'd jubilee the creatures keep,
Which but endures, whilst tyrant-man does sleep:
When a sedate content the spirit feels,
And no fierce light disturbs, whilst it reveals;   40
But silent musings urge the mind to seek
Something, too high for syllables[8] to speak;
Till the free soul to a compos'dness charm'd,
Finding the elements of rage disarm'd,

2. The nightingale.
3. Newly grown.
4. Ferns.
5. Anne Tufton, countess of Salisbury, with whose family Anne Finch lived briefly after the Glorious
   Revolution of 1688.
6. Plural of *cow.*
7. Shore birds.
8. Poetry, or simply words.

O'er all below a solemn quiet grown, 45
Joys in th' inferior world, and thinks it like her own:
In such a night let me abroad[9] remain,
Till morning breaks, and all 's confus'd again;
Our cares, our toils, our clamors are renew'd,
Or pleasures, seldom reach'd, again pursu'd. 50

To the Nightingale

Exert thy voice, sweet harbinger[1] of spring!
 This moment is thy time to sing,
 This moment I attend to praise,
And set my numbers to thy lays.[2]
 Free as thine shall be my song; 5
 As thy music, short, or long.

Poets, wild as thee, were born,
 Pleasing best when unconfin'd,
 When to please is least design'd,
Soothing but their cares to rest; 10
 Cares do still their thoughts molest,
 And still th'unhappy poet's breast,
Like thine, when best he sings, is plac'd against a thorn.

She begins, let all be still!
 Muse, thy promise now fulfill! 15
Sweet, oh! sweet, still sweeter yet
Can thy words such accents fit,
Canst thou syllables refine,
Melt a sense that shall retain
Still some spirit of the brain, 20
Till with sounds like these it join.
 'Twill not be! then change thy note;
 Let division[3] shake thy throat.
Hark! Division now she tries;
Yet as far the Muse outflies. 25
 Cease then, prithee, cease thy tune;
 Trifler, wilt thou sing till June?
Till thy bus'ness all lies waste,
And the time of building's past!
 Thus we poets that have speech, 30
Unlike what thy forests teach,
 If a fluent vein be shown
 That's transcendent to our own,

9. Away from home.
1. Forerunner.
2. Tune her poetry to the bird's song.
3. In music, the singing of a rapid melodic passage.

Criticize, reform, or preach,
Or censure what we cannot reach.   35

Glass

O Man! what inspiration was thy guide,
Who taught thee light and air thus to divide;[1]
To let in all the useful beams of day,
Yet force, as subtle winds, without thy sash to stay;
T'extract from embers by a strange device,   5
Then polish fair these flakes of solid ice;
Which, silver'd o'er, redouble all in place,
And give thee back thy well or ill-complexion'd face.
To vessels blown exceed the gloomy bowl,
Which did the wine's full excellence control,   10
These show the body, whilst you taste the soul.
Its color sparkles motion, lets thee see,
Tho' yet th'excess the preacher warns to flee,
Lest men at length as clearly spy through thee.

Fragment

So here confin'd, and but to female clay,
Ardelia's soul mistook the rightful way:
Whilst the soft breeze of pleasure's tempting air
Made her believe, felicity was there;
And basking in the warmth of early time,   5
To vain amusements dedicate her prime.
Ambition next allur'd her tow'ring eye;
For paradise she heard was plac'd on high,
Then thought, the court with all its glorious show
Was sure above the rest, and paradise below.[1]   10
There plac'd too soon the flaming sword[2] appear'd,
Remov'd those pow'rs, whom justly she rever'd,
Adher'd too in their wreck, and in their ruin shar'd.
Now by the wheel's inevitable round,
With them thrown prostrate to the humble ground,   15
No more she takes (instructed by that fall)
For fix'd, or worth her thought, this rolling ball:[3]
Tow'rds a more certain station she aspires,
Unshaken by revolts, and owns no less desires.

1. Cf. Genesis 1:4–7.
1. Ll. 9–10: The court of James II and Mary of Modena, where Finch ("Ardelia" in l. 2) was a maid of honor; she draws on the idea that monarchs were God's intermediaries on earth.
2. See Genesis 3:24.
3. The earth; this world.

But all in vain are pray'rs, ecstatic thoughts,   20
Recover'd moments, and retracted faults,
Retirement, which the world *moroseness* calls,
Abandon'd pleasures in monastic walls:[4]
These, but at distance, towards that purpose tend,
The lowly means to an exalted end;   25
Which He must perfect, who allots her stay,
And that, accomplish'd, will direct the way.
Pity her restless cares, and weary strife,
And point some issue[5] to escaping life;
Which so dismiss'd, no pen or human speech   30
Th'ineffable recess can ever teach:
Th'expanse, the light, the harmony, the throng,
The bride's attendance, and the bridal song,[6]
The numerous mansions, and th' immortal tree,[7]
No eye, unpurg'd by death, must ever see,   35
Or waves which through that wond'rous city[8] roll.
Rest then content, my too impatient soul;
Observe but here the easy precepts given,
Then wait with cheerful hope, till Heaven be known in Heaven.

On the Death of the Queen[1]

Dark was the shade, where only could be seen,
Disasterous yew[2] that ever baleful green,
Destructive in the field of old when strung,
Gloomy o'er graves of sleeping warrior's hung;
Deep was the wild recess that not an ear,   5
Which grudged her praises, might the accents hear;
Where sad Ardelia mourn'd Urania's[3] death
In sighs which seem'd her own expiring breath;
In moving syllables so often broke,
That more than eloquence the anguish spoke;   10
Urging the tears which could not give relief,
But seem'd to propagate renewing grief.
Lamira[4] near her sat and caught the sound,
Too weak for echoing rocks which fixed the bound,

---

4. "Wye College in Kent, formerly a Priory" (Finch's note).
5. Way of going out; meaning, profit.
6. See Revelation 22.
7. Tree of knowledge, lost with the fall; "mansion" is a word Milton uses to describe Eden before the fall, and the human desire to return to paradise after the fall (see *Paradise Lost* XII.585–86).
8. The New Jerusalem.
1. Maria Beatrice d'Este (Mary of Modena, 1658–1718), second, Catholic wife of James II. This poem was not published until the twentieth century.
2. Dark green tree, associated with mourning.
3. "Ardelia": Finch's poetic persona; a minor character in Katherine Philips's Society of Friendship (see p. 341 above). Urania was the heavenly Muse, and Milton's muse in *Paradise Lost*.
4. Anne Tufton, countess of Salisbury.

For cliffs that overlooked the dangerous wave,   15
Th' unhappy vessels or the sailors' grave;
The pitying nymph whom sympathy constrain'd
Asked why her friend thus heavily complain'd;
Why she retired to that ill-omen'd spot,
By men forsaken and the world forgot;   20
Why thus from light and company she fled,
And living sought the mansions of the dead.
Her head reclined on the obdurate stone,
Still uttering low but interrupted moan,
In which Urania she to all preferr'd,   25
And with her seem'd unactive or interr'd;
As if all virtues of the polished mind,
All excellencies of the female kind,
All winning graces in Urania join'd;
As if perfection but in her was seen,   30
And her least dignity was England's Queen.

Thou hast describ'd her, pleas'd Ardelia cry'd,
As thou hadst known her awful without pride;
As thou in her domestic train hadst stood,
And seen her great and found her warmly good;   35
Duly maintaining her exalted place,
Yet condescending with attractive grace.
Recall'd be days when ebon locks[5] o'erspread
My youthful neck, my cheeks a bashful red,
When early joys my glowing bosom warm'd,   40
When trifles pleas'd and every pleasure charm'd;
Then eager from the rural seat I came
Of long trailed ancestors of worthy name,
To seek the court of many woes the source,
Completed by this last, this sad divorce;   45
From her to whom myself I had resign'd,
The sovereign mistress of my vanquished mind,
Who now survive but to attend her hearse
With dutious tribute of recording verse;
In which may truth with energy be found,   50
And soft as her compassion be the sound.
Blessed were the hours when thro' attendance due,
Her numerous charms were present to my view;
When lowly to her radiant eyes I bowed,
Suns to my sight but suns without a cloud;   55
Towards me their beneficial aspect turn'd,
Impressed my duty and my conduct warn'd;
For who that saw the modest airs they cast,
But from that pattern must be nicely chast[e].

5. Black hair.

Peculiar souls have their peculiar signs,   60
And thro' the eye the inward beauty shines;
Then who can wonder if in hers appear'd
Superior sense to be rever'd and fear'd;
Endearing sweetness to her happy friends,
And holy fire which towards the altar tends;   65
Blessed my attention was when drawing near
(My place's claim) her crowded audience chair,
I heard her by admiring states addressed,
With embassies in different tongues expressed;
To all that Europe sent she gave replies,   70
In their own speech most eloquent and wise,[6]
Soft was her talk and soothing to the heart,
By nature solid, perfected by art;
The Roman accent, which such grace affords,
To Tuscan language harmonized her words;[7]   75
All eyes, all list'ning sense upon her hung,
When from her lovely mouth th' enchantment sprung:
What Livia was when Rome Augustus sway'd,
And thro' a woman's wit the world obey'd,[8]
What Portia was, when fortitude and love   80
Inflicted wounds, which did her firmness prove,
And forcing Brutus to applaud her worth,
Drew with the steel th'important secret forth;[9]
Such was Urania where they most excell'd,
And where they fail'd by nobler zeal[10] upheld.   85
What Italy produced of glorious names,
Her native country and her kindred dames,
All virtues which antiquity could boast,
She equal'd but on stormy Britain tossed;
They lost their value on a northern coast,   90
Yet who can wonder if to her we grant
What poets feign when they Diana[11] paint,
What legends write when they enthrone a saint;
What now Ardelia speaks with conscious sense
Of real worth and matchless excellence.   95
Never such luster strove against the light,
Never such beauty satisfied the sight,
Never such majesty on earth was found,

---

6. Mary of Modena was fluent in four languages; her court was famous for supporting continental artists and musicians.
7. Her native language was Italian.
8. Livia (Julia Augusta, b. 58 B.C.), wife of the Roman emperor Augustus. He was said to value her political counsel.
9. Like her husband, Marcus Brutus, Portia was an ardent republican; she stabbed herself in the leg to prove worthy of her husband's trust in the plot against Julius Caesar.
10. Religious fervor, often in a pejorative sense.
11. Roman goddess of hunting. She was often depicted as the leader of warrior women, a group to which Mary of Modena and her attendants were sometimes compared.

As when Urania worthily was crown'd;
As when superior airs declared her birth   100
From conquerors[12] o'er the monarchs of the earth,
And large excuse did for their maxim bring,
That Roman ladies stoop'd to wed a king.
If royalty had then arose from choice,
And merit had compell'd the public voice,   105
All had allow'd Urania claimed the most,
In view of whom all other charms were lost;
Hers in meridian strong[13] in their decay,
But sweetly sinking like declining day;
In grief but veil'd, as when a rainy cloud   110
The glorious sun does yet transparent shroud;
And whilst it softens each resplendent beam,
Weeps o'er the land from whence the vapor came;
O'er Britain so her pious sorrows fell
Less for her woes than that it could rebel;[14]   115
Yet thence arose the shades her life o'ercast,
And worldly greatness seldom made to last;
Thence in a foreign clime her consort died,[15]
Whom death could never from her thoughts divide;
Thence sable weeds and cyprus walks[16] she chose,   120
And from within produced her own repose,
Yet only pray'd for those she could not calm,
As fragrant trees tho' wounded shed but balm;
Nor ceased to live till vindicated Heaven
Show'd that in vain were such example given;   125
Who held her light to three great kingdoms forth,
Who gave her sufferings to dilate her worth,
That Gallia[17] too might see she could support
Monastic rules and Britain's worst effort;
Now peaceful is the spirit which possessed   130
That never blemished, that afflicted breast;
Closed are such eyes as paradise might boast,
Seen but in Eve e'er innocence she lost.
The solemn grave with severence[18] takes her down,
And lasting wreaths succeed th' unstable crown;   135
For rude huzzas in mercenary streets,
All hail in her triumphant way she meets,
Who shall in silent majesty repose
Till every tomb shall every guest disclose;

12. She was daughter of Alfonso IV, duke of Modena, who descended from the Este family.
13. "in meridian strong": strong like noon.
14. Anne Finch opposed the Glorious Revolution of 1688.
15. James II died in France in 1701.
16. "sable weeds . . . cyprus walks": traditional signs of mourning.
17. France, where Mary of Modena went into exile after the Glorious Revolution in 1688.
18. Severity (an irregular usage); or separation, in a formal or legal sense.

Till Heaven which does all human loss repair,   140
Distinguishing the atoms of the fair,
Shall give Urania's form transcendent beauty there,
And from the beams irradiating her face
(Which here but wanted that suspended grace),
Shall show the Britains how they strove in vain,   145
To strip that brow which was consign'd to reign;
Tho' politicians strove to guide the round
Of miscall'd fortune and prescribe its bound,
Till the contested earth should be no longer found.

Here she concludes, Lamira thinks it just,   150
Such pious tears should wait such royal dust.

TEXTUAL NOTES

Copy-text: *Miscellany Poems* (1713) for all poems included in that volume, since Anne and Heneage Finch oversaw its publication. All significant variants in earlier and/or manuscript versions are included in the textual notes below:

{words added later}
⟨words canceled⟩
[copy-text emended by CB]

In both text and notes, Finch's italics have been eliminated, except where they are necessary for emphasis.

Editions and Abbreviations

1713	*Miscellany Poems, On Several Occasions. Written By a Lady.* (London: printed by J[ohn] B[arber], 1713).
Finch-Hatton	Octavo Manuscript, "Poems on Several Subjects Written by Ardelia," Finch-Hatton 283, Northamptonshire Record Office, Delapre Abbey.
Folger	Folio Manuscript, "Miscellany Poems with Two Plays by Ardelia," Folger Library N.b.3.
Wellesley	Finch Manuscript, Special Collections, Wellesley College Library.
NYPL	"An Elegy on the Death of K. James. By a Lady [Anne Finch]." New York Public Library copy (NCI p.v. 15).
BL	"On the Death of King James. By a Lady." British Library copy (11613.e.35).
Barash	"The Political Origins of Anne Finch's Poetry," *Huntington Library Quarterly* 54 (1991): 237–51.
McGovern	Barbara McGovern, *Anne Finch and Her Poetry: A Critical Biography* (Athens: Univ. of Georgia Press, 1992).
Reynolds	Myra Reynolds, ed., *The Poems of Anne, Countess of Winchilsea* (Chicago: Univ. of Chicago Press, 1903).

"The Introduction": Copy-text: Folger, 1–2. "The Introduction" was transcribed as the first poem in both the Finch-Hatton and Folger manuscripts, suggesting that Finch intended her critique of gender as a frame for reading the poems that follow (McGovern 2–6).

Textual Variants:

l. 16   To write, or read] To read, or write (Finch-Hatton)
l. 20   outmost] utmost (Finch-Hatton)
l. 26   The holy] That holy the Land] His Land (Finch-Hatton)
l. 46   she triumphs] His triumphs (Finch-Hatton)
l. 47   the subject] His subject (Finch-Hatton)

"On Affliction": Copy-text: Folger, 212. First published in *Miscellanea Sacra*, vol. 1 (1696).

Textual Variants:

l. 3   that rock] this rock (Finch-Hatton)

"On My Selfe": Copy-text: Finch-Hatton, 34–35.

"Ardelia to Melancholy": Copy-text: Folger, 16.

Textual Variants:

Title   Areta to Melancholy (Finch-Hatton)
l. 10   who hast] that hast (Finch-Hatton)
ll. 27–8   ⟨earlier version canceled and illegible⟩ (Finch-Hatton)
ll. 41–2   ⟨earlier version canceled and illegible⟩ (Finch-Hatton)

"To the Echo": Copy-text: Folger, 18.

"A Letter to Daphnis April 2nd 1685": Copy-text: Folger, 4.

Textual Variants:

Title   A Letter to ⟨word canceled⟩ Daphnis from Westminster Ap: the 2nd: 1685

"To Mr. F. now Earl of W.": Copy-text: 1713.

Textual Variants:

Title   To Mr. F. now Earl of W.] To Daphnis (Folger)
          Written . . . 1689 (not in Folger)
l. 1,5   Flavio] Daphnis (Folger)
ll. 19–20   That Piks [Pix] and Manl[e]y strove in vain
          With all that dull pretending train, (Folger)
l. 25   Yet] But (Folger)
l. 39   Had never yet] Till then had ne'er (Folger)
l. 54   With mention of a] ⟨To hear the name of⟩ With mention of a (Folger)
l. 56   Negative] ⟨word canceled⟩ Negative (Folger)
l. 62   of late had] had lately (Folger)
l. 63   often] headlong (Folger)
ll. 64–65   Had for ⟨word canceled⟩ Preferment been so spurr'd,
          He'd since, not from the Stable stirr'd, (Folger)
l. 67   given a Bond] given Bond (Folger)
l. 72   additional stanza follows in Folger:
          Another (tho' a trifling Muse)
          New Titles was employ'd to chuse;
          And in Preambles draw
          How some had fought, like Hardy Knute,
          Whilest others, like the Roman Brute
          Kept their own Witts in awe.

l. 82   ev'ry tender] ⟨each endearing⟩ ev'ry tender (Folger)
l. 85   Post] ⟨two words cancelled⟩ Post (Folger)
l. 89   Flavio] Daphnis (Folger)
l. 92   The harmlesse sweets, of married Joys, (Folger)
   "The Tree": Copy-text: 1713.
Textual Variants:
l. 1   *Tree!*] Tree, (Folger and Finch-Hatton)
l. 5,6   do'st] doest (Folger and Finch-Hatton)
l. 22   Which] that (Finch-Hatton)
   "Fanscomb Barn": Copy-text: 1713.
   "Elegy on the Death of King James": Copy-text: NYPL.
Textual Variants:
25   In chosen Lines] In ⟨—?⟩ chosen Lines (Folger).
66   whilst our Records] whilst ⟨Your⟩ our Records (Folger).
102–105]   canceled (Folger).
115]   Twelve additional lines follow in Folger:
              And if one had reveal'd his Private Life
              How had it been of all our Pens the Strife
              ⟨—?⟩
              Of vanquishing [half line illegible]
              Had thus the Conqueror (tho with Teares Bewayl'd
              That words were wanting e're his Ardour fail'd)
              But inward rais'd his too ⟨—?⟩ Thought
              Age and ⟨—?⟩ Ambition 'twoud have Wrought
              In his own Breast a Rebel Work'd to Find
              Where such embattl'd troops of Vices grew
              [So?] the Subduer did at Length subdue
              Who forward bent his Course, but left that war behind.
   The political significance of these lines is discussed in Barash (341–42).
137]   draw the veil] draw the Rate (BL).
142]   Two additional lines follow in Folger:
              (Lest Ruin'd by their complicated Charms
              Mankind had laid on Fate their unprevented Harms)
161   Happier Kings] ⟨happyer⟩ Rightfull Kings (Folger).
   "The Spleen": Copy-text: 1713.
Textual Variants:
Title   The Spleen (Folger)
l. 1,11   dost] doest (Folger)
l. 21   (now] now (Folger)
l. 22   And all] (And all (Folger)
l. 57   (Thro . . . Eyes) (Folger)
l. 58   her] the (Folger)
l. 66   born with him] (born with him) (Folger)
l. 99   whom ev'ry Fool admires] (whom ev'ry Fool admires) (Folger)
ll. 116–7 all . . . below] (all . . . below) (Folger)
l. 130   Indian Leaf] Indian Plant (Folger)
l. 146   too . . . Thought] (too . . . thought) (Folger)
   "Adam Pos'd": Copy-text: 1713. First published (along with five other Finch poems) in Jacob Tonson, ed., *Poetic Miscellany* (1709); three of Finch's

poems appear between anonymous poems by Swift and Pope's "Pastorals" (McGovern 93).

"Friendship between Ephelia and Ardelia": Copy-text: 1713.

Title   The table of contents calls the poem "Ephelia to Ardelia."

"The Circuit of Apollo": Copy-text: Folger, 43–45.

l. 12   ⟨Women⟩ Females

l. 42   ⟨But⟩ Yet

l. 45   Two canceled lines follow:
        And plainly declar'd, so unskill'd in the rules,
        Cou'd not reach to the wits, nor wou'd stoop to the Fools.

l. 48   ⟨writing⟩ composing

l. 76   ⟨no pair⟩ Himself

"A Nocturnal Reverie": Copy-text: 1713. It is the last poem in the volume before the play *Aristomenes*.

"The Nightingale": Copy-text: 1713.

Textual Variants:

In Folger the spacing of the poem is different, with ll. 1, 8, 9, 14, 19, 20 and 30 indented three spaces; and a single stanza break after l. 13.

l. 6   Musick, short] Tune, concise
        Two additional lines follow:
        If, thru Repetition Joy
        Verse redoubl'd shall reply; (Folger)

l. 11   Cares . . . molest,] (Cares . . . molest) (Folger)

l. 12   th'unhappy] the anxious (Folger)

l. 17   fit,] fit? (Folger)

l. 19   that] which (Folger)

l. 21   join.] join? (Folger)

l. 26   Cease then, prithee] Prithee, cease then, (Folger)

l. 29   Three additional lines follow in Folger:
        Hiding thus, in night, thy head,
        Sure, thou'rt to some Faction Wed,
        Or to false opinions bred.

l. 31   Unlike . . . teach,] (Far from . . . teach) (Folger)

l. 33   That's] But (Folger)

"Glass": Copy-text: 1713. "Glass" and "Fragment" (and also the unauthorized poem Reynolds calls "The Bird and the Arras") were both originally part of a long, meditative poem Finch called "Some ocasi[o]nal Reflections Digested tho' not with great regularity into a Poeme" (Folger, 291—93). For the 1713 edition, or perhaps earlier, Finch took the longer, unwieldy poem and turned it into the shorter, lyric poems for which she was well known throughout the eighteenth century. See Barash, *English Women's Poetry, 1649—1714,* 276–78.

"Fragment": Copy-text: 1713. On the Folger version, see textual note to "Glass," above.

Textual Variants:

Title   1713 table of contents calls this poem "A Fragment"

l. 2   Ardelia's] As much my (Folger)

l. 7   next] then (Folger)

l. 13   in their Ruin] {in} their ⟨deep⟩ Ruin (Folger)

l. 15   With them thrown] {With them} Thrown ⟨stupid and⟩ (Folger)
l. 16   that] ⟨her⟩ that (Folger)
l. 17   or worth her thought] ⟨words illegible⟩ (Folger)
          Two canceled lines follow in Folger:
          She feeds a hope that ⟨2 words illegible⟩ mortal birth,
          Or ⟨word illegible⟩ from her tho' framed of Royal Earth.
l. 38   easie] ⟨laws and⟩ easie (Folger)
l. 39   chearful] steadfast (Folger)
    "On the Death of the Queen": Copy-text: Wellesley, 68–71.

BIBLIOGRAPHY

Editions

Barash, Carol, ed. *The Poems of Anne Finch, Countess of Winchilsea.* Oxford: Oxford Univ. Press, forthcoming.

D'Allesandro, Jean M. Ellis, ed. *The Wellesley Manuscript Poems of Anne Countess of Winchilsea.* Florence: privately printed, 1988.

Murry, John Middleton, ed. *Poems by Anne, Countess of Winchilsea, 1661–1720.* London: Jonathan Cape, 1928.

Reynolds, Myra, ed. *The Poems of Anne Countess of Winchilsea.* Chicago: Univ. of Chicago Press, 1903.

Rogers, Katharine, ed. *Selected Poems of Anne Finch, Countess of Winchilsea.* New York: Ungar, 1979.

Thompson, Denys, ed. *Selected Poems.* Manchester: Fyfield, 1987.

Secondary Works

Anderson, Paul B. "Mrs. Manley's Texts of Three of Lady Winchilsea's Poems." *Modern Language Notes* 45 (1930): 95–99.

Ault, Norman, ed. *Seventeenth-Century Lyrics from the Original Texts.* 2d ed. New York: Sloane, 1950.

Barash, Carol. *English Women's Poetry, 1649–1714: Politics, Community, and Linguistic Authority.* Oxford: Clarendon Press, 1996.

———. "The Political Origins of Anne Finch's Poetry." *Huntington Library Quarterly* 54 (1991): 327–51.

Bonnell, Thomas F. "Collins, Lady Winchilsea, and Pursuit of the Muse." In *Teaching Eighteenth-Century Poetry.* Ed. Christopher Fox. New York: AMS Press, 1990. 273–89.

Brower, Reuben A. "Lady Winchilsea and the Poetic Tradition of the Seventeenth Century." *Studies in Philology* 42 (1945): 61–80.

Buxton, John. *A Tradition of Poetry.* New York: St. Martin's Press, 1967.

D'Allesandro, Jean M. Ellis. "Lady Anne Winchilsea's *Preface* and the 'Rules of Poetry.'" *Filologia Moderna* 10 (1988): 103–30.

Doody, Margaret Anne. *The Daring Muse: Augustan Poetry Reconsidered.* Cambridge: Cambridge Univ. Press, 1985.

Ezell, Margaret J. M. *Writing Women's Literary History.* Baltimore: Johns Hopkins Univ. Press, 1993.

Greer, Germaine. "Wordsworth and Winchilsea: The Progress of an Error." In *The Nature of Identity: Essays Presented to Donald F. Hayden by the*

Graduate Faculty of Modern Letters. Ed. William Weathers. Tulsa, Okla.: Univ. of Tulsa, 1981. 1–13.

Hampsten, Elizabeth. "Poems by Ann [*sic*] Finch." *Women's Studies* 7 (1980): 5–19.

Hinnant, Charles H. *The Poetry of Anne Finch: An Essay in Interpretation.* Newark: Univ. of Delaware Press, 1994.

———. "Song and Speech in Anne Finch's 'To the Nightingale.'" *Studies in English Literature* 31 (1991): 499–513.

Johnstone, Lesley. "Winchilsea's 'Nocturnal Reverie,' Lines 4–6." *Explicator* 41 (1983): 20.

———. "Winchilsea's 'Nocturnal Reverie,' Lines 25–28." *Explicator* 41 (1983): 20–21.

McGovern, Barbara. *Anne Finch and Her Poetry: A Critical Biography.* Athens: Univ. of Georgia Press, 1992.

Mallinson, Jean. "Anne Finch: A Woman Poet and the Tradition." In *Gender at Work: Four Women Writers of the 18th Century.* Ed. Ann Messenger. Detroit: Wayne State Univ. Press, 1990. 34–76.

Mermin, Dorothy. "Women Becoming Poets: Katherine Philips, Aphra Behn, Anne Finch." *ELH* 57 (1990): 335–55.

Messenger, Ann. "Adam Pos'd: Metaphysical and Augustan Satire." *West Coast Review* 8 (1974): 10–11.

———. "Publishing without Perishing: Lady Winchilsea's *Miscellany Poems* of 1713." *Restoration* 5 (1981): 27–37.

———. "Selected Nightingales: Anne Finch, Countess of Winchilsea, et al." In *His and Hers: Essays in Restoration and Eighteenth-Century Literature.* Lexington: Univ. of Kentucky Press, 1986.

Rogers, Katherine. "Anne Finch, Countess of Winchilsea: An Augustan Woman Poet." In *Shakespeare's Sisters: Feminist Essays on Women Poets.* Ed. Sandra Gilbert and Susan Gubar. Bloomington: Indiana Univ. Press, 1979. 32–46.

———. "Finch's 'Candid Account' vs. Eighteenth-Century Theories of the Spleen." *Mosaic* 22 (1989): 17–27.

Salvaggio, Ruth. *Enlightened Absence: Neoclassical Configurations of the Feminine.* Urbana: Univ. of Illinois Press, 1988.

Sena, John F. "Belinda's Hysteria: The Medical Context of *The Rape of the Lock.*" In *Psychology and Literature in the Eighteenth Century.* Ed. Christopher Fox. New York: AMS Press, 1987. 129–47.

———. "Melancholy in Anne Finch and Elizabeth Carter: The Ambivalence of an Idea." *Yearbook of English Studies* 1 (1971): 108–19.

Thompson, Denys. "Anne Finch." *PN Review* 8 (1982): 35–38.

Wittreich, Joseph. *Feminist Milton.* Ithaca: Cornell Univ. Press, 1987.

Woolf, Virginia. *A Room of One's Own.* New York: Harcourt Brace Jovanovich, 1929.

THE SWETNAM CONTROVERSY AND THE
DEFENSE OF WOMEN

Although low regard for women was a continuing feature of Western culture, during the late sixteenth and early seventeenth century misogynistic attacks on women became particularly virulent. Beginning with John Knox's infamous attack on Mary Tudor and running to the end of the seventeenth century, women were vilified in sermons, pamphlets, poems, plays, and elsewhere. What is significant in the *querelle des femmes*, as it was called, is the fact that women began to write in response to such attacks, and in doing so began to articulate what modern scholars acknowledge as profeminist ideals of worth and identity, as well as new and trenchant arguments against submission to patriarchal dominance.

In the early seventeenth century the traditional debate concerning women took on renewed vigor with the publication in 1615 of Joseph Swetnam's *The Arraignment of Lewd, Idle, Froward and Unconstant Women*, a compilation of misogynistic commonplaces mostly borrowed from other writers. Swetnam wrote his treatise under the pseudonym of Thomas Tel-Troth, and it may have been partially inspired by the misogyny sanctioned by James I. Offering to his male readers the spectacle of the "Bear-baiting of Women," he also challenged women to respond. There were three direct rebuttals to Swetnam's work: Rachel Speght, *A Muzzle for Melastomus* (1617); Ester Sowernam, *Ester Hath Hang'd Haman* (1617); and Constantia Munda, *The Worming of a Mad Dog: or, A Sop For Cerberus the Jailer of Hell* (1617). There was one indirect rebuttal, Daniel Tuvil's *Asylum Veneris; or, A Sanctuary for Ladies* (1616). Additionally, there was an anonymous play (possibly by Thomas Heywood), *Swetnam. The Women-hater, Arraigned by Women* (1620), which presents Swetnam (as Misogynos) confronted by a court of women who unmask his identity, convict, and torture him.

The first response to Swetnam, *A Muzzle for Melastomus* (or "black mouth"), stands out for a number of significant reasons. The daughter of a London schoolmaster, Rachel Speght was not yet twenty when she published her answer to Swetnam under her own name, in defiance of the constraints against publication by women. Her response is a clear, logical answer to Swetnam's poorly written and illogical work. By criticizing Swetnam for his misuse of the Bible, Speght initiated a new type of defense of woman as the equal of man, a response grounded in solid historical and interpretative strategies. Speght was fully conscious of herself as a literary woman in writing her tract. Although she does not fully separate her belief in the spiritual equality of the sexes from her acceptance of the social and political inferiority of women assigned to them by the patriarchal system, she realized that if progress were to be made she must find a way to redeem Eve from the traditional assignment of sole guilt attributed to her in the misogynistic biblical and literary tradition.

The second response to Swetnam was *Ester Hath Hang'd Haman* (1617), written under the female pseudonym, "Ester Sowernam," a pun on

"Swe[e]tnam." Sowernam claims to be "neither Maid, Wife nor Widow, yet really all, and therefore experienced to defend all." According to this riddling formula, the author could be either a man or woman. The text itself is open to multiple interpretations: the female persona is that of an older woman who condescendingly refers to the lack of experience demonstrated by the "maid" Speght. Using the legal terminology of arraignment, Sowernam cleverly turns Swetnam's metaphor back against him. Yet the persona's reference to a return to London "this last Michaelmas term" may suggest that the author is a law clerk or an associate of the inns of court. Nevertheless, Sowernam outlines elements of an emerging feminism in a devastating attack on a double standard for men and women. Like Speght, Sowernam displays serious knowledge of the Bible and classical literature, which the author employs effectively in undermining Swetnam's illogical arguments.

RACHEL SPEGHT
(1597?–?)

FROM *A Muzzle for Melastomus* (1617)

*Not unto the veriest Idiot that ever set Pen to Paper, but
to the Cynical Baiter of Women, or Metamorphosed
Misogunes,[1] Joseph Swetnam.*

From standing water, which soon putrefies, can no good fish be expected. For it produceth no other creatures but those that are venomous or noisome, as snakes, adders, and such like. Semblably, no better stream can we look should issue from your idle corrupt brain than that whereto the ruff of your fury (to use your own words) hath moved you to open the sluice. In which excrement of your roaring cogitations you have used such irregularities touching concordance, and observed so disordered a method, as I doubt not to tell you that a very accidence scholar[2] would have quite put you down in both. . . .

Many propositions have you framed which (as you think) make much against women, but if one would make a logical assumption, the conclusion would be flat against your own sex. Your dealing wants so much discretion, that I doubt whether to bestow so good a name as the dunce upon you. But minority bids me keep within my bounds; and therefore I only say unto you that your corrupt heart and railing tongue, hath made you a fit scribe for the devil.

In that you have termed your virulent foam *The Bear-baiting of Women,* you have plainly displayed your own disposition to be cynical, in that there appears no other dog or bull to bait them but yourself.[3] Good had it been for you to have put on that muzzle, which St. James would have all Christians to wear: "Speak not evil one of another";[4] and then had you not seemed so like the serpent Porphyrus[5] as now you do; which, though full of deadly poison, yet being toothless, hurteth none so much as himself. For you, having gone beyond the limits not of humanity alone, but of Christianity, have done greater harm unto your own soul than unto women, as may plainly appear. First, in dishonoring of God by palpable blasphemy, wresting and perverting every place of Scripture that you have alleged; which by the testimony of Saint Peter[6] is to the destruction of them that so do. Secondly, it appears by

---

1. Misogynos, derived from *misogynist.*
2. A person who studies grammar or knows the rules of grammar.
3. Speght puns on the original meaning of "cynic" as "dog-like."
4. James 4:11.
5. According to Aelian, Porphyrus was a serpent in India that lacked teeth, but whose vomit was poisonous.
6. 1 Peter 3:16.

your disparaging of, and opprobrious speeches against, that excellent work of God's hands, which in his great love he perfected for the comfort of man. Thirdly, and lastly, by this your hodge-podge of heathenish sentences, similes, and examples, you have set forth yourself in your right colors unto the view of the world. And I doubt not but the judicious will account of you according to your demerit. As for the vulgar sort, which have no more learning than you have showed in your book, it is likely they will applaud you for your pains. . . .

Of Woman's Excellency, with the Causes of her Creation, and of the Sympathy Which Ought to Be in Man and Wife Each toward Other.

To the first of these objections I answer that Satan first assailed the woman because where the hedge is lowest, most easy it is to get over, and she being the weaker vessel[7] was with more facility to be seduced, like as a crystal glass sooner receives a crack than a strong stone pot. Yet we shall find the offence of Adam and Eve almost to parallel. For as an ambitious desire of being made like unto God was the motive which caused her to eat, so likewise was it his; as may plainly appear by that *Ironica,* "Behold, man is become as one of us."[8] Not that he was so indeed; but hereby his desire to attain a greater perfection than God had given him was reproved. Woman sinned, it is true, by her infidelity in not believing the Word of God, but giving credit to Satan's fair promises, that "she should not die."[9] But so did the man too. And if Adam had not approved of that deed which Eve had done, and been willing to tread the steps which she had gone, he being her head would have reproved her and have made the commandment a bit to restrain him from breaking his Maker's injunction. For if a man burn his hand in the fire, the bellows that blowed the fire are not to be blamed, but himself rather, for not being careful to avoid the danger. Yet if the bellows had not blowed, the fire had not burnt. No more is woman simply to be condemned for man's transgression. For by the free will, which before his fall he enjoyed, he might have avoided and been free from being burnt or singed with that fire, which was kindled by Satan and blown by Eve. It therefore served not his turn a whit afterwards to say, "The woman which thou gavest me, gave me of the tree, and I did eat."[10] For a penalty was afflicted upon him, as well as on the woman, the punishment of her transgression being particular to her own sex and to none but the female kind. But for the sin of man the whole earth was cursed. And he being better able than the woman to have resisted temptation, because the stronger vessel, was first called to account, to

---

7. The phrase is from 1 Peter 3:7 and was used in the Homily on Matrimony.
8. "Ironica": irony; see Genesis 3:22.
9. Genesis 3:4.
10. Genesis 3:12.

show that to whom much is given, of them much is required, and that he who was the sovereign of all creatures visible should have yielded greatest obedience to God. . . .

Secondly, the material cause or matter whereof woman was made was of a refined mold, if I may so speak. For man was created of the dust of the earth,[11] but woman was made of a part of man, after that he was a living soul. Yet was she not produced from Adam's foot, to be his too low inferior; nor from his head to be his superior, but from his side, near his heart, to be his equal; that where he is Lord, she may be Lady. And therefore saith God concerning man and woman jointly, "Let them rule over the fish of the sea, and over the fowls of the heaven, and over every beast that moveth upon the earth."[12] By which words he makes their authority equal and all creatures to be in subjection unto them both. This being rightly considered doth teach men to make such account of their wives, as Adam did of Eve: "This is bone of my bone, and flesh of my flesh."[13] As also, that they neither do or wish any more hurt unto them, than unto their own bodies. For men ought to love their wives as themselves, because he that loves his wife loves himself:[14] And never man hated his own flesh (which the woman is) unless a monster in nature. . . .

The other end for which woman was made was to be a companion and helper for man. And if she must be a helper, and but a helper, then are those husbands to be blamed, which lay the whole burden of domestical affairs and maintenance on the shoulders of their wives. For, as yoke-fellows they are to sustain part of each other's cares, griefs, and calamities. But as if two oxen be put in one yoke, the one being bigger than the other, the greater bears most weight. So the husband being the stronger vessel is to bear a greater burden than his wife. And therefore the Lord said to Adam, "In the sweat of thy face shalt thou eat thy bread, till thou return to the dust."[15] And Saint Paul saith, "That he that provideth not for his household is worse than an infidel."[16] Nature hath taught senseless creatures to help one another; as the male pigeon, when his hen is weary with sitting on her eggs and comes off from them, supplies her place, that in her absence they may receive no harm, until such time as she is fully refreshed. . . . Seeing then that these unreasonable creatures by the instinct of nature bear such affection each to other, that without any grudge, they willingly, according to their kind, help one another, I may reason, *a minore ad maius*,[17] that much more should man and woman, which are reasonable creatures, be helpers each to other in all things lawful, they having

11. Genesis 2:7.
12. Genesis 1:26.
13. Genesis 2:23.
14. Ephesians 5:28.
15. Genesis 3:19.
16. 1 Timothy 5:8.
17. From the smaller to the greater.

the law of God to guide them, his word to be a lanthorn[18] unto their feet and a light unto their paths, by which they are excited to a far more mutual participation of each other's burden, than other creatures. So that neither the wife may say to her husband, nor the husband unto his wife, I have no need of thee,[19] no more than the members of the body may so say each to other, between whom there is such a sympathy, that if one member suffer, all suffer with it. . . . Marriage is a merry-age and this world's Paradise, where there is mutual love. Our blessed Savior vouchsafed to honor a marriage with the first miracle that he wrought, unto which miracle matrimonial estate may not unfitly be resembled.[20]

TEXTUAL NOTES

Copy-text: Huntington Library copy (22250) of Rachel Speght, *A Mouzell for Melastomus, The Cynical Bayter of, and foul mouthed Barker against EVAHS SEX. Or an Apologeticall Answere to that Irreligious and Illiterate Pamphlet made by Jo. Sw. and by him Intituled, The Arraignment of Women* (1617). Spelling and punctuation are modernized. Some archaic forms have been kept, while obvious typographical errors have been silently corrected. In some cases punctuation has been altered in order to make complete sentences. Biblical quotations are indicated with quotation marks, rather than italics, and marginal biblical references are included in the notes.

18. Lantern.
19. 1 Corinthians 12:21.
20. John 2.

ESTER SOWERNAM

FROM *Esther Hath Hang'd Haman*[1] (1617)

Chapter II. What Incomparable and Excellent Prerogatives God Hath Bestowed upon Women in Their First Creation.

It appeareth by that sovereignty which God gave Adam over all the creatures of sea and land, that man was the end of God's creation. Whereupon it doth necessarily, without all exception follow, that Adam, being the last work, is therefore the most excellent work of creation. Yet Adam was not so absolutely perfect but that in the sight of God he wanted a helper: Whereupon God created the woman, his last work, as to supply and make absolute that imperfect building which was unperfected in man, as all divines do hold, till that creation of the woman. . . . It is furthermore to be considered, as the maid[2] in her *Muzzle for Melastomus* hath observed: that God intended to honor woman in a more excellent degree in that he created her out of a subject refined, as out of a quintessence.[3] For the rib is in substance more solid, in place as most near, so in estimate most dear, to man's heart, which doth presage that as she was made for a helper, so to be a helper to stay, to settle all joy, all contents, all delights, to and in man's heart, as hereafter shall be shown.

That delight, solace and pleasure which shall come to man by woman is prognosticated by that place wherein woman was created. For she was framed in Paradise, a place of all delight and pleasure. Every element hath his creatures, every creature doth correspond the temper and inclination of that element wherein it hath and took his first and principal *esse* or being.[4] So that woman neither can or may degenerate in her disposition from that natural inclination of the place in which she was first framed. She is a Paradisian, that is, a delightful creature born in so delightful a country.

When woman was created, God brought her unto Adam and then did solemnize that most auspicious marriage betwixt them with greatest majesty and magnificence that heaven or earth might afford.[5] God was the Father which gave so rich a jewel: God was the Priest which

---

1. In the Book of Esther Haman condemned the Jews to death. Esther interceded with King Ahasuerus, who then hanged Haman.
2. Rachel Speght.
3. The most perfect embodiment of something; a pure essence. The term is common in alchemical and hermetic thought.
4. Sowernam employs terminology common to medieval natural philosophy. "Temper" is the distinctive quality of an element, while "inclination" is the general characteristic of the surrounding element.
5. A marginal annotation states, "Men are worldlings, Women paradicians."

tied so inseparable a knot. God was the Steward which provided all the pleasures, all the dainties, all the blessings, which his divine wisdom might afford in so delightful a place. . . .

There is no love (always excepting the transcending love) which is so highly honored, so graciously rewarded, so straightly commanded, or which being broken, is so severely punished, as the love and duty which children owe to their parents. Yet this love albeit never so respective, is dispensed withal in respect of that love which a man is bound to bear to his wife. "For this cause," saith Adam (as from the mouth of God), "shall a man leave father and mother and cleave only to his wife."6 The word "cleave" is uttered in the Hebrew with a more significant emphasis than any other language may express; such a cleaving and joining together, which admitteth no separation. It may be necessarily observed that the gift of the woman was most singularly excellent, which was to be accepted and entertained with so inestimable a love, and made inseparable by giving and taking the ring of love, which should be endless.

Now, the woman taking view of the Garden, she was assaulted with a Serpent of the masculine gender; who, maliciously envying the happiness in which man was this time, like a mischievous politician he practiced by supplanting of the woman, to turn him out of all. For which end he most craftily and cunningly attempteth the woman and telleth her that therefore they were forbidden to eat of the fruit which grew in the midst of the Garden, that in eating they should not be like unto God. Whereupon the woman accepted, tasted, and gave to her husband. In accepting the Serpent's offer, there was no sin, for there was no sin till the fruit was eaten. Now, albeit I have undertaken the defense of women, and may in that respect be favored in taking all advantages I may, to defend my sex.

There are many pregnant places in the Scripture which might be alleged to extenuate the sin of the woman in respect of the sin of Adam. It is said, "Sin had his beginning in woman,"7 *ergo,* his fullness in man.

Saint Paul saith, "By one man's sin death came into the world,"8 without mention of the woman. The same Saint Paul writeth to the Corinthians, to whom he affirmeth, "that all die in Adam,"9 in which the fullness and effects of sin are charged upon Adam alone, not but that woman had her part in the tragedy, but not in so high a degree as the man.

When Adam had eaten and sin was now in fullness, he beginneth to multiply sin upon sin. First he flieth from the sight of God. Next, being called to account, he excuseth his sin and doth expostulate (as it were)

---

6. Genesis 2:24. Sowernam follows the Geneva Bible rather than the King James version here.
7. Ecclesiastes 7:25–26.
8. Romans 5:12.
9. 1 Corinthians 15:22.

with almighty God and telleth him, "That woman which thou gavest me, gave me and I did eat." As who should say, if thou hadst not given the cause, I had not been guilty of the effect; making (herein) God the author of his fall.

Now what is become of that love which Adam was bound to bear towards his wife? He chargeth her with all the burden, so he may discharge himself. He careth little how he clog[10] her.

God having examined the offenders, and having heard the uttermost they could allege for themselves, he pronounceth sentence of death upon them, as a punishment in justice due and deserved. Justice he administered to Adam. Albeit the woman doth taste of justice, yet mercy is reserved for her, and of all the works of mercy which mankind may hope for, the greatest, the most blessed, and the most joyful is promised to woman.

Woman supplanted by tasting of fruit, she is punished in bringing forth her own fruit. Yet what by fruit she lost, by fruit she shall recover.

What more gracious a gift could the Almighty promise to woman, than to bring forth the fruit in which all nations shall be blessed? So that as woman was a means to lose Paradise, she is by this made a means to recover heaven. . . .

Chapter IV. At What Estimate Women were Valued in Ancient and Former Times.

What travail? What charge? What study? Do not men undertake to gain our goodwill, love, and liking? What vehement suits do they make unto us? With what solemn vows and protestations do they solicit us? They write, they speak, they send, to make known what entire affection they bear unto us. That they are so deeply engaged in love, except we do compassion them with our love and favor, they are men utterly cast away. One he will starve himself, another will hang, another drown, another stab, another will exile himself from kindred and country, except they may obtain our loves. What? Will they say that we are baser than themselves? Then they wrong themselves exceedingly, to prefer such vehement suits to creatures inferior to themselves. . . .

In no one thing men do acknowledge a more excellent perfection in women than in the estimate of the offenses which a woman doth commit. The worthiness of the person doth make the sin more markable. What a hateful thing is it to see a woman overcome with drink, when as in men it is noted for a sign of good fellowship? And, whosoever doth observe it, for one woman which doth make a custom of drunkenness,

10. "clog": a large piece of wood attached to the leg or neck of a person or animal in order to impede or prevent movement.

you shall find a hundred men. It is abhorred in women, and therefore they avoid it. It is laughed at and made but as a jest amongst men, and therefore so many do practice it. Likewise, if a man abuse a maid and get her with child, no matter is made of it, but as a trick of youth. But it is made so heinous an offense in the maid that she is disparaged and utterly undone by it. So in all offenses those which men commit are made light and as nothing, slighted over. But those which women do commit, those are made grievous and shameful and not without just cause. For where God hath put hatred betwixt the woman and the serpent, it is a foul shame in a woman to curry favor with the devil, to stain her womanhood with any of his damnable qualities, that she will shake hands where God hath planted hate.

Joseph Swetnam in his pamphlet aggravateth the offenses of women in the highest degree, not only exceeding, but drawing men into all mischief. If I do grant that woman degenerating from the true end of womanhood prove the greatest offenders, yet in granting that, I do thereby prove that women in their creation are the most excellent creatures. For corruption, *boni pessima*[11] the best thing corrupted proveth the worst, as for example, the most glorious creature in heaven is by his fall the most damned devil in hell. All the elements in their purity are most precious, in their infection and abuse most dangerous. So the like in women, in their most excellent purity of nature, what creature more gracious! But in their fall from God and all goodness, what creature more mischievous? Which the devil knowing he doth more assault woman than man because his gain is greater by the fall of one woman than of twenty men. Let there be a fair maid, wife, or woman in country, town, or city, she shall want no resort of serpents, nor any variety of tempter. Let there be in like sort a beautiful or personable man, he may sit long enough before a woman will solicit him. For where the Devil hath good acquaintance, he is sure of entertainment there without resistance. The Serpent at first tempted woman. He dare assault her no more in that shape. Now he employeth men to supply his part, and so they do. For as the Serpent began with Eve to delight her taste, so do his instruments draw to wine and banqueting. The next, the Serpent enticed her by pride and told her she should be like to God; so do his instruments. First, they will extol her beauty. What a paragon she is in their eyes. Next, they will promise her such maintenance as the best woman in the parish or country shall not have better. What care they if they make a thousand oaths and commit ten thousand perjuries, so they may deceive a woman? When they have done all and gotten their purpose, then they discover all the woman's shame and employ such an author as this (to whose *Arraignment* I do make haste) to rail upon her and the whole sex. . . .

---

11. The corruption of the best is worst. An old proverb.

Chapter VII. The Answer to All Objections Which Are Material, Made against Women.

Let me now see how you can free these men from dishonest minds, who are overtaken thus with beauty, etc. How can beauty hurt? How can it be a cause of a man's ruin, of itself? What, do women forcibly draw? Why, men are more strong. Are they so eloquent to persuade? Why, men are too wise. Are they mischievous to entice? Men are more holy. How then are women causes to bring a man to ruin? Direct causes they cannot be in any respect. If they be causes, they are but accidental causes: a cause as philosophers say, *causa sine qua non:*[12] a remote cause, which cause is seldom alleged for cause, but where want of wit would say somewhat, and a guilty conscience would excuse itself by something. Philosophers say, *Nemo leaditur nisi a se ipso,* no man is hurt but the cause is in himself. The prodigal person amongst the Grecians is called *Asotos,*[13] as a destroyer, an undoer of himself. When a heart fraught with sin doth prodigally lavish out a lascivious look out of a wanton eye; when it doth surfeit upon the sight, who is *Asotos?* Who is guilty of his lascivious disease but himself? *Volenti non fit injuria,* he who is wounded with his own consent, hath small cause to complain of another's wrong. Might not a man as easily and more honestly when he seeth a fair woman, which doth make the best use that she can to set out her beauty, rather glorify God in so beautiful a work, than infect his soul with so lascivious a thought? And for the woman, who having a jewel given her from so dear a friend, is she not to be commended rather that in the estimate which she showeth, she will as carefully and as curiously as she may set out what she hath received from Almighty God, than to be censured that she doth it to allure wanton and lascivious looks? The difference is in the minds, things which are called *Adiaphora,*[14] things indifferent, whose qualities have their name from the uses, are commonly so censured, and so used, as the mind is inclined which doth pass his verdict. A man and a woman talk in the fields together, an honest mind will imagine of their talk answerable to his own disposition, whereas an evil disposed mind will censure according to his lewd inclination. When men complain of beauty, and say, "That women's dressings and attire are provocations to wantonness and baits to allure men," it is a direct means to know of what disposition they are. It is a shame for men in censuring of women to condemn themselves. But a common inn cannot be without a common sign. It is a common sign to know a lecher by complaining upon the cause and occasion of his surfeit; who had known his disease, but by his own complaint? It is extreme folly to complain of another when

12. A necessary cause.
13. From Luke 15:13, meaning a profligate.
14. A theological term for things indifferent, that is, aspects of ritual and theology for which there were no specific policies.

the root of all resteth within himself. Purge an infected heart, and turn away a lascivious eye, and then neither their dressings nor their beauty can any ways hurt you.

TEXTUAL NOTES

Copy-text: Huntington Library copy of Ester Sowernam, *Ester hath hang'd Haman: or, An Answere to a lewd Pamphlet, entituled The Arraignment of Women. With the arraignment of lewd, idle froward, and unconstant men, and Husbands* (1617). Same editing principles as used for Speght text.

BIBLIOGRAPHY

Editions

Crandall, Coryl, ed. *Swetnam the Woman-Hater: The Controversy and the Play.* West Lafayette, Ind.: Purdue Univ. Studies, 1969.

Henderson, Katherine Usher, and Barbara F. McManus, eds. *Half Humankind: Contexts and Texts of the Controversy about Women in England, 1540–1640.* Urbana: Univ. of Illinois Press, 1985.

Shepherd, Simon, ed. *The Women's Sharp Revenge: Five Women's Pamphlets from the Renaissance.* New York: St. Martin's Press, 1985.

Secondary Works

Beilin, Elaine V. *Redeeming Eve: Women Writers of the English Renaissance.* Princeton: Princeton Univ. Press, 1987.

———. "Writing Public Poetry: Humanism and the Woman Writer." *Modern Language Quarterly* 51 (1990): 249–71.

Benson, Pamela Joseph. *The Invention of the Renaissance Woman: The Challenge of Female Independence in the Literature and Thought of Italy and England.* University Park: Pennsylvania State Univ. Press, 1992. 205–30.

Brown, Meg Lota. "Rachel Speght." *Dictionary of Literary Biography.* Ed. M. Thomas Hester. Vol. 126, Seventeenth-Century British Nondramatic Poets. Columbia, S.C.: Bruccoli Clark Layman, 1993. 246–49.

Crandall, Coryl. "The Cultural Implications of the Swetnam Anti-Feminist Controversy in the Seventeenth Century." *Journal of Popular Culture* 2 (1968): 136–48.

Dunn, Catherine M. "The Changing Image of Woman in Renaissance Society and Literature." In *What Manner of Woman: Essays in English and American Life and Literature.* Ed. Marlene Springer. New York: New York Univ. Press, 1977. 15–38.

Hull, Suzanne W. *Chaste, Silent and Obedient: English Books for Women, 1475–1640.* San Marino, Calif.: Huntington Library, 1982.

Jones, Ann Rosalind. "Counterattacks on 'the Bayter of Women': Three Pamphleteers of the Early Seventeenth Century." In *The Englishwoman in Print: Counterbalancing the Canon.* Ed. Anne M. Haselkorn and Betty S. Travitsky. Amherst: Univ. of Massachusetts Press, 1990. 45–62.

Jordan, Constance. *Renaissance Feminism: Literary Texts and Political Models.* Ithaca: Cornell Univ. Press, 1990. 286–307.

Kelly, Joan. "Early Feminist Theory and the *Querelle des Femmes,* 1400–1789." *Signs* 8 (1982): 2–28.

Kelly-Gadol, Joan. "Did Women Have a Renaissance?" In *Becoming Visible: Women in European History.* Ed. Renate Bridenthal and Claudia Koonz. Boston: Houghton-Mifflin, 1977. 137–64.

Kusunoki, Akiko. " 'Their Testament at Their Apron-Strings': The Representation of Puritan Women in Early Seventeenth-Century England." In *Gloriana's Face: Women, Public and Private, in the English Renaissance.* Ed. S. P. Cerasano and Marion Wynne-Davies. Detroit: Wayne State Univ. Press, 1992. 185–204.

Lewalski, Brabara K. *Writing Women in Jacobean England.* Cambridge: Harvard Univ. Press, 1993.

Lewis, Jayne. "Compositions of Ill Nature: Women's Place in a Satiric Tradition." *Critical Matrix* 2 (1986): 31–69.

Maclean, Ian. *The Renaissance Notion of Women: A Study in the Fortunes of Scholasticism and Medical Science in European Intellectual Life.* Cambridge: Cambridge Univ. Press, 1980.

Purkiss, Diane. "Material Girls: The Seventeenth-Century Woman Debate." *Women, Texts, and Histories, 1575–1760.* Ed. Clare Brant and Diane Purkiss. London: Routledge, 1992. 69–101.

Rogers, Katharine. *The Troublesome Helpmate: A History of Misogyny in Literature.* Seattle: Univ. of Washington Press, 1966.

Travitsky, Betty. "The Lady Doth Protest: Protest in the Popular Writings of Renaissance Englishwomen." *English Literary Renaissance* 14 (1984): 255–83.

Woodbridge, Linda. *Women and the English Renaissance: Literature and the Nature of Womankind, 1540–1620.* Urbana: Univ. of Illinois Press, 1986.

Wright, Louis B. *Middle-Class Culture in Elizabethan England.* Chapel Hill: Univ. of North Carolina Press, 1935.

CONTRIBUTORS

Poet and critic **Carol Barash** has a B.A. from Yale University and a Ph.D. from Princeton University. She is a professor of English at Seton Hall University. She has published *English Women's Poetry, 1649–1714: Politics, Community, and Linguistic Authority* (1996) and (editor) *An Olive Schreiner Reader: Writings on Women and South Africa* (1987). She is currently completing the first standard edition of *The Poems and Plays of Anne Finch, Countess of Winchilsea* and beginning a study of religion and eighteenth-century poetry.

Eugene R. Cunnar, associate professor of English at New Mexico State University, received his Ph.D. from the University of Wisconsin–Madison. He has published on a wide range of Renaissance authors, including Wyatt, Donne, Jonson, Crashaw, An Collins, Herbert, and Milton, among others, and articles in art history on Vermeer, Zurbaran, and Thomas Cole. He is currently completing a book on Richard Crashaw and work on the *Variorum Edition of John Donne's Poetry.*

James Fitzmaurice is Professor of English at Northern Arizona University. He holds a B.A. from Occidental College and a Ph.D. from the University of Iowa. He was a visiting research fellow at Gonville and Caius College, Cambridge University, during the Easter Term of 1996. Journal publications include pieces on Thomas Carew, Dorothy Osborne, Margaret Cavendish, and Aphra Behn. His edition of the *Sociable Letters of Margaret Cavendish* appeared in 1996, and he is working on a book on the literary interactions of men and women in seventeenth-century England.

Nancy A. Gutierrez, associate professor of English and Women's Studies and current chair of the English Department at Arizona State University, received her Ph.D. from the University of Chicago. Author of *English Historical Poetry, 1476–1603: A Bibliography* (1983), she has also published articles on Shakespeare and Thomas Heywood, as well as on early prose fiction and history writing. She is currently at work on a study of the representations of starving women in early modern discourse.

Josephine A. Roberts, who was William A. Read Professor of English Literature at Louisiana State University, received her B.A. from the College of William and Mary and her Ph.D. from the University of Pennsylvania. She edited *The Poems of Lady Mary Wroth* (1983; 2d ed. 1992) and *The First Part of the Countess of Montgomery's Urania* (1995). She wrote *Architectonic Knowledge in the "New Arcadia"* (1978), as well as numerous articles on women's writing and Renaissance literature. During the summer of 1996, she completed her edition of the second part of Wroth's *Urania,* based on the holograph manuscript at the Newberry Library, Chicago.

Index